Sex and Sexuality
in Latin America

Sex and Sexuality in Latin America

Edited by
Daniel Balderston
and Donna J. Guy

NEW YORK UNIVERSITY PRESS
New York and London

The editors are grateful to the staff of New York University Press, particularly our editor, Tim Bartlett, and managing editor, Despina Gimbel, for their dedication to this project. Thanks are also due to Elizabeth Smith, who prepared the index.

NEW YORK UNIVERSITY PRESS
New York and London

© 1997 by New York University
Chapter 2 © 1997 by Roger N. Lancaster

Library of Congress Cataloging-in-Publication Data
Sex and sexuality in Latin America / edited by Daniel Balderston and
    Donna J. Guy.
        p.   cm.
    Includes bibliographical references (p.   ) and index.
    ISBN 0-8147-1289-4 (cloth: acid-free paper)
    ISBN 0-8147-1290-8 (pbk.: acid-free paper)
    1. Sex—Latin America.   2. Sex customs—Latin America.
    3. Sex role—Latin America.   4. Sex in literature.   5. Sex in
    motion pictures.   I. Balderston, Daniel, 1952– . II. Guy, Donna J.
    HQ18.L29S49   1997
    306.7'098—dc20   96-35697
                        CIP

New York University Press books are printed on acid-free paper,
and their binding materials are chosen for strength and durability.

Manufactured in the United States of America

10 9 8 7 6 5 4 3 2 1

For our mothers,
Judith Braude Balderston (1926–1993)
Yvette Guy (1918–1996)
in loving memory.

Contents

Daniel Balderston and Donna J. Guy

Introduction

Are sex and sexuality embedded solely in the body, or are they linked to mind, culture, race, and ethnicity? Are sex and sexuality different in Latin America than in other parts of the world? Can we talk about any aspect of Latin America without including consideration of gender and sexuality? This volume is an effort to open conversations among those interested in sexuality studies and Latin American studies.

This is more than a volume about gender and sexuality. It explores the process of crossing over: crossing over visually so that apparel can disguise, reveal, determine, erase, or dynamize a particular moment in time and place. We are crossing over into the minds of writers, judges, doctors, lawyers; women and men; gays, lesbians, bisexuals, heterosexuals, and those who are not fixed in a given "preference" or "orientation." We examine events that range from the imaginary to the all too real, from stories of the Monja Alférez in the colonial period to a Cuban film of the 1990s. From La Difunta Correa, a popular saint in Argentina, to a contemporary painting of Simón Bolívar in drag, from sodomy cases in early-twentieth-century Brazil, from the performance of Chavela Vargas, the lesbian Costa Rican/

Mexican singer: from all of these we can learn about the deployment of sex, sexuality, and gender in Latin America.

By crossing over we can accept that Argentine truck drivers pray to a saint in a red dress, her breast exposed to view, because they believe she personifies the ideal wife and heterosexual partner. We can believe that even though prostitution regulations in Brazil were hidden from the rest of the world, the police and public officials made sure that poor female prostitutes knew where to live and what were the rules of the game. We can dismiss the criticism of *Bom Crioulo*, the story of a tragic love affair between a black sailor and a white cabin boy, as unrealistic because it can be shown to be closely paralleled by testimony in courts martial of the time. We can come to understand the ways in which "heterosexual" intercourse in a novel by José Donoso requires the full range of the "polymorphous perversity" of desire. We can examine how the construction of masculinity in Latin American letters of the early twentieth century, as well as in such different spaces as the tango ballroom, the football stadium, and the "mean streets" of the Nuyorican novel, is permeated by homosexual desire.

Believing is only one part of understanding the dynamics of sex and sexuality in Latin America. We must also find a way to integrate this knowledge into more traditional methods of teaching about both sexuality and Latin America. Gender and sexuality were never central preoccupations for early Latin American specialists, but their strong interest in interdisciplinary approaches to this geographic area provided the field with a degree of flexibility that would ultimately enable others to approach these topics. The advent of feminist studies has shifted the ground in the field to an important extent, privileging questions of women's history and writing, women's participation in the political process, and so forth (see, for instance, the early book by Ann Pescatello on male and female in Latin America, on voting patterns, the gendering of politics, and related topics). There is now a very substantial bibliography on women's and gender studies in the several disciplines in Latin American studies (in our final bibliography, see the entries by Stoner; Castro-Klaren, Molloy, and Sarlo; Acosta-Belén and Bose; Kaminsky; Sommer; the Seminar on Feminism and Culture in Latin America; Lavrin; Miller; and so forth).

The paradigm shift that is now under way, and that this book is necessarily a part of, is to look at "gender" and "sexuality" in a broader context, refocusing a number of earlier questions and debates, in a conscious effort to link gender studies and gay and lesbian studies in ways that transcend to some extent the questions of identity politics that provided the initial impetus to these efforts. Interestingly, the stimulus for some of these discussions in Latin American studies has been the opening up of the question of the configuration of masculinity in Latin America, one that has encouraged a more pluralistic vision of what constitutes gender in the region.

From the perspective of gender and sexuality studies as they have emerged, the need to consider cultural variations in different parts of the world is beginning to be explored. Cultural biases inherent in much of Anglo-American gender and sexuality studies have meant that some culture-bound characteristics have been taken to be universal; cross-cultural (and interdisciplinary) work in gender and sexuality studies is a useful corrective to this tendency. Among the most important recent work, however, is that concerned with places and periods where different paradigms of identity and behavior competed for hegemony, such as George Chauncey's pathbreaking *Gay New York*, which studies the different patterns of male sexuality that coexisted in New York City depending on national origin and class. This sort of paradigm conflict is also central to work on male homosexuality in Latin America by Joseph Carrier, Tomás Almaguer, Roger Lancaster, and Stephen O. Murray. Because of the uneven modernity that characterizes Latin America, as well as the fissures opened by differences of race, ethnicity, class, and religion in the constitution of Latin American cultures, the constructions of sex and gender are spaces of conflict, revelatory of culturally significant issues.

This volume begins by questioning the nature of sexual identity in Latin America. Roger Lancaster sets the tone by raising some fundamental questions about how we perceive sexuality in others in Latin America as well as in ourselves. His experiences in Nicaragua lead him to develop his thoughts about "trans-vestics," that is, the way we sort out sexuality issues through performance and play. He asks how we should interpret signals that others give us about their sexuality. His answer: with great care and with attention paid to nuanced actions. Not everything is as concrete and clear as we would like, and we, like Roger, sometimes play the "straight" man to someone else's performance. Yvonne Yarbro-Bejarano similarly explores the ways in which desire and fantasy respond to the strong gendered and sexualized, and powerfully transgressive, performances of Chavela Vargas. Ben Sifuentes examines the complex construction of the transvestite and of sexual desire in Donoso's *El lugar sin límites*, suggesting in terms similar to Lancaster's that transvestic performance unsettles fixed identities.

The next section explores the state and hegemonic efforts to "police" or sanitize sexuality (Beattie, Caulfield, Montero, Buffington, and Quiroga). These essays are linked not only by issues of policing but also by the crossing of historical documentation with literary and cultural discourse. Despite certain differences, they are united by their willingness to question the meanings of historical events and to remind us that truth can be a slippery slope on which we must tread carefully. Peter Beattie uses "evidence" regarding Brazilian military prosecutions of sodomy to show fissures and ambiguities in this modernizing process. Why should a society intent on making the military an honorable space for young males simultaneously try men for homosexual practices yet refuse to eject those convicted from the armed forces? From the perspective of a secret history of prostitution control in Rio de Janeiro, Sueann Caulfield questions how race and nationality were constructed. The documents she examines reveal, as is often the case in Latin America, that race is as much socioeconomic as biological. Equally important, gendered perceptions of physical beauty anchor all discussion of race and prostitution. Oscar Montero examines one of the most "homosocial" of cultural movements in Spanish America, the "modernismo" of the late nineteenth and early twentieth centuries, to show how homosexual desire is policed and censored but never wholly erased. Rob Buffington asks how criminologists determined the relationship between criminality and sexuality in Mexico. To these thinkers, homosexuality signaled degeneration and disorder. How "scientific" was their scientific evidence? Finally, José Quiroga examines the constructions of homosexuality in revolutionary Cuba, where the discourses of repression and the radical use of stereotyping paradoxically made male homosexuality visible, as exemplified in Tomás Gutiérrez Alea's film *Fresa y chocolate*.

Family values, that slogan of recent U.S. discourses around sexuality, provide the context for the next section. But what do we mean by the Latin American family? And what is "typical"? Donna Guy asks what is "natural" about the reproductive sexuality that is constructed in political, medical, and religious discourse in Argentina. State efforts to promote hygienic motherhood in the late nineteenth and early twentieth centuries prioritized goals of producing healthy children, goals that often limited the "natural" power and authority of male heads of households. So men sought other models through popular Christianity. Nina Menéndez examines Cuban women's fiction and other texts of the late 1920s, showing the debates about women's roles in the home and in the public sphere; the "family romance" in the novel she studies is fractured by these debates, as well as by a tacit lesbian subplot. Daniel Balderston studies the contradictory messages at play in another "family romance," that of the complex mother-son relation in the Mexican film *Doña Herlinda y su hijo*. The film refuses self-definition in favor of a broad spectrum of sexual—and personal—possibility. Eduardo Archetti examines tango lyrics and the chants of football fans in Argentina for their implicit construction of an imaginary individual and an imaginary family, strikingly different from the conventional or the supposedly typical. The "family values" revealed in his and the other essays in this section call into question many of the commonplaces that circulate about the family in Latin America.

The final section consists of three papers that redefine the questions of identity often posed in relation to gender and sexuality. Francine Masiello looks at the ways in which citizenship is constructed by dress, from without instead of from within; the cases she examines range from the eighteenth century to the late twentieth. Arnaldo Cruz unsettles the often heroic narratives of resistance in Nuyorican fiction and theater by showing how masculinity is constructed through abjection, a term he takes from the work of French psychoanalyst Julia Kristeva. And Sylvia Molloy looks at the diversion or refusal of the sexual (and specifically of the lesbian) in an extraordinary text by the Argentine poet Alejandra Pizarnik. These final "redefinitions" seek to open, not to close, the questioning of identity and practice that has characterized much recent work in sexuality studies, as in the initial essay in this volume by Roger Lancaster.

The essays in this volume query only a limited number of the cultural sites that could be usefully examined. Future research could explore the uses of butch/femme roles in Latin American lesbian culture (a topic already discussed in U.S. Latina lesbian culture by Yarbro-Bejarano, Moraga, Trujillo, and others); the breaking down of the supposedly traditional active and passive roles in male homosexuality in contemporary Latin American culture; what Jonathan Ned Katz has called the "invention of heterosexuality" in its Latin American forms; questions of the ethnic, racial, and religious contexts in which gender and sexuality are constructed; the culturally central role that bisexuality in its diverse forms plays in Latin America; and how identities are constructed in relation to gender and sexuality.

Also, there are obviously countries and regions that have not been examined from these perspectives here or elsewhere to the extent necessary (Central America, Colombia, Venezuela, and the Andean countries); similarly, there has been insufficient attention to indigenous and other nonwhite cultures in the Spanish- and Portuguese-speaking countries and elsewhere in the region. Much of the work represented here is in historical, anthropological, and literary studies; Latin American popular culture and the visual arts deserve far more attention than they have received to date.

We hope that these reflections serve as a springboard for discussion in basic courses in gender and sexuality studies as well as in Latin American studies, from literature to politics. How can these topics spark discussion of new critical issues in introductory courses? Can we continue to think of the formation of the modern nation-state without contemplating its impact on the construction of gender and sexual identity, or without interrogating the idea of the national as a figure of desire? How have concepts of masculinity and femininity been constructed differently in different places and times? How are gender and sexuality constructed vis-à-vis class, race, religion, and ethnicity? Posing these questions may reveal new dimensions of Latin American realities. These are the challenges we present to our readers in the hope that they will provide some of the answers.

Part One

Questioning Identities

2 *Roger N. Lancaster*

Guto's Performance

Notes on the Transvestism
of Everyday Life

• THE BLOUSE

It was early evening at the end of a typically sweltering day in Managua.[1] Aida, my *comadre*, had returned home from work with an exquisite rarity in Nicaragua's devastated economy: a new blouse, a distinctly feminine blouse, soft to the touch, with good threadwork and careful attention to detail. It had been sent from the United States—not to Aida but to one of her coworkers by a relative living abroad.

In Nicaragua, if commodities could speak, they'd recount peripatetic tales of endless digressions. How Aida had obtained the blouse is its own circuitous story. She had netted this enviable catch through a complex series of trades and transactions involving the blouse's designated recipient and two other coworkers: four transactions in all. Such were the convolutions of everyday economic life at the end of the revolutionary dispensation.[2]

When Aida arrived home, she beckoned everyone come see her new raiment. Her teenage brother, Guto, arose from where he had been lounging shirtless in the living room, watching the standard TV fare. The drama that ensued took me completely by surprise. With a broad yet pointed gesture, Guto wrapped himself in the white, frilly blouse, and began a coquettish routine that would last for fifteen or twenty minutes. Sashaying about the three cramped rooms of his mother's house, the seventeen-year-old added a purse and necklace to his ensemble. Brothers, sisters, even his mother, egged on this performance, shouting festive remarks: *¡Qué fina, bonita, muñequita!*—these cries punctuated by whistles and kissing noises. Someone handed Guto a pair of clip-on earrings. With cheerful abandon, he applied a bit of blush and touch of makeup. His performance intensified, to the pleasure of the audience. After disappearing for a moment into the bedroom, he returned wearing a blue denim skirt. "*Hombrote*" (big guy), he shot in my direction, nuancing his usually raspy voice as though to flirt with me.

I was astonished, and no doubt my visible surprise was part of the clowning of the evening. "See, Róger," Aida kept remarking. "Look, Guto's a *cochón*," a queer. At first, I had imagined that such banter might dissuade Guto from his increasingly extravagant performance—that the sting of the term, *cochón*, might somehow discipline his unruly antics. Not so. If anything, the challenge prodded him to new heights of dramaturgic excess. The young man luxuriated in femininity. His sisters played the role of macho catcallers, hooting their remarks. Laughing, teasing, everyone seemed to enjoy the ritual. Guto beamed.

• THEORY AND LAUGHTER

Both body and meaning can do a cartwheel.

—Mikhail Bakhtin, *Rabelais and His World*

When later, in solemn seriousness, I tried to "interview" participants on what had transpired, no one would give me a *straight* answer. Reviving the spirit of the evening, jest, mockery, and levity colored the responses: "Maybe Guto's queer," his sister Clara laughed. No one had ever seriously suggested such an opinion before. Quite the contrary, it was typically Guto who taunted his younger brother, Miguel, calling him a *cochón*.[3] "Of course, he's a little queen," his mother said, tossing off a laugh. "I was flirting with you, stupid," Guto told me, winking.

How to describe adequately such antics? Or better yet, what exactly has happened here?

The demands of classical ethnographic description seem to set before us a series of mutually exclusive options: Either this was a serious performance or it was playacting. Either the onlookers were approving or they were disapproving. Obviously, these are not the terms of a purely "descriptive" approach—whatever that might be. They are in fact already full-fledged *analyses* of events: claims about perception, staged in terms of an event, its references, and its broader context.

Theorizing these capers proves no less problematic, for theory, too, would put before us a set of dreary options: Either Guto was making fun of women or he was celebrating femininity. Either this was a screen for homosexual flirtation or it was a way of getting rid of those very desires. Either the audience was making fun of *cochones* or it was suspending the usual prejudices to celebrate them. Either Guto was transgressing gender forms or he was intensifying them. Such acts either constitute a radical challenge to the system of gender norms or merely effect a periodic blowing off of steam that enables the system to reproduce itself despite its many tensions.[4] With such options, we are invited to choose sides, to pick a team, and to play a game whose outcome is already decided.

An interpretive apparatus, an analytical technology, hums its familiar noise: parody or praise, subversion or intensification, deviation or norm, resistant or enabling, play or serious. A series of claims, a chain of diagrams. All the parts are already in place; a syntax is prepared; categories are allotted. One need do no more than mark off the performance, catalogue its parts, and fill in the details. Such tedious work! Guto's delirious gestures and swirls would thus be packaged into neat little boxes—theoretical closures, as final as the denouement of a familiar play.

In a famous passage, Geertz argued that "thick description" is telling the difference between a wink and a twitch.[5] Surely, nuance is everything in the phenomenology of a transvestic performance. But what if a dramatic moment *en cours* is overwhelmed by nuance and ambiguity? And how does one think through a continuous play of winks and gestures, looks and movements, to read what lies behind it all: from the twinkle in Guto's eye to the tone of women's laughter?

It is indeed a slippery task to think about the slipperiness of copycat gestures. The whole point of such fun and games is that a final meaning evades us.

What I want to offer here is a set of closely woven arguments about performances of the sort just described, and about those rituals of masquerade cast on the wider stages of Carnival. Guto was indeed playacting—and play is fun or it is nothing at all. But play is not a trivial thing, and the simultaneously destructive and creative power of laughter should never be underestimated. An essay, then, in praise of folly, and some questions about the utility of extravagance.

• THE CLOSET OF EPISTEMOLOGY:
INTENTIONAL AMBIGUITIES

Now I can scarcely frame my own presence out of the events I've recounted.[6] I was part of the audience, and such performances are always intended, if not exactly *for* an audience, then always *with* an audience in mind. My flat-footedness when everyone else knew the steps, my not getting it when others were in on a joke, was clearly part of the evening's merriment. In the argot of show biz, I played the "straight man."

Or did I? Is it possible that my reactions were being probed here, that Guto and his family were attempting to clarify, by reading my reactions, what I was determined to keep ambiguous if not secret? Certainly, events are more or less consistent with this logic. Although the subject of my own sexual preferences almost never came up as a direct topic of query, I am relatively certain that suspicions circulated.

However, I am not willing simply to settle on this reading of the situation, for one's social identity is scarcely a unidimensional or straightforward matter. If implicitly conducted as something of an experiment in which I was the subject, my hosts might have been trying to get some insight into my reactions as a person of unknown sexuality. Or, they might have been probing my reactions as a representative North American, as a white person, as a college-educated man, as a somewhat awkward person. The possible bases of inquiry, the kinds of questions that might be posed, are perhaps too numerous to count.

To make matters yet more complicated, cultural differences occlude the medium of communication, problematizing any notion of a straightforward inquiry into stable identities. As I was constantly reminded, my own conceptions of homosexuality did not exactly match up with that of my informants.[7] It is not even quite clear to me what would have constituted a "queer" response on my part—to play along, as the *cochón*'s macho companion? Or to join in the transvestic frolic? To stand agape?

These are questions that one cannot settle definitively or unequivocally, for what would count as evidence? The word of one's informants counts for something, but in this case those words were double-edged (and necessarily so, as *playful* speech). And even assuming a serious response, how would one weigh divided or shifting subject matters? More vexing still, the acts of not just one but of plural *others* almost never offer themselves up as a transparent window on intention. And when plural others are *playing*, ambiguities multiply geometrically. In such situations, by their very nature, the one intention conceals the other, takes refuge in the other, leads to another.

I dwell on this point to put aside the obvious temptation toward ready finality and easy closure.

In both cultural feminism and in a section of gay/lesbian studies, it has become commonplace to offer one's *own self* up: as subject, evidence, argument, and analysis.[8] Like Descartes's philosophical introspections, this approach begins with what is most proximate and can—presumably—be best known: one's own self, one's own body, one's own experiences. From a fortified interior, one can then venture generalizations about an exterior—about others, about the social world.

Only a naive and vulgar model could delude us into thinking that the self enjoys some special access to its-self. In the first place, the presence of the self, and its effects on others, are necessarily occulted. We can never quite see our own eye seeing, hear our own ear hearing, or touch our own finger touching.[9] A self, then, cannot directly observe itself. Precisely *because* all knowledge filters through a situated self, that self, the nature and scope of its effects, constitutes something of a blind spot—and necessarily so. It is a problem no mirrors or interlocutions can ultimately solve (for they can provide only additional refractions, each with its own blindspots).

In the second place, a self is ever only partially revealed, even to the self, for consciousness is always "consciousness of something." A self exists because it projects into the world. If a self tries to trap itself, "[i]f consciousness tries to recover itself, to coincide with itself, all warm inside with the shutters closed, it becomes nothing. This need of consciousness to exist as consciousness of something other than itself is what Husserl calls 'intentionality.'"[10] As a swarm of intentions, interlacing with the world, the self is always beyond itself. Its effects are infinitely refracted, in the world and through other selves.

To narrow the practice of interpretation to one or two singular dimensions, as recollected from the position of an authoritative self, is to short-circuit everything that goes into the complexity of a moment, the richness of a situation, the contingencies of self-understanding, and the very *sociability* of the *social*, for much of what happens in the give-and-take of social life is tentative, unarticulated, inarticulate. Meanings are negotiated: we don't quite know what we meant until a response comes from someone else. Our best thinking is serendipitous: we're not quite sure what we suspected until some evidence appears. We're not quite sure what we're looking for until we find it. A gaze roves until it catches something unexpected, as we might have expected. What is self, no less than what is other, is out there, in the world, between us, and in play.

Unless it is to decompose into a virtual parody of its nemesis, positivism, reflexivity, too, must practice a sort of reflexivity—and be modest in its pretensions. In the end, I cannot say whether Guto's performance was a test *for me*, and if so, how it was conceived, or even how the evidence would have been read; whether it was an a priori event, and my reactions were probed ex post facto; whether it would have happened in my absence; whether it was staged for my benefit or for others' amusement. It happened, and I was there, a part of it. That is all.

• EXISTENTIAL FUZZ: A DRAMATIZATION

So I can only begin to fathom the complexities of intention that lay behind Guto's performance. This is a problem not just of audience reception but also of performative conception. Transvestism lends itself to performances of gender and sexuality, race and class, desire and repulsion, ego and alter—not to mention the physical body, its carnal practices, and its ideal representations. Such practices are multiply nuanced—and without doubt, complexly intended.

I hope I am being clear about the nature of this enigma. It is really an extension of the blindspots of self-knowledge just described—as seen from the other side. If one's own identity is always and necessarily complex, compound, and multifaceted; if one's own intentions are therefore somewhat ambiguous, even to one's own self; and if one's own self, and its effects, are therefore multiply refracted in the world of others, then one can hardly expect less from others.

If *ambiguity* rules a wide continent of the self, its intentions, its refractions through others, then *ambivalence* is the degree zero of such performances that dramatize and intensify everyday existential fuzz. In such moments, identity, identification, and intention are simultaneously revealed, concealed, performed, manipulated, and denied.

To leave matters in their properly productive ambiguity: Guto was acting the part of a woman, no doubt. He was also imitating queers, as the audience's cries suggest. But he was also playing the role of a man in drag—that is, he was performing a performance. And that is something too, and not at all the same thing, simply *practicing* a gender or sexuality, for in reality, what woman, what queer, what *cochón*, really acts that way, unless deliberately underscoring the action with a broadly performative gesture, too? No matter who acts them out, such performative performances can never simply *imitate* or *mimic* some original practice, person, or type, for they are always *in excess* of their target. That is what distinguishes them as "performances." This "excess" invariably slides around: Guto is now a woman, now a *cochón*, now a low-class prostitute, now a refined and affected matron, now *negra*, now *blanca*, now just Guto, his own self, in a dress, now something else entirely.

In this manner, transvestic performance is multiply transversal. It effects a rapid shuttle between shifting subject matters: between male and female, between femininity and effeminacy, between the real and the imaginary, between the given and the improvised. It is thus not quite correct to say that transvestism defines a space of parody or transgression.[11] Nor is it correct to say that it represents a ritual of intensification. Rather, it represents a profound equivocation. It takes up a space in-between. Contrary, even antagonistic, intentions are held in suspension, but nothing is canceled out. Not only are multiple intentions refracted through a given gesture but, moreover, many possible selves—and others—are always *in play*. The performative performance is a rich, nuanced, and *crowded* practice.

• PHENOMENOLOGY OF TRANSVESTISM

A movement is learned when the body has understood it.
> —Merleau-Ponty, *Phenomenology of Perception*

Such is the everyday world of transvestic performance, a mode of physical simulation far wider than literally cross-dressing—and far broader than any genre of gay camp.

A man quotes a woman. He pitches his voice high to mimic a woman's speech; he thereby takes her part in some reported conversation. Neither in Nicaragua nor in the United States is this an unusual occurrence. Men do this all the time. Or, to seal an argument or establish the reality of a claim, a man extends his gestures a little further than usual to affect either a feminine or homosexual role: a roll of the eyes, a flick of the wrist, a toss of the head. In recounting events or developing an argument, he thus slides into a genre of transvestic performance: that is, he strikes a pose intended to act out the part of some other person, some other role, some other being. He thus models his body's demeanor and disposition in the style of another. In these everyday miniature theaters, a sort of momentary stage arises: the performer necessarily monitors his audience, his interlocutors, to see whether a performance is working or misfiring, to gauge whether his act is appreciated or resented, to know whether it is amusing or annoying, and to decide how far he can take the conceit.

A woman does the same when she enacts the presumed radical alterity of *cochones*: a gesture in the air, a swirl of the hands, a facial expression, a mincing gait, an inflection understood as "effeminate." A glance at the audience, out of the corner of her eye. And in a less parodical context, women are always appropriating what are otherwise marked as "male" words, male speech patterns, male roles: "I am the head of the family now," I told my children, "the mother and the father, and what I say goes." Thus Doña Jazmina recounts herself speaking to her children in a new paternal voice after the death of her husband, just before taking a job in a factory to do "men's work."[12] Her statement itself is a kind of doubly transversal act: she is quoting herself at some past moment affecting a man's role: a performance of self performing another gender. My own citations keep the circuitry going—triply, quadrupally.

Like ventriloquism, these practices "throw" one's voice, one's gestures, one's demeanor—one's self—into the position of another. This happens more often than we might at first acknowledge. Conversation would likely be impossible without such give-and-take, for transvestic figuration is almost implicit in "reported speech," which is itself a necessary component of dialogue.[13] If we thus marked as "transvestic" every iteration, quotation, and pantomime that crossed the lines of gender or sexuality, we would understand such performances in all their startling density: as routine, habit, convention, and second nature.

These trans-vestics, whether linguistically or theatrically performative—whether affected through words, tone of voice, or physical comportment—all involve what Judith Butler describes as a kind of "citationality."[14] In other words, they trade against some representational convention or shared image: a standard gender, a normal body, a scripted role, the usual way some being is thought to act. But as long as the analysis remains fixed at this preliminary level, the analyst can choose between only two equally improbable options: either the performance *enacts* or it *violates* an ideal script.[15] Performativity becomes a variant of normativity, and we fall into the familiar trap of seeing every practice as the blossoming forth of an idea. Because everything happens on the plane of an abstract and disembodied concept, we fail to understand, and cannot even really pose, the question of performance in its carnal materiality. At the same time, we forget what physical fun it is to play. A more impractical understanding of practice and more disembodied approach to the body would be hard to imagine. For the moment we reduce carnal perception to symbolic language, the body becomes nonsense. In making the body one representation, one meaning, among others, we necessarily withdraw analysis to a contemplative retreat far removed from all those carnal ways of knowing and making the world that ought to focus properly the constructionist interrogative from the start: namely, how human subjects are crafted through the practical engagements of living flesh with the fabric of the world.

Before treating performance as a question of citation, then, it might be more productive to think through how a being moves, perceives, and practices. For what occurs in any transvestic performance is an extension and dramatization of rather more mundane movements, themselves implicit in the work of perception and in the logic of the senses.

Telescoping arguments from Merleau-Ponty,[16] "to perceive" something is "to figure" it: to foreground it while backgrounding everything else. Perceptual attention thus draws us both "toward" and "into" the thing attended. Necessarily, we do not attend to the eye when seeing but *from* the eye *to* what is seen.[17] In reaching, we do not know the body but, rather, what is touched or grasped. In the absorption of observation, subject/viewer and object/viewed are momentarily fused. We thus lose ourselves in finding the object, only to recover ourselves among objects, which become extensions of our own limbs, "incrustations in our own flesh."[18] The "operational intentionality"—or better yet, the carnal "ecstasis"[19]—of sense-perception means that we are always entangled with others, with objects, with the world; that by its very nature, the body locates itself only by going beyond its place of standing; that we find ourselves and lose ourselves in the same gesture, the same glance.

Now, if this work of the senses is interactive and creative; if in the primacy of perception we are always losing and finding ourselves; if our bodies are open to the experiences of other bodies, then the senses themselves are given to carnal crossovers, to physical empathies, and—if you will—to assorted trans-vestics and poly-morphics.

Every act of attention, every physical appropriation, every empathic power of the flesh, involves a kind of crossing over, a loss and recovery of the self. These quotidian practices are continuous with a host of other crossover desires, and would seem implicit in the social structure of perception. It could not be otherwise. Because we are social creatures, "self" is always found in an "other." And because our sociability is carnal in its very nature, the desire for another, the desire to be another, is part of the fundamental magnetism the world exerts on us.

Perhaps the full impact of these arguments ought to be stated carefully. First, *all* reported conversation, even self-reportage, and *all* instances of acting out—even the acting out of one's own self—entail a kind of crossover. Therein lies the power, and the risk, of the practice. Second, *all* practice, insofar as it engages the senses, lays the body open to the world and to others in the fashion dramatized—starkly but not uniquely—by transvestic performance. Finally, no one learns (or unlearns) anything—a gender or a sexuality or an identity or even a meaning—except through some process of physical modeling, sensuous experimentation, and bodily play. In the least perception, we are perpetually crossing over and becoming entangled, finding and losing the self, making and dissolving the world.

• HOSTILE MIMICRY AND PLAYACTING

When gays perform drag, when straights pantomime gays, when men mimic women, when children act out adult roles, what often happens is a mockery or a burlesque. We need not imagine that these acts are complimentary.

Yet even in the worst-case scenario—even in, say, a homophobic performance of homosexuality, a misogynist enactment of femininity, in clear cases of hostile mimicry—a certain *other* lesson is also, undeniably, drawn, or, at any rate, made available for those who might draw it. For to act out the part of the other plays off the contingencies of identity: it implies that one's body is malleable; that these gestures are, after all, just extensions of the gestures one already makes—indeed, that everyone is capable of making. As a problem of movement, the transversal performance is an exploration of a space not appropriate but proximate to the space already known. One attempts to abandon one's own horizon so as to see another's horizon, a different landscape. In inhabiting that space, the other is a possible self given to extravagance and excess.

Performances can, of course, "misfire." As Austin shows in his catalogue of performative types[20]—a typology organized precisely around how performances might fall short of or exceed their intended mark—the definition of a misfire depends on nonperformative constraints: on context. In gay camp, one mimics the gesture or words or another (even if that other is sometimes the self)—not quite literally but *ironically*. The audience must both see the irony and find it amusing. In this case, a performance misfires when its irony is lost or when its intention is judged too mean or too obvious. (Of course, all these judgments are relative to the taste, sophistication, and demands of the audience.)[21]

In certain Drag Balls, however, a "good" performance is a *convincing* one. As deBarge intimates, and as every commentator on "Paris Is Burning" has noted, effective drag produces "the effects of the real." In this case a misfiring is one that fails to achieve the illusion of "reality."

For a parodically intended straight male performance of either women or gay men, however, a "misfired" performance is one in which the style of being of the other all too readily sticks to the self of the performer. The act is all too convincing, for not enough space lies between the actor and the

acted. The parody thus lacks its intended irony—or, that irony is deliberately denied as a countermove in the game of negotiated meanings. A hostile
critic of the transvestic performance in this case might note: "It is altogether
quite conceivable that this is the way you act, that you are at home in this
style, that these gestures become you, that this is the way you *are*. Your gestures, your own body, give you away." This implies, further, a category of
"nonvoluntary performances"—by definition, misfirings of attempts to
affect one or another effect.

To return to the performance that stimulated these arguments: It would be
altogether too easy to understand Guto's drag act as hostile mimicry. There
was that, no doubt—but there was also an affectionate, almost sentimental
staging of the stock-figure queen, *la loca*. There was, certainly, the sense
that the transvestic *cochón* is exotic—but attractively, copiably so, with a
force that draws imitation. There was indeed the indication that such antics
are extreme—but in pleasurable senses: in physical abandon, visceral mirth,
creative frivolity.

Performances of this type suggest a variant of trans-vestics, partly taking
in several other genres and making them all possible. It involves trying
things on, trying things out. Playful, exploratory, and ambiguous, this mode
belongs to the genre of children's games, to free play, to friendly banter, and
to Carnival. I shall call this variant by its familiar name, *playacting*. As
infectious as laughter itself, it necessarily invites us to play along. Guto's
performance was almost certainly an example of this genre.

• CARNIVAL DREAMS: BENT-OVER ACTS
AND CROSSOVER DESIRES

"Let's go to *Carnaval* to see the *cochones*," people often say upon
the approach of Masaya's harvest festival. Someone will invariably note,
without apparent irony or guile: "The *cochones* at Carnival are very, very
beautiful." And then someone else will launch into a generous enumeration
of the characteristics and qualities of transvestic beauty, perhaps illustrating
his argument with a mincing gait, or by clutching an imaginary skirt.

The pleasures we partook in Guto's performance were very much in the
spirit of *Carnaval*, "the festival of disguises." Indeed, his antics set people
talking for several days about the visual and visceral joys of that much-antic-
ipated ritual. At Carnival, audience reaction to *cochones* is much what it
was with Guto's Carnivalesque performance: solicitous festivity, teasing
banter, and good-spirited encouragement.

Many of the *cochones* performing on the stage of Carnival are indeed "queers" in real life. But some are men who are not. The difference is not always apparent. Some affect their role with regal demeanor and glamorous adornment. Others are just men in rather plain dresses. No matter. Although onlookers clearly savor flamboyance over simplicity, all are graced with the familiar sobriquet "queer." The best performers receive this mockery in the good spirit of Carnival humor, giving as good as they get. A stately queen approached me at one Carnival procession coquettishly, flirtatiously, but upon closer approach, sharply reactive, as though a bad odor were emanating from me. Theatrically, she took leave, to gales of laughter from onlookers. Such is Carnival's humor, with its turning of tables and inversion of expectations.

One could make selective sense of Carnivalesque festivities through the idioms of gender and sexuality, which are visibly salient features of the experience. Carnival is, in part, the Revolt of the Queers. Much of its whimsy plays off slippages, contradictions, and ambiguities in the propositions of the prevailing sexual culture. Much of its "gay ambivalence"[22] plays off reverses of the usual valences associated with queers, homosexuality, effeminacy, and desire. Things hidden somersault into the open; passivity and activity exchange places; bad sport becomes good humor. In the ensuing vertigo, everyone becomes a little bit queer. The whole world is flaming.

But Carnival also—wildly—exceeds questions of gender and sexuality. One might say that the theory and practice of the flesh renewed each year at Carnival time *subtends* questions of gender and sexuality. If Carnival lends itself to ritual reversals in the performance of *gender and sexuality*, it no less takes up questions of *race, class, and ethnicity*. The famous peach-complexioned masks of Monimbó, with their rosy cheeks and pencil mustaches, recall the Spanish gentry and reveal the colonial dimension of Carnival's history: Indians take on the color, wear the face, mimic the dances—and thereby mime the powers—of white Spaniard rulers.[23] More modern Carnival images likewise traffic in depictions of class, administrative, or neocolonial power. Images include a transvestic whiteface jazzercise class, white-coated physicians with vaudevillian implements, bankers, politicians, *internacionalistas*.

Carnival, then, is the occasion for remembering, interrogating, and *playing with* the history of systems of domination. This reading locates Carnival in its proper historical and political-economic context. But such an approach still remains limited. The danger of leaving matters here is the danger of a false reduction, where everything is settled even before a question can be posed. Like transvestic performance, Carnival becomes either a

contestation or a ratification of the forms of power it so clearly dissects—
yet we have short-circuited the whole inquiry. We never understand *how* it
could, in and of itself, perform either function, or *why* the other should be
so fascinating to start with.

An alternative reading: When Carnaval comes to Masaya, when the Fiesta
de Santo Domingo is celebrated in Managua, or when any of a dozen such
festivities come to towns and barrios across Nicaragua, what happens is a
profusion of masks, a merry confounding of intentions, and a proliferation
of crossover desires. In Carnival time, "gay ambiguity" embraces not just
the imagery of the social, political, and economic world but also the physical world, the natural world. Carnival's working materials are sights, colors,
smells, and tastes. Its repertoire is the entire sensorium, an ever-shifting
kaleidoscope.

Consider, then, a host of other images. Humans take on animal forms,
and people become fantastic creatures: cows, bulls, birds, insects, Diablos,
and Diablitos. Saints walk among savages, alongside an occasional beast
made of sparklers and fireworks. Images pile up, not as a composed and
singular picture but as a work in progress, as an unfinished process of
experimentation, excess, and play. These images play at sacrilege: a traves-
tied crucifixion scene, with a transvestic Jesus and two drag thieves, all
bearing crosses. They also risk a rupture with coherence altogether: ani-
mated objects gambol perplexingly among funny monsters, fused bodies,
and creatures that are half-human and half-animal—like the stirrings of a
psychedelic dream. Trans-vestics becomes pan-vestics, as social discrimina-
tions oscillate, natural distinctions blur, and the contours of the body are
stretched and tested.[24]

Bakhtin's discussion of the sensibility of the mask is instructive:

> The mask is connected with the joy of change and reincarnation, with gay
> relativity and with the merry negation of uniformity and similarity; it rejects
> conformity to oneself. The mask is related to transition, metamorphoses, the
> violation of natural boundaries, to mockery and familiar nicknames. It con-
> tains the playful element in life; it is based on a peculiar interrelation of reality
> and image, characteristic of the most ancient rituals and spectacles.[25]

Beside Bakhtin's celebration of Carnival metamorphosis, we might set
Merleau-Ponty's understanding of the body in its very existence, for it is
precisely in metamorphosis, fusion, and confusion—in that space in-
between perceiver and perceived—that body and self take shape. "A human
body is present when, between the see-er and the visible, between touching

and touched, between one eye and the other, between hand and hand a kind of crossover occurs, when the spark of the sensing/sensible is lit."[26]

Like the "mirror's phantom" contemplated by Merleau-Ponty, the mask "draws my flesh into the outer world, and at the same time . . . my body can invest its psychic energy in the other bodies I see. Hence my body can include elements drawn from the body of another, just as my substance passes into them."[27] Reflections of beings, infinitely refracted, Carnival whimsy plays off those powers of perception that extend the body beyond its contours, to consolidate the body in and through the world—in the very act of dispersing it.

Masks—crossovers, transvestics—no less than mirrors "are instruments of a universal magic that converts things into spectacles, spectacles into things, myself into another, and another into myself."[28]

The horizons of Carnaval are as wide as perception itself and as sensuous as practice itself. Intentionality and identity are caught up in playful equivocations that are simultaneously productive, destructive, and instructive. Abandoning the self-conformity of our own contours, our own horizons, we try out other bodies, other horizons, all possible worlds. Hand with eye, and body to world, the Carnival celebrant grapples with the problem of aesthetics in its original and broadest sense: the perception of reality.[29] Through non-sense, we unmake a sense of self while making a new sense of reality—in open air, as play.

Seen in the context of Carnivalesque festivity, impersonations like Guto's are most richly understood not as discrete representations nor even as enactments of gender or sexuality alone but as practices continuous with the expression of other crossover desires. Such performances turn on physical excess, carnal ambivalence, and gay ambiguity. They model a body exposed to the gravitational pull of other bodies; an open, ambiguous body given to all kinds of crossovers and reversals; a body malleable and in flux because perception opens it to the world; a self thus lost, and recovered, but only in others and in the world.

▪ THE SOCIABILITY OF THE SOCIAL: GAY LAUGHTER

A helicopter passes overhead. A bad omen, the helicopter, in wartorn Nicaragua. On its first pass, it drops loads and loads of dirt on us. It turns, preparing for a second pass. With grit in our mouths and shaking dirt from our hair, we Carnival celebrants scramble to take refuge under the awnings of the buildings that line Masaya's narrow, cobbled streets. But on its second pass, the helicopter drops gently scented flower petals, which slowly rain on the panicked people left stranded in the street. And now we are laughing, all laughing—at life, at ourselves, at our bodies, at our fears no less than our pleasures. Carnival is like that: it assaults you and it pleasures you; it plays bait and switch with your sensibilities; it plays tricks on you, and it makes you laugh. I always leave these festivities more than a little giddy: intoxicated from so much laughter, and largely unable to explain later just what was so funny.

Laughter—deep, visceral laughter—resonates throughout the Carnival experience. An intimate breath reverberates from the belly, acquires a voice, gushes through the air, and flows from body to body. Like that very "respiration of Being" Merleau-Ponty writes about,[30] this inspired laughter erases the distinction between see-er and seen, performer and audience, laugher and laughed-at. Such laughter is the very medium of Carnival connectivity, its carnal form of sociability. This laughter is *felt*, intimately and viscerally, but is also shared and universal. In the dialectical play of opposites described by Bakhtin, laughter lifts us up even as it debases; it "dooms the existing world to the regenerating flames of Carnival."[31] All the popular genius of Carnival, all its mastery of visual tricks and physical games, comes to so much funny playing, so many ways of trying things out.

▪ THEORY *POST-FESTUM*: PLAYING AND KNOWING

Guto, of course, was just playing around. At first I dismissed his eruption as an unusual and marginal occurrence, until I considered just how densely such ludic interludes punctuate daily life. Guto's performance suggests that Carnivalesque leaps of body and meaning are implicit in a wide range of figurings. And just what happens when these everyday suspensions of the normal break out? What happens when people play act? What might it imply to get "carried away" by an act, a mask, a dramatic moment? Are we transported, as it were, bodily, to another space? Do we *live*, if only for a moment, that which we *do*?

Taken as a total situation and seen in the wider context of Carnival, Guto's performance and his audience's interactions suggest the special affinities between play and exploration, knowledge and jest. There was a practical knowledge, a kind of familiarity, to it all, and everyone—save me—seemed to know their parts. Once Guto initiated the evening's gag, my hosts all played along, with a physical understanding, much as one might follow the steps of a dance. There was a joke—it was all so much tomfoolery—but it is precisely the "gestic" or gestural element of jest that, in catching the *gist* of what it mimes, allows it to conceal so many obscure truths, so much manifold sobriety, such a detailed and carnal knowledge of the world.[32]

Huizinga's classic, *Homo Ludens*, provides a set of useful insights for thinking about the relationship between play and other forms of practice, and for theorizing play as both a human universal and as a base condition of culture. In a narrow sense, play is easily distinguished from routine activity and work. Play is "fun." It is some surplus exertion beyond utility and in excess of reason: unproductive, impractical, even irrational. As superfluous activity, voluntarily chosen, play is "free," and this "quality of action" distinguishes it from the practices of ordinary life. Thus, play is bounded against nonplay: as a playtime, on a playground.[33]

But in a broader sense, play has consequences far beyond its own space and time, and any distinction between play and nonplay begins to waver. As a functional matter, play and rules imply each other. Through repetition, variation, and memory, "play creates order, is order"; at the same time, an action becomes playful only through the gridwork of certain expectations, certain regularities. If "play" and "rules" thus come into being simultaneously, the forces they set in motion are anything but trivial.[34]

Huizinga's generalist anthropology traces the play-spirit through a variety of serious practices. Play's affinities with ritual are especially compelling: both are time-bounded activities, restricted to a special place, simultaneously rule-governed and rule-generating. As suspensions of the ordinary, both involve a "*loss of self*" in the *action of the event*. Despite its "imaginary" or "make-believe" character, play is efficacious: it creates a community of players, a community that lingers after the play is over—just as ritual leaves in its wake a community of believers.[35]

Finally, as an open-ended alternation of give-and-take, move-and-countermove, play is *tense*.[36] It solicits us. Poised to move in response, we want to see what happens next. This dynamic of tension and solution both gives play its fascination and fosters the cultivation of certain habits, the development of certain skills. The conduct of play brings together physical attention, mental alertness, bodily exertion, carnal learning, and tests of performative competence. As a result, the player's body and dispositions are, to varying degrees, reshaped by his or her engagement with sport.

From Huizinga's perspective, play embraces culture: it comes before it; it lies beneath it; and it is spread out before it. If the play-spirit lies at the origin of aesthetics, art, myth, ritual, and religion, then it is difficult to think of any "higher-order" activity that is not infused with the spirit of play. *Play is the very quality of action that both encompasses structure and makes it possible.*

Is it such a far step to ask whether what social constructionism attempts to describe is also a kind of play? Would it really be so outlandish to suggest that play is "the matrix of identity,"[37] that very surplus of activity whose consequences entail "subjects," "selves," and "groups"?

It no doubt goes too far to suggest that we *literally become* what we play at being, that we *make* the make-believe become the real. Only a charlatan or a madman asserts that. Play, *by itself*, has no power to make anything happen. "Play is *tense*" means, in part, that sinew and fiber resist certain activities. The freedom of play is meaningful, and faculties are reshaped by its exertions, precisely because both body and world are encountered as obstacles, resistances, counterforces. Play is exhilarating because it is experienced counter to work, to routine, to other practices. Huizinga's heuristic origins stories aside, we are never in the position of the first to play. We thus play our games freely, but we are not free to play them just any way we choose.

And yet, play does come to something. Put another way: Play is a special genre of practice—that form most perfectly aligned with what Marx calls "sensuous practice," or "practice as sensuous activity."[38] It embodies practice at its freest and most creative. In this engagement of body and world, we test the plasticity of the world against the dexterity of the body, not "to do" something else (as in work) but for no good reason at all. Play can either follow or violate a script, but that is not the major point. If play has some part in making the world, as Huizinga argues, it also has a part in unmaking the world, as Bakhtin shows. Either alternative is possible because play engages sense, body, and world in a particularly *impractical* way—and thereby liberates practice from its seriousness, its commitment to a given end, its inertia. In the form of play, practice displays its most potent possibilities (but not its most direct results).

In the model suggested here, play is to identity as sense is to body: it locates and orients us, but it also goes beyond and exceeds us. In this making of identity, the body is neither "given" nor "made up." A body is a self "not by transparency, like thought, which never thinks anything except by assimilating it, constituting it, transforming it into a thought—but a self by confusion, narcissism, inherence of the see-er in the seen, the toucher in the touched, the feeler in the felt—a self, then, that is caught up in things." [39]

All of existence is caught up together, as an unbroken circuit of perception and practice, but to play is to leap and throw oneself, consciously (if not always voluntarily)—an especially instructive way of being "caught up in things." It is a way of knowing. We learn something when we play. The body remembers it. But against all temptation to see the body as a kind of clay, passively stamped by other forces, and permanently shaped into a closed subject, play also reminds us that plasticity is reciprocal; that body and world come into being together.

• IDENTITY, POLITICS, PRACTICE

In ordinary life, ambiguities and crossovers, the promiscuity of the senses, are held in check. Routine practices constellate narrow and habitual relations between self, others, world. When the world is thus held constant, the polymorphous potential of the flesh is still at work, but its surplus capacities are bracketed off and—as it were—backgrounded. "Being" thus brokers a compromise with the forces of its own composition: we attend *to* certain regularities, and thus *from* a body, a self, held constant. Understood this way, "identity" means nothing more than a temporary cessation of the overflow of the senses. (It is to this side of perception that Bourdieu's theory of practice restricts itself: that is, with what memory *forgets*, with what perception *omits*.)[40]

And yet, in the give-and-take of social life, carnivalized subjects and dispersed intentionalities are perpetually breaking through all that is stable, structural, and singular. In the metamorphic figurations of everyday practice; in the implicitly trans-vestic conceits of reported speech; in speculation on the compound identities and mixed motives of other people; in deconstructive double-talk, pun, and verbal play; in every way of longing for a new identity, another body, a fresh perspective—by myriad such devices, what is alter is also ego, what is "beyond" is also "within," and ambiguity lives at the core of identity. Implicit in the nature of our bond with the world, even the most habituated habitus can be the source of new experiences. Through the magic of perception, even the most objectified object can be dislodged from its inertia to reveal new facets. Even the most consolidated self retains in the senses a perpetually available resource for going beyond its-self. "All flesh, even that of the world, radiates beyond itself."[41]

The kind of playfulness I have been sketching—aesthetic, plastic, and creative—is often understood as a variety of leisure, as an index of education, or as a function of privilege. Bourdieu thus separates critical thought from ordinary perception, and reflection from activity.[42] But perceptual intelligence is not necessarily on the side of the higher orders, with inertia on the side of the lower. No one is ever so impoverished or exploited as to be without capacity for empathy, mimicry, laughter, and double-talk. Even at the height of war, social dislocation, and economic scarcity—especially then—people make time for funny games and Carnival laughter.

Not all cultures publicly elaborate these powers: some celebrate Carnival; others do not. Yet like the existentialist idea of freedom, these capacities are always there, always here, always available for some engagement. Play is always available for some work. Everyday transvestics, assorted plays off ambiguity, and temporary transpositions of identity are simultaneously so germane and so mundane that the work they do often goes unnoticed.

Here, in a nutshell, is my argument about that work: identity, like hermeneutic knowledge, is a matter of locating and stabilizing a *self* by way of the detour of the *other*.[43] Identity, then, is not self-identical. Experience is not a receptacle. Like learning to see or learning to walk, learning a gender or a sexuality—or any other kind of self/identity—relies on physical explorations, carnal transpositions, corporeal learning, and practice. Transvestics and other kinds of body-play are absolutely necessary to secure stable genders, but they also carry the danger that play always implies: a game can, at any moment, run away with the players. In engaging the world and one another, subjects make themselves, but they also—through intentionalities without intention—lay themselves open to risks without which they could not "exist" at all.

This volatile and creative capacity is not simply "given," a force outside history, society, and meaning. Like language, it is a human capacity that must nonetheless be learned and developed in all its specifics, in all its variable forms. Although it is "volitional," it represents the will of no given subject; rather, it is that plurality of wills through which subjects are realized. It takes distinctive forms but is not just a terminal form of social practice; it is also both a medium and a *font* of sociability. Surely, it is meaningful, but not in the purely "conceptual" sense of Saussurean semiotics; it is, rather, that creative and slippery way of grounding meaning, through perception, at the interface between flesh and world. This "ecstatic" power, then, belongs to history, but not the way an object fits in a box. We should say, rather, that this capacity—what we do when we play no less than when we labor—is both constitutive in and constituted by history. It is the flesh and blood of history.[44]

Because playful practice is a social power, its effects are differentially distributed. The politics of play is thus anything but a straightforward matter. Fascist Right no less than antiauthoritarian Left embodies a kind of play-spirit. No one wants to be on the receiving end of certain kinds of play, to be "toyed with" as a "play-thing." Doña Jazmina is being inventive, but she is not being funny when she appropriates a partly masculine identification. Cross-dressing has different social implications, depending on who crosses to what, for whom, and in what context. Men and women, rich and poor, "straight" and "queer," all *play*, but they do not and cannot all play the same way, with the same intentions, to the same effects.

Understood in this sense, such fun and games become difficult to distinguish rigorously from ritual at its most solemn—or from the seriocomic practices of gender in everyday life. In this wider sense, Guto's performance was neither the exception nor the rule. Rather, it embodied the kind of practice capable of making or breaking rules. These practices locate us at the heart of practice and in the matrix of identity—not where identity is "produced" or directly made as the consequence of some activity but where unmotivated intentionalities are caught up with unintended consequences; not where signifier joins signified nor where a code is either cited or parodied but, rather, where sense both precedes and exceeds meaning; where hand and eye connect to world; where, between eye and hand, body and world, ego and alter, a kind of combustion occurs; where the creative powers of perception bear witness to the birth of the world; and where the world is made new again at every moment.

These practices happen, unnoticed, all the time. Hand to substance, we give something shape; we know it by its touch and feel. We then indicate that something with a gesture, when the word escapes us. Hand with eye and touch to matter, we learn a technique of labor or a style of expression. We know something because we have explored it from all its angles; we have passed into it, and it into us. There is no cultural activity that is without some element of physical play and corporeal learning. Applying hand to object, we learn the materiality of things. Applying sense memory to body image, we practice at being someone.

This is not to say that transvestism lies at the origin of culture, which is Marjorie Garber's provocative claim in *Vested Interests*.[45] People have argued that stranger things lie at the origin of culture, but it seems to me that this staging of the claim puts the terms backward. Undoubtedly, transvestism is implicit in any gender system—and is likely necessary for gender to exist at all. But it might be better to say that the kind of manipulation, learning, and play that goes into a transvestic ritual goes into every other cultural practice as well; that where there is gender, there must also be transvestism.

Sometimes this playful practice or sensuous epistemology is understood as "mimesis."[46] But as Huizinga notes, play is less "mimetic" (imitative representation) than *methectic*: "a helping out of the action." Its efficacy implies less a distinctive "play instinct" or "mimetic faculty" than the general powers of perception and practice.

It would also be too straightforward to assert simply that all identity is playfully performative—that, for a moment there, Guto really *was* a *cochón*, or a woman, or a transgendered person; that play *directly* makes things happen; that play *is* construction; that gender *is* transvestism. Rather, it might be better to say that playful practices put us at the fulcrum of a phenomenological vector, into a position from which we might spring in any number of different directions. To play act, to play at Carnival, to play at transvestism, is to explore those possibilities.

• GUTO'S "BREASTS": THE TRANSVESTISM OF THE BODY

There are several ways for a body to be body.

　　　　　—Merleau-Ponty, *Phenomenology of Perception*

I do not want to close out this essay with a sense of finality, a notion opposed, at any rate, to Carnival play. I do not even know whether it is germane—how does one ever claim to know such things?—to mention this. After adolescence, Guto, like some other boys in his extended family, had begun to grow small breasts. His older brother Charlie claimed that his own nipples sometimes produced *leche*, milk, as I discovered one day when I encountered him, concentratedly squeezing his nipples and asked him what he was doing. Now, other than Guto's small "breasts," and Charlie's occasional "lactation," the young men's physiques were scarcely "feminine." If anything, their solidly muscular frames could be seen only as "masculine." I surmise that, because Doña Flora's family had come from a rural province, where they lived until moving to Managua, her children may have been exposed to pesticides, including DDT. Some pesticides, when they decompose, mimic the effects of estrogen, giving rise to such phenomena as "breasts" in young men.

When Guto acted out his transvestic part, he had recently undergone a minor operation to remove the breasts. A pair of small, crescent-shaped scars cupped his nipples. Guto made no effort to conceal them, and did not seem self-conscious about these odd-looking marks, which resembled nothing so much as happy-face smiles inscribed on his chest.

• NOTES

Thanks to Florence Babb, Dan Balderston, John Beverley, Samuel Colón, Lois Horton, Micaela di Leonardo, Jean Franco, Donna Guy, Ann Palkovich, Ileana Rodríguez, and Paul Smith for critical readings of early drafts. Additional thanks to those who were collegial during trying times at Columbia, and who gave my work in gay/lesbian studies supportive criticism and helpful feedback: Caroline Bynum, Elaine Combs-Schilling, Linda Green, Jean Howard, Katherine Newman, and Gayatri Spivak. Students rarely get the credit they deserve for stimulating a professor's thinking; special thanks are in order for Andy Bickford, Alex Costley, and Marcial Godoy. And of course, thanks to all the cultural studies students at George Mason University. Finally, my work is indebted to Judith Butler's sharp and disciplined formulations—when departing from them no less than when applying them.

1. Some readers may recognize these characters, the subjects of my book *Life Is Hard: Machismo, Danger, and the Intimacy of Power in Nicaragua* (Berkeley: University of California Press, 1992).

2. Ibid., 52–68.

3. Ibid., 245.

4. Transvestism, transsexuality, and related forms of transgression have lent themselves to various interpretations. See, for instance, Judith Butler, "Critically Queer," *GLQ* 1.1 (1993): 17–32, esp. 21–24; Judith Butler, *Bodies That Matter: On the Discursive Limits of "Sex"* (New York: Routledge, 1993), esp. 121–40; Marjorie Garber, *Vested Interests: Cross-Dressing and Cultural Anxiety* (New York: Routledge, 1992); Esther Newton, *Mother Camp: Female Impersonators in America* (Chicago: University of Chicago Press, 1972, 1979), Janice Raymond, *The Transsexual Empire: The Making of the She-Male* (Boston: Beacon Press, 1979); Nancy Scheper-Hughes, *Death without Weeping: The Violence of Everyday Life in Brazil* (Berkeley: University of California Press, 1992), 490–97; Judith Shapiro, "Transsexualism: Reflections on the Persistence of Gender and the Mutability of Sex," in *Body Guards*, ed. Julia Epstein and Kristina Straub (New York: Routledge, 1991), 248–79.

5. Clifford Geertz, "Thick Description," in *The Interpretation of Cultures* (New York: Basic Books, 1973), 3–30, at 12, 16.

6. The heading of this section is used with apologies to Eve Kosofsky Sedgwick, whose *Epistemology of the Closet* (Berkeley: University of California, 1990) continues to inspire thinking about the closed and the open, the hidden and the revealed.

7. Lancaster, *Life Is Hard*, 235–78.

8. See Roger Lancaster, "The Use and Abuse of Reflexivity," *American Ethnologist*, forthcoming.

9. See Maurice Merleau-Ponty, *Phenomenology of Perception* (London: Routledge & Kegan Paul, 1962), 90–91; see also Drew Leder, *The Absent Body* (Chicago: University of Chicago Press, 1990), an extended investigation into how the body "disappears" as a function of sensuous engagements.

10. Jean-Paul Sartre, "Intentionality" (1939). Reprinted in Jonathan Crary and Sanford Kwinter, eds., *Incorporations* (New York: Zone, 1992), 387–91, at 389.

11. See Judith Butler, *Gender Trouble: Feminism and the Subversion of Identity* (New York: Routledge, 1990), 128–49; Butler, *Bodies That Matter*, 121–40. See also Eve Kosofsky Sedgwick, "Queer Performativity: Henry James's *The Art of the Novel*," and Butler, "Critically Queer," *GLQ* 1.1 (1993): 1–16 and 17–32, respectively.

12. Lancaster, *Life Is Hard*, 179–80.

13. I am extending Volosinov's ideas, from the end of *Marxism and the Philosophy of Language* (1929; Cambridge: Harvard University Press, 1986).

14. See especially Butler, *Bodies That Matter*, 12–16.

15. See Sedgwick's arguments in "Queer Performativity."

16. I am drawing freely on various texts by Merleau-Ponty: *Phenomenology of Perception*, *The Primacy of Perception* (Evanston: Northwestern University Press, 1964), *Sense and Non-Sense* (Evanston: Northwestern University Press, 1964), and *The Visible and the Invisible* (Evanston: Northwestern University Press, 1968).

17. See Leder's precise discussion of "the From and the To" in *The Absent Body*, 15–17.

18. Merleau-Ponty, "Eye and Mind" [1960], in *The Merleau-Ponty Aesthetics Reader*, ed. Galen A. Johnson (Evanston: Northwestern University Press, 1993), 121–49 at 125.

19. If the term *intentionality* carries the Cartesian baggage of an implicitly "mental" (not "physical") act, the word *ecstasis* "describes the operation of the lived body. The body always has a determinate stance—it is that whereby we are located and defined. But the very nature of the body is to project outward from its place of standing" (Leder, *The Absent Body*, 21–22). Readers may note that throughout this essay, I have gradually unfolded these concepts, beginning with Sartre's description of Husserl's "intentionality," working toward the "operative intentionality" of Merleau-Ponty's early work, and ending with the "ecstasis" that occupied Merleau-Ponty's later writings.

20. J. L. Austin, *How to Do Things with Words*, 2d ed. (Cambridge: Harvard University Press, 1975).

21. For wide-ranging analyses of gay camp, see David Bergman, ed., *Camp Grounds: Style and Homosexuality* (Amherst: University of Massachusetts Press, 1993).

22. Felicitously and throughout the text, the English translator of Bakhtin's *Rabelais and His World* gives such terms as "gay ambiguity," "gay ambivalence," "gay laughter," and especially "gay matter." These terms—with their emphasis on change, flux, and carnal engagement—are fully resonant with the perspective of this essay.

23. See Roger N. Lancaster, "The Festival of Disguises," *Progressive*, November 1986, 50.

24. See Georges Bataille, *Theory of Religion* (New York: Zone, 1992), 54.

25. Bakhtin, *Rabelais and His World*, 39–40.

26. Merleau-Ponty, "Eye and Mind," 125.

27. Ibid., 130.

28. Ibid.

29. See arguments by Susan Buck-Morss, "Aesthetics and Anaesthetics: Walter Benjamin's Artwork Essay Reconsidered," *October* 62 (1992): 3–41.

30. Merleau-Ponty, "Eye and Mind," 129.

31. Bakhtin, *Rabelais and His World*, 394.

32. On "gest," see Bertolt Brecht, *Brecht on Theatre: The Development of an Aesthetic*, ed. John Willet (New York: Hill & Wang, 1964). On "gesture," see Merleau-Ponty, esp. *The Primacy of Perception*, 7.

33. Johan Huizinga, *Homo Ludens: A Study of the Play Element in Culture* (Boston: Beacon Press, 1944, 1955), 2–3, 8, 9–10.

34. Ibid., 10ff.

35. Ibid., 12, 18–27.

36. Ibid., 11.

37. To invoke a much-used concept. See, for instance, Butler's formulations in *Bodies That Matter*, esp. 7–8, 31.

38. See especially the "Theses on Feuerbach" in *Karl Marx: Selected Writings*, ed. David McLellan (Oxford: Oxford University Press, 1977), 156–58; see also Marx's arguments about sense, sensuousness, human sense, corporeality, and practice in *The Economic and Philosophical Manuscripts of 1844* (Buffalo: Prometheus Books, 1988).

39. Merleau-Ponty, "Eye and Mind," 124.

40. Pierre Bourdieu, *The Logic of Practice* (Stanford: Stanford University Press, 1980), esp. 52–97.

41. Merleau-Ponty, "Eye and Mind," 145.

42. Bourdieu, *The Logic of Practice*.

43. See Diana Fuss's fine discussion of perspectives from Freud and Lacan, through Sedgwick, Butler, and others on "identity" and "identification" in *Identification Papers* (New York: Routledge, 1995), 1–19.

44. See Merleau-Ponty's discussion of praxis theory, "Marxism and Philosophy," in *Sense and Non-Sense*, 125–36.

45. Garber, *Vested Interests*, 34.

46. See especially Michael Taussig, *Mimesis and Alterity: A Particular History of the Senses* (New York: Routledge, 1993).

3 *Yvonne Yarbro-Bejarano*

Crossing the Border with Chabela Vargas

A Chicana Femme's Tribute

In her public lesbian identification and performance style, singer Chabela Vargas creates a space for a U.S. Latina lesbian reading within Mexican and Latin-American popular music.[1] In this essay, I wish to focus on a specific strategy of cultural representation, that of "queering" heterosexual cultural codes.[2] When I speak of representation, I imply producers and consumers, transmission and reception. Among the transmitters, I include both the artist Chabela Vargas and Orfeón records as marketer of the popular cultural "myth" of Chabela Vargas.

Chabela Vargas allows me to participate in different ways in a form of popular culture that is at once dearly beloved, because of the emotional response and pleasure it evokes, and alienating, because of the (hetero)sexism of its lyrics, and the heterosexual public spaces of its *bailes*. Chilean filmmaker Valeria Sarmiento, in her *Un hombre cuando es hombre* (A man when he is a man), examines the connection between the myths of romantic love in Mexican popular culture, especially music, and rigid gender roles, and violence against, and even murder of, women in Costa Rican culture. But it is important to struggle for meaning here because popular music is a site of body-centered pleasures and cultural identifications I would be loath to "give up to the enemy"!

The mythic images offered for identification, rejection, or negotiation in popular culture make different subject positions available for different consumers. Because of her public sexual positioning as a lesbian, Chabela Vargas appropriates or undermines many of the gendered subject positions in Mexican popular songs, even as she illuminates how impossible it is to conceive of Mexican/Chicana lesbian identities and desires completely outside these culturally specific imaginings about men and women, masculinity and femininity. Although Latina lesbians have always had their own private strategies for appropriating their favorite songs for their favorite fantasies, Chabela Vargas, as a publicly identified lesbian, creates what Emma Pérez calls *sitio* for me within Mexican popular music, a space/place for my mestiza lesbian subjectivity, desire, and sexuality.[3] This occurs for me in Chabela's lesbianizing of the music and lyrics, especially of the heterosexual male subject of desire, and in her public image and performance of sexual identity. Vargas's recordings, photographs, and performances, passed around among Latinas in the United States, have caused lesbian images and an oral lesbian history to merge into the mythic highway of Mexican popular culture. The inventive playfulness of these stories interests me more than their "veracity" or "accuracy" in the conventional historical sense.

Chabela Vargas was an active proponent of the first wave of the Latin-American "rescate del folclor" (rescue of folklore) movement. The Costa Rican writer and poet Alfonso Chase has recently disproved the popular belief that Vargas is Mexican, documenting her birth near the Costa Rican capital.[4] Chase reports that the singer, like other Latin-American "personalities" of the time (read "queers" in the broadest sense), moved to Mexico in the 1950s "en busca de comprensión y espacio" (in search of comprehension and space). In the wake of her nomadic travels throughout Latin America and the world, poets and writers such as Nicolás Guillén, Miguel Angel Asturias, and León de Greiff have praised Chabela for her voice and interpretations.[5] Chabela's heyday in Mexico came in the first half of the 1960s, in the "bohemian" atmosphere of clubs frequented by established and future cultural patriarchs of the Mexican intelligentsia.

At the same time that Chabela Vargas was idolized for her passionate interpretation of Mexican and Latin American popular song, she cut a scandalous figure because of her performance of her out lesbianism. Anecdotes abound of her flamboyant "entrances" on motorcycles and in sports cars and her blatant flirting with women in the audience. She was ultimately blacklisted because of her so-called obscene behavior. In the early 1970s she made her Mexican comeback, performing in a queer-friendly venue for political theater artists called El hábito in Coyoacán, a reference to nuns' (and possibly other) habits.

In 1993, at the age of seventy-four, Chabela Vargas rode the crest of a second comeback in Spain referred to as "El chavelazo" (Chabela-mania), enjoying the adoration of a third generation of Spanish fans:[6] "Dejó al público gozosamente traspuesto, con el pulso desmayado y en estado catártico" (she left the public joyfully transported, with faint pulses and in a cathartic state).[7] Besides this image of a ravished fandom, the press resorted to the lexicon of religious worship: *La Jornada* referred to director Almodóvar as one of the priests who preach Chavelism, and *ABC* intoned, "Bienaventurados los que consiguieron entradas para ver a Chavela Vargas" (Blessed are those who got tickets to see Chavela Vargas). She recorded two albums during her seven-recital tour, making the contemporary scene in the company of queer director Pedro Almodóvar, whose filmmaking esthetic includes using popular Mexican songs, either over the credits or, as with Agustín Lara's "Piensa en mí" in *Tacones lejanos* (High heels), as part of the narrative.

The reports of the tour in the Spanish press add fuel to this avid femme's fantasies, aiding in the imaginative re-creation of Chabela's stage persona. Undaunted by the punishment meted out for her blatant public sexuality in the 1960s, Chabela opened her recital in Madrid with a provocative double entendre, declaring her tireless dedication to "musical" passions: "Cuando a uno le gusta algo, debe practicarlo durante toda la noche" (When you like something, you should do it all night long).[8] It is also fun to note the new tonality of the present scene; instead of flirting with women in the audience, Chabela exchanged innuendos with Almodóvar, seated at a table with actresses Victoria Abril and Bibí Anderson of *Tacones*, who wept their way through Chabela's rendition of "Piensa en mí." When Chabela suggested to Almodóvar from the stage that they get married and have lots of "Pedritos" [little Peters], the director's reply queered the religious lexicon of the Spanish press coverage, calling attention to the singer's advanced age and his/their own sexuality: "Ay Chavela, tú eres capaz de hacer milagros" ([Oh Chavela, you are capable of making miracles)].[9]

Chabela Vargas has recorded more than eighty albums.[10] I am proposing a limited reading of four of her albums with Orfeón, whose commodification of the singer is marked by ambivalence and contra-diction. In the liner notes, in tandem with the cover photos, Orfeón appears anxious to reconcile two aspects of its presentation of Chabela Vargas that are radically at

odds: her "difference" and her emblematic status as "la intérprete más sim-
bólica" (the most symbolic interpreter) of the sentimental Mexican soul.
In spite of Orfeón's rather desperate marketing strategy, Mexicans would
much sooner recognize an earlier singer, Lucha Reyes, as the most representative interpreter of Mexican popular song rather than the idiosyncratic
and iconoclastic Vargas. (Reyes was rumored to be lesbian but did not publicly identify, as did Vargas.) Ironically, by 1993 Chabela *is* the soul of
Mexican identity for her third-generation Spanish fans.

Even a cursory glance at the images of her on the covers of these records
establishes an incontrovertible fact: femme she's not. I realize that the terms
butch and *femme* cannot be applied unproblematically to Mexican culture,
but I will use them because as a bicultural Chicana living in the United
States, my readings of lesbian texts and my own erotic positionings are
informed by butch-femme as well as Mexican and Chicana/o cultural
dynamics; besides, it's *my* fantasy. I offer here a Chicana femme take on
Chabela Vargas.[11] Vargas's first name is spelled at times with a "v" and at
times with a "b," the latter evoking "lo popular" (the people). I prefer to use
the "b," for "butch."

None of the four photos shows her in a dress or a skirt. On her first
album, *Noche bohemia* (Bohemian night), she is wearing the garb adopted
by many in the bohemian scene affiliated with the folklore movement: the
poncho and the huaraches of the male Mexican Indian, rather than femi-
nine-gendered apparel. The marketing strategy here also appeals to those
who want something "raro" or "different," coded in the reference to the
"ambiente nocturno y bohemio" (nocturnal and bohemian atmosphere) of
the clubs. The notes on *Noche bohemia* call attention to Chabela's face and
stance: "una mujer de rostro intensamente interesante, muy hierático, pero
lleno de vida tras su máscara de aparente indiferencia" (a woman with an
intensely interesting face, very hieratic, but full of life behind her mask of
apparent indifference). The control and containment of her public butch
persona contrast with the unusual intensity of her singing (even by Mexican
standards). Her hair is long but pulled back severely, and she is holding a
guitar. Although the esteemed guitarist Antonio Bribiesca is prominently
featured on all four albums as her accompanist, this masculine-identified
agency is attributed to her in the photo, which supports the other signifiers
that make up her butch image.

The butch image on her second album, *Hacia la vida* (Toward life), consists of the hairstyle, the baby-blue shirt, and, in particular, that certain posture with the cigarette from the repertory of butch self-stylings that signal
erotic capabilities. At the same time, her butch darkness in the photograph

engages my desire as a mestiza femme. Consumption of this image provides both femmes and butches what Valerie Traub calls "erotic identifications," meaning a sense of self as erotic subject or object.[12] Because eroticism is not a fixed identity but a sum of erotic practices, the position taken at any given moment in any erotic encounter can switch. In other words, though power transfers characterize the realm of the erotic, the positions of giving and taking are mobile. Even so, individuals tend to have a "general erotic script." *Chabela: "b" for butch.* The liner notes' references to her "strong personality" and how she "lives for her public" are richly ironic, in light of the anecdotal performance tradition I referred to earlier.

The image on the third album, *Chavela Vargas*, food for many a fantasy, is a close-up of her face and hand, shirt buttoned at the throat (no skin visible). The photo, which even looks like it could be on a package of cigarettes,[13] closely identifies her with the smoking culture that permeates Mexican popular music and its marketing. Here the erotic signifier of the cigarette is accompanied by the *short* short fingernails. Her hand rests on the guitar, traditionally the sexualized female body upon which the heterosexual male lover plays. Taken together, the short nails so near the guitar amount to an erotic advertisement of butch sexual expertise. Orfeón makes explicit the marketing strategy of the second album: what is unique and strange can also be "exclusive," accessible only to "aquellos privilegiados que saben apreciar" Chabela Vargas's "estilo único y extraño" (those privileged ones who know how to appreciate Chabela Vargas's unique and strange style).

On *La original Chavela Vargas*, from the early 1970s, she takes on the stature of a veritable Latin American monument, through camera angle, upturned positioning of the chin and face, and the red Peruvian-style ruana that covers her body. It is this strong, handsome Chabela that we see in the Spanish press photos, twenty years later. Again, the monumentalizing impulse in her presentation as interpreter of "el más profundo y arraigado sentimiento del pueblo" (the most profound and deep-rooted sentiment of the people) fails to jibe entirely with the emphasis on her unique style.

The "strangeness" of Chabela Vargas's style is consistently explained in the liner notes in terms of her voice and her idiosyncratic interpretations, although "certain" readers are expected to read between the lines to her "other" difference. Chabela Vargas uses her voice and her body to express marginalized lesbian desire and longing, sexual giving and taking, delight and suffering, seduction and rejection. This unsettling, coded, but undeniable connection between her interpretations and her physicality (the unique vocal technique to infuse emotions into the songs, her body in performance) must be turned comfortingly back to the realm of musicianship. The startling conflation of Chabela Vargas as "estampa de México" (hallmark of Mexico) and butch-desiring subject is quite satisfying, for it includes lesbian subjectivity within the definition of what is considered "authentically" Mexican!

There is a way in which just the public knowledge of Vargas's lesbianism suffices for this femme listener/viewer to appropriate the entire repertory of songs Chabela sings for lesbian desire. Certainly, many such songs, whether "Tatuaje" (Tattoo) in Amalia Mendoza's lush passionate voice or Trío Los Panchos's classics in Edie Gorme's snappy vocal style, are susceptible to lesbian readings because of the lack of gendered pronouns, as also happens with the studious avoidance of pronouns in Mexican gay singer Juan Gabriel's work, which makes subject positions available for gay male consumers. Some heterosexual female singers, such as Tania Libertad, systematically change the pronouns of the classical male songs to align the desire of the text along a heterosexual axis. Still, precisely because Tania Libertad or Amalia Mendoza represent heterosexual female *desire*, they provide femme identifications and engage butch desire. One feminine gender position Paquita la del Barrio does particularly well is the abandoned but tough woman who scornfully trashes no-good former lovers, exposed as worth less than a cigarette. But she also aligns herself behind the punitive male voice of patriarchal authority, dispensing judgments on "malas mujeres" (bad women) in her strong, matronly voice.

But it is precisely in the play of the pronouns that the most radical appropriations are made; they are key to the ways certain listeners are included and others excluded. Chabela Vargas's most transgressive interventions are those in which the voice of the song is either unmarked or identified as male, and the object of desire is marked as female in the text. Because traditionally such songs have been sung by male singers, in these texts, Chabela Vargas dons a kind of musical drag, writing/ speaking/singing lesbian desire through the butch appropriation of the active heterosexual male subject position. Such texts, in which the object of desire is marked as "she," are open to lesbian and male heterosexual readings but limit female heterosexual or gay male identifications. This is not to deny possibilities of bisexual or queer identifications or a butch gay male reading of a femme object of desire but merely to point out that the specific dynamic here appears to be between a particular construction of heterosexual (especially masculine) gender roles and their use as a vehicle for lesbian erotic identifications.

I want to illustrate this with two musical texts, "Macorina" and "La china," which both sing of erotic nocturnal encounters.

MACORINA

Ponme la mano aquí, Macorina,	*Put your hand here, Macorina*
Ponme la mano aquí. (2X)	*Put your hand here.* (2X)
Tus pies dejaban la estera	Your feet left the mat
Y se escapaba tu saya	And your skirt escaped
Buscando la guardarraya	Seeking the boundary
Que al ver tu talle tan fino	On seeing your slender waist
Las cañas azucareras	The sugar canes threw
Se echaban por el camino	Themselves down along the way
Para que tú las molieras	For you to grind
Como si fueses molino.	As if you were a mill.
Ponme la mano . . .	*Put your hand . . .*
Tus senos carne de anó'	Your breasts, soursop fruit
Tu boca una bendición	Your mouth a blessing
De guanábana madura	Of ripe guanabana
Y era tu fina cintura	And your slender waist
La misma de aquel danzón	Was the same as that dance
Ponme la mano . . .	*Put your hand . . .*
Después el amanecer	Then the dawn
Que de mis brazos te lleva	That takes you from my arms
Y yo sin saber qué hacer	And I not knowing what to do
De aquel olor a mujer	With that woman scent
A mango y a caña nueva	Like mango and new cane
Con que me llenaste al son	With which you filled me at
Caliente de aquel danzón.	The hot sound of that dance.
Ponme la mano . . .	*Put your hand . . .*

The insistent refrain of "Macorina" is "Ponme la mano aquí, Macorina, ponme la mano aquí" (put your hand here, Macorina, put your hand here). Of course the answer to the question "where?" depends on the body of the speaking/singing subject, heterosexual male or butch lesbian. In performance, Chabela Vargas would engage the gaze of a woman in the audience and put her hand on her own crotch when singing this line. This claiming of the spaces of Mexican popular music for the female/lesbian sexual body is given a highly erotic charge by the lyrics of the song. Sensual images of tropical fruits and sugar cane associating the female body with certain tastes, forms, and smells are cast definitively into the realm of the sexual through the image of the sugar cane throwing themselves down for her to "grind" (moler). The song gets away with this in part through the articulation between having sex and dancing (the references to "aquel danzón"). The voluptuous inventory of the female body, with its movements, fragrances, and ripe flavors, generates a lot of heat.

In "La china" Chabela sings through the subject position of the male lover returning to the domestic feminine space of the rancho in joyful anticipation, using a heterosexual gender role to assert lesbian erotic agency.[14]

LA CHINA

Mi china me conoce	My darling knows me
Ya hasta en los pasos	By my footsteps
Pero si piso juerte	But if I walk hard
Se queda en duda	She is in doubt
Si voy tarde en la noche	If I go late at night
Piso despacio	I walk slow
Me saco las espuelas	I take off my spurs
Pa' no hacer bulla.	To avoid making noise.
Chinita de mi vida	*My little darling, my love*
Vení, vení	*Come, come here*
No seas tan huraña	*Don't be so skittish*
Que sos pa' mí	*For you belong to me*
Ya lo saben todos	*Everybody already knows*
Que como yo	*That no one loves you*
Naiden te quere.	*Like I do.*
Cuando voy pa' mi rancho	When I get to my ranch
Tarde en la noche	Late at night
Desensillo el caballo	I unsaddle the horse
Junto a la puerta	Next to the door
Y mi china me espera	And my darling awaits me
Con su reproche	With her reproach
Pero cuando me acuesto	But when I get in the bed
Se queda quieta.	She's quiet.
Chinita . . .	*My little darling . . .*
Yo soy jinete viejo	I'm a seasoned rider
Pa' los amores	When it comes to loving
No concibo palenque	I take no bad female
Pa' hembra mala	To the hitching post
Como conozco el serape	Just like I know the serape
Por sus colores	By its colors
También conozco la yegua	I also know the mare

Desde montarle.	From riding her.
Chinita ...	*My little darling* ...

Besides the reference to the woman's reproach at her lover's late arrival fading away when they get into bed, and the transparent metaphors of riding and walking hard or slow, much of the sexual energy in the song is produced by the desirous modulations of singer's voice as she draws out the syllables of the first line of the refrain. The drag effect I mentioned earlier is activated here as the listener imagines Chabela taking off her spurs. The song becomes the site of butch-femme erotic transactions and rhythms: waiting and return; "fuerte" (strong, hard) and "despacio" (slow, soft); noise (spurs, footsteps, reproaches) and silence (acquiescence, arousal); withholding and surrender. The feminine gender role in the text offers a femme erotic identification in the register of waiting and receiving, but this desire is by no means passive.[15]

Only hearing Chabela Vargas can clarify the articulations among her body (including her voice), the intensity of her emotional register, lesbian desire, and erotic style.[16] Musically, her iconoclasm consists of extreme contrasts in tempo and volume and the artful manipulation of the whole range of the human voice: whispers, cries, growls, laughs, shouts, and murmurs of desire. In his analysis of Michael Jackson's appeal, Kobena Mercer identifies a similar use of the voice that goes beyond the semantics of lyrics to communicate emotions and eroticism centered in the body of the singer:

> Jackson's vocal performance is characterized by breathy gasps, squeaks, sensual sighs and other wordless sounds which have become his stylistic signature. The way in which this style punctuates the emotional resonance and bodily sensuality of the music corresponds to what Roland Barthes called the "grain" of the voice—"the grain is the body in the voice as it sings."[17]

We find a similar grain of the voice in Vargas when sudden outbursts of affect break with the verbal register, interrupting rather bland interpretations of clichéd songs (for example, in her recording of "No te importe saber"). These unexpected surges create an effect of excess that disrupts the conventional level of the lyrics, opening the music to other readings, and other pleasures. This physical investment of the lesbian voice and heart in the song makes the body of the text female and homoerotic for this femme listener. And in the realm of performance, imagination, or fantasy, Chabela Vargas takes the stage for a body that is both sexual and mestiza.

As the myths and images of Mexican popular culture circulate back and forth across the U.S. border, I take my pleasures there, bending these diverse imaginings to my needs and desires. Chabela Vargas offers me a whole gamut of identifications along the axes of butch erotic subjectivity and heterosexual masculinity: radiant happiness, abject wallowing in self-pity, the anguish of loss and rejection, the good woman/bad woman dichotomy, the possessive kind of romantic love that slides so easily into violence, seductive desire, wrenching solitude, and the longing for the other. Chabela's music has seen me through good times and bad times, and for this gift I offer her my tribute. On the earphones, entre las girlfriends, and in my fantasies, she makes a cherished repertory of Mexican and Latin American music uniquely mine.

• NOTES

1. The present essay is a version of a paper first presented at "Gender, Sexualities and the State: A Hispanic/Latino Context," University of California, Berkeley, March 1993. Of course, my title also salutes Latina anthropologist Ruth Behar's tribute to another Latin American woman, *Translated Woman: Crossing the Border with Esperanza's Story* (Boston: Beacon Press, 1993). I would like to thank my colleague Cynthia Steele for sharing her knowledge and love of Chabela with me.

2. Nayland Blake, "Curating in a Different Light," in *In a Different Light: Visual Culture, Sexual Identity, Queer Practice*, ed. Nayland Blake, Lawrence Rinder, and Amy Scholder (San Francisco: City Lights Books, 1995), 43.

3. Emma Pérez, "Sexuality and Discourse: Notes from a Chicana Survivor," in *Chicana Lesbians: The Girls Our Mothers Warned Us About*, ed. Carla Trujillo (Berkeley: Third Woman Press, 1991), 159–84.

4. Alfonso Chase, "Reivindican a Chavela Vargas costarricense," *La Jornada*, 29 May 1993.

5. Juan Luis Pavón, "*Chavelazo* en Sevilla," *ABC*, 15 May 1993.

6. Francisco Giménez, "*Felipistas y chavelistas*, la división en España," *La Jornada*, 20 May 1993.

7. Pavón, "*Chavelazo* en Sevilla."

8. Giménez, "*Felipistas y chavelistas*."

9. Ibid. See Smith's review of Almodóvar's (tongue-in-cheek?) disavowal of homosexuality in his films, "Laberinto de pasiones (Labyrinth of passion)," *Sight and Sound*, February 1993, as well as his *Unlimited Desire: The Cinema of Pedro Almodóvar* (London: Verso, 1994).

10. Pavón, "*Chavelazo* en Sevilla."

11. See the pioneering work of Joan Nestle (*A Restricted Country* [Ithaca: Firebrand, 1987]), and Cherríe Moraga and Amber Hollibaugh ("What We're Rollin Around in Bed With: Sexual Silences in Feminism," in *Powers of Desire: The Politics of Sexuality*, ed. Ann Snitow, Christine Stansell, and Sharon Thompson [New York: Monthly Review Press, 1983], 394–405) in the recuperation of butch-femme gender stylings and erotic practices in the face of middle-class lesbian feminism's squeamishness and censure. Recently, the deserved focus on the lives and experiences of butches, who bear the brunt of society's hostility and violence (as in "it's a bitch to be butch"), has yielded to a consideration of femmes' issues, as in the inver-

sion of the usual pairing "butch-femme" in the title of Nestle's anthology, *The Persistent Desire: A Femme-Butch Reader* (Boston: Alyson, 1992), or in the new collection *The Femme Mystique*, ed. Lesléa Newman (Boston: Alyson, 1995).

12. Valerie Traub, "Desire and the Difference It Makes," in *The Matter of Difference*, ed. Valerie Wayne (New York: Harvester Wheatsheaf, 1991), 81–114.

13. Arnaldo Cruz, personal communication.

14. In Latin America, *china* or *chino* is a term of affection with racial connotations of Indian, mestizo, or mulatto, and class connotations of peasant or servant.

15. Victoria Baker, "Femme: Very Queer Indeed," in *The Femme Mystique*, ed. Lesléa Newman (Boston: Alyson, 1995), 53.

16. In his statement that "esta mujer canta de donde le sale el coño," Almodóvar seems to recognize this conflation of voice, emotion, and the female body (Giménez, *"Felipistas y chavelistas"*).

17. Kobena Mercer, "Monster Metaphors: Notes on Michael Jackson's *Thriller*," *Welcome to the Jungle: New Positions in Black Cultural Studies* (New York: Routledge, 1994), 34.

Ben Sifuentes Jáuregui

Gender without Limits

Transvestism and Subjectivity in *El lugar sin límites*

Si era hombre tenía que ser capaz de sentirlo todo, aún esto . . .
—José Donoso, *El lugar sin límites*

El lugar sin límites is a simple story, indeed.[1] A cold Sunday, in the middle of nowhere, the famed madam la Manuela learns that the very macho Pancho Vega has returned to town. A year earlier he had tried to beat her but failed; the rumor now was that this time he was "going to get her." The entire day is full of anxiety, but Manuela tries to run her errands as if nothing were at all different. In the course of the day, she decides to fix her red flamenco dress, in the event that she might need it to entertain Pancho that evening. This act paradoxically shows that though she fears him, she very much wants to come face-to-face with him. She often thinks about that passion that she unleashes in other men. This passion is hard to articulate because it is unconventional: la Manuela is, after all, a transvestite. That evening Manuela makes every effort to appear calm; she imagines that if there is any trouble, the town's patriarch, don Alejo, will come as before to her rescue. She is unsuccessful at pretending that her safety is assured, for with the inevitable arrival of Pancho at the whorehouse that night, she runs and hides in a chicken coop. It is there that she remembers another day—eighteeen years earlier—when she was raped, and how she and her partner, la Japonesa, "won" the (whore)house where she has lived since.

An analysis of that rape scene shows the construction of the body politic and the structure of sexual and gender domination that operate throughout the text. In this essay, I perform a series of readings of the ways in which the transvestite's body becomes an object through which other subjects rethink their own subjectivity. For example, how la Japonesa Grande forges her "masculinity," how don Alejo exercises his (heterosexual) authority, how Pancho Vega erases his homosexuality, and how critics of the novel expand other theoretical preoccupations; all of these impositions happen as a misreading of transvestism.

• READING RAPE

La Manuela remembers that fateful night. After much partying, the men go to the whorehouse take la Manuela, exhausted from dancing, to the canal and throw her in. When she is pulled out of the water, the men get a little surprise, amazed "ante la anatomía de la Manuela" (by la Manuela's anatomy).[2] Stripped of her red flamenco dress with white polka dots, la Manuela emerges as Manuel; her coming out as a man is certified to the abusive men by the size of the transvestite's large penis. For them, the penis is undoubtedly the most obvious marker of masculinity; the men's comments bear witness to this tautology: "Mira que está bien armado" (Look he is well armed [or endowed]). And, "Psstt, si éste no parece maricón" (Psstt, this man doesn't even look like a faggot). Another man warns, "Que no te vean las mujeres, que se te van a enamorar" (Make sure the women don't see you; they are going to fall in love with you).[3] The men's reactions merit some explanation. Let us go back. First, the "unveiling" of the penis happens at a moment of torture of la Manuela; she had been thrown in the water after her debut performance at la Japonesa Grande's brothel. In a victory celebration party for don Alejo, the famous dance scene begins when la Manuela takes center stage, only then to be passed around the guests. First she dances for/with don Alejo, then the mailman, the station chief, and finally with another man, who attacks her, pulling up her skirt.[4] More than a striptease, the assault on la Manuela's body represents a moment of pleasure as well as shame for the men. Shame because of the pleasure. La Manuela's body literally becomes the site and sight of a homosocial event.[5] This homosocial exchange is apparent from the very beginning when the several community leaders (don Alejo, the mailman, and the station chief) fight over la Manuela as if trying to establish their authority. Also, the men's cracks are meant not only for la Manuela but, importantly, for one another. That the men insist on dancing with her and "discoursing" through her is quite something. To begin with, they already knew that "she" was a "he," so what exculpates any trace of homosexual panic—that is, the panic that results from the possibility of being identified as homosexual—is the *communal* aspect of their homosocial desire. In other words, la Manuela is a woman because that is what the men want; moreover, she is a woman the way they want her to be—in a "straight" jacket (allow me the pun in English). One man's ambiguous exclamation, "Está caliente" (She is horny. Or, she is angry), unwittingly blurs any compromising position in which the men might find themselves. Ambiguity in language tropes off the body of the transvestite. As a matter of fact, the whole narrative structure of the novel hinges on the ambiguity signified by the transvestite's body. Transvestism is thus seen by the men as merely *ambiguity*, which permits them to do whatever they want.

I would like to point out that nowhere is the misreading of transvestism as plain "ambiguity" more prevalent than in the critical reception of the novel. To wit, it is baffling that almost every critic has discussed la Manuela's transvestism as a symptom of something else: transvestism as Bakhtinian carnivalesque or ambivalence,[6] transvestism as a distorting of "reality,"[7] and transvestism as homosexuality.[8] Garber's highly suggestive "third term"[9] is pertinent, for within its description we manage to locate the importance and the relevance of transvestism as a sexual and political figure in and for Latin America.[10] We cannot ignore the importance of context and referentiality that produce a subject—and the reverse is true.

• THE PLACE WITHOUT LIMITS; OR, LOOKING FOR LOVE IN ALL THE WRONG PLACES

If there is, indeed, a place *without limits*, it is the scene of the family romance: we learn that la Manuela and her daughter, la Japonesita, are the owners of a bordello, which is frequented by the men of the small town.[11] To view the bordello as a place only of economic exchange would be limiting. It is paradoxical, however, that in the lost and diminishing space of Estación El Olivo, which has been forgotten by the *políticos* as another barren area in the provinces of Chile, it is a place of political and sexual—in the broadest sense of the word—production. When the patriarch don Alejo wins election as the area's deputy, all of the men go celebrate at the bordello and "the women of the town agreed not to protest for having to stay in their homes that night."[12] They knew that don Alejo would appreciate and might even reward their husbands for being there with him in his moment of triumph. The men's visit represents more than a rite of passage, more than a boy's fancy to "get it" for the first time; they go there to garner political, social, and sexual leverage. The bordello is and has always been a space for re-creation; the fact that it is owned by a transvestite and her "virgin" daughter does not lessen the powerful exchanges and transactions that we witness there; strangely enough, the owners' own sexual predilections and fantasies heighten the degree to which the bordello is privileged as a site of sexual, social, and political commerce. In other words, the men of the town go to see others and to be seen. It is a space of spectacle and voyeurism.

As a matter of fact, it was an unbridled moment of voyeurism that transferred proprietorship of the bordello from don Alejo to la Japonesa Grande and la Manuela. Don Alejo mocked la Japonesa Grande's womanliness and femininity and made her an offer that she would not resist, that she bed down with la Manuela while the men all watch their *tableaux vivants*. It is, then, in a bout of rage, that la Japonesa Grande asks for the house. To don Alejo's initial reluctance about such a request, la Japonesa Grande challenges don Alejo to keep the promise he made in front of witnesses.[13] She calls into question his word and, in the context of his election to deputy, his authority. He agrees. What is most important in this exchange—besides the conditions of the bet—is the way in which both la Japonesa Grande and don Alejo radically call into question each other's "femininity" and "masculinity." Don Alejo wanted la Japonesa to show off her sexuality. She wanted him to keep his word and "no se me corra," translated here as both "don't run out on me" and "don't come"—and by extension, "don't get limp." So, not to keep his word would mean that he was not a man. Their struggle to retain their social stature means questioning the other's sexual prowess.

This obsession with sexual prowess and performance is the same one that the men had when they first saw la Manuela naked. What is at stake in the sexual performance of others? What do the men get watching others perform sexually? Do they get off? To what degree and in what manner does the sexual performance between a prostitute and a transvestite satisfy the sexual appetite of heterosexual men?

It is following the rape of la Manuela that the bet has been made. La Japonesa Grande begins her seduction. After finding la Manuela crying in the kitchen, la Japonesa joins her and tries to console her. La Manuela explains that she is used to being mistreated. It is amazing to see how la Manuela has already become used to the violence against her, how she has to a greater or lesser degree internalized the pain of rape. There is a hint of self-awareness when she uses the third-person form to refer to her sexuality, "saben que una es loca" (they know that *one* is queer).[14] Manuela seems to be saying that her masquerade is doomed to the violence of strangers. Another thing that strikes us about the transvestite's explanation and exculpation of the men's behavior is the repetition of the phrase, "I don't know why." This repeated ignorance seems more dramatic especially when she tells us why it is that they beat her: "they [the men] were afraid." She knows that the men are afraid of her, not simply of what she is but rather of what she represents unconsciously in their lives. The question here is not what la Manuela's performance means for the transvestite but what her performance means for the men. The beatings, the psychological violence, the death wish against the transvestite signal perversely her "success" as a woman. For the men, however, la Manuela's successful performance represents a sinful erasure of the sexual and gender boundaries that they have neatly drawn. She is right: the men were afraid that she could get them excited, *calentarlos*, thus discounting for them the impossibility of homosexuality. As a consequence, la Manuela's words signify on the men and on us: "they know that one [*una*] is queer."

It is precisely this *locura*, queerness, this strange and untranslatable sexuality that the men want to see in the *tableau vivant* that don Alejo demands as proof. Let us imagine for a second what one would call the sexual scenario between a prostitute and a transvestite. Let us call it a heterosexual relationship. Or, perhaps, a lesbian relationship? But as we shall see these terms—*heterosexual*, *lesbian*, among others—prove inefficient when describing the seduction and the orgasm. Also, what the men want by witnessing this event needs to be explained. The difficulty of talking about what a transvestite and a prostitute might do in bed lies in the fact that we have failed to account adequately for what might commonly be called sexual practices, erotic imagination, or the theater of sexuality. Accordingly, let us pinpoint what the actresses project.

• BASIC INSTINCT

La Japonesa Grande's seduction of la Manuela is not easy. From the outset the very idea of sleeping with a woman repulses la Manuela: "¿Estás mala de la cabeza, Japonesa, por Dios? ¿No ves que soy loca perdida? Yo no sé. ¡Cómo se te ocurre una cochinada así!" (My God, Japonesa, are you sick in the head? Can't you see I'm a hopeless fag? I don't know. How dare you think up such a disgusting thing!).[15] We see that after questioning la Japonesa's mental health and her vision, la Manuela focuses on the sexual act itself as some perversion that the former devised. This sets up the scene for what follows. La Japonesa tries holding la Manuela's hand, who pushes it away. The failure of this back-and-forth touching and pushing away opens up a textual space where competing narrative voices struggle to arrive at an accord.[16] Denial, comedy, fear, the narrative voices battle to set the terms of a new pact. Of the distinct voices that we can discern, nothing is more surprising than the reversal of roles that we hear. On the one hand, la Japonesa Grande's persuasive strategy to bring the whole event to the level of a comedy, of performance. On the other hand, la Manuela resists this performance, most strikingly, for misogynist reasons. La Japonesa's view of the scene is reduced to nothing ("no, no, no"); I suspect that this attitude responds to her professional regard for sexuality as a performance for men. She seems to realize that sexuality—especially, in this case—is constructed and located to please men, that women's role in the sexual act is liminal, almost subliminal. If we anchor the sex show in this rigid framework of what sexuality might mean for a prostitute, we can then begin to understand la Manuela's aversion to women's bodies. The misogynist voice we hear, then, is really Manuel's, here and now a "militant" homosexual so involved with his own conception of "masculinity" that women's bodies bother him. Women's bodies—what the compulsory heterosexual mind attributes and assigns as his ultimate desire, reemergence, and appropriation—bother him.

La Manuela thinks of women's bodies as a threat to his peculiar "masculinity." Of course, this does not solve his dressing up as a woman; in fact, on the surface, it complicates the whole scene of transvestism. How do we explain this conflict: la Manuela dresses up as a woman, insists on being called a woman, yet finds women's bodies a threat. I find the explanation that a transvestite is not a "real" woman, hence not a "real" threat for la Manuela, banal—to say the least. That the masquerade of transvestism is an act of appropriation as a means for Manuel to control his biggest fear also rings too simplistic. Transvestism is not about appropriating "woman" but rather about reinscribing (fantasizing and rewriting) the excess of "woman," of "femininity." Again, linearity presents an obstacle to finding a solution. I suggest that la Manuela lacks language to describe her sexual subjectivity. She conceives her *liaison* with la Japonesa as the primal scene, as an original moment and screen upon which to mount the dynamics of her sexual persona and to re-present sexual identity. Her (paradoxical) gender trouble[17] could more fully be explained by arguing that la Manuela is (or *effects* the role of) a homosexual male. Yet given the specific and narrow cultural definition of what it means to be a homosexual—that is, a man who is like a woman—in the context of Latin America, the subtleties of gender are lost. National language (Spanish, in this case) both opens up and exacerbates the notion of gender almost literally to a *letter*, thus setting certain limits or possibilities of subject formation. As a side note, through and with the power of language, the "national" constructs the closet.

Consequently, la Manuela (ad)dresses and disguises her sexual orientation with clothing, the very codes of gender. In other words, *la Manuela's only way of being a homosexual is being like a woman.* Once more, la Manuela lacks language, so she assigns culturally defined gender signs to mark the parameters of the sexual. At this crucial point we can unfold and understand the outrageousness (*locura*) and limits of the homosexual male body politic in Latin America. Certainly, there is a relationship between sexuality and gender, however, given the instability of that relationship, it behooves us to suspend the different conceptualizations of each axiom to see the texture and complexity of a *transvestite-homosexual matrix* that la Manuela designs. Her basic instinct is to (con)fuse the two practices into one. Perhaps it is this insight that makes la Japonesa Grande realize that, in the end, la Manuela is a man like the others, another vision of masculinity, and she warns him: "Oye, Manuela, no te vayas a enamorar de mí" (Listen, Manuela, don't go falling in love with me).[18]

• ORGASMS IN UNISON

The sex scene between la Japonesa Grande and la Manuela is one of the most erotic and explicit in Latin American literature. La Japonesa Grande tries to make la Manuela feel at ease. It is not easy because la Manuela cannot perform as is demanded of her. The only things that la Manuela senses are the smells of the cheap wine, of la Japonesa's breath, of her sweat. She feels nothing, but sees don Alejo watching. It is important to understand here don Alejo's position in the erotic scene, in the erotic triangle. He, too, is a participant insofar as he choreographs this primal scene revisited.

La Manuela's description of the event (using a male shifter of meaning: *muerto*), her attention to detail as she lies in bed, shows that she is literally trapped in bed, being forced to put on a role that she does not want or enjoy, performing as the "heterosexual man" don Alejo would like her to be. This imposition of gender and sex roles accounts for her anxiety, for her nonperformance. But what is marvelous about *El lugar sin límites* and this scene in particular is seeing how la Japonesa manages to seduce la Manuela to deliver a performance that neither would ever forget. To accomplish this, La Japonesa uses incredible skills of rhetoric to make la Manuela come (out as a man).

At every turn, la Manuela resists la Japonesa's advances. La Japonesa begins with verbal tenderness.[19] What we see here is la Japonesa's attempt to remove or pacify the fear that la Manuela has by stating that "we are not going to do anything." This phrase is then repeated over and over by la Manuela trying to literalize it. This process of literalization through repetition subverts and momentarily disarms la Japonesa Grande. The delirious repetition of "nothing is going to happen, it's for the house, nothing more, for the house" shows an economic structure of production, "something for nothing," that is a central trademark of transvestism. To be sure, the process of recycling the excesses of language permits the transvestite a unique talent that often confuses play with reification, fantasy with materiality. If I have not been careful to notice that the expression "it's a show" is repeated by la Japonesa and la Manuela incessantly, it is because I want to show that the expression is an empty signifier; it functions also like saying "nothing is going to happen." It would be too formulaic and reductive to assume by this turn of phrase that the narrator seeks to explain away the whole event as some carnivalesque moment. Indeed, in spite of the fact that la Manuela says it to herself, this sexual encounter with la Japonesa is rather tragic—and not comedic at all. Furthermore, to suppose that this sexual encounter is representative of a "show" of the world upside down is wrong, considering the fact that the operative heterosexual structure has been stated or reinstated as the norm. Interestingly, it is this turn of phrase, "it is a show," that la Manuela cannot subvert; this is so because of her positionality as a transvestite, a marginal figure, within the broader social context of what represents the "normal." Subversion of the signifier "show" would represent for la Manuela a deconstruction of her very own subjectivity. She must maintain the illusion of "realness," or proprietorship and authority, within the confines of her own discourse, otherwise she is dead. Her resistance to the clear-cut demands of compulsory heterosexuality is an act of psychic survival that must continue throughout the seduction. La Manuela imagines:

A ella le gusta hacer lo que está haciendo aquí en las sábanas conmigo. Le gusta que yo no pueda: con nadie, dime que sí, Manuelita linda, dime que nunca con ninguna mujer antes que yo, que soy la primera, la única, y así voy a poder gozar mi linda, mi alma, Manuelita, voy a gozar, me gusta tu cuerpo aterrado y todos tus miedos y quisiera romper tu miedo, no, no tengas miedo Manuela, no romperlo sino que suavemente quitarlo de donde está para llegar a una parte de mí que ella, la pobre Japonesa Grande, creía que existía pero, que no existe y no ha existido nunca, y no ha existido nunca a pesar de que me toca y me acaricia y me murmura . . . no existe, Japonesa bruta, entiende, no existe.

(She [la Japonesa] likes what she is doing between the sheets with me. She likes the fact that I can't: with no one, tell me so, pretty Manuelita, tell me that never with any woman before me, that I am the first, the only one, and that way I can enjoy myself my pretty, my soulful Manuelita, I'm going to enjoy this, I like your body afraid and all your fears and I would like to break that fear, no, don't be afraid Manuela, not break it but softly remove it from where

it lies to get to that part of me that she, poor Japonesa Grande, thought existed
but, that no longer exists and never has existed, and never has existed even
though she touches me and strokes me and says quietly to me . . . it doesn't
exist, you stupid Japonesa, don't you understand, it doesn't exist.)[20]

La Japonesa Grande's sexual appetite makes la Manuela suspect that the
woman enjoys the man's impotence; la Manuela's paranoia goes so far as to
portray la Japonesa as a sadist. La Manuela is confused; in effect, it is not
that la Japonesa cares whether or not la Manuela can perform but whether
she is a virgin. The whole line of thinking that la Japonesa insists upon,
"with no one, tell me so, pretty Manuelita, tell me that never with any
woman before me, that I am the first, the only one, [and so on]" inaugurates
the framing of a different mode of seduction. It is no longer a perfunctory
act (a comedy that means nothing), but more directly, it acquires a literally
comic turn, that is, la Japonesa takes on actively the traditional role of a man
trying by all means to woo a woman. By reinscribing a heterosexual,
"repro-narrative"[21] of a conventional first or wedding night, la Japonesa
Grande hopes to return (or rewrite) la Manuela to her role as a woman,
specifically as a virgin. How the repro-narrative laces this scene of seduction is quite obvious; for example, when la Japonesa talks about breaking la
Manuela's fear, it sounds as if she were breaking her hymen and, later, when
she corrects herself, saying that she would "softly remove it." It does not
cease to amaze how flagrantly repro-narrativity dominates any discourse of
seduction; I insist that this accounts for the seductive failure again. La
Manuela's abrupt response that *that* passion which la Japonesa seeks does
not exist, accosts any pretension about the centrality of repro-narrativity.
How la Japonesa ultimately seduces la Manuela satisfies the risky essential-
ist question: Can one seduce the Other in a language other than her or his
own?

As, perhaps, a desperate measure to all of the resistance that she encounters, la Japonesa ventures to suggest that it is

como si fuéramos dos mujeres, mira, así, ves, las piernas entretejidas, el sexo
en el sexo dos sexos iguales, Manuela, no tengas miedo al movimiento de las
caderas, la boca en la boca, como dos mujeres cuando los caballeros en la casa
de la Pecho de Palo les pagan a las putas para que hagan cuadros plásticos . . .
no, no, tú eres la mujer, Manuela, yo soy la macha, ves cómo te estoy bajando
los calzones y cómo te quito el sostén para que tus pechos queden desnudos,
y yo gozártelos, sí tienes Manuela, no llores, sí tienes pechos, chiquitos como
los de una niña, pero tienes y por eso te quiero.

(it's as if we were two women, look, like so, you see, the legs intertwined, a
sex member in the other, both sexes the same, Manuela, don't be afraid the

movement of the hips, the mouth in the mouth, like two women when the gentlemen at the Ice Princess's house {another bordello} pay the whores to put on a show . . . no, no, you're the woman, Manuela, I'm the butch [*macha*], you see how I am pulling your panties and how I take off your bra so that your breasts become naked, and I can enjoy them, indeed you have breasts Manuela, don't cry, you have breasts, small ones like a girl, but you have them and that is why I love you.)[22]

Substituting a new lesbian erotics and discourse for repro-narrativity frees the tired, unproductive mise-en-scène, while it presents and maintains it for the men watching the illusion of "normal" heterosexuality. I play with the very notion and call into question the "normal" state of the heterosexual tableau because something else is going on. To wit, I am talking not only about the "secret" lesbian relation that has developed but, provocatively, that there are men watching and talking. Their voyeurism constitutes a (per)version of heterosexuality—and here I refer to the casting of a prostitute and a transvestite in the heterosexual matrix as well as the erotics involved in the process itself of framing. Let us look in more detail at the newly articulated version of a *homosexual* matrix, then move on to the question of the erotics of revising the heterosexual matrix—or the family romance.

La Japonesa has had sex with other women before. Her words unwittingly leak that secret: "look, like so, you see, the legs intertwined" and also "I'm the butch [*macha*]." Furthermore, she chooses as a point of reference the Ice Princess's house,[23] a bordello where la Manuela has been working. This shows that lesbian sex tableaux are commonplace, and that they are part of male sexuality and erotic imagination. As an aside, one can see that at this specific discursive sexual moment, questions about the gender, sexuality, and sexual orientation of la Manuela are difficult to fasten: is la Manuela imagining herself as female, as a lesbian, as a passive man? These questions of subjectivity that are customarily well secured by the signifiers "heterosexual," "woman," "sadomasochist," and so on become irrelevant unless there is a clear understanding of how and under what conditions these signifiers are constructed, and what impact the performance of these signifiers effects. In other words, and perhaps reiterating the gist of gender studies today, gender, sexuality, and sexual orientation are axioms that define identity; they are historically and culturally produced, cannot be grounded, only effected.

The seduction is subtle, to the extent that la Japonesa knows that she must define her role as "butch," *macha*, while convincing la Manuela that she is a girl. When she says to la Manuela "you see how I am pulling your panties and how I take off your bra so that your breasts become naked," she pronounces a speech act; she "reads" a lesbian erotica for la Manuela: "yo soy la macha y tú la hembra, te quiero porque eres todo, y siento el calor de ella que me engulle, a mí, a un yo que no existe" (I am the butch [*macha*] and you are the femme [*hembra*], I love you because you are everything, and I feel her warmth that engulfs me, me, an "I" that does not exist).[24] The seduction continues and builds up. La Manuela sees herself as part of the lesbian act that la Japonesa has designed. That line "I am the butch one [or the manly woman] and you are the femme" conveys the complexity of the roles with which each woman identifies. First, la Japonesa would embody the virility and masculinity that will attract la Manuela later. The sexual figure and imagination of la Japonesa will appear later in the plot of the novel not as a *macha* but as the *macho* Pancho Vega, very butch, very masculine, and very repressed, with whom la Manuela will fall in love. Second, as la Japonesa talks, la Manuela *se calienta*, gets an erection, and becomes the man Don Alejo wanted to see: in an oppositional movement, la Manuela identifies at that specific moment with the role of the woman (*hembra*). The temporality of subjectivity hinges on an awareness of difference that is lucidly articulated by la Manuela, "me," an "I that does not exist;" these fleeting moments where identity is registered climax at the almost existential realization by la Manuela. It would only make sense then for la Manuela, who denies her subjectivity, to deny or reinterpret her ecstasy. One image is striking: shame. It is not the shame of being watched, for, as we might imagine, the transvestite's obsession with specularity, with being seen and praised, is known. La Manuela specifies that it is the "vergüenza de las agitaciones" (shame of the agitation), of the commotion that she is causing. This is a major and perspicacious recognition of the transvestite's power to transform herself and the subjectivity of others. Shame replies to an epistemological disjunction, a crisis in the categorization of gender—to use a phrasing introduced by Garber to describe a transvestite effect.

It is this shame that affects how la Manuela expresses her orgasm; "hasta estremecerme y quedar mutilado, desangrándome dentro de ella" (until I shudder and become mutilated, bleeding inside her):[25] she is castrated, she bleeds. It is also la Manuela's first and last period. She has lost her penis, her "period," as well as her phallus, her "words melt." This loss of authority can be seen in the very narrative structure of the event. Her phrases are joined by a series of conjunctions; language has lost its grammar; genders have lost their grammar. La Manuela's delirious grammar creates a palimpsest of this and that and something else. This layered discourse repeats and structures the very trials of subject formation and the writing of the text. Meaning is found not only within each morphological sign but, importantly, between the relationship and deployment of each. Transvestism continuously reifies that conjunction and rearrangement.

Returning to the scene of the crime: la Manuela is quick to deny that what happened happened. And la Japonesa tells her not to worry, that they won the house, really that la Manuela won the house for her. Nevertheless la Manuela is fixated on one and only one issue, that it not happen again.[26] The end of the bet is important for two reasons. First, we are taken forward to the chicken coop, where la Manuela is hiding from Pancho Vega, who has tried to rape her. The winning bet contextualizes (gives texture to) the present. Here she is shaking and fearing for her life, holding onto her famous red flamenco dress. She remembers that occasion when she was that virile "man" who impregnated la Japonesa—or, as she sighs nostalgically, "that 'I' that I need so much now [and who] doesn't exist." Second, la Manuela conjures up this performance of masculinity so that she may face this brute Pancho Vega, just another of "those big men with thick eyebrows and harsh voices [who] are all the same: as soon as dusk comes, they begin manhandling you."[27] In other words, if la Manuela is going to meet this man face-to-face, then she must do so in his terms.

Who are those big men? What do they want? Earlier I suggested that the same *tableau vivant* represented a double perversion of the idea of heterosexuality. On one level, heterosexuality sets itself up as a polar opposite of lesbian sexuality; on another level, male heterosexuality eroticizes the process itself of framing this binarism. In other words, the direction and choreography of lesbian sexuality by men spotlight a special relationship between the men themselves—call it homoeroticism. The pleasure for the men is not so much in watching two "women" having sex but, rather, in having the power to force them into this situation. Likewise, pornography is not necessarily the representation of sexualities but a structural relation of power. Furthermore, with respect to the tableau, the men's relationship is not one of inclusion but of exclusion and exclusivity. Homosocial bonding happens as the first step of defining heterosexuality; the homosocial is a discursive space created by repression along the lines of gender within the heterosexual matrix. The next step, of course, which conventionally ensures the enterprise of the "heterosexual," is homophobia, another repressive measure that hinges on and delimits the sex coordinate. The archeology of heterosexuality, then, can be a palimpsest of repressions, which makes for a difficult articulation of referentiality. Cutting through this complex called "normal" heterosexuality is messy, always uncovering unsuspected gender and erotic fantasies.

• TRANSVESTITES AND OTHER VERSIONS OF MASCULINITY

La Manuela, who had been shaking in the chicken coop, conjuring up the strength to face Pancho as that "man that no longer exists," chooses to face Pancho otherwise as a woman. She becomes the martyr, the woman who returns to the scene of the crime to face the criminal again. This painful moment that has been foreshadowed and internalized already by the transvestite as just "part of men's entertainment" does not stop surprising us. This threat of violence is disregarded by almost everyone; any physical or verbal abuse that la Manuela gets is taken for granted. Even la Japonesita at the end of the novel has stopped worrying about la Manuela, just saying that her father will return after a couple of days, that she is used to her father's behavior. It could be argued that this compulsion to repeat (or rehearse) obeys a desire to return to the original moment or event, where the subject "failed," and now tries to repair or resolve the "event." However, I argue that why the scene of violence repeats itself has to do with the transvestite's entrance into the pleasures of sadomasochism. La Manuela's return as la Manuela reconfigures a structure, upon which her subjectivity depends. I am not arguing that she is solely asking to being beaten and brutalized for its own sake but, rather, that she seeks within this violence the pleasure that the scene of sadomasochism gives her. Pleasure is dislocated from the climax of compulsory heterosexuality and woven into the process of framing narratives in the text of sadomasochism.

What is difficult to conceive is that when la Manuela enters the bordello as a woman, she is not really what Pancho desires: he wants a man. La Manuela dances for Pancho, and he reveals his passion. "That thing," as Pancho refers to la Manuela, becomes "the old faggot."[28] The inchoate and unrecognizable body of the transvestite becomes engendered at the moment that Pancho begins to desire. Pancho wants la Manuela's dancing to touch him; he wants to feel the transvestite's body against his own. The writhing of the body—or, as the silent Spanish "h" would have me saying—the writing of the body that la Manuela displays for her man is, indeed, "that thing" that Pancho wants. Pancho wants to re-dress himself. In other words, he wants to be like her. He wants to be her. The gender ambiguity of the language that he uses blurs the identity of the subject "he" in the last line, "it is no longer a cause of laughter because it is as if he, too, were coveting." He is Pancho. He is la Manuela. He is Pancho and la Manuela. Desiring the Other is not a case for laughter. To laugh is to construct the Other as a parody. Laughter destabilizes the very unity of the Self. In the following scene we can see Pancho's initial desire for la Manuela turn into paranoia of being identified with her, which then clearly becomes homosexual panic, the desire that his friend Octavio not learn of his arousal by la Manuela. Despite all of the excitement that has caused Pancho to get an erection, he is paranoid, afraid even, that Octavio will learn or discover that la Manuela's "hysteria" is doing something to him. The desire *and* denial that Pancho has for the drag queen is such that he almost seems to resist that it is happening in a peculiar way; he says that "dejándose sí, pero desde aquí desde la silla donde está sentado nadie ve lo que le sucede debajo de la mesa" (he will allow himself to be touched yes, but from here from the chair where he is sitting no one sees what happens under the table).[29] Pancho talks about himself in the third person, passively and literally "under the table" negotiating the eroticism between himself and the old flamenco dancer. I argue that Pancho's twisted reconstruction of the event is a desperate attempt to create a closed scene of writing and reading, of desire and denial, all these moments of anguish provide the necessary space for the "literary."

I would like to reevaluate Pancho's "readerly" moment of panic, a classic example of homosexual panic, in other terms. What is at stake in this scene is that Pancho wants not to explain away his desire but simply to desire within himself. Pancho's reasoning of not wanting to be seen is, in effect, another way of coming to terms with his homosexuality. No matter how perverse this explanation may be, Pancho is playing with a new identity. The *macho* is trying to recapture a loss of his subjectivity; the panic that he shows is a symptom of male hysteria. I define the term *hysteria* as a moment of loss, as a crisis of agency, where the "I" cannot comfortably locate itself; in other words, the hysteric results from the act of denial of a "traditionless Self."[30] Pancho suffers from male hysteria when he begins referring to himself in the third person, "he"; this shift to the third-person pronoun should not be confused with the "third term" because Pancho's own representation occurs as an act of denial rather than one of affirmation. If we could revisit the important "third term": it is important to underline its condition of affirmation of agency and subjectivity. Here the "third" is more than just another category; it is an epistemological challenge. Male hysteria is, then, that moment of psychic death that comes about through the failure to recognize and affirm a subjectivity that is new and changing.

A poignant moment that illustrates Pancho's denial of his homosexuality is when he takes another prostitute's hand and places it on his penis. How important it is to see here that his heterosexuality is performed through the use of a real woman's body. In other words, Pancho normalizes his homosexual desire by putting his penis under a woman's hand. This turning of the screw shows, as Juliet Mitchell argues, that "hysteria sometimes presents not the negative of the sexual perversion but the negative of a perverse knowledge."[31] Pancho's action negates not the transvestite but his homosexuality, a perverse knowledge.

• A KISS BEFORE DYING

Upon leaving the bordello, la Manuela leaned toward Pancho and tried to kiss him.[32] When la Manuela tries to kiss Pancho, that is, when she takes action, she becomes a threat; as long as she behaved as the two men wanted, everything was fine. Being caught or seen with the drag queen is all right; however, when she implicates and threatens the players with the possibility of homosexuality, she must be released. Pancho is gay and afraid. Faced with the name-calling—and, certainly, in the place without limits naming signifies affiliation—, Pancho will begin questioning la Manuela in every single respect. That questioning becomes a major issue for Octavio: "¿Lo besaste o no lo besaste?" (Did you or didn't you kiss him?).[33] In this particular line or question, Octavio locates "being" as a performance. A beating follows la Manuela's answer, "Pura broma" (It was just a joke);[34] this suggests that transvestites cannot put into motion or articulate a parody because their very positionality invalidates whatever they might say. And so the transvestite must die.

The death of the transvestite comes as a brutal awakening:

> Octavio la paralizaba retorciéndole el brazo, la Manuela despertó. No era la Manuela. Era él Manuel González Astica. Él. Y porque era él iban a hacerle daño y Manuel González Astica sintió terror.
>
> (Octavio paralyzed her twisting her arm, [then] Manuela woke up. She wasn't la Manuela. She was he, Manuel González Astica. He. And because it was he they going to hurt him and Manuel González Astica felt terror.)[35]

In this painful event la Manuela discovers that her body is not that of a woman but of a man. She realizes that her body is deployed, developed, and disposed however others want. Pancho draws upon the different uses that the transvestite has for him when he tells her that she went too far in trying to kiss him.[36] La Manuela's body is used to define the subjectivity of the men, not her own. She is fully baptized Manuel González Astica, the face of a terrified man. Her "masculinity," like that of all the men, is told to us as an experience with the *uncanny*, a strange familiarity.

Manuel manages to escape and runs to don Alejo's vast vineyards, hoping to find some protection. However, going to don Alejo's refuge is the greatest of ironies because we know the futility that it represents, to seek cover by the very institution that oppresses one. He runs in the sure belief that don Alejo awaits for him. But he will not get there. The men catch up with Manuel and beat her ruthlessly.[37] The men weigh heavily on la Manuela; they attack her, "bocas calientes, manos calientes, cuerpos babientos y duros hiriendo el suyo y que ríen y que insultan y que buscan romper y quebrar y destrozar y reconocer ese monstruo de tres cuerpos retorciéndose, hasta que ya no queda nada" (hot mouths, hot hands, spitting and hard bodies hurting Manuela's own and they laugh and insult and seek to rip and break and destroy and recognize that three-bodied monster writhing until there is nothing left).[38] Back in the bordello, la Japonesita holds the fort. Unaware of la Manuela's fate, she imagines that her father will return as he always does. La Manuela's escapades are nothing new. She will return, according to la Japonesita, after a couple of days of "triumphs."[39] The still-virgin prostitute will go to bed in the dark, ignorant that la Manuela has been raped again.

The metaphorics of rape, to which I have alluded throughout this essay as acts of misreading of transvestism, take a literal turn in this scene. The danger of the metaphor is that it suspends the possibility and actualizing of the event. If the men could no longer figuratively rape la Manuela, using their pen(ises) to write on the transvestite, their ultimate alternative—and it is not really an "alternative" per se but their unequivocal desire—is to rape, "seek[ing] to rip and break and destroy and recognize" and to rename by force. But, transvestism is not a voluntary or involuntary imposition, it is also a desire that seeks recognition.

The men beat la Manuela for the perverse pleasure of affirming their uncanny sexual "integrity." They want a single story to be told about them; ambiguity is out of the question. Nonetheless, what is absolutely fascinating about *El lugar sin límites* is the trial and error, the attempting to tell the story right. I mentioned the shifting narrative voice in the text; this voice meanders desperately through the passions of the mind and the body trying to capture who we all are. The event in and of itself is always uncanny and inaccessible. But language allows us to survey the different voices that construct that "event." Transvestism prefigures the assurance that subjectivity is unique through the echoes of many voices. And trying to be univocal, that is, imposing a single voice, strangles the transvestite.

• NOTES

The writing of this essay has benefited from my ongoing discussions with Sylvia Molloy, Patrick J. O'Connor, Daniel Balderston, Donna J. Guy and Will H. Corral. I would like to thank them for their perspicacious readings, helpful criticisms, and encouragement.

1. I cite from the 1987 edition of José Donoso's 1966 novel *El lugar sin límites* (Barcelona: Editorial Seix Barral, 1987). This text has been translated as *Hell Has No Limits* by Hallie D. Taylor and Suzanne Jill Levine (New York: Dutton, 1972). However, given the specific questions of gender that this essay takes up, all translations are mine. Donoso's *El lugar sin límites* has been classified as a minor text; a displacement occasioned by Donoso himself, who suggested that it was not his best work. He designated his Gothic *El obsceno pájaro de la noche* as his contribution to that hard-to-define period we know as the "Boom."

2. Donoso, *El lugar sin límites*, 80.

3. Ibid., 80–81.

4. Ibid., 79.

5. I am using the term *homosocial* as developed in the work of Eve Kosofsky Sedgwick, especially in *Between Men: English Literature and Male Homosocial Desire* (New York: Columbia University Press, 1985). By "homosocial," I understand the relationship between men where any "sexual" component has been erased by ignorance, denial, or repression.

6. See Diana Palaversich, "The Metaphor of Transvestism in *El lugar sin límites* by José Donoso," *AUMLA: Journal of the Australian Universities Language and Literature Association* 73 (1990): 156–65. Palaversich argues that the presence of the transvestite gives the novel its carnivalized discourse, in other words, the transvestite serves only to illuminate, dramatize, and explain the narrative difficulty of the text.

7. See Hernán Vidal's discussion in his *José Donoso: Surrealismo y rebelión de los instintos* (Gerona: Ediciones Aubí, 1972), esp. chap. 3.

8. Only one article discusses—though not very thoroughly—the relationship between transvestism and homosexuality: Bernhardt Roland Shultz, "La Manuela: Personaje homosexual y sometimiento," *Discurso literario* 7.1 (1990): 225–40. The article's main problem lies in the fact that it merges synonymously homosexuality and transvestism; as a matter of fact, it insists on placing *El lugar sin límites* in the context of "recent gay narrative" (225) without really exploring the critical and theoretical dimensions of that literary historical situation and troping.

9. Marjorie Garber, *Vested Interests: Transvestism and Cultural Anxiety* (New York: Routledge, 1991), 10.

10. Furthermore, one could possibly argue that the invention of Latin America as a geographic and political construct itself mirrors the figuration of the transvestite.

11. Sharon Magnarelli argues that the place without limits is language, "the locus of the logos": *Understanding José Donoso* (Columbia: University of South Carolina Press, 1993), 67–68. I hasten to add that the place without limits is *gender* and *sexualities* as a function of desire in language.

12. Donoso, *El lugar sin límites*, 64.

13. Ibid., 83.

14. Ibid., 85. I have taken the liberty of translating *loca* as "queer." It is important before I continue, however, to note that the word in Spanish means "crazy woman" and is also a derogatory term for a gay man, like "faggot," "queen," and the like. I do not ignore the fact that in the Spanish, la Manuela uses the feminine form of "one," "*una*." She does this as part of her ongoing project of representing herself always as

a woman; however, I have taken the liberty again of blurring the translation to show effectively the subtle way in which the transvestite implicates us by her performance, revealing our own performances of gender. Though in his study of "gay and lesbian themes" David William Foster attempts to give an all-encompassing view of alternative representations of sexuality, he fails to consider the complexity of la Manuela's *locura*. He observes narrowly that "La Manuela does not rise above being a stereotypical *loca*: hysterical, ludicrous, alternately sentimental and viper tongued, coquettish." He rather wants to describe transvestism as a "disruptive" element to patriarchy: it is why transvestism must be eliminated to normalize the social order. See *Gay and Lesbian Themes in Latin American Writing* (Austin: University of Texas Press, 1991), 92–93. For Foster, the place without limits is don Alejo's land and world as a metaphor for patriarchal power (88). I argue that the place without limits is la Manuela's body and her gayness.

15. Donoso, *El lugar sin límites*, 85.

16. Ibid.

17. Judith Butler, *Gender Trouble: Feminism and the Subversion of Identity* (New York: Routledge, 1990).

18. Donoso, *El lugar sin límites*, 89.

19. Ibid., 108.

20. Ibid.

21. I am borrowing this term from Michael Warner, "Introduction: Fear of a Queer Planet," *Social Text* 29.9.4 (1991): 3–17.

22. Donoso, *El lugar sin límites*, 108–9.

23. A note on this translation: I have translated La Pecho de Palo's name as the Ice Princess to connote the figurative meaning of her name—cold, detached, also wretched. However, it is worth mentioning that *pecho de palo* may also means "flat-chested," and from this I am tempted to speculate that she too was a transvestite.

24. Donoso, *El lugar sin límites*, 109.

25. Ibid.

26. Ibid.

27. Ibid., 15.

28. Ibid., 126.

29. Ibid.

30. I borrow this term from Juliet Mitchell, "From King Lear to Anna O and Beyond: Some Speculative Theses on Hysteria and the Traditionless Subject," *Yale Journal of Criticism* 5.2 (1992): 104.

31. Donoso, *El lugar sin límites*, 104.

32. Ibid., 129.

33. Ibid., 130.

34. Ibid.

35. Ibid.

36. Ibid.

37. Ibid., 132.

38. Ibid., 132–33.

39. Ibid., 138.

Part Two

Policing
Sexuality

5 *Peter Beattie*

Conflicting Penile Codes

Modern Masculinity and Sodomy in the Brazilian Military, 1860–1916

Only one thing vexed the cabin-boy [Aleixo]—the black man's sexual whims. Because [the black sailor known as] Bom Crioulo was not satisfied merely with possessing him sexually at any hour day or night. . . . He obliged the boy to go to extremes, he made a slave of him, a whore of him. . . . The first night he wanted Aleixo to strip, to strip right down to the buff. . . . Aleixo replied sulkily that that was not something you ask a man to do! Anything but that.

—Adolfo Caminha, *Bom Crioulo*

In 1895 former navy officer, ardent republican, and novelist Adolfo Caminha shocked Brazilian readers by deftly using his knowledge of navy life to produce a detailed romance between a black man who escaped slavery only to be pressed into navy service and a blond-haired, blue-eyed fifteen-year-old cabin boy.[1] Caminha's audacious exploration of the homosexual taboo, one that also challenged racial biases, led most of his contemporaries to ostracize him. His best novel, *Bom Crioulo* (literally, good nigger), remains outside the canon of classic Brazilian literature.[2]

It is useful to look back at Caminha's novel for several reasons. First of all, it tells of a time and place when alleged homosexual behavior in the Brazilian military rarely led to expulsion. Second, *Bom Crioulo* links literature to historical documents because it is possible to examine nineteen court-martial cases involving sodomy in the Brazilian army and navy from 1861 to 1908.[3] Fact united with fiction, medical theory, and law all reveal conflicting conceptions of masculinity and honor among officers and *praças* (a Portuguese term that lumps together the ranks of noncommissioned officers and common enlisted men). In the midst of these hierarchically and racially informed tensions, reformers sought to rescue enlisted service from associations with social and sexual deviance.

These efforts formed part of a larger drive to modernize the military. Officers struggled from 1874 to 1916 to execute new laws replacing arbitrary impressment (coercive manhunts) with a Prussian-inspired draft lottery. The draft would target a better class of recruits, hence to render enlisted service more acceptable to the public, reformers strove to improve its status and conditions to make it an honorable manly duty unencumbered with innuendos of deviance. Stories like *Bom Crioulo* reinforced unflattering assumptions about the culture of enlisted service and hampered reformers' efforts to establish and then to enforce conscription after it began in 1916.

These "reformist" officers were increasingly influenced not only by German military models but also by German ideas of appropriate masculine sexuality. If the Brazilian case is indicative, it could be that the Prussian-inspired military reformism that swept most of the twentieth-century world was an important conduit of a cross-cultural restructuring of sexual identity.

• SEXUAL IDENTITY, GENDER, AND HONOR

For most nineteenth-century Brazilians, individuals were neither homosexuals nor heterosexuals per se. Sodomy was an immoral act rather than an abstract identity shaped by sexual preference. The term *homosexual* became common only in the 1950s; it first appeared in English in 1892 as translated from a German text. Meanwhile authorities referred to intercourse between two males as "sodomy, pederasty, libidinousness, sexual inversion, and immoral acts," as it was similarly defined in turn-of-the-century Brazilian military documents.[4]

Most assumed intercourse between males consisted of anal sex between a dominant and a passive partner. The active partner took on a manly identity as a sexual aggressor, while the passive partner attained an emasculated femininity or, at best, an attenuated masculinity as a "boy." As Aleixo despaired, to stand exposed for another's sexual pleasure was not "something you ask a *man* to do" (my emphasis). Similarly, during the same decade that *Bom Crioulo* was written, drunken and belligerent Private Horácio Veloso accosted and offered Private João Estácio five réis to "serve him as a woman," João hotly replied that he "was not a young boy [*gury*] nor a woman to serve such ends." When Horácio continued to taunt João, a struggle ensued that cost Horácio his life and João eight years in prison.[5] These examples reflected a common belief that women and children were sexually passive and men were sexual actors. This created a sexual hierarchy in which penetrators dominated the penetrated. Shame rested mostly with passive partners because active partners often boasted of illicit sexual conquests as proof of virility. Not everyone (including *praças*) viewed sexuality in this manner, but it seems to have been prevalent among all social classes in Brazil, and remains prominent in Latin America.[6]

Nineteenth-century physicians came to view homosexual acts and even masturbation as dangerous to health and psychological stability. In *Bom Crioulo*, Caminha describes a cabin boy caught masturbating: "Herculano had just committed a real crime, not one in the rule-books, a crime against nature, pouring out uselessly, on the dry and sterile deck, the generative juice of man."[7] Caminha and other like-minded reformists sought to stigmatize all nonreproductive sexual acts whether passive or active.

Brazilian society held sexual honor at a high premium. A male was responsible for protecting his family, dependents, and himself from real or putative sexual aggressions by other males. Dishonor tainted the victim and the victim's protectors. Unavenged, dishonor could potentially make the victim and mate, employer, and family the subject of scurrilous rumors and more overt forms of public ridicule that undermined claims to respectability, opportunity, and support. Seduction or rape could invite private vengeance to reestablish honor, but authorities encouraged citizens to resolve these disputes in court.[8]

Military culture reinforced this code of honor by promoting the cult of machismo. General Nelson Werneck Sodré described attitudes toward honor and sexuality among students in the late 1920s at the Colégio Militar in Rio (a gateway to the Military Academy and an officer's rank):

> A man could not admit that his sister was the object of the same pleasure he sought from another's, and cuckolded husbands were victims of ridicule that no one accepted for themselves or their family . . . one could only save himself from ridicule by killing the woman. Separation of a couple . . . was always assumed to be linked to the husband's sexual inadequacies. . . . The military education at the Colégio Militar demanded the elevation of the cult of machismo and sought to perfect to the maximum these . . . prejudiced tendencies.[9]

Dishonor left a "man" few options because caustic affronts could greet him at every turn if he did not follow the code. Cases of wife and consensual-mate murder among *praças* indicate that enlisted men accepted a similar code of ethics.[10] Among men engaged in ongoing homosexual relationships, the rules and roles of sexual honor could also apply to active and passive partners.

Honor is an arena where dominance and social status could be contested among individuals, families, and nations. For military men, sexual honor took on a peculiar collective significance. National honor was often depicted as a virtuous female. Society entrusted enlisted men to defend her from foreign aggressors and medizing insurgents. An 1867 Brazilian cartoon depicted "national honor" as a beautiful kneeling woman besieged by specters labeled "war, hunger, Urquiza [an Argentine general] and Cholera." The figure of a male Tupi Indian warrior interposed himself to defend Brazil's feminized honor. To inspire recruits, an 1865 Brazilian editorial described invading Paraguayans as those who "assailed, violated, and dishonored virgins and married women, and . . . killed innocent children." The rape of the innocents by rampaging "barbarians" has long been a rallying cry for war mobilization.

Brazilian national honor was thus linked and charged with deep-seated preoccupations with sexual power and dominance. An 1872 medical thesis linked the fate of "nations" throughout history to their management of prostitution and "unnatural" copulations. With the rise of nationalism throughout Latin America, this rhetoric became even more pronounced because it fetishistically promoted the heterosexual nuclear family as the primary building block of social order and metaphor for the nation.[11] During war, the metaphor implied that defeat produced a nation of cuckolds unable to protect collective virtue.

Ironically, in Brazil those who defended national honor came mostly from the "dishonorable" ranks of the *desprotegidos* (unprotected ones): vagrants, former slaves, orphans, criminals, migrants, unskilled workers, and the unemployed. Officials coerced approximately half of all recruits into service against their will, and most volunteers signed on to escape unemployment, hunger, homelessness, and sometimes slavery. Almost all *praças* were Brazilian-born and included blacks and whites, but most were of mixed race. As Brazil made a transition from slave to wage labor from 1850 to 1888, enlisted service was identified with marginality and captivity. As Bom Crioulo mused, "a sailor and a black slave, in the long run, they come down to the same thing."[12]

The ignominy of impressment placed the military barracks at the opposite end of the spectrum of values represented by the family home. Brazilians associated the home with honor, order, marriage, safety, family, and private power, while the street implied disgrace, chaos, illegitimacy, danger, vagrancy, and vulnerability to the vagaries of impersonal public authority.[13] The very term for enlisted men, *praças*, derived from the Portuguese word for public square, linguistically locating them in the street. In colonial times, the term *soldado* (private) was a euphemism for a male criminal sent into exile; it also designated an unmarried man.[14] This marked the traditional exemption from military service that married men enjoyed (if they could document their status), and the use of exiled criminals to serve in colonial regiments.

Marriage remained an important badge of status in post-Independence Brazil. Poor men who violated their marriage vows or trifled with virginity threatened this touchstone of status and were sometimes summarily punished with military impressment.[15] Unlike private homes, barracks segregated mostly unmarried men "promiscuously" into crowded common abodes, as did the slave quarters of plantation society. Like slaves, unmarried *praças* needed their superiors' consent to marry or establish a family, a privilege not granted lightly.

The belief that unmarried men living together led to promiscuity prompted one physician to assert that the military and boarding schools produced the majority of "active" sodomites: "In the military . . . sodomy has developed to such an extent that rare are those who do not practice it. . . . Rare is the officer without one or two *camaradas* [privates designated as an officer's personal servants] who provide these dishonest services." In 1906 another physician noted that imperial presidios, jails, barracks, and military apprentice schools (where authorities often placed abandoned children and juvenile delinquents) produced "many dedicated homosexual practitioners."[16] The association between dishonorable status and enlisted service was strengthened during the Paraguayan War (1864–1870), when the state manumitted hundreds of slaves and freed scores of convicts to fill depleted ranks.

In some ways, prior to 1916, the barracks functioned as the male equivalent of the bordello: both attempted to isolate dangerous men and women from honorable households.[17] Impressment protected "respectable" family homes from dangerous single men by congregating and watching over them. Barracks were a suspect social space: a place for orphans, seducers, vagrants, perverts, and thieves but not for the "men or sons of families." Recruitment threatened honorable poor families because it meant comparatively low wages and often the relocation of a household head or a productive adolescent. This posed serious hardships for modest households. Vulnerability to recruitment implied a lack of manhood and misfortune.

Certainly many career *praças*, their families, and friends held a different, more positive perspective on enlisted service. Veterans who risked their lives to defend national honor could identify themselves with the fashionable European ideology of the "nation in arms" that depicted the military as a microcosm of the nation.[18] Although this was a minority opinion, it was a view draft advocates hoped recruitment reform would make predominant.

Enlisted service constituted a semicoercive public labor system and a protopenal institution, but the state tried to alter this function by implementing a national draft lottery first legislated in 1874. The new law made most men eligible for the draft. Significantly, married men were no longer exempted from military service.[19] Honorable poor families fervently resisted this law because it threatened to subject their protectors to the humiliation and hardships of enlisted service and expose the family to dishonor. Their actions thwarted conscription's immediate implementation. In the meantime, impressment continued. The State succeeded in implementing the draft only in 1916, spurred by the uncertainties of World War I.

- ## *BOM CRIOULO* AND MILITARY INQUIRIES: WINDOWS ON MASCULINITY

Most army and navy officers repressed homosexual acts in the ranks, but almost all military men were cognizant of a partially submerged culture of same-sex relations in the military. Military tribunals sometimes asked and pursued men accused of homosexual acts, and some told about their sexual liaisons with other soldiers. Tradition-bound Brazilian officers and *praças* felt sodomy to be an abominable sin. Some reformist ones, like Adolfo Caminha, understood it as a result of degenerative medical pathology. Others at least partially rejected these views and partook of forbidden sexual liaisons themselves.

At certain levels, Caminha's story suggests that Bom Crioulo's "inverted" sexual drive resulted from slavery's inhumanity, later compounded by degrading conditions and corporal punishments he suffered as a *praça*. The uneducated and abused Bom Crioulo believed his own sexual desires to be "natural."[20] As a parallel, Caminha depicted a highly esteemed navy captain, a well-educated scion of the imperial nobility, as

> a man completely indifferent to the fair sex, who sought out his innate, ideal model of beauty in male adolescents. . . . [He] preferred to live in his own way, with his own people, with his sailors. And there was always a touch of respectful hypocrisy, of malicious hesitation when the captain was mentioned. [But] no one spoke disrespectfully of him. Everyone wanted him to remain as he was . . . gentle at times, an implacable disciplinarian, a model officer.[21]

In this and other passages, Caminha presents an ambivalent view of sodomy among sailors. He makes it clear that the captain and Bom Crioulo desired young males to the exclusion of women. Even though sailors furtively smirked about the captain, they respected and feared his authority, as they did Bom Crioulo's. The captain and Bom Crioulo were the active partners in their homosexual couplings, implying virility and even a rugged individuality.

Caminha selected an aristocratic sodomite to vent his republican animus toward the monarchical Brazilian Empire (1822–1889). He insinuated that slavery, impressment, and aristocratic privilege created a "degenerate" social and sexual order. The old regime's extreme social inequities reversed the "natural" desires of the most privileged and most exploited.[22]

Although a fierce abolitionist, Caminha's depiction of Bom Crioulo also expresses doubts about Brazil's "race" and national destiny. A black sailor seducing and "enslaving" a white cabin boy was calculated to shock racial sensibilities that placed whites on top of Brazil's social and sexual hierarchies. But it complemented bigoted Brazilian medical assertions that Africans and Indians brought pederasty to the *bagaceira* (the sugar plantation's lax moral environment) and "contaminated" the Portuguese with this "perversion."[23] Bom Crioulo's apartment held Emperor Pedro II's portrait, a reference to the support many poor blacks maintained for the deposed monarch even after the Republic's promulgation in 1889. Caminha implies that Bom Crioulo's ignorance, race, and depravity made him a natural monarchist, an enemy of the new Republican order.[24]

Caminha draped his accusations of racial degeneration and homosexual depravity with the fabric of pseudoscientific studies of homosexuality and masturbatory insanity. He was particularly familiar with the works of German sexual "science" by Richard von Krafft-Ebing (1886), Kurt Moll (1893), and Ambroise Tardieu (1857). His reliance on German theory marked a break with earlier Brazilian medical literature on sexuality that borrowed heavily from similar French "science."[25]

Once again, the reliance on German thought suggests a link between Brazilian sexual science and Prussian military ideals. Caminha and other Brazilians probably became aware of these works as the German military emerged as a world model. Brazilian officers were among many who made pilgrimages to Berlin; others avidly studied German military journals at home. Those who backed the adoption of a Prussian-inspired draft seem to have also been exposed to German ideas on male sexuality and its relationship to martial capability. Brazilians developed their own critical interpretations of a far from monolithic European literature on sexuality. Their efforts to promulgate a draft law borrowed German rhetoric and shared similar concerns with securing the respectability of enlisted service. When Brazil's 1874 military-recruitment law reform passed, a police chief praised it: "The army will gain discipline and morality when the flower of the nation flows into its ranks. . . . [It will] cease to be a receptacle for vagrants and *perverts*."

The government's inability to implement a draft, however, meant the enlisted ranks remained a penal dumping ground until 1916, but officers continued to look to Franco-Prussian models for guidance.[26]

Although Caminha alluded to science that condemned homosexuality as degenerative, Bom Crioulo is a sympathetic character with admirable sentiments. As one critic noted, Caminha's depiction of homosexual love is more dignified than his rather "comic" portrayal of Aleixo's heterosexual affair with Carolina, a plump Portuguese prostitute.[27] Bom Crioulo was a handsome physical specimen whose "colossal, savage figure" defied with "formidable muscles, the diseased softness and weakness of a whole decadent, enervated generation." He exhibited a nobility of physical strength and dexterity: "a man to be watched," who exercised a "decisive influence over the crew" despite his low rank.[28] The sailor was also generous, hardworking, tolerant, and philanthropic; in most respects, he was a Brazilian Billy Budd.[29] These positive traits, however, are corrupted by injustice, making Bom Crioulo's fate tragic. When flogged or unfairly treated, he became "lazy" and "rebellious," given to drinking too much *cachaça* (sugarcane brandy) and provoking fights.[30] He was also consumed by a gnawing jealousy over Aleixo. The choice of such a controversial tragic hero to condemn impressment, slavery, corporal punishment, the empire, and homosexuality befuddled Caminha's republican contemporaries.

Subsequently, some dismissed Caminha's novel as a distorted depiction of enlisted life. On closer examination, however, Aleixo and Bom Crioulo's relationship bears a strong resemblance to courts-martial transcripts. Though Caminha used archetypical characters to dramatize his critique, these protagonists were also human and complex. His literary license does not disqualify his portrait's accuracy. Similarly, military inquiries reveal contentious interpretations of events that must be interpreted with subtlety. But whether soldiers accused of sodomy were victims of malicious character assassination or not, the testimony speaks to what military men felt was believable. Thus, *Bom Crioulo*'s naturalism and courts-martial cases yield rare glimpses of the clashes and compromises between differing visions of appropriate masculine sexuality.

• THE WAR ON SODOMY

Like Caminha's *Bom Crioulo*, military-court cases revealed a multidimensional approach to adjudicating sex crimes. Military discipline repressed homosexuality at two levels. *Praça* records show that officers often took summary actions to castigate homosexual behavior without recourse to formal courts martial. At times, however, accusations of attempted or consummated homosexual acts led to full-blown trials.

In 1900 Private Manoel Cardoso do Nascimento was jailed for six days for having beaten a woman. Two months later, he was kept in isolation for eight days after attempting "immoral acts" in the stockade's group cell with a comrade. Attempted sodomy received a sterner censure than beating a lower-class woman, but in terms of regimental discipline, eight days in the stockade was not severe. Similarly, in 1891 Private Antônio Moreira Ignacio was imprisoned for a fortnight without daily supper for abandoning his post guarding the company arms. He was discovered on top of the fort's gate practicing immoral acts with a comrade. Officers often applied mild penalties to those caught performing homosexual acts, indicating that there was a certain degree of tolerance and expectation that such couplings would occur.[31]

These disciplinary actions were tame compared to the 1891 Código Penal e Disciplinar da Armada (Naval disciplinary and penal code, adopted by the army in 1899), which specified that "any individual who acts against the honesty of a person of either sex by means of threat or violence with the goal of satisfying lascivious passions or for moral depravation or by inversion of the sexual instinct" be punished by one to four years imprisonment.[32] The term *inversion* echoed a French one coined in 1882, but the law criminalized only coerced sex. The Prussian Count von Lippe's 1763 code (the basis of Brazilian army law of 1899) made no specific mention of sodomy, but medieval traditions stipulated death for this "nefarious sin." Imperial and republican civil law did not define homosexual acts performed in private between consenting adults as crimes.[33] It seems sodomy was not a legitimate state concern if consensual and performed in private. But if committed with a minor under age sixteen, it constituted statutory rape. Military and civil law defined homosexual rape as a serious crime, but few were tried on these charges. Many victims probably found it too hard to substantiate the charge or too humiliating to report.

Only one extant trial record shows a conviction for homosexual rape: Navy Coalman José Joaquim de Sant'Anna and Sailor Antônio Ferreira da Silva were accused of raping Navy Coalman Pedro Cavalcante in 1893. The three had gone out drinking together on Môcangüe Island in Rio, where the navy's correctional company for "incorrigible" sailors was located. On their return, Antônio, José, and Pedro entered an abandoned house, where a struggle ensued. An initial report noted that Antônio and José forcibly stripped and bound the "younger and weaker" Pedro and proceeded to satisfy their lascivious desires upon him.

The judges were able to convict these men only because of Pedro's willingness to testify—victims rarely admitted they had been raped. Others corroborated his testimony, observing that when Antônio returned he stated: "Whoever wants to go can, I am already finished." Antônio allegedly boasted that he had had his way with Pedro, callously inviting others to do the same. Only three years earlier, Antônio had been tried and absolved for injuring a comrade whom he allegedly intended to force to "practice immoral acts." In 1893, however, the court martial sentenced José and Antônio to four years, the maximum sentence, and absolved Pedro.[34]

This case illustrates important themes. First, Antônio boasted about his domination and violation of Pedro. In a number of cases, active partners allegedly bragged about their sexual conquests. Pedro made it clear that he had struggled to defend his honor, but even so, he was courageous to admit that his honor had been violated. Rather than seek vengeance, he relied on the authorities to avenge his shame. Another recurring theme was the liberal consumption of *cachaça* by *praças* on bases, at sea, in homes, taverns, barracks, and brothels. Some were accused of intentionally plying comrades with alcohol in the hopes of currying favor, weakening inhibitions, and enticing them to submit to their "lascivious" desires.[35] If persuasion failed, as in Pedro's case, alcohol facilitated coercion. *Praças* asserted their manhood by drinking hard without succumbing to inebriation, but one incapacitated by grog put his honor at risk.

Booze, pride, and the exigencies of evidence made sodomy difficult but not impossible to prove. From 1870 to 1925 official sources record seventy-nine courts martial for sexual offenses (many for homosexual acts), although, as stated above, only one of these was for homosexual rape. More than one-third of the known sentences resulted in convictions (some for officers).[36] *Praças* with bad disciplinary records or "reputations" were probably more susceptible to court martial proceedings. Take the 1884 case of Second Sergeant Gabriel Coutinho Brazil, a twenty-year-old navy carpenter. Gabriel had emerged from the notoriously picaresque world of the navy's apprentice schools. At age nine, Gabriel's "protector" presented him to the navy arsenal, but his apprenticeship was not promising. He was frequently jailed for fighting, drunkenness, skipping his geometry class, and failing to fulfill his duties. In 1882 his wages were suspended because he was found in his quarters practicing "immoral acts." The next month Gabriel deserted and then returned voluntarily two months later. Probably as a punishment for desertion, he was transferred to the regular navy. Apparently, Gabriel turned a new leaf. He was promoted to corporal and then to second sergeant in 1883. In 1884, however, he was accused of being an "active pederast," busted to a private's rank, and brought to trial.[37]

Nine witnesses, mostly *praças* in Gabriel's regiment, alleged that the second sergeant had maintained a relationship with Private José Theotonio de Oliveira. According to a first sergeant, "It was known throughout the battalion that Sergeant Brazil lived immorally with Private Theotonio." Others testified that Gabriel bragged publicly about his relations with Theotonio and even "dared to mistreat his comrades with words, all because of jealousy for Theotonio." One asserted that Gabriel openly declared that "Theotonio belonged to him because he supported him, giving him clothes, money, cigarettes, and other things." It was alleged that Gabriel let it be known that Theotonio was his "*protegido*" (client), assigned him light duties, and sometimes excused him from roll calls. When interrogated, Gabriel simply stated that there was no proof of his guilt. Most of the seven officers serving on the court martial agreed. A plurality of votes absolved Gabriel. The officers noted that "to be punished it is indispensable that the defendant be caught in the act or at least that some of the witnesses had seen [Gabriel] performing the act."[38]

The sergeant's "intimacy" with a younger private reveals that *praças* replicated the system of patriarchal protection common to larger Brazilian society. Many sought out patrons or *pistolões* (big shots) for protection and to ameliorate the conditions of enlisted life. These client ties could be strengthened by or conditioned by sexual intimacy. Protection could come at a price, however; several witnesses indicated that Gabriel had beaten Theotonio and destroyed some of his property in fits of jealous rage. Interestingly, Theotonio did not testify, nor did a number of other *praças* accused of having been the passive partners in sodomy inquiries. When they did testify, victims normally insisted that they had struggled to defend themselves. No "man" willingly submitted to another man's sexual desire.

The depiction of Gabriel and Theotonio's relationship resembles *Bom Crioulo*'s plot. Immediately drawn to recently inducted Aleixo, Bom Crioulo beat up a sailor who treated the cabin boy badly. For fighting, the black sailor was flogged. For Aleixo, "The idea that Bom Crioulo had suffered physically for him made such an impression on the Cabin-boy's mind and heart that he now considered him a true, unselfish protector." Bom Crioulo bestowed favors and flattery on Aleixo. Then one evening the two hung their hammocks together and cuddled in an isolated room aboard ship, and Aleixo felt

> his own blood impulses that he had never felt before, a sort of innate desire to give in to the black man's wishes . . . a vague relaxation of the nerves, a longing for passiveness. "Go ahead!" he whispered and rolled over. And the crime against nature was consummated.[39]

Caminha's depiction of Aleixo's sexual awakening via Bom Crioulo's advances emphasizes Aleixo's "longing for passivity," stereotypically a feminine sentiment. This reflected the perception that all intercourse was undertaken not by equals but by active and passive partners.

From then on, the black sailor protected Aleixo and provided his lover with gifts and a room they shared on shore leave. Most of their comrades were probably aware of their relationship but feared to provoke Bom Crioulo's wrath. Such relationships were probably not uncommon in the sometimes dangerous enlisted ranks. Some accepted the passive role in the hopes of gaining ongoing protection, sexual and emotional fulfillment, and favors, or because they enjoyed playing a transgressive role. These desires were not mutually exclusive.

Bom Crioulo took pride in his relationship with Aleixo, but Caminha's narrative indicates that the black mariner's homosexual activity had serious medical consequences. As with classical Greek drama, Bom Crioulo's tragedy lay in his inability to recognize his transgression. As the black seaman carried on an affair with Aleixo, he inexplicably grew thin and weaker. Bom Crioulo became seriously ill and desperate when transferred to a steamship whose aristocratic captain refused him shore leave and flogged him. During their separation, Aleixo, ashamed of his sexual domination by the black man, did not seek Bom Crioulo out and proudly began a "manly" affair with a female prostitute. Bom Crioulo learned of Aleixo's betrayal in the navy hospital from a comrade. In the end, the black Jack Tar deserted the hospital in a demented state and brutally took Aleixo's life to avenge his honor. The cautionary tale implies that deadly physiological and psychological consequences resulted from this "waste" of a man's "generative juices" in nonreproductive copulations.

Military law condemned homosexual rape but did not expressly condemn homosexual acts between consenting adults performed in private. In 1884, however, a tribunal punished two men, one of whom admitted to homosexual liaisons. Three witnesses found Honório Hermeto Carneiro Leão and José Moreira da Cunha practicing "immoral acts" in Rio's navy hospital latrine. The older Honório was the active partner (*agente*); José, the passive (*paciente*). In 1880 José had been sent to the navy apprentice school by Paraíba's police chief, who estimated his age to be fourteen. Three years later, he was transferred to Rio as a cabin boy. When the crime occurred, Honório was serving a six-year sentence for seriously injuring a comrade but was often in the navy hospital recovering from illness.

Honório denied his guilt, but José, who declared he was only fifteen, stated that "having committed the infraction" and judging himself guilty, he "had nothing to allege in his favor."[40] José did not say that Honório forced him to submit, indicating that he had willingly consented. Was José unashamed of being a "passive sodomite," flying in the face of conventional conceptions of honor? Or, did he indeed feel that he was guilty of a crime against nature? By emphasizing his age, fifteen (making him three years younger than his record estimated), did José hope to attenuate his punishment by implying statutory rape? The latter interpretation seems more likely. José is the only *praça* of more than twenty interrogated in extant case records who admitted to engaging voluntarily in this "offense." The hospital's court martial found both guilty but said it did not have the competence to pass sentence. The Conselho Superior Militar e de Justiça, responsible for reviewing all cases, condemned both Honório and José to six months in prison.[41] In this instance, the high court did not recognize the passive "minor" as any less culpable than the active adult partner; both acts were equally shameful for the court.

Unlike civilian juries, military tribunals rarely dismissed murder cases in which *praças* claimed defense of honor. Most officers probably believed that few *praças* had honor to lose. But even though many Brazilians regarded soldiers as degraded individuals, enlisted men did not agree. For the most part, they accepted and upheld as best they could the code of honor common to civilian society. Deadly fights could erupt between *praças* when one accused the other of being a "passive sodomite" or more typically of "serving as a woman" for another man's lascivious desires. This was the ultimate insult to "manly" honor. The macho culture promoted by the military pressured soldiers to prove, at least periodically, their dominance. Documenting virility often came at the expense of a comrade's honor.[42] Thus, the macho code of ethics encouraged confrontations detrimental to discipline.

Reformist officers, some influenced by German ideas on sexuality, hygiene, and discipline, sought to discourage this disruptive behavior by stigmatizing both partners as homosexuals. Modern military discipline and an overweening sensitivity to personal honor are incompatible. By implementing a draft law, reformers hoped to sublimate the *praças*' concern with their personal honor in favor of a proud institutional association with national honor.

The conflict between traditional conceptions of masculine honor and modern military science became more apparent as the recruitment reform effort accelerated in the early 1900s. Conditions of service were substantially altered: minimum service contracts dropped from six years to one, corporal punishments were abolished (earlier in the army than in the navy), the *camarada* (the assignment of privates as officers' domestic servants) was eliminated, and general conditions improved. Moreover, the image of soldiering and sailoring became more respectable to "honorable" poor families through propaganda that extolled enlisted service as an expression of masculine duty. In 1916 a promilitary service tract attacked the prejudice against sexually segregated institutions: "How is one to have an idea of fatherland if he does not have a home or a family?! Everyone disparages the honest celibacy of the priest and the soldier . . . for the miserable life they lead; if they are not sexually deviant, they are [assumed to be] eunuchs."[43] This statement demonstrates the distrust of segregated male institutions that contrasted the monastery (or priesthood), the barracks, and the *senzala* to the normative sexuality of the house. Even the "honorable" celibacy of the priest was suspect because many believed that the male's sexual urges required a release. The monastery and the barracks presumably attracted those with "abnormal" sexual proclivities and "corrupted" others. Reformers addressed the specific prejudices that shrouded the barracks in a sinister aura of social castration and sexual perversion. They strove to dispel these perceptions, and enumerated how the draft and military discipline would fortify family values, the work ethic, and masculine virtue. Previous attempts to implement conscription had not been accompanied by efforts to sell the new system to the public and recast soldiering's image. Unlike World War I mobilization in the United States, where draft dodgers were subject to gender ridicule and labeled as emasculated "slackers," in Brazil, propagandists had to convince the public that army service was manly.[44]

The Brazilian military became more and more self-conscious of its public image as it successfully pushed for conscription's implementation in 1916. Officers portrayed barracks as "honorable" houses where officers, who acted as caring parents, made the military a virtuous family.[45] In the 1930s, when the military took on a high-profile role in politics and tightened up draft enforcement, officers became even more defensive. Thus, it is not surprising that the navy sought to ban distribution of a new edition of *Bom Crioulo*. Unsuccessful, some sought to discredit Caminha's realism. Gastão Penalva's 1939 biography of Caminha dismissed the accuracy of his portrayal of 1890s navy life: "The navy of *Bom Crioulo*, the scenery in which the novel takes place, the facts and characters that animate the plot are not real. . . . What influenced him [Caminha] were literary reminiscences, exploits of other lands and peoples, and the fallacious oral tradition, which ruins history and misinterprets myths." The casual way that sailors and officers in *Bom Crioulo* regarded homosexual acts seemed a damning allegation to the conscripted military of the 1930s. Whether they knew it or not, Caminha shared most of their dismal views on homosexuality.[46]

CONCLUSIONS

All this asking, telling, and pursuing in the Brazilian military through the early 1900s is laden with ironies. How could men be punished for "criminal" sexual acts when enlisted service constituted a semicoercive labor system and a protopenal institution? After serving their sentences, only those who committed heinous crimes were expelled. Before 1900 most convictions required *praças* to serve out their contracts after finishing prison stints, forfeiting all the time previously served. Thus, convictions extended rather than reduced required service. Because many men were punished (some for sexual offenses) with army service, excluding men from military service for practicing or claiming to have practiced homosexual acts would have been a reward rather than a punishment.[47] Unlike more recently in the United States, asking, telling, and pursuing rarely led to expulsion from the Brazilian military in the late 1800s.

After 1916 conscription slowly elevated enlisted service from a punitive to a preventative reform institution. Even so, the middle and upper classes legally and illegally dodged enlisted service because it continued to carry the stigma of humble social origins. The conscripted military recruited a larger cross section of Brazilian youths from more "honorable" poor families for short stints of duty. The state now granted more timely discharges and could more easily expel troublesome recruits. Officers could also more effectively instruct troops in nationalist doctrine, hygiene, physical exercise, morality, and civic duty. More research is needed to determine the extent to which officers spoke out against homosexuality as an "illness" as part of this program.

Government efforts to improve the soldier's image succeeded in gaining greater public acceptance and tighter draft enforcement, but reformers were less successful in propagating new sexual identities that equally stigmatized active and passive homosexual partners. For most, the shame still rested with the passive partner. In the late 1920s Nelson Werneck Sodré recalled that among Colégio Militar cadets:

Homosexuality . . . was only shameful when one was the passive partner, the active partner was seen almost as a demonstration of virility. Passive partners were few, but couplings were common, almost always inconsequential—most of the time for reasons of ostentation—among cadets. In two or three cases, these couplings were the object of rumors, provoking fights and jealousies; in one case, the passive partner was one of these exceptional cases of an indecisive nature between [a preference] for one sex or another.

Sodré condemned such "cloistered regimes" because they "mutilate" people.[48] He and many others continued to associate sexual deviance with sex segregation, affirming that army propaganda had not overcome the perception that the barracks promoted homosexual acts. While homosexuality was a part of military and civilian life, passive partners remained the main object of derision.

The sources examined here indicate significant connections between rising militarist nationalism and efforts to define appropriate masculine sexuality. To my knowledge, there has been no explicit affirmation that a particularly useful avenue for future research would be investigating links between the rise of the Prussian-inspired recruitment reforms and the dissemination of new sexual identities.[49] The new culture of a conscripted military based on the principle of universal male military service spurred authorities to grapple with male sexuality and adjust concepts of family and nation.

The impact of recruitment reforms provides a unique avenue for developing a more rigorous and nuanced cross-cultural understanding of changing conceptions of masculinity because the militaries of most nations underwent similar reforms in the late nineteenth century and early twentieth. Conscription allowed states to move sexual "science" out of medical journals and to apply hygienic and eugenic theory to a large cross section of a nation's male population. Certainly, militarist movements of both the Right and Left in Latin America and beyond have demonstrated an obsessive concern with purifying "national morality" by defining and repressing those who practice "unnatural" sex.[50]

The history of Brazilian military recruitment reform suggests that similar national case studies should reveal links between the European martial reformation and the institutionalization of new conceptions of and policies toward male sexuality in Latin America.

• NOTES

Abbreviations used in the notes: Arquivo Nacional, Rio de Janeiro (ANR); Conselho Superior Militar e de Justiça (CSMJ); Suprema Tribunal Militar (STM).

1. Adolfo Caminha, *Bom Crioulo: The Black Man and the Cabin Boy* (1895), trans. E. A. Lacey (San Francisco: Gay Sunshine Press, 1982), 74–75.

2. Raul de Sá Barbosa, introduction to Caminha, *Bom Crioulo*, 6–9; Gastão Penalva, *Subsídios para a história da Marinha* (Rio de Janeiro: Imprensa Naval, 1939), 2:385–474.

3. *Relatório da Repartição dos Negócios do Ministério da Guerra apresentado ao Parlamento* (Rio de Janeiro: Imprensa Nacional, 1870–1889), appendixes;

Relatório da Repartição dos Negócios do Ministério da Guerra apresentado ao Congresso (Rio de Janeiro: Imprensa Nacional, 1891–1925), appendixes.

4. David M. Halperin, "Sex before Sexuality: Pederasty, Politics, and Power in Classical Athens," in *Hidden from History: Reclaiming the Gay and Lesbian Past*, ed. Martin Duberman et al. (New York: Meridian Press, 1989), 38; George Chauncey Jr., "Christian Brotherhood or Sexual Perversion? Homosexual Identities and the Construction of Sexual Boundaries in the World War One Era," *Journal of Social History*, 1985, 189–211; Peter Fry, in *Para Inglês Ver: Identidade e Política na cultura brasileira* (Rio de Janeiro: Zahar, 1982), 93–94, argues that homosexual identities developed in the cities of southern Brazil only in the late 1960s.

5. ANR, STM, *maço* 13224, *processo* 236, João Estácio, São Gabriel, Rio Grande do Sul (1897), 47.

6. Richard G. Parker, *Corpos, prazeres, e paixões: a cultura de sexo no Brasil contemporâneo* (São Paulo: Best-Seller, 1991), esp. 70–71; Roger Lancaster, *Machismo, Danger, and the Intimacy of Power in Nicaragua* (Berkeley: University of California Press, 1992), esp. 237–71. George Chauncey Jr.'s work on the U.S. Navy in 1919 Newport, R. I., suggests that a similar division between passive and active partners in homosexual couplings existed; see "Christian Brotherhood," 196.

7. Francisco Ferraz de Macedo, "Da prostituição em geral" (Rio de Janeiro: Academica, 1872); Francisco Manuel Soares de Sousa, "Generalidades médicas acerca de recrutamento" (Rio de Janeiro: Typ. do Brasil, 1845); Miguel Antônio Heredia Sá, "Algumas reflexões sobre a copula, onanismo, e prostituição" (Rio de Janeiro: Typ. Universal de Laemmert, 1845). Navy Corporal Thomaz da Cruz Ferrari, from Pelotas, Rio Grande do Sul (a city associated with homosexuality in Brazilian lore), suffered heart palpitations and frequent illness attributed to "the vice of *onanismo*" or excessive masturbation. *ANR, STM, processo* 4, *maço* 13199, Thomaz da Cruz Ferrari, Rio de Janeiro (1896). Daniel A. McMillan analyzes German nationalist views on masturbation in "Dealing from Strength: Manliness and Citizenship in the German Gymnastics Movement, 1811–1871" (AHA conference paper, Chicago, 6 January 1995). Also see Caminha, *Bom Crioulo*, 31–32.

8. Peter M. Beattie, "Transforming Enlisted Army Service in Brazil, 1864–1940: Penal Servitude versus Conscription and Changing Conceptions of Honor, Race and Nation" (Ph.D. diss., University of Miami, 1994), chap. 8. Marta de Abreu Esteves, *Meninas Perdidas: Os populares e o cotidiano do amor no Rio de Janeiro da Belle Epoque* (Rio de Janeiro: Paz e Terra, 1989). See also Sueann Caulfield, "In Defense of Honor: The Contested Meaning of Sexual Morality in Law and Courtship in Rio de Janeiro, 1920–1940" (Ph.D. diss. New York University, 1994).

9. Nelson Werneck Sodré, *Do Tenentismo ao Estado Novo: Memórias de um soldado*, 2d ed. (Petrópolis: Vozes, 1986), 41.

10. One soldier who came home to find his wife engaged in adultery with a comrade, killed both, but he repeatedly stabbed his wife to completely repudiate his dishonor: Beattie, "Transforming," 458–61.

11. "Os espectros da atualidade," *O Arlequim*, 14 July 1867, 8. Ferraz de Macedo, "Da Prostituição," 163. Donna J. Guy, *Sex and Danger in Buenos Aires: Prostitution, Family, and Nation in Argentina* (Lincoln: Nebraska University Press, 1991). Doris Sommer, *Foundational Fictions: The National Romances of Latin America*

(Berkeley: University of California Press, 1991), 33–51. Michel Foucault, *A History of Sexuality: An Introduction*, trans. Robert Hurley (New York: Vintage Books, 1980). Benedict Anderson, *Imagined Communities: Reflections on the Origin and Spread of Nationalism* (London: Verso, 1983). Junandir Freire Costa, *Ordem médica e norma familiar*, 3d ed. (Rio: Graal, 1983), 240.

12. Caminha, *Bom Crioulo*, 80.

13. Roberto da Matta, *A casa e a rua: espaço, cidadania, mulher, e morte no Brasil* (Rio: Ed. Guanabara, 1987), 31–69. Roberto da Matta, *Carnavais, malandros, e heróis: Para Uma sociologia do dilema brasileiro*, 5th ed. (Rio: Ed. Guanabara, 1990), 43–68. Gilberto Freyre, *Sobrados e macumbos: decadência do patriarcado rural e desenvolvimento do urbano* (1936), 7th ed. (Rio: José Olympio, 1985), 1:34–41. Peter M. Beattie, "The House, the Street and the Barracks: Reform and Honorable Masculine Social Space in Brazil, 1864–1945," *Hispanic American Historical Review* (forthcoming).

14. Timothy J. Coates, "Exiles and Orphans: Forced and State-Sponsored Colonizers in the Portuguese Empire, 1550–1720" (Ph.D. diss., University of Minnesota, 1993), 113–15; M. N. Pearson, "The Crowd in Portuguese India," in *Coastal Western India*, ed. M. N. Pearson (New Delhi: Concept, 1981), 42.

15. Joan E. Meznar provides examples from Paraíba in "The Ranks of the Poor: Military Service and Social Differentiation in Northeast Brazil, 1835–1875," *Hispanic American Historical Review* 72.3 (1992): 342–44.

16. Herculano Augusto Lassance Cunha, "Dissertação sobre a prostituição na cidade do Rio de Janeiro" (Rio: Typ. Imparcial de F. Paula Brito, 1845). Ferraz de Macedo noted high sodomy rates among soldiers in "Da Prostituição," 115–21, 167. José Ricardo Pires de Almeida, *Homossexualismo (A libertinagem no Rio de Janeiro* (Rio: Laemmert, 1906), 75–76, 85. Luiz Mott, *Escravidão, homossexualidade e demonologia* (São Paulo: Icone, 1988). In the 1890s the Santa Casa da Misericordia's director made a public outcry when numerous military apprentices appeared for the treatment of anal syphilis sores at his hospital: Pires de Almeida, "Homossexualismo," 85. In 1875 the director of Bahia's Arsenal was removed for "giving himself to the vice of pederasty by corrupting and forcing himself on minors": ANR, IG¹128, War Ministry Correspondence, Salvador, 10 June 1875, *folha* 1031. I thank Hendrik Kraay for generously sharing the last citation.

17. Doctors advocated regimenting prostitution in publicly supervised bordellos: Ferraz de Macedo, "Da Prostituição," 121; Francisco Manuel Soares de Sousa, "Generalidades médicos acerca de recrutamento" (Rio de Janeiro: Typ. J. J. da Rocha, 1845); Magali Engel, *Meretrizes e doutores: Saber médico e prostituição no Rio de Janeiro* (São Paulo: Ed. Brasiliense, 1988), chap. 4. For Buenos Aires, Donna J. Guy describes the barracks-like quality of state-run bordellos in *Sex and Danger*, 39.

18. Frank D. McCann, "The Nation in Arms: Obligatory Military Service during the Old Republic," in *Essays Concerning the Socioeconomic History of Brazil and Portuguese India*, ed. Dauril Alden and Warren Dean (Gainesville: University Presses of Florida, 1977), 211–43.

19. *Collecção das leis do Império do Brasil* (Rio de Janeiro: Typ. Nacional, 1875), 1:64–66.

20. Soares de Sousa, "Recrutamento," 5.

21. Caminha, *Bom Crioulo*, 100.

22. Caminha was not the first to suggest this connection. Soares de Sousa, "Recrutamento," 20; Ferraz de Macedo, "Da Prostituição," 115–21.

23. Pires de Almeida, *Homossexualismo*, 75–76, 85.

24. Thomas E. Skidmore, *White into Black: Race and Nationality in Brazilian Thought*, 2d ed. (Durham: Duke University Press, 1993). Nancy Leys Stepan, *The Hour of Eugenics: Race, Gender and Nation in Latin America* (Ithaca: Cornell University Press, 1992), 36. In the emperor's presence at his graduation, Caminha insulted the monarch by praising Victor Hugo's implacable republicanism. See Caminha, *Bom Crioulo*, 7, 81; Michael R. Trochim, "The Brazilian Black Guard: Racial Conflict in Post-Abolition Brazil," *Americas* 44 (1988): 93–104; Carlos Eugênio Líbano Soares, *A Negregada instituição: Os capoeiras no Rio de Janeiro* (Rio de Janeiro: Biblioteca Carioca, 1994), 185–245.

25. Caminha remarked: "After all, what is *Bom Crioulo*? Nothing more than a case of sexual inversion as studied in Krafft-Ebing, Moll, Tardieu and the books on forensic medicine!" Cited in Robert Howes, "Adolfo Caminha's *Bom Crioulo*," in Caminha, *Bom Crioulo*, 14. On sexuality, armed forces, and nation in France, Robert A. Nye, *Masculinity and Male Codes of Honor in Modern France* (New York: Oxford University Press, 1993), chap. 6.

26. *Relatório do Presidente da Província de Pernambuco Henrique Pereira da Lucema* (Recife, 1 March 1875), 35. Frederick Nunn, *Yesterday's Soldiers: European Military Professionalism in South America* (Lincoln: University of Nebraska Press, 1983).

27. Howes, "Adolfo Caminha's *Bom Crioulo*," 15.

28. Caminha, *Bom Crioulo*, 43, 33.

29. Caminha probably read Herman Melville's sea novels, which also portrayed or suggested homosexuality among sailors. See Melville, *Billy Budd, Sailor: An Inside Story* (rpt. Chicago: University of Chicago Press, 1962); *Moby Dick; or, the White Whale* (rpt. New York: Harper, 1950); *White Jacket or the World in a Man of War* (New York: Harper, 1850).

30. Brazilian doctors in the 1800s deplored corporal punishment and advocated moral persuasion: Costa, *Ordem médica*, 197–204.

31. ANR, STM, *caixa* 13.390, *processo* 396, Manoel Cardoso de Nascimento (1980), 59); ANR, STM, *caixa* 13.349, *processo* 750, Antônio Moreira Ignacio (1904), 10. One report noted that pederasty and masturbation should not be punished severely because this "contributes" to further sexual "abuses" by sailors. It recommended moderate punishments: Arquivo Público do Estado da Bahia, Seção de Arquivo Colonial e Provincial, 5367, Relatório, Commissão de Saude do Segundo Distrito Naval, Bahia, 4 April 1863. I thank Hendrik Kraay for sharing this citation.

32. *Código Penal e Disciplinar da Armada: regulamento processual e formulário do processo criminal militar* (Rio de Janeiro: Imprensa Nacional, 1914), 58.

33. On the French origin of "invert," see Nye, *Masculinity*, 108; Raimundo José da Cunha Mattos, *Repertório da legislação militar* (Rio de Janeiro: Typ. Nacional, 1837), 3:161; José Severiano, *Código penal da República dos Estados Unidos do Brasil* (Rio: Jacintho Ribeiro dos Santos, 1923), 391–95, 421.

34. ANR, CSMJ-CGM, *maço* 13191, *processo* 1922, (1893), 17–18, 57–59.

35. In 1894 Agripino Antônio da Costa was imprisoned for eight days for allowing a corporal to enter barracks at 3:00 A.M. under his watch to intoxicate one of his comrades for libidinous ends. *ANR*, STM, Agripino Antônio da Costa, *caixa* 13309, *processo* 434 (1896), 6–7.

36. Beattie, "Transforming," 408–75. The extant records of only two inquiries record final convictions and none preserve trials for officers.

37. ANR, CSMJ-CGM, *maço* 13183, *processo* 1368, Gabriel Coutinho Brazil, 11–12.

38. Ibid.

39. Caminha, *Bom Crioulo*, 46, 74–75.

40. ANR, CSMJ-CGM, *maço* 13182, *processo* 1346, Honório Hermeto Carneiro Leão and Jose Moreira da Cunha (1884), 17–22, 40.

41. In the Articles of War, Article 6 specified that sailors could be convicted of "blasphemy, false and profane testimony, hexing, immodesty, or other scandalous acts" but gave no sentencing guidelines. An 1883 guideline specified: "Practicing acts offensive to morality that are not foreseen in article six of the Articles of War," could be punished either by twenty-five lashes or solitary confinement. *Regimento Provisional da Armada Real de 1825* (Rio de Janeiro: Typ. Nacional, 1825), 98; *Collecção das leis do Império do Brazil de 1883* (Rio de Janeiro: Typ. Nacional, 1884), 1:381–84.

42. Private José Domingues dos Santos was tried for insubordination after attacking a corporal. He declared, however, that the corporal was a "pervert" who woke him to perform libidinous acts and then attacked him in the barracks: ANR, STM, *caixa* 13203, *processo* 176, José Dominguez dos Santos (1896). Private Antônio Manoel Rodrigues killed a comrade he declared had twice tried to force him to perform libidinous acts. He died before a decision could be reached on his case: *ANR*, STM, *caixa* 13214, *processo* 624, Antônio Manoel Rodriguez (1896).

43. Domingos Ubaldo, *A Greve Militar* (n. p., 1916), 3.

44. Beattie, "Transforming," 168–69. The U.S. Navy waged a similar propaganda campaign. Southern prohibitionist politician and navy secretary Josephus Daniels preached in 1914, "I am the father of more than 50,000 young men . . . and there is nothing more upon my heart than to see them of strong Christian character, living clean lives for home and kindred and country." See Frederick S. Harrod, *Manning the New Navy: The Development of a Modern Naval Enlisted Force, 1899–1940* (Westport, Conn.: Greenwood Press, 1978), 26–31, 34–48. Gerald Edwin Shenk, "Work or Fight: Selective Service and Manhood in the Progressive Era" (Ph.D. diss., University of California at San Diego, 1992).

45. Beattie, "The House."

46. Barbosa, introduction to Caminha, *Bom Crioulo*, 10. On attempts to ban *Bom Crioulo*'s distribution, see Braga Montenegro, "Adolfo Caminha," *Clã* (Fortaleza), 17 June 1958, 96–100, cited in Howes, "Caminha," 13.

47. Meznar, "The Ranks of the Poor," 342; Beattie, "Transforming," chap. 2.

48. Sodré, *Memórias*, 40.

49. Brazilian courts martial contrast with the 1919 cases analyzed by George Chauncey Jr. of American sailors in Newport. In Brazil, convictions focused on the "active" partner; in Newport, navy investigators focused on "queens." Perhaps this

strategy reflected different assumptions about seduction and sexual roles in the two cultures. In Brazil, the active partner claimed bragging rights of sexual conquest as well as most of the blame for his success if prosecuted; in the United States, the passive partner was both denigrated and held as the primary culprit (See Chauncey, "Christian," and Lancaster, *Life*, 238.) In another important study of sexual identity, *Gay New York: Gender, Urban Culture, and the Making of the Gay Male World 1890–1940* (New York: Basic Books, 1994), Chauncey notes the importance of military mobilization for invigorating gay culture in New York, but he does not ruminate on the possible cross-national implications of conscription.

50. Lancaster, *Life*, chap. 18. Martin Leiner, *Sexual Politics in Cuba: Machismo, Homosexuality, and AIDS* (Boulder: Westview Press, 1994). Sandra McGee Deutsche analyzes gender and left- and right-wing reaction in four nations in "Gender and Sociopolitical Change in Twentieth-Century Latin America," *Hispanic American Historical Review* 71.2 (1991): 259–306.

6 *Sueann Caulfield*

The Birth of Mangue

Race, Nation, and the Politics of Prostitution in Rio de Janeiro, 1850–1942

From the early nineteenth century until the 1860s, many European countries promoted state regulation of prostitution to control the spread of venereal disease during wartime. Others wanted to identify deviant women in rapidly urbanizing areas. Thereafter moral reform campaigns targeted state-regulated prostitution, particularly in postcolonial nations, as old-fashioned. In the late nineteenth century and early twentieth, Brazil's desire to portray itself as a modern nation involved obscuring prostitution control in its capital city, Rio de Janeiro. How could Brazil regulate prostitution and still be considered modern? While prostitution became an astonishingly frequent topic of debate among diverse groups of public officials and professional elites, control measures in Rio were never clearly delineated. Official regulation was considered by legislators to contradict both Catholic morality and civil liberties guaranteed by Brazilian law. Nevertheless, pressures to "clean up" the city so that elite families and foreign visitors would not have to view prostitutes forced the police follow extralegal policies. Their actions, including the relocation of some prostitutes to less visible and less desirable parts of the city, reflected the racial, ethnic, and class prejudices that informed elite ideals for the nation.

The result was the birth of Mangue, an infamous red-light district. Located on the margin of downtown Rio, Mangue was populated by poor prostitutes, most of whom police conveniently identified as Jewish Europeans or Brazilians of color. Once a neighborhood shared by prostitutes, small businesses, and working-class residents, Mangue was overtaken by brothels and bars after 1920, the year the king and queen of Belgium visited Rio. Police, instructed to "clean up" areas that their royal highnesses would tour, rounded up lower-class prostitutes, held them in jail for vagrancy until the royal visit ended, and then crowded them into the existing brothels on Mangue's nine crisscrossing streets. There, a few kilometers inland from Guanabara Bay and comfortably out of sight of the city's modernized commercial core, began a series of experiments in police administration of vice.

By the late 1920s, prostitution in Mangue had evolved into a unofficial system by which police registered sex workers and intervened in the administration of brothels. This regime directly contradicted the "abolitionist," or antiregulatory, disposition of Brazilian law. In part because of the weakness of Brazil's central government, however, legislators never defined prostitution policies clearly. This vagueness fostered debates on prostitution policy, kindled by the struggles of diverse professionals for the authority not only to shape municipal administration but to determine Brazil's cultural identity and political future. In the meantime, Rio's police worked with or against politicians, jurists, public health authorities, social workers, and other professionals to define and implement diverse, often conflicting, policies. Prostitutes took advantage of these conflicts, whether by gaining allies who could help defend their individual or collective interests or by slipping through the cracks of incoherent control mechanisms.

• SOCIAL HIERARCHIES OF PROSTITUTION, 1850–1920

The story of "the zone" (*a zona*), as Mangue was known, began well before the 1920s. From the mid-nineteenth century, police had organized increasingly vigorous, though sporadic, campaigns to confine lower-class prostitutes to areas the police considered appropriate. In particular, police tried to keep prostitutes away from tramlines and reputable commerce, and beyond the gaze of respectable citizens. They acted in response to increasing pressure from sensationalist press campaigns and from medical and legal authorities to protect "honest families" and the city's international reputation from the proliferation of poor prostitutes in fashionable downtown areas.

Campaigns to control prostitution were sparked by fears of increased crime, epidemic diseases, and social disorder in Rio. These problems seemed to be exacerbated after the demise of slavery in 1888, when a massive influx of rural migrants and foreign immigrants strained the city's housing and sanitary facilities.[1] Influential upper-class residents tended to associate the city's real health threats and abysmal living conditions with the moral and racial degeneracy attributed to the largely African-descended population. They hoped that European immigration would reverse this degeneracy by "whitening" the population. Imagine the distress of elite residents who discovered large numbers of poor white European prostitutes mingling with prostitutes of African descent on the city's streets! Rio was Brazil's most important political and cultural center, seat of the Brazilian Empire (1822–1889) and capital of the Republic (1889–1930). National leaders wanted the city to serve as a showcase of their civilization for the rest of the world as well as for the rest of Brazil. Poor prostitutes epitomized the moral and physical contagium that undermined their attempts to "civilize" the population and construct images of Brazil's cultural and social progress.

The relationship between prostitution and Rio's international image, however, had an ambiguous history. Prostitutes had figured prominently in both negative and positive images of Rio's tropical sensuality throughout the nineteenth century. Slave women who were forced into prostitution by their owners provided fuel for abolitionists who depicted Rio as thoroughly corrupted by Brazil's slave system.[2] Many upper-class men, on the other hand, received lessons in cosmopolitan fashion and social mores from high-class European, especially French, *cocottes*. French courtesans and artists followed the cultural missions that the Portuguese emperor João VI imported from Paris after transferring his court to Rio in 1808. More French artists and courtesans followed in subsequent decades. By the late nineteenth century, a number of these women, capitalizing on their French nationality, prospered in "luxury prostitution" and related businesses such as nightclubs, cabarets, and cafes frequented by wealthy men and their mistresses.

This world of public leisure was similar in many ways to cosmopolitan European capitals, particularly Paris. Brazilian elites, in fact, consciously sought to consume French culture and it was reflected in architecture, city planning, fashion, and behavior. Some historians have explained the remarkable prominence of *as francesas*, as French prostitutes were known in turn-of-the-century Rio, as only the most ostentatious display of Brazilian elite pretensions to "Europeanize" Brazil.[3]

As many contemporaries recognized, however, when Rio's population embraced European cultural icons, they both mimicked and parodied them.

This was perhaps most evident in elite carnival parades that displayed prostitutes in fanciful European regalia. This ironic imitation also characterized the two zones that became sites of eroticized male leisure during the early twentieth century: Lapa and Mangue. The former, an older neighborhood near the heart of the reconstructed downtown, became the center of early-twentieth-century bohemia. The latter, part of the "New City" that was created out of swamplands in the nineteenth century (*mangue* means swamp in Portuguese) to accommodate Rio's burgeoning lower-class population, represented in many ways Lapa's poorer, more sordid counterpoint. These two zones would, in the 1920s and 1930s, come to represent both the essence and the limits of Rio's uniquely sensual and exotic identity.

Both Lapa and Mangue had cosmopolitan airs in the early twentieth century, though not of the type that the city planners hoped to cultivate. According to police and public health statistics available for 1923, about 33 percent of prostitutes working in brothels in Mangue and probably a slightly higher proportion in Lapa were foreign-born.[4] Few of the Lapa prostitutes, and even fewer of those in Mangue, were sophisticated *francesas*. Most were lower-class Eastern Europeans, many of whom were Jewish, who accompanied the very large European immigration to the Americas in the late nineteenth century and early twentieth.[5]

The visibility of foreign prostitutes and class differences among them, gave new meaning to national labels. *Polaca* (a derogatory term for Polish woman) was used for lower-class European prostitutes. Because a Jewish international prostitution ring specializing in poor eastern European women had operated since the late nineteenth century, *polacas* were usually assumed to be Jewish, although most were not. Similarly the *francesa* (a favorable term for higher-class European prostitutes) was not always French. Brazilian prostitutes of color were similarly differentiated, but with racial rather than national labels. *Mulata*, a term evoking sexual desirability, was generally used for those who achieved higher-class status through luck, talent, or physical endowments but not necessarily lighter skin. *Preta* (black) denoted a degraded lower-class woman of color. Although the *francesa* and the *mulata* were tolerated and even admired, the presence of *polacas*, who worked alongside poor black Brazilian prostitutes, provoked consternation among those in positions to influence state policy. National and religious identities thus interacted with conceptions of race and class to create social hierarchies among prostitutes.

The "spectacle" of sexual commerce of unacceptable European and non-white women not only offended "honest" bourgeois families but also competed with licit commercial establishments for rental space and business. Merchants therefore joined ranks with physicians, jurists, politicians, and especially journalists to pressure municipal authorities, especially the police, to eliminate the spectacle.[6] There was consensus that prostitution had to be brought under control, but little agreement on how this should be accomplished.

• LEGAL STRUGGLES TO DEFINE PROSTITUTION POLICIES

Brazilian professionals generally defined prostitution policies according to European classifications: "prohibitionist" criminalized prostitution; "regulatory" controlled prostitution through state-regulated brothels; and "abolitionist" neither criminalized nor regulated prostitution. "Prohibitionist" legislation had very few advocates in Brazil, as was the case in most officially Catholic nations.[7]

There was less agreement regarding the propriety of state-authorized medically supervised brothels. In practice in Paris from 1804 until 1946, this system had been tried and abandoned in several European capitals by the early twentieth century, after which most physicians and jurists declared it ineffective. Some Brazilians advocated state-run brothels, but most favored less visible government control.

Brazilian law, both before and after the overthrow of the monarchy in 1889, therefore remained staunchly "abolitionist." Imperial and republican legislators preferred to wash their hands of the problem by considering prostitution control part of the maintenance of public order, a responsibility of Rio's police chief since the mid-nineteenth century. The city council repeatedly rejected proposals to regulate prostitution but handed police "reasonable arbitrary power" to repress "scandalous prostitutes."[8] Yet each time successive police chiefs tried to implement this power, they met with resistance not only from prostitutes and brothel owners but also from the Brazilian medical association, the municipal council, and individual jurists who occasionally declared illegal police harassment of prostitutes and attempts to regulate or close down brothels.

Ironically, the "arbitrary power" police commanded in Rio expanded after the establishment of a democratic republic in 1889. Successive republican regimes gave police chiefs the power to act semiautonomously to maintain order, especially during the frequent states of siege imposed to combat political opposition and social unrest. The contradiction between the Republic's ostensively democratic political institutions and its authoritarian enforcement of order surfaced in laws and policies regarding prostitution.

The 1890 Penal Code permitted prostitution, punishing only its "facilitation," or pimping. Poor prostitutes, however, continued to mar the image Brazil's leaders wished to project, especially because alarm escalated among

Europeans about the Rio market for "white slaves," European women brought by organized international vice networks to work as prostitutes. In response, Congress ratified a 1904 international anti-white-slave trade treaty and, in 1915, passed legislation to deport foreign pimps and make it illegal to "operate houses of tolerance [casas de tolerância]" and to "rent rooms to facilitate prostitution."[9] The eleven-year gap between treaty and law, due to continual arguments about its wording, illustrated once again the legislature's ambiguity on these issues. Once passed, the law engendered copious opinions on definitions of "facilitation" and casa de tolerância. They also debated the legality of deporting foreign pimps without a criminal trial. Police chiefs in Rio continued efforts to regulate prostitution, and repeatedly called for legislation that would clearly delineate their duties.[10] Efforts to legitimize their de facto powers, however, were largely unsuccessful because of hostile reactions by many legislators and jurists. Police were left in the awkward position of carrying out the mandates of authoritarian regimes criticized by many influential professionals and public officials.

To add insult to injury, many of the city's best-known "madams"—mostly foreign women who had risen from the prostitute ranks, some with assistance from organized vice networks—gained the protection of powerful politicians and jurists who frequented high-class brothels. Other brothel keepers and prostitutes turned to jurists who believed prostitutes' rights were guaranteed by law. Renowned labor and civil-rights attorney Evaristo de Moraes, for example, successfully defended many prostitutes affected by a series of high-profile police evictions in the late 1890s. As a result of these and other incidents, the boundaries of "tolerated" areas and their internal regulation fluctuated erratically, and arrests and relocations remained arbitrary and inconsistent. Police were also often frustrated in efforts to prosecute procurers because prostitutes, whether out of solidarity or fear, rarely testified against their pimps.[11]

Police may have been unable to control prostitution completely, but they were able to concentrate some of the most conspicuous sex workers to areas designated for "tolerated prostitution," such as Mangue. Some of the city's humbler prostitutes relocated to these zones by their own choice or by the dictates of pimps and brothel keepers.[12] Mangue attracted many newly arrived foreigners and "black" Brazilians because police tolerance allowed them to work more aggressively toward building a client base, and they made up for low rates by serving large numbers of men. Prostitutes who were considered less coarse, "whiter," and more attractive gained a firmer hold on higher-income markets, and generally chose to avoid Mangue. They worked instead in the more discreet brothels or private apartments or houses known as rendez-vous in Lapa or in Glória, an adjacent upper-crust zone. Most prostitutes, however, continued to work clandestinely in "moralized" areas, hiding from or bribing patrol officers or waiting out the short-lived moralization campaigns.

Legal ambiguity thus allowed police to continue policies to confine and "supervise" prostitution, but their effectiveness was limited by prostitutes' resistance, police corruption, setbacks in court, and the growing opposition to authoritarian public policy. During the first two decades of the twentieth century, when police were repeatedly called upon to repress popular protests and political militancy, the situation became critical. In 1917 Police Chief Aurelino Leal responded to increasingly vehement criticism of his abuses of authority by organizing a "Juridical-Police Conference." There he defended the thesis that "police power" was a legitimate branch of public administration.[13] Leal declared that police had the authority to design social policies, including prostitution control, even when not specifically mandated by law. Conveniently, this authority could be extended to other "dangerous" groups, such as the labor activists who were a primary target of police repression. After lengthy debate, conference participants, including the minister of justice and other powerful jurists, approved Leal's thesis. Once again, attitudes toward police powers were not unanimous. A significant number of jurists, together with many journalists, physicians, and opposition politicians, believed that such arbitrary authority made a mockery of republican civil liberties and democratic institutions.

Critics of extralegal police authority pointed to the mass arrests and relocation of prostitutes to Mangue in preparation for the visit of the Belgian king and queen in 1920 as a low point in republican politics. It conveyed the emptiness of the liberal democratic self-image, as Evaristo de Moraes pointed out in an article published two months after the departure of the royal couple. Concerned that "the scandal of poor prostitutes would demoralize us before King Albert," government leaders put aside liberal democratic principles and condoned illegal police violence and repression.[14] Extravagant arrangements to "beautify" the capital created an image of prosperity and homogeneity that belied the impoverishment and diversity of the city's majority. Censorship, a tight security apparatus, and arrests of labor militants, meanwhile, silenced political opposition.[15]

Police cleanups of the downtown were not only coercive, violent, arbitrary, and illegal, Moraes argued, but ineffectual, even counterproductive, as a measure of "moral hygiene." The vast majority of prostitutes, moreover, were never affected by police regulation of prostitution. The "moralized homage to the hero-king" was thus nothing more than a temporary façade.[16]

• LAPA AND MANGUE IN THE "GOLDEN ERA" OF SUPERVISED PROSTITUTION (1920s–1930s)

After the campaign to sanitize Rio for the royal visit had ended, Lapa and Mangue embodied the contrasting realities of Carioca prostitution. Lapa, the lively center of Rio's much-acclaimed bohemian nightlife since the 1910s, was part of the façade that Brazilian officials exhibited to King Albert and Queen Elisabeth. Remembered as "our little improvised Montmartre in the tropics," the neighborhood included an assortment of "German bars," or beer houses, pool halls, cabarets, and café-concerts with Old World names like "Blue Danube," "Vienna-Budapest," and "Alcazar."[17] Lapa's fame, however, derived from its white-suited malandros (rogues or con-men), mulatas, and samba music—all of which would later become icons of Brazilian popular culture. In Lapa, symbols of French erotica blended into a distinctively Carioca[18] space of moral transgression, a place where middle- and upper-middle-class men, including some of the city's most influential intellectuals, artists, journalists, and politicians, escaped the confinement of bourgeois family life. The neighborhood characterized Rio's sensual identity for the men who gathered to drink, eat, listen to samba, rub elbows with malandros, enjoy the paid company of waitresses and prostitutes, or purchase sex.

In contrast, Mangue represented another generation of men and a different style of sexual commerce. Younger and poorer men frequented the less distinguished and more remote streets of Mangue, the location police chose to deposit the "scandalous" prostitutes they wished to hide from King Albert and Queen Elisabeth. The neighborhood, which covered about the same geographical area as Lapa (six or seven city blocks long and two blocks wide), held a higher number of prostitutes: in 1923 police registered 436 in Lapa and 674 in Mangue.[19] Like Lapa, Mangue had its share of samba musicians and malandros. In fact, the zone was adjacent to "little Africa," the lower-class, largely Afro-Brazilian neighborhood where samba was born. Lapa evoked a cleaned-up, cosmopolitan version of an exotically sensual local culture for middle-class consumption; for urban authorities, Mangue represented the moral degradation of the city's unsightly lower class. Police vigilance of Mangue brothels was therefore more intense, and the commercial establishments there were less varied.[20]

If Lapa was seen as the territory of sophisticated francesas and exotic mulatas, Mangue was the reputed zone for polacas and pretas. This perception was clear in a report by Betty Rice, a U.S. nurse contracted to organize home visits and make surveys of prostitutes for an antisyphilis campaign in the 1920s.[21] Distressed by a 1925 police "moralization" campaign that relocated 1,300 prostitutes from Lapa and the downtown to Mangue, she described Mangue as "the worst section of the city, with poorly constructed and dilapidated, dimly-lit structures, poorly ventilated, almost in ruin. . . and 600 women of the worst caste, the majority of them of the black race!" Rice was horrified that "whiter" and higher "caste" Lapa prostitutes were forced to live in such surroundings.

Not all observers shared Rice's opinion of Mangue as unsanitary, sordid, and degenerate. Many of its houses were frequented by sons of the middle classes. Mangue was also the favorite spot of both soldiers and many young military officers. Nelson Werneck Sodré, a young military officer who frequented the zone from 1929 to 1933, remembered this period in Mangue as "a splendid phase, with such outstanding and picturesque aspects that Mangue was even a tourist attraction."[22]

Among the picturesque aspects Sodré mentioned were frequent street fights between clients, particularly soldiers and sailors. Partly because of its rowdiness and the class and racial makeup of its prostitutes, and partly because it was considered a remote area where "scandalous" activities would not offend "families," Mangue became the center of increasingly systematic police regulation in the late 1920s. Police also continued to close hotels and brothels outside Mangue.[23] As a result of both the booming business in Mangue and more systematic record keeping by police, the number of registered prostitutes swelled to 1,735 by 1929, more than five times the 1923 number.[24]

In the midst of invigorated police regulation in Mangue, Brazil's official "abolitionist" posture allowed representatives to international conferences to boast of their nation's advanced legislation. Brazilians also took pride in Rio de Janeiro's progressive public health project to combat venereal disease. The project monitored the spread of venereal disease, provided free, voluntary treatment, and included a special project for educating and treating prostitutes.[25] The campaign, along with Brazil's officially abolitionist prostitution laws—or better put, the absence of clear prostitution-control regulations—was extolled in international medical and juridical articles.[26] This tribute bolstered campaigns by legal and medical professionals who insisted that they, rather than the police, should design social policies.

Attempts by physicians and other professionals to influence public policy intensified after a military revolt overthrew the Republic in 1930 and handed power to former opposition politician Getúlio Vargas. Struggles by diverse factions to chart the political course of the new regime were quelled, however, after 1937, when Vargas instituted a dictatorship he called the *Estado Novo* (New State).

Vargas's social policies featured the repression of political opposition, control of labor unions, and deportation of so-called foreign agitators. The policies were conceived as part of an official ideology of state paternalism, disseminated through censorship and a propaganda campaign stressing "organic" links between centralized state power, national honor, and the "traditional Brazilian family." Nationalist ideologues attacked the "Europeanizing" pretensions of the republican period and promoted instead a homogenized Brazilian identity that incorporated "cleaned-up" representations of popular culture such as carnival and samba.

Not surprisingly, the New State supported police campaigns to "moralize" public leisure in the capital. Police were finally given free rein to confine and supervise prostitutes, and they did so with unprecedented vigor. They shut down the remaining brothels outside Mangue and required prostitutes in the zone to carry identity cards and undergo regular gynecological examinations. Now it made little difference that public health physicians were almost unanimously opposed to police coercion as an instrument of public health campaigns.

Police also enforced the segregation of different "categories" of prostitutes. By 1942, police limited prostitutes working in Lapa to a small "elite" force of 262, relocating those they considered unsightly or insubordinate to Mangue. Nonetheless, the number of prostitutes registered in Mangue, 1,210, had dropped slightly since the late 1920s.[27] Although it is not possible to determine how accurately this number reflects the number of prostitutes actually working in the zone, contemporary observers and later memorialists agreed that the zone had gone into decline by the late 1930s and had lost its appeal, especially for higher-paying clients.[28] The decline was probably partly caused by the oppressive police presence, but it also reflected a shift in Rio's urban geography, as the bulk of residences and nocturnal leisure spaces moved from the downtown to the southern coast or the northern suburbs. Although Lapa, too, had lost its bohemian character and Old World charm by the 1940s, prostitutes there earned about four times more than their counterparts in Mangue, according to a 1943 study, and police frequently used the threat of removal to Mangue as a means of coercion in Lapa. Mangue prostitutes, in turn, could be "rewarded" for "good behavior" by a transfer to Lapa—provided they passed "certain physical requirements" not specified in the study.[29]

As Evaristo de Moraes had pointed out in the early 1920s, the vast majority of prostitutes in Rio were not confined by police zoning policies or regulation. Many worked in unregulated brothels in the center of town, subject to sporadic police "cleanup" campaigns. Most, however, worked independently of brothels, through "clandestine" *rendez-vous* and other arrangements. In the late 1930s, for example, public health officials estimated the number of prostitutes in the city at 20,000 to 30,000, yet only 1,472 were registered in 1942.[30]

It seems as though police finally won support for prostitution control just as economic, demographic, and social conditions were changing in Lapa and Mangue. By the 1940s, the face of prostitution in Rio had been transformed, and police actions played only a small part in the changes. Brothels were becoming unfashionable with the expansion of nocturnal social spaces designed for both female and male patrons, particularly in the burgeoning new beachfront center of tourism and middle-class leisure, Copacabana. Increasing numbers of prostitutes, particularly those who could attract higher-income clients, moved there and worked independently, leaving the inconveniences of police supervision to women of lesser resources. Most of the latter were poor migrants from other regions of Brazil.[31] Finally, the two major issues affecting prostitution policy during the previous century, the "white slave trade" and rising mortality by venereal disease, seemed close to resolution. Immigration of poor Europeans to Brazil was no longer significant, and the remaining *francesas* and *polacas* were growing old; police in Buenos Aires and Rio de Janeiro had dismantled the most active foreign prostitution rings in the early 1930s; and effective treatment for syphilis was on the horizon.[32]

Political winds were also shifting. As the Vargas dictatorship began to turn away from police repression of opposition and toward new strategies to attract popular support, the notoriously repressive chief of police Filinto Müller, in power since 1933, was replaced by Alcides Etchegoyen in 1942. Etchegoyen, less preoccupied with political opposition, paid even more attention to moralization efforts. By this time, however, regulation in Mangue had proven embarrassing for the police, whose officers were accused of various abuses of power in the zone, where pimping, numbers running, and drug trafficking flourished. Mangue, moreover, was considered more overcrowded, unsanitary, and sordid than ever. The new police chief, informed by legal counsel that regulation had always been illegal, ordered brothels shut down and prostitutes dispersed. The first set of police experiments with regulation in Mangue thus came to an abrupt end.

• CONCLUSION

If Mangue's official birth and death were marked by the actions of police and other municipal authorities, its life and afterlife were shaped by prostitutes, who responded to police measures and market opportunities in a variety of ways over the decades. In large measure, the history of the zone is a history of conflicts and negotiations between police and prostitutes. Neither police nor prostitutes, however, acted in a vacuum. Indeed, the nation's major political conflicts had found their way into Mangue ever since its swamp had been drained in the nineteenth century.

From the start, concern with public morality, expressed most forcefully in debates over prostitution, influenced government projects to accommodate the city's burgeoning poor population in newly urbanized areas and to create a showcase of Brazil's progress and civilization in the older downtown. Moreover, Brazil's struggle for international prestige as well as conflicts of authority among groups of professionals, legislators, and police officials shaped theoretical debates on prostitution and the administration of vice in Mangue. The history of Mangue's gradual conversion into a police-regulated red-light district, in contradiction to the letter and spirit of the law, thus reveals power struggles at the center of both municipal and national politics. Ambiguous legislative decrees and erratic juridical decisions regarding police powers to regulate prostitution during the First Republic reflected the relative weakness of centralized authority during that period and the lack of homogeneity among the professional and political classes that sought to guide the course of the new nation. While the executive relied upon the police to carry out authoritarian public policy, many influential professionals and even public officials, particularly jurists, contested police powers. It was under the authoritarian New State that police were able to carry out "moralization" and "confinement" policies in a systematic way. Their conflicts with prostitutes and with groups of juridical and medical authorities, however, were never definitively resolved, either in practice or in law, and continued to surface in erratic juridical decisions and police policies regarding prostitution. Although police regularly harassed prostitutes in diverse areas of the city, their direct intervention in administration of brothels was limited to Mangue, where a small fraction of the city's prostitutes worked. Nonetheless, precedents set in the 1930s for police administration of prostitution in Mangue help explain the persistence of the zone as a controversial urban landmark for nearly half a century after its reconstitution in 1945.

The story of this period of the "Republic of Mangue," which ended in 1979, remains to be written. It seems clear, however, that the story will illuminate ongoing struggles to define police powers and civil liberties, as well as the ways race, ethnicity, and class continue to intersect with sexuality to create images of the Brazilian nation. *Polacas* and *francesas* no longer occupied the extremes of the social hierarchy of prostitution in Rio de Janeiro after 1942. But although city officials and tour agencies since the 1930s have promoted images of alluring women lounging on beaches and exotic *mulatas* dancing samba as tourist attractions, lower-class prostitutes, particularly those of color, continue to represent the negative limit of commercialized sex.[33]

• NOTES

1. The city's population grew from 274,972 in 1872 to 522,651 in 1906. During the same period, population density increased even more dramatically, from 247 to 722 per square kilometer. See Eulália Maria Lahmeyer, *História do Rio de Janeiro* (Rio de Janeiro: IBMEC, 1978), 2:469.

2. Many of these slaves were able to gain their freedom in court, taking advantage of abolitionist support and the desire of some police officials to "moralize" the city and the slave system. See Sandra Lauderdale Graham, "Slavery's Impasse: Slave Prostitutes, Small-Time Mistresses, and the Brazilian Law of 1871," *Comparative Studies in Society and History* 33–34 (1991): 669–94.

3. Jeffrey Needell, *A Tropical Belle Epoque: The Elite Culture of Turn-of-the-Century Rio de Janeiro* (New York: Cambridge University Press, 1987), chap. 5.

4. Police and public health records roughly coincide in estimations of the foreign contingent of Mangue prostitutes (36 percent of 674 prostitutes and 32 percent of 578, respectively) but differ sharply on Lapa estimates: police reports show 25 percent of 436 Lapa prostitutes were foreign, compared to 45 percent of 591 prostitutes in the syphilis campaign data. The discrepancy is probably due to the way prostitutes were counted: the syphilis data probably included many prostitutes who escaped police supervision, which focused on casas de tolerância. See Theophilo de Almeida, "Syphilis e prostituição no Rio de Janeiro," *Arquivos da Fundação Gaffree-Guinle* (1929): 2:21–52; esp. chart on 48; Nelson Hungria, "Relação das mulheres que exercem o meretrício em zona do 12o districto policial," Arquivo Nacional, Ministério da Justiça e Negócios Interiores, *Caixa* 6C751A; Franklin Galvão, "Mappa descriminativo das meretrizes moradoras sob a jurisdição do 9o districto," Arquivo Nacional, Ministério da Justiça e Negócios Interiores, *Caixa* 6C751A. I am greatly indebted to Claudio Batalha and Marcos Brettas for drawing my attention to the police documents and making copies available to me. The total proportion of foreign women in the city of Rio de Janeiro, according to the 1920 census, was 19 percent. See *Recenseamento do Brazil realizado em 1 de setembro de 1920*, 2, 1a parte (Rio de Janeiro: Directoria Geral de Estatística), xxxix.

5. According to both police and public health statistics for 1923, about 70 percent of the foreign prostitutes in Mangue were eastern European. The statistics diverge sharply for Lapa: in the police list, 40 percent of foreign prostitutes in Lapa were eastern European and only three were French; in the antisyphilis campaign data, 45 percent of Lapa prostitutes were foreign, of which 23 percent were eastern European and 31 percent French.

6. Numerous petitions and proposals concerning prostitution submitted to the municipal council from 1853 to 1910 by residents, merchants, professional groups, and police chiefs, along with the council's responses, are held in Arquivo Geral da Cidade do Rio de Janeiro, Coleção Series Documentais, "Prostituição no Rio de Janeiro" (hereafter AGCRJ/CSD/PRJ).

7. For a discussion of differences among Catholic, Protestant, and Jewish positions on prostitution, see Donna J. Guy, *Sex and Danger in Buenos Aires: Prostitution, Family and Nation in Argentina* (Lincoln: University of Nebraska Press, 1991), 12–35.

8. AGCRJ/CSD/PRJ, Cod. 48-3-59.

9. Articles 278 and 279 of the 1890 Penal Code, modified by law n. 2.992 of 25 September 1915. See Jorge Severiano, *Código Penal da República dos Estados Unidos do Brasil* (Rio de Janeiro: Jacintho Ribeiro dos Santos, 1923), 415–17; and Vicente Piragibe, *Dicionário de jurisprudência penal* (Rio de Janeiro: Freitas Bastos, 1938), 1:529–83. Pimping had been included as a justification for the minister of justice to deport foreigners. Legislative decree 1641 of 7 January 1907 authorized deportation of "foreigners who, for whatever motive, threaten national security or public tranquility." See "Atos do poder legislativo," in Brasil, Federal Government, *Leis do Brasil* (1907), 1:24–25. See also Eduardo Espínola, "O 'habeas-corpus' e a expulsão do estrangeiro," *Pandectas brasileiras* (Rio de Janeiro: Casa Gráfica, 1929), 210–21; Lena Medeiros de Menezes, *Os estrangeiros e o comércio do prazer nas ruas do Rio (1890–1930)* (Rio de Janeiro: Arquivo Nacional, 1992), 74–75.

10. For a summary of these efforts by police chiefs from the mid-nineteenth century, see Leonidio Ribeiro Filho, "Os problemas médico-legaes em face da reforma da polícia"; speech, reprinted in *Gazeta Policial*, 16 June 1931. The best work on the white slave traffic to Latin America is Guy, *Sex and Danger*, chap. 1, 5–35. See also Margareth Rago, *Os Prazeres da noite* (Rio de Janeiro: Paz e Terra, 1985), 249–309. For a fictional account of the trade in eastern European Jewish prostitutes in Rio de Janeiro, see Esther Largman, *Jovens polacas* (Rio de Janeiro: Rosa dos Tempos, 1993).

11. Anésio Frota Aguiar, police delegate responsible for combating pimping in the 1940s, complained of this frustration in *O lenocínio como problema social no Brasil* (Rio de Janeiro: n. p., 1940).

12. For a journalistic account of the strategies of French prostitution networks in the 1920s, see Ricardo Pinto, *Tráfico das brancas: Observações em torno dos caftens francezes que vivem no Rio de Janeiro* (Rio de Janeiro: n. p., 1930).

13. *Annaes da conferência judiciária-policial convocada por Aurelino de Araujo Leal* (Rio de Janeiro: Imprensa Nacional, 1918), 1:403–24, 2:265–67.

14. The article was published on 6 November 1920, and reprinted in Evaristo Moraes, *Ensaios de patologia social* (Rio de Janeiro: Leite Ribeiro & Maurillo, 1921), 279–84.

15. Ibid., 280.

16. Ibid.

17. Luis Martins, *Nocturno da Lapa* (Rio de Janeiro: Civilização Brasileira, 1964), 149.

18. The term *Carioca* is used to designate people and things from Rio.

19. Hungria, "Relação das mulheres"; Galvão, "Mappa descriminativo das meretrizes."

20. See the report of Ministry of Justice and Internal Affairs official C. Jiqurica, "Polícia Civil: Relatório de 4–11–1930 a 4–11–1931," National Archive, Docket IJ6-401, 1932.

21. Quoted in Almeida, "Syphilis e prostituição," 27. Almeida was a physician who worked with Rice's team. He summarizes her 1923 and 1924 reports on pages 22–36. Apparently, Rice's belief that physical decay was related to the "black race" blinded her to the findings of her own 1923 report, which classified only 16 percent of Mangue prostitutes as "black." The remainder were classified *parda*, or mixed race (30 percent), and white (54 percent). The same report classified 4 percent of Lapa's prostitutes as black, 22 percent *parda*, and 72 percent white. Similar proportions were reported in 1924. See ibid., 48–49. The statistics do not indicate how "color" was determined. It is not possible to compare them with police data, which did not include color categories.

22. Nelson Werneck Sodré, *Do tenentismo ao Estado Novo: Memórias de um soldado* (Petropolis: Vozes, 1986), 52.

23. Coriolano de Araujo Goes Filho, *Relatório da polícia do Districto Federal* (Rio de Janeiro: Imprensa Nacional, 1928, 1929, 1930).

24. See the report of Ministry of Justice and Internal Affairs official C. Jiqurica, "Polícia Civil."

25. The best sources on the antisyphilis campaign are the journal *Arquivos da Fundação Gaffree e Guinle* (1927–1935) and *Anais da Primeira Conferencia Nacional de Defesa contra a Sífilis* (Rio de Janeiro: Imprensa Nacional, 1941).

26. For a discussion of Brazil's participation in several of these forums and an overview of the medical position on prostitution and public health, see Ribeiro Filho, "Os problemas médico-legaes em face da reforma da polícia."

27. Manoel Odorico de Morais, "Estado atual da prostituição no Rio de Janeiro," *A Folha Médica* 23.13 (1942): 148–52. This article reproduces sections from Helio Gomes, "O problema da prostituição sob o ponto de vista sanitário e jurídico," *Anais da Primeira Conferencia Nacional de Defesa Contra a Sífilis* (Rio de Janeiro: Imprensa Nacional, 1941), 423–35.

28. See, for example, Sodré, *Do tenentismo ao Estado Novo*, 52; Armando Pereira, *Prostituição: uma visão global* (Rio de Janeiro, 1976), 65–67.

29. Moraes, "Estado atual," 150–51.

30. Ibid., 148.

31. There are no comprehensive data on Mangue prostitutes in the 1940s, but a 1959 study shows that only 2.5 percent of 1,460 registered prostitutes were foreign-born; 19.4 percent were from the city of Rio; the remainder were migrants from Rio de Janeiro or other states. Maria Luiza Alves de Mattos, "Situação da prostituição no Rio de Janeiro," in *Lenocínio e prostituição no Brasil*, ed. H. D. Barruel de Lagenest (Rio de Janeiro: Agir, 1960), 23–42.

32. Penicillin, discovered in 1939, was first tested in the early 1940s and used to treat soldiers infected with venereal disease during World War II. It became available in Brazil shortly after the end of the war. See Claude Quetel, *History of Syphilis* (Baltimore: Johns Hopkins University Press, 1990), 249–51.

33. This has been clear in recent concern that "prostiturism," in which prostitutes are the major consumption item for economy-class male tourists, is replacing Rio's declining high-class tourist industry. See Rodolfo Alberto Rizzotto, "Prostiturismo," *Jornal do Commércio*, 23 February 1992; "Turismo sexual atrai mais estrangeiros," *Jornal do Brasil*, 12 January 1996, 5.

7   *Oscar Montero*

Modernismo and Homophobia
Darío and Rodó

Homosexuality has not been a prominent topic in histories and critical studies of Spanish American *modernismo*, in the way that the topic of so-called sexual deviance has been studied in recent work on English and American literatures of the nineteenth century.[1] The two terms *homosexuality* and *modernismo* seem to belong to two distinct traditions, two mutually exclusive branches of knowledge and cultural production. Apples and oranges, as the saying goes. *Homosexuality* was one of many terms for same-sex desire created by nineteenth-century "sexual pathologists."[2] Like homosexuality, *modernismo* is an all-encompassing cultural category but, of course, in the realm of literary production, not in the realm of sexual behavior. Initially a rather imprecise synonym of *Symbolism*, *decadentism*, and even *impressionism*, *modernismo* went on to become a prestigious chapter in Spanish American literary history.[3]

Modernismo, a handy, journalistic label in its beginnings, was appropriated by the Spanish American poets of the fin de siècle, especially the Nicaraguan poet Rubén Darío (1867–1916). As Darío's reading of the legacy of French Symbolist poet Paul Verlaine (1844–1896) reveals, *modernismo* had to be cleansed of troubling signs of sexual deviance, associated with the so-called decadent school, unofficially headed by Verlaine. Uruguayan critic José Enrique Rodó (1871–1917) finished off the job with a double strategy. In Rodó's hands, *modernismo* became a style of writing, coupled with a body-hating ideology of rectitude and a somber sense of duty and decorum. The play, and the excesses, of *modernismo* were finished.

Modernismo entered the academy embalmed by Rodó. The most obvious aspects of its style, especially its Hellenism, aestheticism, and preciosity, were ultimately rejected by the followers of *vanguardismo*, Latin America's diverse versions of the avant-garde movements. *Modernismo's* erasure of homosexuality is as foundational to Latin American culture as the erotics of politics discussed by Doris Sommer.[4] The following pages look at two specific instances in the writings of Rodó and Darío, perhaps the two most influential *modernistas*, where the topic of homosexuality is approached and at the same time either erased or recast in more acceptable forms. In dealing with the topic of homosexuality, Rodó and Darío display a type of cultural manipulation whose influence on the development of possible homosexual identities in Latin America has been as unmentionable as it has been enduring. A critical reading sensitive to such manipulation by two of our canonical writers may throw light on the roots of Spanish American homosexuality and homophobia. At the same time, it may suggest new ways of reading the legacy of *modernismo*.

For nineteenth-century men of science, homosexuality was a disease with identifiable symptoms, especially when the body was found to be marked by sores, chancres, or other evident signs of supposed deviance. At the same time, homosexuality was considered to be a social disease capable of infecting the rest of the population, the same metaphoric slippage at work in current AIDS-phobia. In 1888 a Cuban doctor by the name of Benjamín Céspedes published *La prostitución en La Habana* (Prostitution in Havana), a sociomedical treatise about prostitution, including male prostitution, in the Cuban capital.[5] The treatise by includes an interview with a young pederast and a prologue by Enrique José Varona (1849–1933). Varona, the Cuban heir of French positivism and British empiricism, was an influential thinker (*pensador*) and critic at the turn of the century. In his prologue, Varona praises Céspedes because he invites us to approach a dissection table, to contemplate cancerous sores with a naked eye, to discover the tissues attacked by the virus.[6] The somatic metaphors have an evident source in the body of the young pederast interviewed by the doctor, but Varona wastes no time in applying such anthropomorphic metaphors to the city. The homosexual body is the source of metaphors of illness and social contamination. It is also the locus of imitation and deceit, for homosexuals are said to mimic heterosexual behavior. The portrait of the homosexual sketched by Céspedes and Varona is characteristic of the medico-legal discourse of the period. It proved to be a lasting portrait whose outlines are still very much a part of our cultural and political landscape. In Varona's comments, the connection between contamination and deceit in the homosexual body in turn influences a correlative metaphoric web used to describe cultural productions. Artistic and literary productions become decadent, and thus threatening to the integrity of the American republics, when they favor "external adornment," in short, when they do not signify clearly. The argument is as evident in Max Nordau's *Degeneration*[7] as it is in Varona's influential cultural politics.

The most important regulator of the excesses of the *modernismo*, criticized by Varona and other thinkers of the period, was the Uruguayan critic José Enrique Rodó. Ironically, Rodó's style, brilliant at its best, was itself strained by the florid excesses of *modernismo* he sought to correct. If Rodó's version of the *modernista* style seems as current today as the stuffy furniture of a Victorian parlor, his vague ideology of optimism, virtue, and solidarity continues to surface in diverse affirmations of Latin America's claim as an "imagined community," Bolívar's failed political dream recast as shared cultural sublime. In his appeal to the virtues of friendship, cooperation, and solidarity among Latin Americans, Rodó often relies on images of antiquity, "that image of antiquity," writes Benedict Anderson, "so central to the subjective idea of the nation."[8] At the same time, Rodó's native recipe for classically inspired sweetness and light has a dark side, barely alluded to in the critical tradition and certainly erased from his hagiography. In Rodó's references to antiquity, the inevitable topic of homoerotic friendship is not merely ignored, as was the norm; in his handling of the story of Hylas, the thorny topic is written out of existence.[9]

To be sure, until K. J. Dover's pioneering work, first published in 1978,[10] the subject of Greek homosexuality had not been openly discussed. According to David Halperin, "The ban on speaking about ancient sexual attitudes and behaviors" was still in place in the early 1970s.[11] It is obvious that Rodó's use of the classics corresponds to the tradition of such a ban. However, to leave it at that, in other words, to agree that of course Rodó could not and did not openly refer to the topic of homosexuality, ancient or modern, is to accept the ban in question as the final word.

In Rodó's misreading of the classical tale of Hylas, not even the slightest hint of same-sex desire must remain. Such an erasure is carried out at the expense of a body: that of Hylas, who disappears without a whimper; that of the reader, also silenced into submission; and ultimately that of the writer, banished from the text, an odd move for an heir to *modernismo*'s strong subject. Rodó's erasure of the self helps to explain the anomalous character of his works. At the very opening of literary modernity in Latin America, Rodó's text is curiously anachronistic, as if written decades before. At the same time, erasure of the self inexorably implies the self's abjection. What Diana Fuss has called "the specter of abjection"[12] haunts the contrived optimism of Rodó's works. In the classical tale, the young Hylas, pulled into the brook by amorous nymphs, cries out to his lover. In Rodó's version, that cry is silenced, but the violence of such a gesture, the refusal to allow homosexuality to be even a distant echo, impacts on the writing subject in compelling ways.

A year after Rodó's death, Uruguayan critic Raúl Montero Bustamante distanced himself from "la algarabía de vulgares elogios" (the din of vulgar praises) and faulted Rodó for his vague, gutless sensualism. Rodó's works argue for an incorporeal aesthetic sublime, "de sabor helénico" (with the flavor of the Hellenic), writes Montero Bustamante, a troublesome flavor that prompts the critic to apologize for Rodó: "el diletante en él estuvo siempre vigilado y controlado por un alto sentido moral" (the dilettante in him was always watched over and controlled by a high moral sense).[13] What needed watching and controlling was the erotic charge of Hellenic statuary, reflected in Rodó's gaze yet magisterially written out of existence. Rodó's treatment of the story of Hylas in *Motives of Proteus*[14] reveals what that gaze did not want its mute reader to see. The voice of the master claims to triumph through love and solidarity but in fact does so by doing violence to the reader, who remains perpetually mute. "The rhetorical power to sustain the magisterial voice consists," writes González Echevarría, "in doing violence to an implied other onto whom one's words are to be cut."[15] The silencing of that other is also the erasure of the homoerotic other in Rodó's text. Yet erasures leave traces, and in Rodó's eminently rhetorical text, such traces are sometimes visible, particularly in his handling of the Hellenic tradition.

Rodó's version of the story of Hylas is exemplary in his use of the Hellenic tradition to construct an influential, enduring version of Spanish American identity in which the erasure of same-sex desire is a given, understood by any reader, who at the same time is spared even the condemnation of erotic deviance. As Doris Sommer has persuasively argued, the hero of the Latin American novel of the nineteenth century may be "feminized" the better to serve his country. According to Sommer, erotics and politics cross or tangle in order "to produce a secure knot of sentimentalized men."[16] In Rodó's essays, such a crossover is impossible, for, improbable as it may seem, Rodó's work is neither erotic nor political, willfully abstaining from both the social body and the body proper. When he alludes to the classics,

Rodó recasts same-sex desire as a vague, objectless sublime, and for that very reason the outlines of his rhetorical suppression are rather clear.

If Rodó's homosexual panic may be read by the traces of its erasure, Rodó's notorious misogyny is the other, more visible, side of the coin. According to Mario Benedetti, "la soledad (y su variante: la misoginia) significó una constante en la vida de Rodó" (solitude (and its variant: misogyny) were a constant in Rodó's life).[17] Benedetti's suggestion that male solitude is a "variant" of misogyny hints at the well-worn topic of the lonely but chaste male homosexual. According to Rodó biographer Víctor Pérez Petit, Rodó's shyness, as much as his misogyny, kept him "away from women."[18] It goes without saying that these and other references to Rodó's sexuality are cautious to a fault. Indeed, they must be so, for even in his personal correspondence, at least the part of it that has been published, Rodó avoids the topic with an insistence that is itself telling. Faced with the homoerotic tale of young Hylas, Rodó's strategies of silence and circumlocution have unexpected results. He cannot merely pretend to ignore the topic, as he apparently did in his few personal writings, but must forcefully rewrite it, leaving legible traces of his exercise.

The story of Hylas is one of the many parables that make up Rodó's *Motives of Proteus*, in a sense the expansion of the individualistic message of *Ariel*. According to Rodó, the central theme of his *Motives* is "la cultura del propio yo" (the cultivation of one's own self).[19] If the book is indeed a series of digressions on the cult of the self, the obvious paradox is that *Motives of Proteus* is a highly impersonal book. In his introduction to the Ayacucho edition, Real de Azúa mentions several critics for whom "los pasajes sobre el amor resultan la elaboración libresca de un misógino o la lucubración de un hombre de vida erótica soterrada o insignificante" (the passages on love are the bookish elaboration of a misogynist or the lucubrations of a man whose erotic life is either buried or insignificant).[20] Again, misogyny and a "buried" erotic life are somberly coupled to suggest an image of the writer as abject outsider to the dogged optimism of his works.

Motives of Proteus seeks to fulfill its aesthetic credo in the reader, who is addressed in the familiar *tú*. Moreover, Real de Azúa writes, Rodó's book seeks "la fertilidad emocional del lector, su simpatía, su convicción profunda" (the emotional fertility of the reader, his sympathy, his deepest conviction).[21] According to Real de Azúa, Rodó sought "los artificios comunicativos" (devices for communicating) that would lessen the distance between the book and the reader. This may have been Rodó's stated wish, but in all of his published works, the distance between writer and reader is vast. What González Echevarría says of the reader in *Ariel* may be said of the reader in Rodó's other works: "The reader is always *in statu pupilari* and, though situationally in dialogue, is necessarily mute,"[22] a muteness that is also a kind of emasculation, or more properly an unsexing of the reader, whatever his or her gender. Rodó's common reader has neither sex nor tongue, as if only in their absence can the master's rhetoric rise unchallenged.

Rodó's will to mastery is evident in his violent rewriting of the Hylas story. In Rodó's version, Hylas is barely a pretext for the search, not Herakles' search but that of a host of young people who reenact his search for Hylas every spring. The displacement of the boy's figure is already evident in the *Argonautica* by the Alexandrian poet Apollonius of Rhodes, a contemporary of Theocritus, the Syracusan Greek credited with inventing bucolic poetry about 255 B.C. Theocritus's thirteenth idyll is the first and best-known version of the Hylas story.[23] In the *Argonautica*, an enraged Herakles demands that the noble sons of the city of Cius never cease their search for Hylas.[24] In Virgil's passing mention of the story, set into the song of Silenus, in Eclogue VI, all the sailors cry out for Hylas: "Hylan nautae . . . Clamassent" (mariners for Hylas lost / Shouted).[25] If two is company, three is an allegory, a possibility eagerly seized by Rodó. In the version of the story by Theocritus, the salient topics are the youth and beauty of Hylas and the fact that his loss caused the great hero to display the passion of a mere mortal. In Rodó's version, the familiar topics of the idyll are eclipsed in favor of an allegory of youth and renewal, implicit in the *Argonautica*'s elaborate version of the story and amplified by Rodó.

Significantly, Rodó's version of the Hylas story is preceded by a long discussion on the meaning of love. According to Rodó, it is best not to love whoever does not deserve to be loved, but love itself contains "a spontaneous, liberating principle" that triumphs over an inferior object. What matters, Rodó writes, timidly echoing the *Symposium*, is the quality of love, more than the quality of the object of love. The good sort of love cleanses the lover of any "inmundicia," filth, indecency and any sort of moral deviance.[26] Rodó compares pure love with "el vértigo del amor bastardo" (the vertigo of bastard love), which contains "un principio de descomposición moral, una *idea febrilis*, cuyo proceso sugirió a Alfonso Daudet las páginas despiadadas de su *Safo*" (a principle of moral decomposition, an *idea febrilis*, whose development suggested to Alphonse Daudet the pitiless pages of his *Sapho*).[27] From love as "inmundicia" Rodó moves on to Daudet's *Sapho*, an abrupt yet significant slippage.

By citing the French writer's fiction of Sappho[28] in the prelude to the story of Hylas, Rodó combines the threat of an uncontrollable female sexuality with a hint at the dangers of homosexuality. More significantly, female (homo)sexuality is used to mask its male counterpart and to associate it with "a principle of moral decomposition."[29] By contrast, superior love must bear a principle of order and of sublime discipline. Even when it is violent or tragic, it retains "su virtud purificadora" (its purifying virtue).[30] This disembodied, homophobic love is at the core of Rodó's influential aesthetics of conduct, a love that is no love at all but rather a violent desire for cleansing and purifying what is too filthy to conceive, much less mention. Rodó wrote at a time when the homosexual, certainly in Euro-American cultures, had already become a "species" rather than a "temporary aberration," to repeat Foucault's famous distinction. Paradoxically, as homosexuality begins to manifest itself in cultural productions, it simultaneously disappears, "into the closet," writes Fuss.[31] Attacks on the weakness and effeminacy of the *modernistas* were topical, ultimately mirroring Max Nordau's notorious diatribe against the Symbolist poets and the so-called decadents. Rodó alludes to such polemics in one of his letters,[32] but in *Motives of Proteus*, he retains only the metaphors of cleansing and purifying what is filthy within love, implicitly what may be homosexual within the larger category of love.

The strategy backfires. The "process of negative interiorization" discussed by Fuss reveals, like the negative of a photograph, "the homosexual as the abject, as the contaminated and expurgated insides of the heterosexual subject."[33] Given the nature of such love, which prefaces the tale of Hylas, the presence of the young lover is incidental; indeed, it must be so. In Rodó's version the young man simply "acompañaba a Hércules en la expedición de los Argonautas" (accompanied Herakles in the expedition of the Argonauts).[34] Rodó quickly sums up Hylas's fall into the stream, and then adds that "los compañeros de Hylas bajaron a buscarle, así que advirtieron su tardanza" (Hylas's companions went to look for him, no sooner had they noticed his lateness).[35] They cry out for him, and when Hylas does not appear, they sail away. Thus ends the story of Hylas, which Rodó now turns into an allegory of youthful solidarity: the young people of the village turn the loss of Hylas into a rite of spring. When the first flowers appear, young men and women go out to look for Hylas in a vaguely erotic ritual. The message of the parable is finally a call for solidarity and renewal. "Hylas no apareció jamás" (Hylas never appeared), writes Rodó. "Pero, de generación en generación, se ejercitaba en el bello simulacro la fuerza joven" (But from generation to generation, youthful vigor carried out the beautiful simulacrum).[36] A homosexual couple becomes a heterosexual mob, then a bodiless principle of "youthful vigor" and, implicitly, a principle of historical solidarity, a pillar in the edifice of Latin America's imagined community, so powerfully heralded in Rodó's work.

Rodó was a self-taught man, and his knowledge of the classics was not that of a scholar. However, annotated editions in Greek and Latin were common in the nineteenth century. There is a Spanish translation of Theocritus with a prologue by Menéndez y Pelayo from 1880.[37] There is a French version by Leconte de Lisle from 1861.[38] Whatever version Rodó consulted, he goes out of his way to silence the cry of Hylas and nearly to suppress the name of Herakles, turning the story into an allegory of youth and renewal.

In the section of *Motives of Proteus* that follows the Hylas story, Rodó seems relieved that the boy has disappeared forever: "Pongamos que él no haya de parecer [*sic*] jamás: ¿qué importa, si el solo afán de buscarle es ya sazón y estímulo con que se mantiene el halago de la vida?" (Let us suppose that he will never appear again: what does it matter, if the mere desire to search for him is the spark and the stimulus that allow one to keep the delight of life?)[39] Critics have complained that Rodó's idealism has no object, or that it is an object under erasure. What is less obvious is that Rodó's writing subject is also a disturbing void. If Hylas is the emblem of the homoerotic body, Rodó must write in its absence; or one may suggest that it is the absence of such a body that allows Rodó to write. In his avuncular, magisterial rhetoric, "you" and "I" are not only incorporeal but also faceless and sexless. There is less misogyny in Rodó than a kind of homophobia that blurs sexuality and gender difference. Ironically, for a writer proudly writing of the "essence" of the Latin American soul, Rodó leaves nothing but a written surface, which is quite a lot but not exactly what he had in mind. Rodó's magisterial voice, engraved in stone, echoes in an empty classroom. The body dies so that it may become a cultural monument to a tradition of Latin American identity from which homoeroticism has been violently and radically exiled.

Rodó rewrote the Latin American tradition of the enlightened teacher in the style of *modernismo*; however, as recent studies have reaffirmed, *modernismo* is today less significant as a literary style than as the founding moment of a subject, an "Organizing I," writes Gwen Kirkpatrick,[40] the provisional center of conflicting ideologies, not merely the univocal agent of a dialectic of modernity but the foundation of a shifting center where those conflicts may be played out, where they indeed continue to be represented. It must be added that the subjective center of *modernismo* is also erotic in the broadest possible sense: it passes through the body, whether in illness, in violence and in passion, whatever its object. One need only mention in passing the names of José Martí, Rubén Darío, Julián del Casal, José Asunción Silva, and Delmira Agustini to assert that the legacy of *modernismo* is the erotic body and its ineluctable role in the foundation of a Latin American writing subject. In the work of Rodó, heir apparent to the legacy of *modernismo*, the erasure of the erotic and the fear of the body transform the writing subject into a void, already noted by his earliest critics and apologists.

In Rodó's writing, the fear of the homoerotic body comes home to roost, so to speak. His text is unsettling because it is oddly subjectless for a modern text. Rodó's writing is a kind of incantation on the aesthetic sublime at times seemingly devoid of sense, meaning, and purpose. Rodó transforms the book into the cenotaph of the self. Paradoxically, the very absence of that self demands the return of the mute reader. In Rodó, the devastation of the subject, the abjection not of the other but of the self, is represented in the silencing of Hylas and the correlative muting of the reader. When the reader becomes critic, that is, when he or she writes, the spell is broken, so that one may look sympathetically and dialogically at a text built on the abjection of the body, the boy Hylas, the reader's, and the writing subject's. Rodó's abjection of the erotic body, specifically the homoerotic body associated with Hylas, left him, and generations of readers, empty-handed. Rodó's style produced no subject, and as a writer, he was caught in the void. Rubén Darío was not about to take the same path. Darío's strong subject would keep abjection at arm's length, or turn it into a literary topic. In a series of brilliant, if at times murky, rhetorical ploys Darío pays homage to his most important teacher, while at the same time consigning him to the realm of the abject: the sick, the pitiful, the queer.

Darío's sketches of literary figures were first published between 1893 and 1896, most of them in Buenos Aires's *La Nación*. *Los raros*, a collection of these sketches with a brief prologue, published in Buenos Aires in 1896, October 12 to be exact, sold out in two weeks.[41] At a founding moment in Spanish American literature, Darío weaves a text around an odd canon using a complex strategy of affirmation and concealment, of sympathy and self-identity, on the one hand; of innuendo, coyness, and ambiguity, on the other. Buenos Aires was the perfect setting for Darío's self-promotion. In a city already aspiring to the title of South America's most cosmopolitan capital, Darío cast himself as the ambassador of the latest in European art and literature. To succeed in his adopted city, Darío had to show that he knew the right names, specifically the names of the Parisian cultural elite. Moreover, Darío wanted to suggest that he was in fact one of them; yet he could not belong, when the main one among "them" was Paul Verlaine, the most important European influence on Spanish American *modernistas*. Along with the master Edgar Allan Poe, Verlaine heads the list of the so-called decadents, the core of *Los raros*, with Lautréamont, Villiers de l'Isle Adam, and Jean Richepin among them. However, other inclusions seem deliberately to upset the unity of this list, notably José Martí, dead the year before on the battlefield, and Max Nordau, the popularizer of decadence as artistic and moral corruption. At any rate, two names stand out on in *Los raros*: Verlaine and Nordau, the queer Symbolist and his most influential attacker.[42] *Los raros* wants to set the record straight, in more ways than one.

Los raros was published with all the trappings that a contemporary reader may associate with the launching of a best-seller: advance notices, advertisements, and, once the book came out, a flurry of reviews and an ensuing controversy. A brief, catty review by Manual Ugarte (*El Tiempo*, 25 October 1896) sums it up this way: "Son estudios y comentarios sobre las más famosas personalidades de la escuela decadente y son tanto más interesantes cuanto que ha nacido bajo la pluma de un sectario incondicional de la nueva musa" (They are studies and commentaries about the most famous personalities of the decadent school, and they are all the more interesting because they have been penned by an unconditional disciple of the new muse).[43] There was no "decadent school," as Ugarte calls it, but of course *decadent* is a term inexorably associated with the fin de siècle. For a time, it was a near-synonym of *Symbolism*, *impressionism*, and *modernismo*. Unlike these other terms, however, *decadent* is the only one that cuts through different zones of culture, and the only one that could be applied indistinctly to a cultural artifact and to the behavior of an individual. Ugarte's comments and others like it put Darío in a serious bind. On the one hand, Darío champions an aesthetic sublime brilliantly displayed after *Azul* and perfected in *Prosas profanas*, published the same year as *Los raros*; on the other hand, the esoterism, Satanism, and deviant eroticism associated with the so-called decadents goes against the emerging, and still precarious, cultural values of the new republics. If *Prosas profanas* is the brilliant banner of the new aesthetic, *Los raros* is its rather murky underside.

What unifies *Los raros* is not a coherent aesthetic system but a constantly shifting, often slippery, subjective stance. When critics affirm the book's coherence or apologize for the absence of such coherence, they assume that Darío writes in a critical mode and that, whatever his shortcomings, he wants some measure of clarity and objectivity to show in his work. However, it is helpful to consider the book not as criticism but as self-representation, self-promotion, and, in a sense, self-preservation.

Darío's acknowledged debt to Verlaine is well known. He dedicated a poem to the French Symbolist in his *Prosas profanas* (1896). The poem, titled "Verlaine," begins: "Padre y maestro mágico, liróforo celeste" (Father and magical master, celestial poet). Its verses are followed by a dazzling epitaph: "que sobre tu sepulcro no se derrame el llanto, / sino rocío, vino, miel" (Let no tears flow on your sepulcher, / rather dew, wine, honey).

Taking stock, with an implacable Rodó looking over his shoulder, Darío modifies his paean to the master in "Yo soy aquel": "con Hugo fuerte y con Verlaine ambiguo" (with Hugo, strong; and with Verlaine, ambiguous).[44] At the same time, Verlaine is the central figure in Nordau's influential diagnosis of artistic degeneration. In the "Dilucidaciones" that open *El Canto Errante*, Darío writes, "Tan solamente he contestado a la crítica tres veces, por la categoría de sus representantes . . . ellos se llamaban Max Nordau, Paul Groussac, Leopoldo Alas" (I have only answered my critics three times, and it was because of their stature . . . their names being Max Nordau, Paul Groussac, Leopoldo Alas). An article published by Nordau in *La Nación*, 5 March 1903, had provoked Darío's reply, published the following month.[45] Darío has always been seen against Nordau, Nordau as the utilitarian inquisitor and Darío as the defender of art and its weaker, less fortunate, practitioners. However, in the portrait of Nordau in *Los raros*, Darío's take on Nordau is more complex than a mere defense. In *Los raros* Darío's Nordau complements his Verlaine in more ways than one. For Darío, Verlaine is the master, the one who by distancing himself from the rigors, both stylistic and moral, of the Parnassians, opened up the possibility of a new poetic idiom. Moreover, the impact of Rimbaud on Verlaine's drift from wife and family toward a poetic odyssey they both shared is well known. Verlaine's "case" is central to Nordau's attack on Symbolism, which, to make a long story short, he turns into degeneration, because it is the work of a queer.

One critic has written that the essay on Verlaine is "almost exclusively biographical."[46] From the start, Darío zeroes in on Verlaine's illness and on his death, which had occurred in January of 1896, nine months before the publication of *Los raros*. Darío writes: "¡oh, pobre viejo divino! Ya no padeces el mal de la vida, complicado en ti con la maligna influencia de Saturno" (Oh, poor, divine old man! You no longer suffer the evil of life, complicated in you by the malign influence of Saturn).[47] The allusion is characteristic of Darío's rhetorical ploy. Some readers may recognize a reference to Verlaine's *Poèmes Saturniens*, but others, who may miss the literary allusion, will certainly think of Verlaine's scandalous affair with Rimbaud. According to Darío, Verlaine is the master of a group of the chosen, spiritual, and, perhaps, erotic followers, as suggested by the mention of Socrates: "rodeado de los tuyos, de los hijos de tu espíritu, de los jóvenes oficiantes de tu iglesia, de los alumnos de tu escuela, ¡oh, lírico Sócrates de un tiempo imposible!" (surrounded by yours, your spiritual children, the pupils of your school, oh, lyric Socrates of an impossible time!).[48] Darío cites a Dutch critic who sees Verlaine "como un leproso sentado a la puerta de una catedral, lastimoso, mendicante, despertando en los fieles . . . la compasión" (like a leper seated at the entrance to a cathedral, pitiful, begging, provoking sympathy among the faithful).[49] Léon Bloy, writes Darío, has also called Verlaine the Leper, with a capital *L*.

In Darío's sketch of Verlaine, the first person delays its entrance, so to speak, in order to establish the image of Verlaine as a sick, leprous, if influential, old man. Darío's I enters grandly of course with a "Yo confieso," proclaiming his "painful love" for the "sad master." Yet between "Yo confieso" and Darío's love for the master, there is a series of clauses beginning with "después de hundirme en el agitado golfo de sus libros, después de penetrar en el secreto de esa existencia única" (after plunging in the stormy waters of his books, after penetrating into the secret of his unique existence), continuing in this vein for a entire paragraph. The effect is to generate more sympathy for Darío than for Verlaine. Darío affirms his candor with the "Yo confieso," but his confession of love and admiration asks for sympathy for having come so close to one so monstrous as Verlaine.

With the image of Verlaine as the leprous "sad master" firmly established, Darío adds that thanks to a mutual friend, he was able to "[penetrar] en algunas interioridades de Verlaine" (to penetrate in some of Verlaine's intimacies).[50] Once again, Darío spares us the details of such intimacies, but everyone knew of Verlaine's scandalous homosexual affair with Rimbaud, subsequently a topic of French literary history and of the history of homosexual identities. Verlaine and Rimbaud were as famous, or as infamous, a homosexual pair as Alice Toklas and Gertrude Stein a generation later. For Darío, ambiguity is the name of the game. Someone in the know, *un entendido*, that is a homosexual reader, would understand Darío's veiled allusions to Verlaine's sexuality. For all the rest, however, Darío had to first show pity, then disgust, for Verlaine and his kind, all the while paying homage to the sad master.

Suddenly, as if on cue, enter Nordau. Darío of course appears to defend Verlaine against his attacker. Darío claims that it was Nordau's *Degeneration*, first published in 1892, that brought to light for the first time "the figure of Verlaine," almost unknown to the general public, and that figure constituted "the most curiously abominable of all portraits."[51] It is true that Verlaine was not exactly welcome in decent Parisian homes, including the homes of some of its most prominent poets; however, the fact is that by the early 1890s he was enjoying the success of a lecture tour that had brought him much-needed funds and considerable recognition among younger poets, both on the Continent and in England. At any rate, it is obvious that whatever his rhetorical defense of Verlaine, Darío wants to give the reader Nordau's version of Verlaine. He cites some of Verlaine's defenders but ends up quoting Nordau for an entire paragraph.

Darío's constant quoting and name-dropping masks the shifts in his own point of view. Toward the end of the sketch, Darío finally gets to the point, referring to the "nebulous legend" in Verlaine's life, and quickly adds, "I will not linger on such miseries." He must conclude for lack of time, an old standby. "De la obra de Verlaine, ¿qué decir?" (About Verlaine's works, what can one say?)[52] Because there is no more time, not much. Darío concludes with a comment on Verlaine's fame in England, the United States, and Italy, contradicting the earlier statement. A promised future study "of the great Verlaine" never came. Darío concludes with a prayer, which is also his coup de grace: "¡Dios lo haya acogido en el cielo como en un hospital!" (May God welcome him into heaven as into a hospital!)[53]

It is not impertinent to consider the implications of homosexual panic in Darío's construction of his poetic persona and in his successful attempt to create an erotic sublime in the context of *modernismo*, safely distant from the implications of sexual deviance aired out in Nordau's and other contemporary attacks on literary modernity. In his sketch of Nordau, Darío finally agrees with Nordau's assessment: "No hay que negarle mucha razón a Nordau cuando trata de Verlaine, con quien—en cuanto al poeta—es justo" (One cannot entirely deny that Nordau is right when he deals with Verlaine, with whom—as far as the poet is concerned—he is just).[54]

Darío's maneuvering among the decadents in *Los raros* comes to safe port, so to speak, with the edition of 1905. Darío makes few major changes with an important exception. He adds an introductory essay based on Camille Mauclair's *L'Art en silence*,[55] a book that moves, Darío writes, toward an absolute moral ideal. Darío calls it a healthy book, *un volumen sano*.[56] Darío praises Mauclair's book, specifically its development of an aesthetic sublime cleansed of the erotic ambiguities of the decadents. Mauclair blames women for the downward spiral of Western culture. Men, feminized by women, were responsible for the so-called decadent literature of the fin de siècle. Mauclair calls for a healthy return to the war of the sexes, in other words for a radical division according to gender. The aesthetic sublime finally endorsed by Darío is grounded on this difference. Feminism and homosexuality are its enemies. Darío and the *modernistas'* reification of woman has certainly been discussed and reconsidered. It must be added that Darío's misogyny is also profoundly homophobic.

Darío's praise of Mauclair's *L'Art en silence* corresponds to the stance he adopts in the prologue to the 1905 edition of *Los raros*. In Darío's characteristically apologetic stance, the word *decadent* again is pulled into service to cover a multitude of sins, both stylistic and moral. *Decadent* is a semantic shifter; one of its many meanings is sexual deviance and the imitative behavior described by Dr. Céspedes when he wrote that late-nineteenth-century homosexuals in Havana held private parties where they mimicked births and baptisms. With his usual modesty, Darío writes that it fell upon him to make Symbolism known in the Americas, "y por ello, y por mis versos de entonces, fui atacado y calificado con la inevitable palabra 'decadente.' . . . Todo eso ha pasado—como mi fresca juventud" (and for that reason, and for my verses of that period, I was attacked and defined with the inevitable word "decadent." . . . All of that is in the past—like the bloom of my youth)]. As he does in "Yo soy aquel," Darío's comments aim to be corrective of a past deviation. He alludes to Verlaine when he says that today, approaching his idols of the past, he discovers "más de un engaño de mi manera de percibir" (more than one deceit in my perception).

Modernismo's aesthetic sublime would be completed, and in more than one sense finished, in a closed circle, where erotic deviance, and specifically homosexuality, had no place, or rather had places assigned beyond the edge of that circle. In the twentieth century, homosexuality would be either crime or illness. Cultural representations of it would be marginal, and many completely forgotten until our day. In Latin American writing, the circle would begin to crack with the works of José Lezama Lima, Virgilio Piñera, Reinaldo Arenas, Severo Sarduy, and Manuel Puig.

The end of abjection for homosexuals lies in the meeting of bodies not in one style or another that may be rejected or appropriated by straight normativity, according to whim or fashion. Nineteenth-century men of science, such as Dr. Céspedes and Varona, put the homosexual body at arm's length, and thus ensured the objectivity as well as the safety of their own sexuality. Rodó damned bodies: Hylas's, the reader's, perhaps his own. Darío made Verlaine's body the locus of deviance and disease, even while he managed to salvage the work of his master. Such parcelings were incorporated into the legacy of *modernismo*, whose aesthetic sublime is at once erotic and homophobic. Queer critics today need not respect the boundaries. From the fringes, from the abjection imposed by science and authority, queer love has emerged in ways that it could not emerge at the time of Darío or Rodó. Queer criticism rereads the aesthetic legacy of *modernismo*, but it does not uncritically endorse the implicit homophobia of its sexual ideology. The result is the possibility of new readings of the *modernista* canon and perhaps the eventual recasting of our own ever-evolving homosexual identities.

• NOTES

1. For example, in works by Michael Moon (*Disseminating Whitman: Revision and Corporeality in Leaves of Grass* [Cambridge: Harvard University Press, 1991])

and Richard Dellamora (*Masculine Desire: The Sexual Politics of Victorian Aestheticism* [Chapel Hill: University of North Carolina Press, 1990]).

2. The term began to gain currency particularly after the publication of Krafft-Ebing's *Psychopathia Sexualis: A Medico-Forensic Study* in 1886 (English trans., H. E. Wedeck; New York: Putnam, 1965). The Spanish cognates are not current until well into the twentieth century. On the development of homosexuality, see George Chauncey Jr., "From Sexual Inversion to Homosexuality," *Salmagundi* 58–59 (1982–1983): 114–46.

3. The influential works of Angel Rama, especially *Rubén Darío y el modernismo (Circunstancia socio-económica de un arte americano)* (Caracas: EBUC, 1970), began to reconsider the complexities of *modernismo*, as have recent works by Julio Ramos (*Desencuentros de la modernidad en América Latina: Literatura y política en América Latina* [Mexico City: Fondo de Cultura Económica, 1989]) and Gwen Kirkpatrick (*The Dissonant Legacy of Modernismo: Lugones, Herrera y Reissig and the Voice of Modern Spanish American Poetry* [Berkeley: University of California Press, 1989]). On the deviant side of Latin American's fin-de-siècle, the bibliography is more scant. See Sylvia Molloy's "Too Wilde for Comfort: Desire and Ideology in Fin-de-Siècle Spanish America," *Social Text* 31–32 (1992): 187–201, and Jorge Salessi's "The Argentine Dissemination of Homosexuality: 1890–1914," in *¿Entiendes? Queer Readings, Hispanic Writings*, ed. Emilie Bergmann and Paul Julian Smith (Durham: Duke University Press, 1994), 49–91.

4. Doris Sommer, *Foundational Fictions: The National Romances of Latin America* (Berkeley: University of California Press, 1991).

5. Benjamín Céspedes, *La prostitución en La Habana* (Havana: Tipografía O'Reilly, 1888).

6. Ibid., xi.

7. Max Nordau, *Degeneration* (1892; New York: Appleton, 1895).

8. Benedict Anderson, *Imagined Communities: Reflections on the Origin and Spread of Nationalism* (London: Verso, 1983), 44.

9. In his attempt to reshape the Latin American imaginary through an appeal to the Hellenic tradition and the virtues associated with it, Rodó was the belated participant in a project of nation-building through artistic production whose roots may be found in eighteenth-century German thought. Like Lessing in the eighteenth century, Rodó is concerned with the positive role of art in the process of defining a national character, or specifically in Rodó's case, the process of defining Latin America's imagined community. On Lessing's *Laokoön* and the homosocial "abjection of the feminine," see Susan E. Gustafson, "Beautiful Statues, Beautiful Men: The Abjection of Feminine Imagination in Lessing's *Laokoön*," *PMLA* 108 (1993): 1083–97.

10. K. J. Dover, *Greek Homosexuality* (Cambridge: Harvard University Press, 1978).

11. David Halperin, *One Hundred Years of Homosexuality and Other Essays on Greek Love* (New York: Routledge, 1990), 2. See also his *Before Pastoral: Theocritus and the Ancient Tradition of Bucolic* (New Haven: Yale University Press, 1983).

12. Diana Fuss, "Inside/Out," *Inside/Out: Lesbian Theories, Gay Theories* (New York: Routledge, 1991), 3.

13. Montero Bustamante, *José Enrique Rodó: Carta al Dr. Gustavo Gallinal* (Montevideo: La Buena Prensa, 1918), 17–18. Montero's book was a reply to Dr. Gustavo Gallinal's *Rodó* (Montevideo: Renacimiento, 1918), one of the books published in honor of the writer a year after his death.

14. Rodó, *Motivos de Proteo*, in *Ariel: Motivos de Proteo*, ed. Angel Rama (Caracas: Biblioteca Ayacucho, 1976). English ed.: *Motives of Proteus*, trans. Angel Flores, intro. Havelock Ellis (New York: Brentano's, 1928).

15. González Echevarría, *The Voice of the Masters: Writing and Authority in Modern Latin American Literature* (Austin: University of Texas Press, 1985), 27.

16. Sommer, *Foundational Fictions*, 33.

17. Mario Benedetti, *Genio y figura de José Enrique Rodó* (Buenos Aires: EUDEBA, 1966), 18.

18. Quoted, ibid.

19. In a letter quoted by Carlos Real de Azúa, "Prólogo a *Motivos de Proteo*," in *Ariel: Motivos de Proteo*, ed. Angel Rama (Caracas: Biblioteca Ayacucho, 1976), xli.

20. Ibid., xlviii.

21. Ibid., lxiii.

22. González Echevarría, *The Voice of the Masters*, 21.

23. Theocritus, *A Translation of the Idylls of Theocritus*, trans. R. C. Trevelyan (Cambridge: Cambridge University Press, 1947).

24. Apollonius Rhodius, *The Argonautica*, with an English trans. by R. C. Seaton (Cambridge: Harvard University Press, 1912), 95–96.

25. Virgil, *Eclogues*, trans. and notes Guy Lee (London: Penguin, 1984), 72–73.

26. Rodó, *Motivos de Proteo*, 252.

27. Ibid., 253.

28. Daudet, *Sapho* (1884; Aix-en-Provence: Edition Alinea, 1992). Also see Joan DeJean, *Fictions of Sappho, 1546–1937* (Chicago: University of Chicago Press, 1989).

29. Rodó, *Motivos de Proteo*, 253.

30. Ibid.

31. Fuss, "Inside/Out," 4.

32. In the rough draft of a letter to Leopoldo Alas, dated 30 June 1897 and quoted by Emir Rodríguez Monegal in his introduction to Rodó's *Obras completas* (Madrid: Aguilar, 1967), Rodó explicitly rejects *modernismo* and "decadentism," or rather *modernismo* as decadentism: "En América, con los nombres de *decadentismo* y *modernismo*, se disfraza a menudo una abominable escuela de trivialidad y frivolidad literarias, una tendencia que debe repugnar a todo espíritu que busque ante todo, en la literatura, motivos para sentir y pensar" (In America, the names of decadentism and *modernismo* often disguise an abominable school of literary triviality and frivolity, a tendency that should disgust any spirit who searches in literature above all for reasons to feel and to think), 85.

33. Fuss, "Inside/Out," 3.

34. Rodó, *Motivos de Proteo*, 255.

35. Ibid.

36. Ibid.

37. The edition to which Menéndez y Pelayo wrote the prologue is a second edi-

tion. An earlier one was published in Mexico by Ipandro Acaico (pseud.), *Poetas bucólicos griegos* (Mexico City: Imprenta de I. Escalante, 1877).

38. *Idylles de Théocrite et odes anacréontiques, traductions nouvelles par Leconte de Lisle* (Paris, 1861).

39. Rodó, *Motivos de Proteo*, 256.

40. Kirkpatrick, *The Dissonant Legacy of Modernismo*, 36.

41. Darío, *Estudios dispersos de Rubén Darío recogidos de periódicos* (La Plata: Universidad Nacional de La Plata, 1968), 55.

42. Darío, *Los raros*, in *Obras completas* (Madrid: Afrodisio Aguado, 1950), 2:245–517.

43. Ugarte, quoted in *Estudios dispersos de Rubén Darío*, 54.

44. On Darío's poetic reply to Rodó, see Molloy, "Ser/decir: tácticas de un autor-retrato," *Essays on Hispanic Literatura in Honor of Edmund King* (London: Tamesis, 1983), 187–99.

45. On Darío and his critics, see Emilio Carilla, *Una etapa decisiva de Darío (Rubén Darío en la Argentina)* (Madrid: Gredos, 1967).

46. Ludwig Schräder, "Rubén Darío, crítico literario en *Los raros*," *El ensayo y la crítica literaria en Latinoamérica* (Toronto: University of Toronto Press, 1970), 96.

47. Darío, *Los raros*, 292.

48. Ibid.

49. Ibid., 293.

50. Ibid., 294.

51. Ibid., 297.

52. Ibid., 298.

53. Ibid., 299.

54. Ibid., 458–59.

55. Camille Mauclair, *L'Art en silence* (Paris: Société d'Editions Littéraires et Artistiques, 1901).

56. Darío, *Los raros*, 249.

8

Rob Buffington

Los Jotos

Contested Visions
of Homosexuality
in Modern Mexico

For late-nineteenth- and early-twentieth-century Mexican criminologists, sexual deviance of any kind was unnatural, antisocial, and linked to innate criminality; criminals constituted an identifiable class with distinct traits that included atavistic homosexual tendencies.[1] Thus, in the criminological imagination, sexual deviance indicated criminality, which in turn threatened national political, economic, and social development. Homosexuality in particular undermined a nation's very existence by fostering unfruitful sexual unions in an era obsessed with national reproduction and the international "struggle for life."[2] Either way, the perceived need to study the problem was urgent.

The Mexican inmate subjects of criminological study had a much different vision of homosexuality than their professional observers. Prison inmates did indeed engage in what criminologists defined as homosexual activities, fairly often by most accounts. Many, like their criminologist counterparts, stigmatized the participants. Upon closer examination, however, the correspondence breaks down. Some sexual acts—especially men taking the passive role with other men—were denigrated by criminologists and inmates alike, although for very different reasons. Other behaviors—men taking the active role with other men—deeply concerned criminologists but bothered inmates hardly at all. The link between sexual and criminal deviance thus proved more complex and more socially (as opposed to scientifically) constructed than criminologists had supposed. Why this was so and what it meant are the subjects of this essay.[3]

The most exhaustive criminological investigation into sexual deviance was conducted at the turn of the century by Porfirian criminologist, journalist, and littérateur Carlos Roumagnac.[4] In the spirit of the era, he began with a dire warning about national degeneration conveyed through the ubiquitous medical metaphor:

> What epidemic [is] more dangerous than that for which we know . . . no hygienic measures with which to combat it and for which quarantines are useless because we carry it inside ourselves, infiltrated in our blood for years and years, and which we transmit to our descendants, passing on to them, without thought but not without guilt, the virus that sooner or later will flower into the bitter blossoms of crime and transgression?[5]

The mixture of melodrama and medical science was not only typical of the period, it also presumed the criminologist/physician's right—as an agent of "social defense" against the contagion of crime—to gaze frankly and intimately into the bodies and lives of his (and early Mexican criminologists were all male) inmate patients. That sexual behavior, especially deviant sexual behavior, would appear as a leitmotiv—a recurring theme—in his study is thus hardly surprising. Sex was after all the unspoken obsession of the Victorian age.[6]

Roumagnac's "scientific" method involved extensive case histories of his inmate subjects compiled in large part from personal interviews conducted inside Mexico City's principal jail, Belén, and the newly built Federal Penitentiary. Inmates were photographed, measured, inspected, and questioned about everything from their extended family's health history to their post prison plans. And, at every opportunity, they were quizzed on their sexual habits. Not surprisingly, given his expectations, Roumagnac's "observations" of individual inmates established a positive correlation between the criminal and sexual deviance of all his subjects: boys, women, and men.

Because youth figuratively and literally represented Mexico's future, the boys' case was particularly revealing. Although Roumagnac acknowledged—as the previous quotation indicates—a powerful link between inherited traits and potential criminality, he also expressed great interest in the environmental (as opposed to genetic) factors that either caused or sparked criminal behavior. These factors, he insisted, played a potent role in transforming Mexico City's legions of "morally" and physically abandoned children into hardened criminals. One of his many case studies, for example, included a thirteen-year-old boy, brought in for assisting a blind beggar, who "didn't know his father and knew of his mother only that she got sick a lot, suffered from rheumatism, and drank and got drunk frequently." "I don't doubt," Roumagnac pessimistically concluded, "that someday he will reappear as a beggar in his own right and blind as well."[7] Alcoholism and sexual promiscuity were problems too. In Roumagnac's professional estimation, these environmental factors—abandonment, alcoholism, promiscuity—thwarted the development of proper moral restraints in children: criminal and sexual deviance was the inevitable and deplorable result.

Roumagnac included five case histories in a chapter on "juvenile criminals" and in each interview he asked his young subjects about sexual practices outside and inside the prison. Most admitted to encounters with female prostitutes before incarceration but vigorously denied engaging in homosexual encounters in prison. "I'm sure," he observed of a fourteen-year-old convicted murderer, "that if I had asked him the question somewhere else, he would have hit me." Nevertheless, Roumagnac persisted, ultimately uncovering the "inevitable" evidence of homosexual behavior: an ongoing relationship between two boys in which the older boy took the active (and often aggressive) role of the *mayate* (dung beetle) while his sometimes unwilling partner acted as the passive *caballo* (horse).[8]

Roumagnac's "objective" style, presenting his data without formal analysis, obscures his reading of this encounter. The general drift, however, was clear. While he stigmatized both parties as "sexual degenerates," Roumagnac, if anything, sympathized more with the younger boy, relating his attempts at resistance (after confession) and attributing "vicious appetites" to his partner. This bias was hardly surprising. For a guardian of public order, passivity and a willingness to reform were positive attributes; aggressive immorality directly challenged proper political and moral authority. Nevertheless, the shame felt by the passive partner—"I'm more of a man than you are," the younger boy shouts at his partner/rapist—indicated that inmates interpreted the situation quite differently (as we shall see).[9]

Roumagnac's investigation of adult male homosexuality followed a similar pattern with one significant difference: overt homosexual behavior was accepted practice (within certain bounds), especially within the poorly supervised confines of Belén. When one director attempted to isolate "all known pederasts" in a separate area to put an end to the "bloody squabbles" of jealous men, targeted inmates responded by "parading in front of other inmates, without bashfulness or shame, making, on the contrary, an ostentatious display of feminine voices and mannerisms."[10] Unlike the young boy forced to "play horse" for his older partner, adult male sexual inverts (as turn-of-the-century observers described effeminate men) flamboyantly asserted their difference, often taking suggestive, feminized nicknames like "la Golondrina" (the swallow) and "la Bicicleta" (the bicycle).[11] For Roumagnac, they were dangerous sexual degenerates. And, in his view, the problem penetrated far deeper into the inmate population.[12] Like the boys, adult-male inmate subjects were quizzed about their sexuality at every opportunity. Like the boys, most had been sexually promiscuous before incarceration. Like the boys, most emphatically denied any involvement in homosexual activities even while acknowledging its presence in the prison. And, like the boys, they maintained their "innocence," even in the face of contrary evidence. One inmate, accused by many others of "pederasty," suggested that his principal accuser was seeking revenge for his refusal to "grant (sexual) favors."[13] Roumagnac, noncommittal as usual, later cited his accuser's allegation that another inmate who "acted as his (the accused's) woman" was contemplating murder in order to stay in prison with his lover.[14] To complicate matters further, the accuser's own brother accused the accuser of seducing him (the brother) as a child and of being a "horse" or passive partner to other inmates.[15] Even without interpretation, these intricate webs of accusations and counteraccusations—as in the previously cited case with the young boys—demonstrated the fundamental deceitfulness of criminals and thus reinforced Roumagnac's efforts to link criminal and sexual deviance. They also, not coincidentally, signaled the need for trained observers to expose these elaborate dissimulations.

One sensational case—a man convicted of murdering a five-year-old boy he had just raped—further cemented this link. Roumagnac identified this as a clear case of "moral insanity." He noted that the subject had begun by watching his sisters undress and observing copulating dogs and had then progressed to pornography and group sex. Coupled with a family history of mental illness and the subject's own alcoholic tendencies, the rape and murder of a child seemed inevitable in Roumagnac's narrative. And, his juxtaposition of this case with other, less dramatic tales of moral decline created a guilt by inference in which all deviants collectively share the blame for the most atrocious of their collective crimes. In this context, even the subject's seeming disinterest in homosexual activities in prison paradoxically suggests that these activities were not isolated sexual phenomena but part of a generalized deviancy that manifested itself in different ways at different times and in different situations: the appearance of any deviant behavior thus signified the hidden presence of its other possible manifestations.[16]

Nor were Roumagnac's observations about deviancy confined to males. Women too felt the probing gaze of the professional criminologist. And their responses were remarkably similar to, if less ostentatious than, those of their male counterparts. Some women, for example, openly acknowledged their sexual relations with other women: according to Roumagnac's informants, "manly" women parted their hair on the right side and their "feminine" partners parted on the left. At the same time, however, most of Roumagnac's subjects denied participating in homosexual activities even while they accused their fellow inmates of *safismo* (female homosexual relations). One particularly vociferous inmate condemned the frequent fights between jealous women and their habit of "kissing, embracing, and nibbling" each other in public.[17] As with boys and men, Roumagnac implied that most of these denials were disingenuous and cited various contradictions and ambiguities in the different accounts. Again, the overall impression was of dissimulating inmates attempting to cover up the rampant homosexual activity that signified their deviance.

As with the men and boys, this deviance had a history. The most prominent of Roumagnac's morality tales, for example, chronicled the fall of a young girl seduced and abandoned by her patron's son, who turned to prostitution, morphine, and sapphism (which she "learned" from two Spanish colleagues) before committing the murder—she killed another prostitute in a dispute over a man—that landed her in jail.[18] This tale and his other narratives of women's "descent into crime" resembled those of the men with one significant difference. For the women, moral lassitude, rather than leading directly to criminal acts, instead increased their vulnerability to unsavory, outside influences—dishonest young men, procuresses, madams, drug dealers, pimps, and Spanish sapphists—who turned them to crime. The assumption that deviant women failed to control their own destinies gave female homosexuality a slightly different spin, especially for the general inmate population which—as we will see—interpreted male homosexual behavior in quite other ways.[19] For Roumagnac, this difference signified much less because female criminality hardly threatened public order; forging the theoretical link between sexual and criminal deviance in both men and women was a far more important undertaking.[20]

By the 1930s, the pioneering efforts of men like Roumagnac had borne their expected fruit. Early criminologists had struggled to find the proper words—sexual inverts (for both sexes), pederasts (for men), sapphists (for women)—to describe what was after all a rather complex set of deviant behaviors. Later generations confidently lumped these variegated phenomena into a new conceptual category they called "homosexuality."

Typically, this new category was closely tied to criminality. In a 1934 article on, "The Anti-Social Character of Homosexuals," written for *Criminalia*, the newly inaugurated professional journal for Mexican criminologists, Dr. Alfonso Millán buttressed Lombroso's old argument about atavistic homosexuals with up-to-date references to Freudian psychology and recent discoveries in endocrinology (the study of hormones). Extrapolating from these prestigious "scientific" sources, he concluded that male homosexuals took on the negative traits of both sexes: "from the man [*macho*] he has a somewhat aggressive, hostile, and vain spirit, while from the woman, the gossipy scheming, the subtle intrigue of the eighteenth-century salon, and traitorous coquetry." These traits resulted in a "psychology . . . that seems more prejudicial than the physical practices themselves." And, although he distinguished between passive and active homosexual types, he added—as Roumagnac had already implied—that active partners were "as or more dangerous" than their passive counterparts because they were more aggressive and difficult to identify.[21] A 1935 article, "Homosexuality and the Dangerous State [*estado peligroso*]" for the same journal, by his Peruvian colleague, Dr. Susana Solano, expanded on Millán's themes. She noted that "other peculiarities like being lazy, indolent, and egotistical augment [the homosexual's] dangerousness." More to the point, she added confidently that "a certain pathological sexual affinity between the insane, criminals, and homosexuals is proven."[22] For these later criminologists (both of them medical doctors as well), Roumagnac's inferences had become criminological doctrine. By 1935, the links between criminal and sexual deviance had been "proven."

Some criminologists went a step further. Since the Revolution (1911–1920), most Mexican social scientists had stressed the social and environmental causes of criminality. This environmentalist bent shifted some of the blame from the criminal to society and committed the national government (at least rhetorically) to improving living conditions for all Mexicans as well as rehabilitating the criminals produced by these social inequities. The rhetorical commitment to social justice for the previously criminalized lower classes also affected criminological discourse.

In this context, sexual deviance and especially homosexuality—which criminologists still considered primarily biological problems—threatened to contaminate "normal" criminals! In his book on criminal methods in Mexico, police reporter José Raúl Aguilar related an anecdote about a *macho* convicted murderer transported to the penal colony at Islas Marías whose voice became increasingly "high-pitched and effeminate after he was forced (literally kicking and screaming) to travel with a group of obviously homosexual convicts."[23] Aguilar's preoccupation with the contamination of a murderer suggests that some criminologists were restructuring the hierarchy of deviance.

In response to the perceived threat of homosexual contamination, Mexican criminologists like Raúl González Enríquez pioneered the "conjugal visit"—which allowed prisoners sexual access to their "spouses"—specifically to alleviate the problem of homosexuality in the all-male world of the prison. In his prize-winning book, *The Sexual Problem of Men in the Penitentiary*, he warned that in some inmates "the taste for fairies [*los jotos*] . . . becomes so ingrained that afterwards they need to mix in illicit acts [*coitos bastardos*] to satisfy their wayward instinct." Like Roumagnac, he recognized fundamental differences between passive "sexual inverts" and aggressive "sexual perverts" while pointing out the specific dangers posed by each group. Inverts, he criticized for introducing young inmates to "unsuspected pleasures." Perverts, he especially condemned for their "violent passions . . . [which] are the source of many acts that could be classified as criminal." To support his point, he cited frequent fights between jealous men and particularly graphic examples of younger inmates raped at knifepoint. As with Roumagnac, the affinity between criminal and sexual deviance appears obvious, but in González's formulation, homosexuality is even more dangerous than criminality because it can permanently corrupt the moral character of a potentially redeemable criminal.[24]

This restructuring of deviance by postrevolution Mexican criminologists underscores the political, even ideological, agenda that underlay criminological "science" and its attitude toward homosexual relations. In the Porfirian period, social scientists had been obsessed with the problem of "order," which seemed the necessary first step toward capitalist economic development. Criminal activities represented a grave threat to public order, threatening economic development by disrupting commerce, encouraging capital flight, and discouraging foreign investment. Crime was therefore a source of considerable concern to Mexican policy makers. This concern translated into a scientific investigation not just of crime and criminals per se but of a generalized state of being, "criminality," that included sexual deviance. Roumagnac's special concerns about the disruptive potential of aggressive homosexuals—González's perverts—are a case in point and make this linkage with Porfirian fears of disorder quite clear. Thus Roumagnac's construction of "homosexuality" was far more ideological than scientific. This conclusion holds true for his successors as well.

Postrevolutionary criminologists shared Porfirian concerns about public order and capitalist economic development but with one significant difference. Ideologically linked to the idea of an inclusive (if not democratic) modern state, their agenda stressed the redemptive possibilities of the new regime and thus doubly condemned congenital (probably unredeemable) states like homosexuality. Criminals might be the by-products of social injustice; homosexuals were (especially in the biological sense) unproductive sexual degenerates whose perversion threatened the moral health of the newly reborn Mexican nation. The wholesale transportation of "undesirable" homosexuals to the Islas Marías penal colony alluded to by Aguilar underscored this new attitude. In the new "revolutionary" Mexico: criminals maybe, homosexuals definitely not.

Criminologists, however, were not the only group that politicized "homosexuality." Their male subjects, for example, constructed the politics of sexual deviance rather differently. Coming for the most part from the popular classes, they generally took a position, common throughout Latin America, that heavily stigmatized effeminate sexual inverts (*los jotos*) but not necessarily their active (and thus more manly) sexual partners.[25] Although they also recognized different homosexual types, criminologists typically lumped criminal activity and all forms of sexual deviance under the rubric "criminality." This conflation of deviances, given the lower-class origins of most Mexican criminals, amounted to a class distinction.[26] For male inmates, on the other hand, the stigma of homosexuality fractured along gender rather than class lines: men who inverted their gender by behaving like women were constantly mocked and harassed (and used) by their *macho* colleagues; men who took the active (male) role in sexual relations usually escaped severe censure.[27]

Active partners denied their participation in homosexual acts to criminologists; it was never publicly acknowledged behavior even if expected. In any case, they rarely questioned their own manhood and vigorously rejected the criminologist's accusation of "homosexuality." For example, one of Roumagnac's adult male subjects felt compelled to "pray to God that in the time I'm here that I don't use one of those men." Another, although he too had resisted temptation, responded with a colorful euphemism—"I'm not saying I won't drink from that well [*de esta agua no beberé*]"—to express his position.[28] Nor did these attitudes change much. Years later, an inmate informed another inquisitive criminologist that many fellow prisoners satisfied their sexual needs by making arrangements with "effeminate men" (*los afeminados*).[29] For active partners, homosexual relations were a vice, even a sin, but not an indicator of their own homosexuality. And under these circumstances, denying homosexual relations was no different from denying any other legal or moral transgression, a kind of denial convicted criminals likely understood quite well.

For most inmates, however, sexual inversion was a different matter altogether. Effeminate men were mercilessly teased and sometimes raped by other inmates. A 1931 account of conditions in Belén, remarked that "male laundry workers were *naturally* the object of ridicule from other inmates."[30] The situation was little different in the Federal Penitentiary, where prison authorities attempted to isolate effeminate inmates. In spite of their isolation, an inmate observer noted that "the others jeer at them." And, asked about sexual relations between active and passive partners in the Federal Penitentiary, another responded frankly that "sometimes the active one pays and other times the passive one; sometimes it's arranged free for reasons of sympathy and other times through the energetic imposition of the macho on the fairy [*del macho sobre el joto*]."[31]

Even through the criminologist's lens, the difference in inmates' attitudes is apparent. An anecdote related by criminologist Carlos Franco Sodi is especially revealing. In a short essay he entitled "Meditating on the Thought of a Prisoner," Franco recalled encountering the following graffito, written in bad Spanish, on a wall in the Federal Penitentiary: "Padese sufre y sobrelleva sin perder la esperanza de reunirte con los tullos para aserlos felises y ser bueno" (Suffer, bear and endure without losing the hope of being reunited with your loved ones in order to make them happy and to be good). For Franco, the message indicated the presence of "a normal individual, honorable and of moral sentiments," an "accidental" criminal whom the justice system could easily and profitably return to civil society. Beside this hopeful message, however, another inmate had boldly scrawled "los jotos" (fairies). The response, Franco noted, was "typical" because for most inmates "manliness consists in feeling at home behind bars, in being firmly resolved to lead a life of crime, and in feeling no remorse for the blood spilled or the deed committed that landed them behind bars."[32]

Franco's interpretation was typical of a guardian of public order. The inmate who scrawled "los jotos" next to the pious thoughts of his fellow prisoner clearly had a different take. And his take was as political as any criminologist's.[33] Deciphering it, however, involves some speculation. In his famous 1950 essay "The Sons of La Malinche," Mexican poet-philosopher Octavio Paz examined the various meaning of the Spanish verb *chingar* (to fuck). In his exposition of its meaning for Mexicans, the sexual politics were quite clear: "The *chingón* is the *macho*, the male: he rips open the *chingada*, the female who is pure passivity, defenseless against the exterior world." In (relatively) polite conversation, *joder* (to screw) stands in for *chingar* and *jodido* (screwed) for *chingada* but with one significant difference. *Jodido* carries the same political message as *chingada* but implies a less permanent, less explicitly sexual condition that implies the possibility of resistance. On the other hand, *joto*, which resembled a bastardized past participle of *joder*,[34] suggests the sexual "passivity" Paz attributes to the *chingada*.[35] Thus, following Paz's construction of *chingar*, the macho inmate who scrawled "los jotos" was expressing deep disdain for the pious soul who accepted his punishment with resignation and remorse.

That disdain likely had little to do with sexual orientation and everything to do with the political situation of Mexico's lower classes: the sexual metaphor conveyed disgust for the complicitous *joto* who passively accepted his own screwing by the dominant political and social system. Criminals might be *jodidos*—screwed by the legal system—but to accept that fate, to show remorse, was unmanly, the act of a *joto* or a "female who is pure passivity, defenseless against the exterior world."[36] Inmate slang (*caló*) for the sex act, *hostigar* (to harass or victimize), clarified the power relations involved in even normative sexual relations.[37] Passive acquiescence in this harassment was considered despicable.

The depreciation of passive femaleness in women and in men who acted like women represented a political (and obviously very sexist) position of resistance to arbitrary authority. The criminologists' construction, which lumped inverts and perverts into a single category of homosexual, attempted symbolically to transform the active, resistant *jodido* into the passive, complicitous *joto*, leaving him no space in which to act out the male rituals of domination (including sexual domination of other men) that gave existence and meaning to his political self. Machismo was thus the quintessential posture of political resistance, especially for otherwise downtrodden lower-class men. It was a posture learned at the feet of oppressive masters and entrenched by centuries of racism, economic exploitation, and political exclusion. Consequently, it was (and is) certainly not a position they would willingly relinquish at the behest of an elitist ideological construct like scientific criminology. Furthermore, if Paz is correct, the inmates' gendered construction of homosexuality was typical, even archetypical, of Mexican society in general. In any case, its potent political symbolism made (makes) it a formidable adversary for modernizing criminologists.

By the same token, because it lacked a strongly politicized subtext, female homosexuality was effectively marginalized: by criminologists because female criminality posed little threat to society, and by male inmates (and probably male society in general) because the female—women and *jotos*—had no political voice.[38] At the same time, the active male partner who "rips open" the *chingada*, the *joto*, or even the unwilling weaker inmate was not a homosexual (which would have lumped him with the *jotos*) but a *chingón* who imposed himself violently upon a hostile world. He resolutely refused to have it any other way.[39]

These distinct, often contradictory, visions of homosexuality suggest the difficulty of discussing issues like homosexuality, sexuality, and criminality outside a political context: in the fluid medium of language and symbols, categorical boundaries shift dramatically with the ideological tide. In Mexico, criminologists and male inmates contested the meaning of homosexuality; the former constructed their vision around politicized notions of class legitimized by science; the latter around politicized notions of gender legitimized by resistance to arbitrary (male) authority. Both groups stressed homosexuality's ideological significance. For both, sex was politics—male politics. The complexities of lived experience became anecdotal evidence in the service of their different visions, or was left unspoken.

• NOTES

I am very much indebted to the editors, Daniel Balderston and Donna J. Guy, for their patience, encouragement, careful reading, and excellent advice.

1. For historical background on early Mexican criminology, see Robert Buffington, "Forging the Fatherland: Criminality and Citizenship in Modern Mexico" (Ph.D. diss., University of Arizona, 1994); Pablo Piccato, "'El Paso de Venus por el disco del Sol': Criminality and Alcoholism in the Late Porfiriato," *Mexican Studies/Estudios Mexicanos* 11.2 (1995): 203–41; and Javier MacGregor Campuzano, "Historiografía sobre criminalidad y sistema penitenciario," *Secuencia: Revista de historia y ciencias sociales* 22 (1992): 232–34.

2. On this obsession with national survival see for example Justo Sierra, "The Present Era," in *The Political Evolution of the Mexican People*, ed. Edmundo O'Gorman, trans. Charles Ramsdell (Austin: University of Texas Press, 1969), 342–68. For a discussion of "scientific politics" in general, see Charles A. Hale, *The Transformation of Liberalism in Late Nineteenth-Century Mexico* (Princeton: Princeton University Press, 1989).

3. The transition from the broadly defined conceptual category of "sexual inversion" to the narrower "medical model of homosexuality" and the categorical confusion that resulted is explored in George Chauncey Jr., "From Sexual Inversion to Homosexuality: The Changing Medical Conceptualization of Female Deviance," in *Passion and Power: Sexuality in History*, ed. Kathy Peiss and Christina Simmons (Philadelphia: Temple University Press, 1989), 87–117. For a contemporary ethnography that explores the complexities of the homosexual experience in Mexico, see Joseph Carrier, *De los otros: Intimacy and Homosexuality Among Mexican Men* (New York: Columbia University Press, 1995).

4. For a more thorough treatment of Roumagnac's investigation into inmate sexuality and its role in prison life, see Pablo Piccato, "Sexuality in the Prison: Mexico City, 1897–1919" (unpublished manuscript, University of Texas at Austin, 1995).

5. Carlos Roumagnac, *Los criminales en México* (Mexico City: Tipografía El Fénix, 1904), 10. His introduction provided a review of European criminology that further developed the implied theoretical link between criminal and sexual deviance.

6. Michel Foucault, among others, argues that Victorians were obsessed with sex even as they pretended to deny it a place in polite society: *History of Sexuality*, trans. Robert Hurley (New York: Pantheon Books, 1978). Peter Gay also disputes the image of sexually repressed Victorians: *The Bourgeois Experience: Victoria to Freud*, vol. 1, *The Education of the Senses* (New York: Oxford University Press, 1984).

7. Roumagnac, *Los criminales en México*, 41.

8. Ibid., 77. The word *mayate* is apparently derived from the Nahuatl *mayatl*, an iridescent green beetle: Marcos A. Morínigo, *Diccionario manual de americanismos* (Buenos Aires: Muchnik Editores, 1965), 405. Also, in classical Nahuatl *mazatl* connotes a "bestial . . . sexual or lascivious person: John Bierhorst, *A Nahuatl-English Dictionary and Concordance to the Cantares Mexicanos* (Stanford: Stanford University Press, 1985), 208. For a glossary of Latin American terms for homosexual acts and actors, see Stephen O. Murray and Wayne R. Dynes, "Hispanic Homosexuals: A Spanish Lexicon," in *Latin American Male Homosexualities*, ed. Stephen O. Murray (Albuquerque: University of New Mexico Press, 1995), 180–92. Murray and Dynes note that the term *mayate* also connotes a "flashy dresser" and is used in Chicano Spanish for a "black pimp" (188). Their translation of *caballo* as "mare" (184) seems dubious; the usual word for mare is *yegua*, and rural Mexicans at least would distinguish clearly between male *caballos* and female *yeguas*. More likely, the imagery reflects a domesticated male animal that is ridden (dominated) by a male rider. Another possible derivation: in Spanish playing cards, the *caballo* corresponds to the "queen" in the standard deck. Although the etymology of these terms is far from clear, my suspicion is that these multiple connotations probably reinforced the use of these particular terms. As we will see, these multiple connotations will also be true of the word *joto*.

9. Roumagnac, *Los criminales en México*, 97.

10. Ibid., 77.

11. Ibid., 210.

12. Homosexual subcultures centered around sexual inversion thrived (and continue to thrive) in many Latin American cities. See, for example, Jorge Salessi, "The Argentine Dissemination of Homosexuality, 1890–1914," *Journal of the History of Sexuality* 4.3 (1994): 337–68; Daniel Bao, "*Invertidos Sexuales, Tortilleras*, and *Maricas Machos*: The Construction of Homosexuality in Buenos Aires, Argentina, 1900–1950," *Journal of Homosexuality* 24.3–4 (1993): 183–219; Rommel Mendès-Leite, "The Game of Appearances: The 'Ambigusexuality' in Brazilian Culture of Sexuality," *Journal of Homosexuality* 25.3 (1993): 271–82; and Richard G. Parker, *Bodies, Pleasures and Passions: Sexual Culture in Contemporary Brazil* (Boston: Beacon Press, 1991).

13. Roumagnac, *Los criminales en México*, 219–20.

14. Ibid., 307.

15. Ibid., 312.

16. Ibid., 296–303.

17. Ibid., 191. He explains the significance of hair parting on 174.

18. Ibid., 104–15.

19. Pablo Piccato argues that women inmates generally had more stable, "supportive" homosexual relationships than the men and boys. See his "Sexuality in the Prison," 25.

20. Female homosexuality was also a problem for national reproduction. See especially Jorge Salessi, "The Argentine Dissemination of Homosexuality." However, in Mexico, fear of female criminality and working women in the public sphere was apparently less of an issue than in Argentina. Roumagnac was one of the few criminologists to give women equal time.

21. Alfonso Millán, "Carácter antisocial de los homosexuales," *Criminalia* 2 (1934): 53–59. Millán was the medical director of a Mexico City insane asylum, the Manicomio General de la Casteñeda.

22. Susana Solano, "El homosexualismo y el estado peligroso," *Criminalia* 2 (1935). The use of the verb "to be," *ser* in the original Spanish, indicates that these are permanent rather than temporary states.

23. José Raúl Aguilar, *Los métodos criminales en México: cómo defendernos* (Mexico City: Ediciones Lux, n.d.), 180–81. The penal colony at Islas Marías (in the Pacific Ocean off Mazatlán) was specifically designed by the Porfirian regime to hold undesirables; by the postrevolutionary period, this category included everyone from political prisoners like Madre Conchita (who allegedly masterminded the assassination of President Alvaro Obregón) to pimps, homosexuals, and communists.

24. Raúl González Enríquez, *El problema sexual del hombre en la penitenciaría* (Veracruz: Editorial Citlaltepetl, 1971), 94–96. González conducted his research, like Roumagnac, in Belén and the Federal Penitentiary. He won *El Universal*'s annual Miguel Lanz Duret prize for the work in 1942, which suggests that it had a fairly broad circulation. This was one of the attractions of a titillating topic, as Roumagnac had discovered earlier.

25. Most anthropologists who study Latin American attitudes toward homosexuality argue that this stigma against sexual inversion is typical, even normative. For an excellent overview of this literature, see Tomás Almaguer, "Chicano Men: A Cartography of Homosexual Identity and Behavior," in *The Lesbian and Gay Studies Reader*, ed. Henry Abelove, Michèle Aina Barale, and David M. Halperin (New York: Routledge, 1993), 255–73. Unfortunately, the anthropological literature tends to ignore the specific historical contexts—political repression, economic exploitation, and social/racial discrimination—that reinforce this "Mediterranean" construction of homosexuality, especially for lower-class men. Almaguer also explains the semantics of the various "contemptuous" Spanish terms for male homosexuals— *maricón, joto, puto*—noting that *joto* and *puto* "are infinitely more derogatory and vulgar in that they underscore the sexually non-conforming nature of their passive/receptive position in the homosexual act" (260). Translating *joto* into English is problematic because although "faggot" carries the contempt, it lacks specificity. For that reason, I have used the somewhat less derogatory "fairy," which stresses sexual inversion.

26. Mexican criminologists, most of them from the professional middle classes, did point out that the overly refined upper class contained many effeminate men.

Thus the image of sexual deviance did double duty by damning the two classes that threatened the rising middle classes.

27. Jorge Salessi argues that even though Argentine criminologists used the broader conceptual category of homosexuality, they preserved the distinction between passive and active roles with the passive "pederast" becoming the "stigmatized category of male sexual deviance." The point is arguable for Mexico as well, but I would suggest a greater difference between the vision of criminologists and the general population. See Salessi, "The Argentine Dissemination of Homosexuality," 367. Richard G. Parker analyzes Brazilian attitudes towards gender in considerable depth in "Men and Women," from *Bodies, Pleasures and Passions*, 30–66.

28. Roumagnac, *Los criminales en México*, 275, 279.

29. Raúl Carranca y Trujillo, "Sexo y penal," *Criminalia* 1 (1933–1934): 26–31. Group activities like movies apparently provided ample opportunities for homosexual relations.

30. Guillermo Mellado, *Belén por dentro y por fuera* (Mexico City: Cuadernos "Criminalia," 1959), 32. My italics. This was Belén's final year as a jail.

31. Carranca y Trujillo, "Sexo y penal," 28.

32. Carlos Franco Sodi, "Meditando sobre el pensamiento de un preso," *Don Juan Delincuente y otros ensayos* (Mexico City: Ediciones Bota, 1951), 12–19.

33. On the political awareness of penitentiary inmates, see Pablo Piccato, "Mexican City Prisoners: Between Social Engineering and Popular Culture" (paper delivered at the Conference on Latin American History 1996 Annual Meeting, Atlanta, Georgia).

34. My suspicion, however, is that *joto* is not derived from *joder* at all but from the name of Cell Block J (*jota* in Spanish) of the Federal Penitentiary in Mexico City, where prison authorities attempted to isolate overtly homosexual inmates; see Sergio García Ramírez, *El final de Lecumberri: reflexiones sobre la prisión* (Mexico City: Porrúa, 1977), 27. This would be another case, then, of the presence of multiple connotations and folk etymologies (as we have seen already with *mayate*).

35. Octavio Paz, "The Sons of La Malinche," *The Labyrinth of Solitude: Life and Thought in Mexico*, trans. Lysander Kemp (New York: Grove Press, 1961), 77. There are numerous feminist critiques of Paz's heavily gendered construction of Mexican identity. See, for example, Norma Alarcón, "Chicana Feminist Literature: A Re-Vision through Malintzin, or Malintzin, Putting the Flesh Back on the Object," in *This Bridge Called My Back: Writings by Radical Women of Color*, ed. Cherríe Moraga and Gloria Anzaldúa (Watertown, Mass.: Persephone, 1981), 182–90.

36. This interpretation supports George Chauncey's argument that medical discourses on sexual deviance "provide us with a key to understanding the politics of sexuality" even when they have little impact on "popular attitudes and the social relations of sexuality": "From Sexual Inversion to Homosexuality," 108.

37. Roumagnac, *Los criminales en México*, 379.

38. Jorge Salessi suggests that concern about working women and immigration (foreign penetration) fueled turn-of-the-century homophobia in Argentina: "The Argentine Dissemination of Homosexuality," 338. Some of this doubtless occurred

in Mexico but not to same extent; other than his observation about hair parting, Roumagnac evinced little interest in the gendered roles of "sapphists," and other observers disregarded women altogether. This marginalization of female homosexuality has persisted. Stephen O. Murray laments the lack of scholarship on "female homosexualities" in his introduction to *Latin American Male Homosexualities*, xiii, n. 3. He also provides a short bibliography (178–79).

39. This reinforces Piccato's argument that "in Belén, male sexuality tended to express itself in violent ways and to be closer to the structure of power" ("Sexuality in the Prison," 34). Interestingly, although manly, "butch," women probably adapted many overtly male behaviors, extreme violence was rare. This, of course, doesn't preclude an aggressive sexuality. See, for example, Almaguer's discussion of Cherríe Moraga's work in "Chicano Men," 268.

9

José Quiroga

Homosexualities in the Tropic of Revolution

- CRYSTAL CUBA

Few countries in Latin America have been as swamped as Cuba by so many who have chronicled the island to itself and to the world: sociologists, economists, political scientists, tourists, filmmakers, critics, historians. Since 1959 the Cuban Revolution and all of its aspects have been written about, analyzed, observed. An ocean of paper circumnavigates the island, and the revolution beckons those armies of the letter relentlessly, with sometimes dramatic panache. "Come to Cuba, come to see what we have done"—so goes the inscription, popular in tourist brochures, naming a revolutionary spectacle, a pride in achievements that may not, under any circumstances, be left unrecorded. But this invitation also signals a mode, a construction, a network of desires, a spectacle that by no means started in 1959. On the contrary, at some level Cuban history can be read in all of its messy complexity as an utterance, a disputation that seeks the complicity of others. Thus, the first socialist republic in Latin America was established on an island whose particular relationship to the United States always played on the libido, articulated by means of tropical clichés of paradise and sex. From the playground of wealthy North Americans seeking fun and frolic in their very own backyard, Cuba, after 1959 took upon itself a much wider representation—that of freedom from imperial machinations of socialism without ideology but with a rhythmic beat and cadence.[1] Before and after, Cuba has always been linked to the outside world by the threads of desire. What I want to explore—and ultimately link *to* the Cuban social theater, is the one issue that has placed itself at the center of Cuban cultural discourse: the polemical relationship of homosexuality to revolutionary culture. Surveying the literature since the early 1960s, one realizes that homosexuality has been at the center of the social process—a process that articulated a critique of all things Cuban in terms of class, culture, and gender but that, when confronted with the issue of sexuality, confined all difference (mainly, homosexuality) to the realm of the private, defining homosexual subjects as disloyal to the brotherhood and solidarity entailed by the revolution, and as suspicious or perverse.[2]

With this context in mind, there are two points of departure for this revisitation on the issue of homosexuality in Cuba. The first is the recent film *Fresa y chocolate*, by Tomás Gutiérrez Alea, based on Senel Paz's short story "El lobo, el bosque y el hombre nuevo." By officially sanctioning a film that zeroes in on one of the more polemical aspects of the revolution, one that gives credence to most of its "enemies" and puts its past apologists in a sort of no-man's-land, the Cuban government has sought to present openly a situation that, on the one hand, plays on the affective subversion of the forbidden but that, on the other, falls behind the social realities of the moment. That Tomás Gutiérrez Alea, the world-famed director of *Memorias del subdesarrollo*, decided to film *Fresa y chocolate* is not without significance. In both, the central character is meant to stand for something at a given moment in revolutionary history: in *Memorias*, the intellectual is literally thrown out of his petit-bourgeois world and forced to ponder his alienation when faced with the growing class consciousness of the population; in *Fresa*, the homosexual mourns the cultural myopia of the Cuban bureaucracy. Whereas the intellectual in the former film walks through the streets of Havana like a parasite who merely recirculates himself in relationship to a thoroughly productive society, the homosexual character in *Fresa* is put squarely within the realm of culture: he is the one who circulates culture as a good whose value is finally understood by the straight object of affection (David) and recharged for revolutionary consumption. Together, *Memorias* and *Fresa* allow us to trace a revolutionary discourse as it changes over time: from the intellectual as revolutionary malcontent in need of integration, to the homosexual. As gay critics, we are all like Diego, the gay character in *Fresa*, inasmuch as he recalls Benjamin's angel of history, looking back and forward at a ruin, taking us back to other moments of crisis where homosexuals appear and disappear from the Cuban scene. The film is, in this sense, perhaps the last chapter of a debate carried on since the early eighties—since the Mariel exodus and the work of the dissident intellectuals who produced *Mariel* magazine and *Improper Conduct* (1984), perhaps the first generation of postrevolutionary dissident writers.

The second point of departure for my essay is more anecdotal. At a recent conference on postmodern discourse at Yale, a famous Cuban writer still residing within the island addressed foreigners' concerns that *Fresa y chocolate* portrayed a stereotypical view of gay men: "In a homophobic country," he said, "I pray for us to at least appear as stereotypes." That statement and the intersection of politics, culture, and homosexuality in *Fresa y chocolate* are at the core of my essay, for I argue that what the comment implicitly marks as a surrender (representation always contingent upon homophobia) should actually be understood in a different light. What is interesting about the film is not that homosexuality appears as a stereotype—that is, in a sense, predictable—but that the homosexual should be essentialized as representing the fate of a revolutionary cultural class. His body, as well as his culture, becomes an emblem. That the homosexual is metonymized in such a fashion may not be surprising, given the history of persecution of Cuban homosexuals after the revolution. But it also may not be, alas, the cause for celebration.

In the introduction to his *Teatro completo*, Virgilio Piñera remarked that no dramatic author could compete with the theatrical pose of Fidel Castro entering Havana, acclaimed by multitudes, adored by all.[3] If at some level the revolution was a theater, homosexuality was the limit of the public theater of revolution and the revolutionary spectacle.[4] It was seen as a parody of sex, and as such it was tolerated or discouraged or simply repressed. Because revolutionary hygiene saw in homosexuality a copy of heterosexual roles into same-sex behavior, homosexuality was almost immediately consigned to an ambivalent realm of privacy—but to a privacy that was public, in any case.[5] This placing of homosexuality in the private realm was contradictory, for the revolution itself rendered the issue of homosexuality *visible* in the first place—visible in the sense of its being transparent to the society as a whole. As early as 1962, seven years before the Stonewall rebellion would mobilize gays out of the closet, the Cuban Revolution already indexed homosexuality as a condition that needed to be extirpated in order to fulfill an economic and political program that in turn became affixed to the nationalist ideology. Rendering homosexuals as part of an economic system that was articulated as "foreign," because it was linked to the demi-monde of prerevolutionary sexual desire for bodies, the revolution joined an economic system to a nationalist project, and social hygiene to revolutionary action. Part and parcel of a system that has never been able to dislodge itself (as government) from its revolutionary acts, the revolution categorized and consigned homosexuals as part of the officially tolerated or officially repressed "gusanera" (literally "worms," the term the revolution gave to all its disaffected elements) or, in the same vein, as part of a lumpen proletariat that, in Marxist terms, was defined as nonproductive circulators of nonvalued goods.

This rendering of political opposition in terms of bodily function appears already in Marx. As Andrew Parker has shown in an illuminating essay, the intersection of class and sex in Marx's *Eighteenth Brumaire* is done at the expense of sex. While producing a kind of sex-inflected analysis of class formation, Parker deconstructs Marx's equation of homosexuality with the lumpen proletariat, and hence with everything anal and excremental, what in Cuba has to be seen as the wider discourse of the *gusanera* as the parasitical class that the revolution discharges or dislodges from its midst. But I argue that the metonymy of *gusanera* in terms of homosexuality cannot merely be assimilated or imposed to homosexuals as a class. *Gusanos* or "worms," parasitical infections are, for the revolution, the *essence* of the fecal discharge—feces and anality the metonymized referent by means of which the homosexual is always named. The *gusano* essentializes the homosexual as its quintessence; the model for the gusano is always the homosexual. It was this discourse, via Marx, and not, as I hope to show, a kind of cultural "atavism" of Cuban homophobia, that inflected the prevalent Cuban orthodoxy after the revolution.[6]

It was no secret that since the 1950s gay men had proclaimed themselves the "custodians" of Cuban culture, as Diego's statement in *Fresa y chocolate*, examined below, reveals. Indeed, the very question of gay intellectuals (as opposed to intellectuals who were gay) had surfaced in Cuban intellectual discourse at the outset of the revolution in the pages of *Ciclón* (1955–1959), the foremost Cuban journal of the time immediately before the revolution, founded by José Rodríguez Feo, an openly gay millionaire, and directed by Virgilio Piñera, an openly gay writer who was not part of the financial elite. Having silenced most of its critics, the revolution could never produce the logical continuation of that critique in the form that it had assumed in France or in the United States. Particularly after the official closing of Ediciones el Puente (1962–1963), Cuban progressive thought would fall back to arguing that its differences in terms of sexuality were due more to atavistic principles than to official policy—this, in a country whose cultural policy after 1959 was directed (if you will pardon the expression) from top to bottom.[7]

Fresa y chocolate narrates a rather simple allegorical story. There are only two flavors—strawberry and chocolate—in the ice cream palace of Coppelia, the site of most gay encounters in Havana. Because only real men eat chocolate, the thirty-year-old gay queen Diego partakes of strawberry as he sits next to David, a budding writer and young Communist Party cadre. The boy-meets-boy plot line is underscored by the political distance between the two men, who also choose different flavors for dessert. But Diego has found a real strawberry in his dish, and he savors it with the only topping he can find: banned books, among them, one by Mario Vargas Llosa, which he exposes to David. Culture, as something that is at the same time possessed and shared, forms the most visible subplot of a sentimental tale that ends with the unjust banishment of the suffering homosexual who, like so many others, leaves the island after he sees his options for living diminished. It is the legacy of that injustice (supposedly taking place in 1979, a year before the Mariel exodus) that the film seeks to address, but not before Gutiérrez Alea treats us to a tour de force account of life in Havana, of its buildings and its poor tenements, of the people's efforts to feed themselves from day to day, his cinematic gaze reproducing Diego's sense of melancholia. Throughout, the film wants the audience to accept the other as different, especially if these others are gay men whose distance from "us" is just the minor point of a quirk in terms of sexual object.

As a morality tale, *Fresa y chocolate* is also what Gutiérrez Alea calls a necessary tale, from his first reading of the Senel Paz story on which the film is based.[8] As such, it has been hailed as opening up the complex issue of homosexuals in Cuba, and any critique on the film has been accused of being blind to the very real problems entailed in making a film like this, given the crucial situation that the Cuban government is going through. Even if the critique is valid (although one could say that the film is precisely made *because* of the difficult situation of the present, as in *Philadelphia*, one would prefer a belated tale rather than no tale at all), what is interesting about *Fresa y chocolate* is how it faces up to its own past by means of transference, by sublimating homosexuality to culture and further sublimating homosexuality to friendship. For, it turns out, homosexuals have not merely circulated their own bodies for the sake of nonreproductive sex, but they have all along circulated culture, something whose value in and of itself can be found only outside the usual value-producing social mechanisms. Like *Memorias*, with its constant internal references, *Fresa y chocolate* is a compendium of the visible and the invisible history of Cuban culture. No longer solely an issue of private behavior versus social mores, homosexuality needs a space because, like culture, it falls outside the parameters of the normative. Essentialized always as culture, or as transmitter of culture but nevertheless not organic in relation to it, the homosexual is deracinated from a context, outside nature.

As a film that deals with homosexuality and with allegory, *Fresa y chocolate* overdetermines authenticity. And because it is a film about visibility and acceptance—a "message" film—it has to be concerned with technique, with the language used in order to express a homosexuality that is presumably not shared by the director or by members of the cast. But it is no secret that visibility is in itself conditioned, constructed, and even fabricated. As Paul Julian Smith has remarked in terms of Néstor Almendros's *Improper Conduct*, even what is self-evident might be subject to competing interpretations.[9] Where Almendros decided to give the illusion of transparency by means of immensely complex technical means, Gutiérrez Alea wants to confer authenticity to a film that is, on all accounts, a game of illusion.

The problem is, of course, that of conferring authenticity to a narration that is at all times allegorical, constructed precisely on claims to representation that are more proper to allegory—characters that *represent* much more than their individual selves, by virtue of the dense ideological context in which they are found.[10] Gutiérrez Alea is conscious at all times of the given compromises and trade-offs between the allegorical character of the story (what made it necessary in the first place) and the fabrication, or the illusion, of film, and throughout, Alea balances illusion and play, as in, for example, not choosing a given locale in order that the viewer not think that the locale itself is the set designer's brainchild.[11] Alea composes in a careful and lyrical language whose fabrication is set precisely on a style that borders, or limns, construction. Talking about how he filmed *Fresa y chocolate*, Alea explains that he put the camera at the service of the actors (so as not to impede the flow of the mise en scène and create a more naturalistic mode of acting), to the extent that technical proficiency gives the illusion that there is no foul play: what is natural—jerky camera movements, for example— would seem in this context to be as contrived as cinema verité. This is why Gutiérrez Alea erred on the side of technique (on the formal sophistication, on the avoidance of reality itself) in order not to disturb the viewer with the intrusion of the real. The criterion of organicity in the tale demands, nevertheless, an amazing amount of technical proficiency. No detail is spared, no rational decision taken outside such contrivance. Balancing limited resources and budget, the imprimatur of style demands the masking of sophistication as spontaneity. The film wants to give the viewer the illusion of the real and not necessarily reality itself.

Questions of style are always related to a particular mode of constructing and representing desire. In terms of Diego, what is important is not why the character is homosexual but how he will be represented. And this is where the claims of spontaneity as well as the claims of fabrication collide. For all of Alea's repeating that he put the camera at the service of the actors, and that he allowed the actors' free play in front of the camera, acting itself ends up producing its own set of problems:

> En cuanto a su gestualidad, no estábamos muy seguros de qué nivel de afemi-namiento debía manifestar el personaje. El cuento de Senel lo describía con modales marcadamente afeminados incluso, en ocasiones, agresivamente desenvelto y provocador. Trabajamos con el actor para ver hasta qué punto era capaz de manifestarse en ese nivel sin que resultara chocante y, sobre todo, sin que se convirtiera en una caricatura. El actor llevó a cabo un trabajo delicado y riguroso hasta lograr que el aire afeminado brotara de una actitud interna más que de una gestualidad importada.

> (In terms of the gestures, we were not very sure as to the level of effeminacy that the character should show. Senel's story described him with markedly effeminate characteristics, even, at some point, as an aggressive and provoca-tive character. We worked with the actor to see up to what point he was capa-ble of manifesting himself in that way without this becoming shocking and, above all, without turning himself into a caricature. The actor's delicate and rigorous work allowed for effeminacy to arise from an internal attitude, more than from imported gestures.)[12]

Effeminacy is treated as a stylistic mark that is meant to underscore the given authenticity of the film, because the question of homosexuality always entails a problem of denotation.[13] In this sense, *Fresa y chocolate* is a Cuban *Philadelphia*, necessary to the extent that it gives official voice to a situation, but utterly redundant, given the more complex realities at hand.

Like *Philadelphia*, *Fresa y chocolate* hinges on the issue of representa-tion in ways that can be directly pertinent only to the non-openly identified heterosexuals in the cast of characters. This is why the film has to be seen in the context of networks of control: what is going to be let out and repre-sented, and what is not going to be represented and why—a sense of control that even anticipates the manner in which the audience is supposed to respond. According to Gilda Santana, who served as consultant to the film, there were at least eleven versions of the script, not including the final version.[14] Each version was subjected to delicate and painstaking analyses that furnished each action with the criteria of believability and motivation. Each action—for example, and particularly, David's going into Diego's private space—is thus the result of a rational decision that needs to be explained on the basis of what would be, at any given point, the essential behavior of the characters. Throughout the subsequent versions of a script that debated at all points not only the form but the content of the tale (whether it was going to be told, as in the story, as a flashback, for example) a minute examination of the characters takes place, a sort of microscopic analysis that cannot help but normalize and completely colonize all illusions of personal freedom.

What is invisible in terms of the seamless narration of the filmic discourse is the series of absolute questions that have to do with every aspect of the characters in the film. Thus, for the sake of balance, the subplot of the hysterical neighbor is added, in order to give David (and, presumably, the heterosexual viewers) some release throughout the film; the plot line of Diego's sculptor friend is fleshed out; and David's conflicts with Miguel, his Communist Party friend, are amplified. These might all seem like minor details—to be expected, perhaps, in any translation from a written to a filmic text. Or perhaps these details are precisely *to be expected* any time the issue of homosexuality is dealt with—in other words, perhaps this is what the presentation of homosexuality (by nonhomosexuals) entails: an absolute degree of dominance that is at pains to show, at the same time, its own sense of authenticity. These issues of stylistic and technical control are related to the issue of a Cuban culture that is also shown as being thoroughly controlled. In this sense, one can say that the film displaces issues of cultural control toward the stylistic constraints brought to bear upon the figure of the homosexual. If culture should circulate freely, as Gutiérrez Alea argues, the film nevertheless also argues that representations should still be subjected to a certain level of control. *Fresa y chocolate* presents Diego as an exemplar of a true and authentic Cuban culture—of *cubanía*—trampled upon by an intolerant milieu that has sought to refashion that same *cubanía* according to modes that are foreign to it. But whereas Gutiérrez Alea and Paz argue for the stability and inner cohesion of the signified (culture) while tampering with the signifier (Diego, homosexuality), their position is not in contradiction to what the party itself seeks to accomplish. The internal cohesion of culture is never put into doubt (as a matter of fact, the film is predicated upon the impossibility of changing the parameters that allow culture to have such an internal cohesion), but its external manifestations are thoroughly controlled. The content is never disputed, but the style in which that content is framed is subject to mechanisms that are thoroughly prefabricated. Only within these parameters can culture move freely—an argument that gave the Cuban government the recourse to its famous subjection of culture to different "parameters" in the early 1970s.[15]

It is in relation to a secret commerce with culture that the film makes its stronger points, points that are generally lost on a non-Cuban audience. Diego's range of knowledge is not limited to Mario Vargas Llosa and contemporary Latin American literature: John Donne and Cavafy, Maria Callas and Giselle, they all coexist with Cuban nineteenth-century women poets, with treatises on Havana architecture, as well as with an incomplete treatise on *bugarrones* and their language in different parts of the city. The relationship between Diego as homosexual and Diego as intellectual is never precisely spelled out, except as violation of the parameters between the private (homosexuality) and the public, and as we see Diego proclaiming himself on the side of a national culture originating from the Cuban poet José Lezama Lima—classifying the different members of society in order to differentiate between them. It is clear that the film attempts to relate the homosexual to the intellectual in one body, seen and narrated by another who is not torn between the contradictions of sex and culture but between two versions (the official and the "dissident"). But what is not clear is how Diego represents to himself the opposition that has been given by the system. In other words, to what extent is his sense of alienation due to homosexuality or to the version and vision of culture that he sustains?

Needless to say, given the situation at hand, one could not expect Diego to distinguish between both. Diego is totally committed to Havana, to its people, to Cuban social problems, and above all, to Cuban culture: "Entre una picha y la cubanía, la cubanía" (If I have to choose between a dick and Cuba, I choose Cuba), he explains at one point. In a remarkable passage that has been excised in the translation from story to film, Diego explains to David the different kinds of desire that exist within what the revolution wants to normalize and categorize as homosexual. Diego's discourse is like that of a modern day Virgil guiding a young Dante through the labyrinths of passion, or of a Petronius voicing the varieties of sexual experience to be found in a tropical Rome:

Los homosexuales caemos en otra clasificación aún más interesante que la que te explicaba el otro día. . . . Esta escala la determina la disposición del sujeto hacia el deber social o la mariconería. Cuando la balanza se inclina al deber social, estás en presencia de un homosexual. Somos aquellos—en esta categoría me incluyo—para quienes el sexo ocupa un lugar en la vida pero no el lugar de la vida. Como los héroes o los activistas políticos, anteponemos el Deber al Sexo. La causa a la que nos consagramos está antes que todo. En mi caso el sacerdocio es la Cultura nacional, a la que dedico lo mejor de mi intelecto y mi tiempo. . . . Los maricones no merecen explicación aparte, como todo lo que queda a medio camino entre una y otra cosa: los comprenderás cuando te defina a las locas, que son muy fáciles de conceptualizar. Tienen todo el tiempo un falo incrustado en el cerebro y sólo actúan por y para él. La perdedera de tiempo es su característica fundamental. Si el tiempo que invierten en flirtear en parques y baños públicos lo dedicaran al trabajo socialmente útil, ya estaríamos llegando a eso que ustedes llaman comunismo y nosotros paraíso. Las más vagas de todas son las llamadas de carroza. A estas las odio por fatuas y vacías, y porque por su falta de discreción y tacto, han convertido en desafíos sociales actos tan simples y necesarios como pintarse las uñas de los pies.

(We homosexuals fall into another classification that is even more interesting. . . . This scale is determined by the subject's disposition toward social duty or toward faggotry. When the scales tip toward social duty, you are in the presence of a homosexual. We are those—I include myself in this category—for whom sex occupies a place in life but not the place of life. As heroes or political activists, we put Duty before Sex. The cause to which we are devoted is before all. In my case my priesthood is national Culture, to which I dedicate the best of my intellect and time. . . . Faggots deserve no separate explanation, as everything which is midway between one thing and another: you will understand when I define queens for you, for these are easy to conceptualize. They have a dick inserted in their brains at all times, and they only act because and for it. . . . The laziest ones of all are the flaming queens. Those I hate because they are fatuous and empty, and because given their lack of discretion and tact they have turned into social defiance simple and necessary acts, such as painting one's toenails.)[16]

The reader understands that this whole discourse is meant to instruct but also to seduce the young David with the blatant truth of a sexuality that is never clear-cut but, rather, one that belongs to different registers, which are in turn explained by the master sociologist, who includes himself in the definition as that type of gay man who is properly called a "homosexual" (as opposed to faggots, queens, and the like, Diego explains) and who presents the revolution with no problem other than those entertained in Gutiérrez Alea's depiction of the scene. It is, as Diego would have it, a question of style, for the cultured homosexual given a choice between a good lay and serious, disciplined research would choose the latter. That Diego wants us to believe this or wants to fool his reader into believing this is a different matter altogether. The truth content of this discourse is apparently not subject to interpretation or disputation, given that it is uttered precisely by a member of the tribal category at hand. In other words, it is irrelevant whether what he asserts is true or not. One may create a different taxonomy where all culture queens lie to themselves and to others, where they like to pretend that they are above the fray, where this is part and parcel of their system of control, of their self-delusion, of their self-hatred, or of their deception: as Diego himself says, quoting from Lezama in the story, "Sé que la bondad de los maricones es de doble filo" (I know that the generosity of queers is double-edged). But the subject who is Diego already speaks from the standpoint of a certain position of implicit power, and as such, it makes no sense to negate it in terms of *ideology* in order to oppose his taxonomies to others that are more real, more "truthful," and, thus, less "ideological" because of his desire to include himself in the category of the intellectual and distance himself from the other "locas" that he does not defend but, rather, condemns.

I argue that this taxonomy is what makes Diego into an emblem, for it is in this static and at the same time dynamic system where the intellectual joins the homosexual and both collaborate with an other to whom the spectacle is offered. Not that one necessarily has to condemn Diego for seeking an alliance with the intellectual class, for it is only from his social and systemic repression that Diego refers back to himself as subject, within ideological parameters that he has inherited from the society as a whole. The point of these different strata of homosexual society is that they have as their aim an identification of the self within a repressive circumstance.[17] It is, always and ultimately the self, the one who produces knowledge, forms discourse, and taxonomizes for his own pleasure. In the end, this perverse instrumentalizing of power is the only one that Diego can fling back at his own society as a response to the repression that he himself has suffered. The fact that he flings it back as sheer pleasure, in perverting the categories of Marxist production for his own benefit, should not prevent us from noticing that his taxonomies of sexual desire clearly demarcate a hierarchy where sex is defined first in terms of its social worth, and then in relation to productivity. The subjects that form part of Diego's exact and exacting taxonomies are fixed even within their apparently fluid construction, which runs the gamut crowned by the culture queen, and ends by categorizing segments of society in terms of their apparent interest or disinterest in "productive" or "unproductive" sex. The apparent neutrality of the taxonomical grid is as a matter of fact quite rigid—no *loca de carroza* can belong to the cultured realm—while in itself producing its own biases for the sake of the reader's pleasure (the more obvious reactionary effect of having Diego critique and participate in terms of the *locas'* painting of their toenails, implying that he does the same thing and wants to do it with impunity, without political motivation, or his constant referring to himself in the feminine gender).

The more perverse reading of this passage concerns precisely the visibility to which it subjects the entire homosexual population, a visibility that is even more important given its absence from the film—Diego is, with one exception, an isolated and alienated character. I am not referring merely to the fact that all of Diego's public and private, visible and invisible behavior differs from the "morally reprehensible" categories that he lists. What I am questioning is how this paragraph functions within the imperative of visibility that guides not only Senel Paz's story (representing homosexuals) but the film to which it is translated. For in spite of all arguments to the contrary, *Fresa y chocolate* and "El lobo, el bosque y el hombre nuevo" show that no behavior can escape or can ever be freed from the constraint of having to be normalized, analyzed, and finally, subjected to taxonomy. Sex can never be anything but something that is permanently other, when the otherness of sex is what distinguishes but not defines the subject.[18]

As an allegory that has been financed, distributed, and filmed by the very state that in the same film points the accusatory finger at itself and accepts the social and political costs of repressing some of its most loyal members solely because of their "flaw" or "difference," *Fresa y chocolate* is, to quote Langston Hughes, a kind of montage of a dream deferred: the possibility for the state and for the illustrated intellectual class to redeem and reform themselves, to say that the state that *is* (at the present) is not the state that *was*, while, at the same time, reserving for itself the right to make claims about what nationality and culture mean. In a sense, the film is interesting precisely because one feels that the unbiased totality of the given situation that it presents has gotten too out of hand for that same literate class to manage at a time when the collapse of the socialist bloc has left Cuba to navigate alone in unfamiliar waters.

But it is precisely within the context of this open address to a messy and conflictive situation that Gutiérrez Alea and Senel Paz are able to present the homosexual. But it is precisely because of this representation of the homosexual that the sense of visibility given in *Fresa y chocolate* must remain suspect, for only in the realm of power could power itself apologize for its own misdeeds: it is the prerogative of the powerful to be magnanimous. Power, Foucault warned, cannot simply be explained away as repressive:

> If power were anything but repressive, if it ever did anything but say no, do
> you really think one would be brought to obey it? What makes power hold

good, what makes it accepted, is simply the fact that it doesn't only weigh on us as a force that says no, but that it traverses and produces things, it induces pleasure, forms knowledge, produces discourse. It needs to be considered as a productive network which runs through the whole social body, much more than as a negative instance whose function is repression.[19]

Thus understood, the point is not to condemn or defend *Fresa y chocolate*, for condemnation and defense belong to the set of moral parameters that are given precisely within the network of power and that force us to participate within its ideological apparatus. The point here, rather, would be at once to decry the *given* state of affairs while also understanding that what is being offered is always a partial view. Because the currency that circulates around the film reveals homosexuality to be principally an issue of intellectuals and not an issue of the *locas de carroza*'s relations to the system, the problem has to be seen as it is inscribed and articulated through culture. *Fresa y chocolate* in this way represents to itself whole areas of Cuban culture whose repression is not the points of origin for a contentious view of Cuban culture but, rather, the point of origin for a sense of nostalgia. Because of this nostalgia, one can only create an ambiguous text that uses as emblem that figure that is the most ambivalent of all: the homosexual. And what is presented as the homosexual can only be an indecisive text, unclear in its melancholia. Its subjects finally cannot explain their actions or behavior to themselves, except by recourse to order. That there would be a different "take" if the acceptance were predicated on other members of the taxonomy is without question.[20] What *Fresa y chocolate* portrays, in a sense, is the homosexual as a fatal sign in the tropic of revolution—fatal precisely because of the central position that he assumes within an accepted and tolerated degree of marginality.

It is within the context of this critique that one can then go back to Argüelles and Rich's canonical understanding of the repressive wave of the late sixties and read it as an apologia for that same cultured class that has taxonomized itself within the system:

> The lesbian and homosexual male intelligentsia, now concentrated in the Cuban Writers and Artists' Union (UNEAC), made no public counter-critique on the issue of homosexuality. The homosexual resistance and survival strategies of the time were largely private, individual in nature, and lacked effective oppositional qualities. As a result, the silence permitted the PSP analysis to assume undisputed hegemony even in intellectual circles. Among many reasons for the absence of any such public gay counter-critique

and resistance in this period, three stand out. Foremost was the lack of a tradition of feminist discourse and, thus, of any liberating and substantive base for discussions of sexual order and gender politics. Another reason lay in the contemporary conception of homosexuality: as a legacy of the pre-revolutionary period, homosexuality was still seen, by both the Cuban gay and straight worlds, as something performed in the dark with little or no nonsexual implications. Self-interest dictated the third reason: many closeted intellectuals who were bringing Cuba international recognition feared the loss of their personal privilege—especially the loss of their ability to travel abroad, which allowed so much latitude in their own sexual expression—if they spoke out against the official stand on homosexuality.[21]

Repression, I argue, was always based on a community whose allegiance was central to the state and to culture—on whose very centrality the issue of the law is predicated. One must forcefully contrast this retrenchment into the closet with the degree of at least ambivalently open polemic entertained both in the prerevolutionary *Ciclón*, as well as in the postrevolutionary *Lunes de Revolución*, since a similar assessment is going on in Cuba at this present time (in the mid-1990s). The impression that one gets is precisely not that there was no available gay countercritique but that every element of a possible gay countercritique was stifled, forced to see its own homosexuality under the sign of a fatality, as a "damned difference." In this sense, the revolution *created* and thus could give us only the *tragic* gay intellectual out of a model present in the poetry of Emilio Ballagas or in Lezama Lima himself—or better still, reinforced the tragedy and the malaise of being homosexual precisely at the point when this malaise was about to come out into the open, out of the dissident members of that same revolutionary situation. This is surely what Argüelles and Rich mean when they talk about pre-1965 homosexuals as seeing their own sexuality as "something performed in the dark." But even a cursory glance at cultural artifacts of the period belies this assessment, for what strikes the researcher is precisely the free-flowing eros of the Havana cultural milieu. Once again, in this case, Argüelles and Rich are prey to their native informants, to the literate homosexuals who appear in Senel Paz's story.

The cultured homosexuals who remained, and who are metonymized in *Fresa y chocolate*, negotiated their position precisely by virtue of their degrees of distance with the *locas de carroza* and *maricones*—those who are the lowest of the low, in terms of gay and straight society. The whole issue begs and precludes the identification with these *locas*, for identifying with them, assuming their plight and their sense of liberty, is denied those whose transactions are with culture.[22] One could imagine that the frustration and hostility of those who are forced to leave, like Diego, would erupt in operatic terms, years later, in a scene not unlike the one Argüelles and Rich recount in horror: "In 1984, when a well-known Cuban writer came to lecture at the University of Gainesville in Florida, he was greeted in the hallway by hostile anti-Castro protesters screaming 'maricón sagrado' [sacred faggot] at him.[23] The point is not to condemn or justify this scene at this point in time but to understand that rather than being the example of some atavistic homophobia, this incident is the unfortunate result of the climate of opportunism and self-interest that homosexual intellectuals became immersed in. The high drama of Revolution produces the comic opera of the screaming furies of exile. In contrast, deception and ambivalence seem to guide the sad melancholias of sons and daughters:

> While their sexuality may be an open secret inside Cuba, many lesbians and gay males who participate in cultural and academic exchanges with the United States become more guarded when abroad, fearful of how homosexual issues are utilized in the war against the Cuban revolution. But many still take the opportunity to visit lesbian and gay bars and bathhouses in New York or San Francisco. Ironically, their own adjustment to a greater social integration in Cuba causes them increasingly to feel out of place in these sites, viewing their sexual consumerism as bizarre. Some, like Jorge, an artist, contend that "for all the repression, there is more true sexuality for gays in Cuba."[24]

Consumers of capitalist sex thus become isolated members of a tribal category whose sexuality is economized within bathhouses, where the simulacra of sex performs an alienation that is less true in relation to its context than that of the repressive regime that forces the brotherhood of socialist queens to integrate themselves within a nominally progressive system that persists in dislodging the expression of gay sexuality for the benefit of social integration—separating style from context, effeminacy from culture.

The progressive position is not, of course, that the minority adjust to the position of the majority but that members of the majority themselves understand that the sense of power invested in sheer numbers forces them to acquiesce and to accommodate the desires of those who otherwise would feel cast off. *Fresa y chocolate* seems to take a step in this direction but does so still arguing for the inner cohesion of a culture—albeit this time not from the point of view of the loud and boisterous theater of collective desires but from the point of view of the minority itself. For it is the culture of *Orígenes* that Diego presents as the essence of *cubanía*—a culture distinguishing between inner and outer realm, consigning privacy and nationhood as essential elements always to be found inside, with its a priori sense of what is Cuban and what is not that paradoxically allows Diego to furnish the system with the same ideology that will continue to expel him from the paradise of others. And it is in this sense that *Fresa y chocolate* can be construed only as the swan song of an intellectual class that will be unable to overcome the parameters that are used to repress its members. This may be the time and place to mourn for those choices, the film seems to argue, but perhaps it is more important to point out the *givenness* of those choices in order not to work against a Cuban gay discourse that could be something other than the reflection of the hyperventilated social opera, with its heavy dose of high drama. The choices, at this point, are equally dramatic and as real as those of the past. The difference is that the future text must render all of its contradictions visible.

• NOTES

1. The particularities of the Cuban relationship to the United States are explored in Louis A. Pérez, Jr., *Cuba and the United States: Ties of Singular Intimacy* (Athens: University of Georgia Press, 1990).

2. The literature on the Cuban Revolution and homosexuality is vast. The most important book is, of course, Allen Young's *Gays under the Cuban Revolution* (San Francisco: Grey Fox Press, 1981). Other important pieces include Lourdes Argüelles and B. Ruby Rich's "Homosexuality, Homophobia and Revolution: Notes Toward an Understanding of the Cuban Lesbian and Gay Male Experience, Part 1," *Signs* 9.4 (1984): 686–87, which produced its share of polemical ripostes that are quoted throughout this essay. Among these, the most important one is found in the special issue of the journal *Mariel* dedicated to homosexuality in Cuba, quoted below. Also useful is the essay by Laura Gotkowitz and Richard Turits, "Liberation Little by Little: Sex and Ideology in Cuba," *Gay Community News* 12.11 (29 September 1984): 8–10, which supports Rich and Argüelles's thesis. Finally, there is Marvin Leiner's *Sexual Politics in Cuba: Machismo, Homosexuality and AIDS* (Boulder: Westview Press, 1994).

3. Virgilio Piñera, "Piñera teatral," *Teatro completo* (Havana: Ediciones R, 1960).

4. The idea of revolution as theater underlies Carlos Victoria's recent novel *La travesía secreta* (Miami: Ediciones Universal, 1994), which recounts the whole period of the late sixties and early seventies in Havana by focusing on an adolescent's interaction with a theater group that wants to produce a traditional, conventional Chekhov play and not Grotowski or Artaud's Theater of Cruelty. The irony is that in not performing the latter and choosing to escape to the nineteenth-century realistic theater, the theatrical troupe, composed of artists alienated from the intellectual milieu, is repressed in the early seventies, along with others who think like them.

5. I would add to the terms of Argüelles and Rich's account of homosexuality as an issue of privacy that privacy ceases to be a criterion when a subject isolates an aspect of his or her life from others. To index sexuality as private because the state or society points it out as a private realm is analogous to publicly stating a silence. It seems to me we should distinguish between these silences and privacy. For a detailed critique of Argüelles and Rich, see Ana María Simo and Reinaldo García Ramos, "Hablemos claro," *Mariel, Revista de Literatura y Arte* 2.5 (1984): 9–10.

6. Allen Young also faults the overreliance on the Soviet model as the principal cause for the desire to "clean up" Cuba. See Young, *Gays under the Cuban Revolution*, chap. 2, 14–33.

7. Simo and García Ramos make a useful distinction at this point. They do not deny that Cuban discourse was immersed in homophobia before the revolution. What they argue, convincingly in my view, is that homophobia after 1959 was institutionalized and politicized out of what the revolution called its general political considerations, namely, its growing militarization, its repressive and homogenizing general character, and the utilizing of homosexuals as a kind of outlet for the frustrations of the population at large. See their "Hablemos claro." This belies what Gotkowitz and Turits examine as the general framework for homosexuality in Cuba, that the state and particularly the National Working Group on Sex Education represent a kind of "vanguard of sexual politics vis a vis its population." To Simo and García Ramos's contextualizing of the repressive state, the following passage from Gotkowitz and Turits, "Liberation Little by Little," is, in itself, ambivalent: "We asked Monika Krause why the books used for sex education were equivocal, and somewhat contradictory. She answered that the revolution has always been careful not to step far beyond the consciousness of the people or to alienate them. 'We have to be patient, making steps forward little by little; in performing our sex education work, we have already very often broken the tolerance limits of our people'" (8). That sex education was itself instrumentalized within the context of an institutional framework but that it nevertheless entertains the notion of itself as part of an enlightened vanguard with regard to which the people ("our people") are more conservative is in itself an equivocal notion.

8. All subsequent quotes from Gutiérrez Alea and Gilda Santana are from a special issue of the Spanish journal *Viridiana* 7 (1994) dedicated to *Fresa y chocolate*. Here I quote from 119.

9. "Almendros and Arenas on the Beach" (unpublished manuscript, Cambridge University).

10. Allegory always entails an excess of meaning. For Angus Fletcher, in *Allegory: The Theory of a Symbolic Mode* (Ithaca: Cornell University Press, 1964), "allegory says one thing and means another. It destroys the normal expectation we have about language, that our words 'mean what they say'" (2). Furthermore, "The whole point of allegory is that it does not need to be read exegetically; it often has a literal level that makes good enough sense all by itself. But somehow this literal surface suggests a peculiar doubleness of intention, and while it can, as it were, get along without interpretation, it becomes much richer and more interesting if given interpretation" (7). A broader reading of allegory is given by Walter Benjamin in *The Origin of German Tragic Drama*, trans. John Osborne (London: Verso Books, 1977), including a brooding meditation on the relationship between allegory and melancholia: "For the only pleasure the melancholic permits himself, and it is a powerful one, is allegory" (185).

11. Clarity and luminosity is underscored throughout Alea's narration of the way in which the film was made, as when Alea talks of the beauty of Havana (120). Throughout the final version of the script, Senel Paz points out how the camera's gaze focuses differently on the city, underscoring what David feels at a particularly given moment.

12. Alea and Santana, *Viridiana*, 121.

13. That this would not be necessarily a problem (or that it would produce a different set of problems) were the film to employ a homosexual actor as such begs the question of representation. The same goes for the given or supposed sexuality of the director or of the scriptwriter. What is not immediately evident in the case of filming is carried over to the choice of actors and to their development on the film.

14. Alea and Santana, *Viridiana*, 131.

15. For a first-person account of the effects of the "parametrización del arte en Cuba," see René Cifuentes "Los parámetros del paraíso," *Mariel* 2.5 (1984), 12.

16. Senel Paz, "El lobo, el bosque y el hombre nuevo" (Havana: Imprenta de la Dirección de Información, Ministerio de Cultura, 1991), unpaged.

17. I would join this passage to the taxonomy that Reinaldo Arenas examines in a Cuban jail in *Before Night Falls*, trans. Dolores Koch (Harmondsworth: Penguin, 1993), where the social classification reproduces, in prison, that of Diego in *Fresa y chocolate*. Arenas's position as a witness of the degrading spectacle of a Cuban prison is related to the definition of the self that tries to hold together self as a writer and as a homosexual. It is clear that the regime arrests Arenas as an intellectual and that, in prison, he can comfort himself with that fact as he examines, with horror, what the system does to jailed homosexuals (see, in particular, 177–201). Arenas also taxonomized, as does Diego, but his taxonomies include areas left out in Diego's discourse. For Arenas, there are "dog-collar gays" who are constantly being arrested, "common gays," "closet gays," and the "royal gays" who "because of close contact with the Maximum Leader or especially important work with the state security apparatus, or any similar reason, can afford to be openly gay, to have a scandalous life, and at the same time to hold an important public office, travel freely at home, leave the country and come back, cover themselves with jewels and clothes, and even have a private chauffeur" (78). The one critique that one could level at Arenas is that of not cataloguing himself within the catalogue, for it is obvious that he does not really belong to any of the categories that he presents.

18. Readers could argue that I have submitted Diego and his situation to the claims of a reality that is not immediately self-evident, given the fact that *Fresa y chocolate* has chosen fiction (or a fictional character with all of his consequent ambivalences) as its mode of presentation. But it seems interesting precisely to examine how the film arises from an intellectual construct that in itself sabotages its own nominally progressive aims. Again, the case of *Philadelphia* is pertinent here (even if we have to nuance our claims because one film comes out of the collusion of private, Hollywood interest and the other out of the hands of the state), for at this point in time and even in the Cuban context, a film such as *Fresa y chocolate* is meant to elicit, from an intellectual audience, an anticipated nostalgia for a time and a possibility that never was.

19. Michel Foucault, "Truth and Power," in *Power/Knowledge: Selected Interviews and Other Writings, 1972–1977*, ed. Colin Gordon, trans. Colin Gordon, Leo Marshall, John Mepham, and Kate Soper (New York: Pantheon Books, 1980), 119.

20. The issue would be different, of course, if this film had chosen to present a gay outlaw in the sense defined by Leo Bersani in *Homos* (Cambridge: Harvard

University Press, 1995), 113–81. Needless to say, such a portrayal was already discarded because of the appeal to a broad proportion of the population that Gutiérrez Alea sought. Still, the film does present Diego as a kind of outlaw, not precisely as one who saves art "from the preemptive operations of institutionalized culture" but, rather, as one who would like to see his own notion of art within the context of the institutions.

21. Argüelles and Rich, "Homosexuality, Homophobia and Revolution," 691.

22. In this sense, Diego is much less moralistic than his Anglo-American counterparts, for he realizes, after his whole disquisition on gayness, that the same parameters hold for the heterosexual side of society, while belying Argüelles and Rich's central tenet as to the degrees of latitude of the revolution: "Homosexuals who chose to stay in Cuba became even more guarded yet continued to believe that the substantial material and emotional benefits they were deriving from the revolution outweighed the pain of repressing or concealing their sexuality" (692).

23. Argüelles and Rich, "Homosexuality, Homophobia and Revolution," part 2, *Signs* 11 (1985): 133.

24. Argüelles and Rich, "Homosexuality, Homophobia and Revolution," part 1, 697.

Part Three

Family Values

10 *Donna J. Guy*

Mothers Alive and Dead

Multiple Concepts of Mothering in Buenos Aires

Mothering has many meanings for Argentines. Some beliefs stem from popular culture and are linked to a higher value placed on birthing than on raising a child. According to popular Argentine religious lore, between 1820 and 1860 in San Juan province, Dalinda Antonia Correa died of thirst on a dusty road with an infant by her side. Miraculously, her breast milk continued after her death, and the suckling and the mother were found by mule-team drivers. No one seems to know what happened to the infant, but many accounts say that he died shortly thereafter.

The fate of the infant seems to be unrelated to that of the mother, who became a popular, uncanonized saint. Except for the last episode, her life was unknown, but as a saint, she was later assigned other good works. La Difunta Correa (the dead Correa, her religious name) was then praised as a woman who had patriotically spoken out against tyrants before her death, as a wife who followed her husband after he was impressed into service by a dictatorial political leader, and as a mother who sustained her infant even in death. According to Juan Draghi Lucero,

> Remembering her glorifies fidelity to an absent spouse and . . . gives meaning to her gift of her breasts to her son in her moment of agony. She is the perfect

woman according to popular definitions. She is submissive and self denying and because of this she feels God at her side in His Holy Glory.[1]

Subsequently, La Difunta Correa became the patron saint of truck drivers. Throughout Argentina roadside altars provide opportunities to leave offerings, usually by men. There are also formal sites where men and women pray for miracles. Although La Difunta Correa's miracles—through not only her miraculous milk but also her responses to prayers—have never been accepted by the formal Catholic Church, she has the most elaborately developed set of shrines and rituals of any popular saint in Argentina. Is this the Argentine paradigm of an ideal mother?[2]

During the same period of civil wars, in 1848, the orders of another Argentine despot, Juan Manuel de Rosas, shattered sensibilities by sending a pregnant mother-to-be to the firing squad. Camila O'Gorman, guilty of marrying a priest, was executed despite the colonial tradition of sparing pregnant women. This time the state intentionally created its own martyr and presented the nation with another dead woman to promote order and stability for Rosas's authoritarian regime. Although Camila has not been celebrated as a popular saint, a movie was made about her immediately after the demise of the military dictatorships in the 1980s.[3]

The depiction of Dalinda's death in religious art and practice, along with the retelling of Camila's death in modern movies, recalls the nineteenth-century practice of using the image of a "dead woman . . . to regenerate the order of society, to eliminate destructive forces."[4] Elisabeth Bronfen has argued that during times of change and instability, the symbolic sacrifice of a woman helps reestablish "an order that was momentarily suspended due to her presence."[5] These women were both real and symbolic, and their sacrifice may have served to stabilize society, but as mothers of the future citizenry, they could never fulfill their patriotic duty. Thus new forms of female patriotism had to be envisioned and constructed to both stabilize society as well as protect the future of the state.

It took many years for state officials to develop these new ideas. Civil wars lasted until 1862, and basic civil, commercial, and penal codes were not fully in place until the 1880s. There was no national public health organization until 1880, and for many years it dealt in the main with the ports and with charting the course of epidemic disease. During this time municipal entities, principally the government of the city of Buenos Aires, devised mothering campaigns that ultimately became incorporated into national policies. The capital city was particularly concerned with the behavior of the many European immigrants who flocked there between 1880 and 1914.

Republican motherhood eventually had little in common with the image of the martyred mother whose child could not serve the nation. Between the nineteenth century when La Difunta Correa displayed her miraculous breasts and Camila sacrificed herself and her child to love, and the first decades of the twentieth century, new images of appropriate mothers were constructed by secular and medical authorities. Their concerns stemmed not from the act of mothering but, rather, from its absence. The modern mother was measured in terms of how well she raised her child, not just how many she bore. She also placed devotion to children above devotion to spouse.

Mothering concepts in Argentina and other nation states embracing modernity in the late nineteenth century were deeply affected by the formation of modern public health campaigns to lower infant mortality rates.[6] Prior to that time, infant death was common and taken for granted. In many Catholic societies elaborate ceremonies marked the funerals of *angelitos*, dead children under the age of seven.[7] Once public health physicians began to define good mothers as well as more antiseptic practices of birthing, and cities constructed adequate sewage and potable-water facilities, infant mortality rates in many cities began to fall. Recent studies of European, North American, and Latin American cities confirm that extensive statistics regarding birth weight and survival were kept in order to confirm progress.[8]

Initially, knowledge of prenatal care was limited. Practical concerns about care for children after birth—how mothers fed them, whether they kept them clean and warm, and whether they had them vaccinated against smallpox—became important components of urban campaigns, ones that gradually spread to the countryside as well. From the perspective of the modern public health physician, good mothers devoted themselves to their children, and the measurement of maternal qualities was linked to the production of healthy youngsters. As Dr. Henry F. Helmholz of the Mayo Clinic announced to representatives of the Eighth Pan American Child Congress in 1942,

> The infant mortality rate is no longer considered the only index of child-health progress. . . . It is not enough that more babies shall survive their first year of life. . . . The objective of child-health work is to protect, promote, and conserve the health of children from the prenatal period through adolescence.[9]

For these reasons a very different view of mothering had appeared in Buenos Aires by 1910. In 1901 María Sampó, an unmarried mother, left three-year-old Luisa Elena at the orphanage Casa de Expósitos operated by the Sociedad de Beneficencia, a charitable organization. Sampó asserted that poor health and insufficient financial resources stood in the way of her raising the child. The society, comprising elite married women, gave Luisa Elena to Señora de Cestino for foster care. In 1910 Sampó had a change of circumstances or heart and went to the Civil Registry to enter the birth of Luisa Elena. She requested the return of her child. Displeased by Sampó's attitude toward mothering, the society, Luisa Elena's legal guardian, went to court to protest removal of Luisa Elena from the custody of her foster parents.

When the judges agreed with the society and ruled that Sampó was unworthy of *patria potestad*, or parental authority over her child, Sampó appealed. The comments of an appeals judge, Dr. Baires, indicated that there were clear standards of good mothering. Sampó, whom he always identified pejoratively as "the actress," had "denied her daughter maternal support ... by failing to recognize her responsibility in terms of her voluntary maternity." Furthermore, she "had failed to carry out other fundamental activities linked to her quality as a mother." These included her reluctance to go to the Civil Register for nine years, as well as her failure to demonstrate "maternal affection for her child." He berated her for having denied her daughter affection (literally her lap [*su regazo*]) and her name for selfish reasons. The appeal was denied. To him the heart and the lap, rather than the breast, were the sites of maternal qualities.[10]

What is a good mother, and who defines women's responsibility toward their children? What type of body image and spiritual characteristics were linked to the modern mother? In Argentina, as in most other countries in the late nineteenth century and early twentieth, motherhood was socially and politically constructed as a result of gender, economic, social, political, and religious factors. As Jane Jenson has pointed out in her comparison of state policies toward working women and infants in France and the United States, the formation of such policies "cannot be simply read off the large-scale changes occurring in many industrial societies at the time." Rather, she continues, "we must locate these programs in the politics of that time, assessing the relationship between strategies of many actors" including public health officials, political parties, organized labor, and moral reformers. In a similar fashion, the study of motherhood involves an analysis to determine how definitions of "a good-enough mother" arise in modern societies.[11]

Religious values are central to the discussion of mothering. As in most Latin American nations, the Roman Catholic religion was officially recognized and served as a powerful cultural and legal force in Argentina. In its formative phase, it idealized the celibate life linked to a spiritual (Father, Son, Holy Ghost) rather than a worldly family. Thus as Clarissa Atkinson observed, notions of Catholic motherhood developed late and often focused on idealizing the suffering and self-abnegation of the Virgin Mary. La Difunta Correa, even though not recognized by the official church, represented a very traditional view of the self-sacrificing mother. Camila, in contrast, defied the rules of celibacy to form a relationship with a priest. The acknowledgment of an activist rather than passive reproductive Catholic motherhood emerged only with the formation of a male medical ideology in the sixteenth and seventeenth centuries, and Catholic countries lagged behind Protestant countries such as Great Britain in the publication of medical manuals devoted to mothering.[12]

The absence of a strong medical literature on mothering in Catholic countries, added to the existence of convents inhabited by celibate women, led to practices of turning unwanted infants over to the church. In turn, the church supported this custom, particularly in conjunction with the use of the foundling wheel, or *turno*, as a viable alternative to infanticide and abortion.[13] In that way the church with its virginal, celibate nuns replaced rather than educated mothers. Thus, in many countries with large Catholic populations, the concept of "a good-enough mother" was defined initially by neither the medical profession nor the church but when civil authorities needed to establish policies to keep poor mothers from abandoning their children.

According to John Boswell's erudite study, in Catholic Europe from the Middle Ages onward, child abandonment was a significant factor that in the nineteenth century became epidemic. Some nineteenth-century Italian convents had to care for thousands of abandoned children—as many as one-third of all children born in some cities. In France and Russia, state authorities had been devising plans to deal with abandoned children since the eighteenth century. Ensnared in the antiabortion stance of the Catholic and other orthodox churches, influenced by legal issues and concepts of honor, and often devastated by poverty, many Catholic women abandoned their children. Confronted with this stark social reality, political and social elites began to examine how different groups viewed the rights, duties, and responsibilities of parents.[14]

Newly independent Argentina faced many similar circumstances. From the late eighteenth century onward, child abandonment in Buenos Aires had been a notable, if grim, feature of urban life. By 1881 the Casa de Expósitos was already housing 1,147 infants.[15] The issue became particularly acute after 1883 when, for the first time, more than 500 infants were left at the city's orphanage in one year. In six years time the number doubled. Between 1870, when there were 186,320 city dwellers, and 1895, when there were 663,854, the average number of abandoned or orphaned children deposited each year at the Society had increased from 644 to 1,817.[16] Child abandonment rates paralleled illegitimacy. By 1889 the number of illegitimate births had reached 2,798, or 12.6 percent. After 1900 the proportion rose to 15 percent, a total of 4,987.[17]

If these statistics alarmed urban authorities, the percentage of women who refused to recognize their illegitimate children was even more disturbing. An 1890 Buenos Aires public health report noted that of 680 illegitimate children born and recognized by one or both parents, fathers recognized 395 infants, whereas mothers recognized only 239. This pattern repeated itself between 1900 and 1909 with 23,456 illegitimate births: fathers, 13,637; mothers, 7,175; both parents, 2,644. Mothers' refusals to recognize their children occurred more frequently because these women, socially castigated because they could not get their partners to acknowledge paternity, were forbidden by Argentine law from taking these men to court and were faced with all the financial responsibilities of raising their children.[18]

In Argentina the plight of abandoned children quickly became a secular problem because the formation of the Sociedad de Beneficencia was the result of early state efforts to stem the power and authority of the Catholic Church. Catholic ideology, however, continued to influence legal attitudes toward families. Furthermore, the society, never given adequate funds to operate its establishments, was forced to seek inexpensive labor. After 1880 it relied upon orders of Catholic nuns to staff its many homes and hospitals.

Despite the strong influence of religious orders within the Sociedad de Beneficencia, Argentine governments continued to assert secular authority in the matter of abandoned children. In 1829 provincial authorities created the Defensor de Menores, a position held by elite men charged with caring for paupers and young children. In December 1890 the mayor of Buenos Aires created the Patronato Asistencia de la Infancia, or Children's Aid Society. This was also operated by elite men allied with women who belonged to the Sociedad de Beneficencia. Only partly subsidized by the city government, the Patronato supported its ambitious plans by raising money to operate day-care centers, schools for mothers, and agricultural education centers. Through the combination of the Sociedad de Beneficencia, the Patronato Asistencia de la Infancia, and the Defensores de Menores, the Argentine political elite attempted to create a hegemonic discourse about mothering. This process combined religious, secular, medical, feminist, and upper-class views defining the parameters of what ultimately became bourgeois notions of parenting, and particularly the role of mothers.[19]

Basic legal parental responsibilities were outlined in the national Código Civil, or civil code, adopted in 1872. Patterned after the highly patriarchal French Napoleonic Codes, the Argentine code defined the family as legally constituted by religious marriage and whose biological descendants had clear title to inheritance. In return for this birthright children had to obey their parents and to perform tasks appropriate to their age and without compensation. Parents had their responsibilities as well. They were obligated to choose their children's professions. They were also responsible for feeding and educating their offspring to the degree that they could afford to do so. Within this family, however, only the father explicitly exercised *patria potestad*, the body of rights and obligations that parents had toward their legitimate children. Moreover, only the father could be brought to justice if he failed to feed minor children.

Only single mothers exercised *patria potestad*; married women were explicitly denied responsibilities that interfered with patriarchal privilege. They were placed in the same category as minors, blind and deaf men, nonresidents, the unemployed, and the bankrupt. This meant that the legal system, if adhered to strictly, rarely gave married women the right to care and protect biological or custodial children. There were also no provisions for complete adoption.[20]

Although the civil code was enacted after the era of La Difunta Correa and Camila O'Gorman, the same legal realities faced married mothers before the consolidation of the state as afterward. Women were needed to produce heirs and citizens, but their responsibilities after birth were unclear. If the state needed nonbiological mothers to care for children, or if it wanted to encourage mothers to be more involved in raising their children, normative practices had to change, and new ways to address legal realities had to be devised. Under these circumstances, problems confronting both the Sociedad and the Defensores were difficult. The Casa de Expósitos, increasingly crowded, offered shelter for infants but never the promise of new parents. Similarly, the Defensores de Menores found it difficult to place older children in foster homes that did not exploit the children as cheap labor. A new definition of motherhood had to be fashioned. For these reasons, the language used in the 1910 court case to deny María Sampó the right to mother her child did not exist in the 1872 law. These ideas developed rather quickly between 1880 and 1910 and were greatly influenced by the actions of feminists, physicians, Defensores, the Patronato de la Infancia and the Sociedad de Beneficencia. In the process it became clear that there was a gendered discourse influenced by class and often contested by the popular classes.

The loss of parents for whatever reason meant that either the state or some other legally defined person assumed responsibility for the child. The Código Civil provided for these cases by establishing the *tutela*, or legal guardianship. Guardians were different from parents because their rights were not inherited, and their wards did not become relatives of their relatives. Widows who did not remarry could become guardians, as could grandparents and elder brothers. Other women were ineligible, again due to unwillingness to share patriarchal privilege with most married women.[21]

Both the Argentine civil code and the institutions gradually established by municipal and national governments that dealt with child abandonment and infant mortality were patterned after institutions created in France during the seventeenth, eighteenth, and nineteenth centuries. This was due to the influence of French code laws, and Argentine liberals' respect for French revolutionary tradition. The Sociedad de Beneficencia, originally formed as a religious organization, was similar to the French Ladies of Charity Society that Saint Vincent de Paul founded in 1638 to care for abandoned children.[22]

The French Revolution of 1789 had been most explicit about the state's commitment to abandoned children:

> The Revolutionary period saw the emergence of more positive attitudes toward abandoned children, and, hence, a new policy designed to benefit them. . . . The Constitution of 1792 "proclaimed for the nation the task of raising the abandoned children" and a law of 28 June 1795 charged the nation "with the moral and physical education of *enfants trouvés*." Euphemistically, in a new egalitarian and national spirit, all *enfants trouvés*, *enfants abandonnés*, and *orphelins* were called *enfants de la Patrie*.[23]

This law was followed by another in 1801 that enabled any mother to abandon her child to a state orphanage. Although these were noble ideas, the ease with which a woman could abandon her child, added to the passage of the 1804 civil code, made it impossible for an unmarried mother to pursue the paternity of her child through the courts, leading to increased rates of abandonment. The ensuing financial burdens resulted in significant modifications in state policy. In the 1850s the French government began to enact a series of measures to make it more difficult for mothers to abandon their children. It now encouraged mothers to develop greater affective bonds with their offspring. Foundling wheels at state orphanages were closed, and more modern concepts of mothering emphasized maternal breast-feeding and more specific parenting roles for mothers.[24]

Protestant-influenced Germany pursued another approach to child abandonment. During the nineteenth century illegitimacy rates in cities like Leipzig were less than those in France and Italy, but infant mortality rates hovered around 30 percent. To deal with abandoned children, German authorities placed them in foster homes rather than setting up large orphanages. Reforms of the civil code in 1890 permitted women to assume "guardianship over persons other than their own children or grandchildren," although married women needed their husbands' permission. This provision, when applied to a foster-parenting system created by Max Taub of Leipzig, in 1883, led to a network of twelve thousand women in three hundred communities who by 1911 had adopted other women's children. This system was based upon the principle that "illegitimate children were often better off with foster families than with their own mothers, . . . described as irresponsible and mentally deficient." At the same time public health physicians attempted to reduce infant mortality by promoting breast-feeding or providing pure milk to more worthy mothers. Once again the breast and maternal milk entered the mothering discourse, not as characteristics of mothers but, rather, as replacements for them.[25]

Argentina, too, had to come to grips with illegitimacy, child abandonment, infant mortality, and wet nursing in its capital city. Like France, it could not afford to replace the system of convents with public orphanages, and unlike Germany, it was unwilling to allow women to assume guardianship over nonbiological children. To deter abandonment and protect children from inappropriate parenting, the state to tried to clarify gendered concepts of parenting.

The Sociedad de Beneficencia directly participated in the construction of mothering through its control over the Casa de Expósitos, Asilo de Huérfanas (Girls Orphanage), and Asilo de Huérfanos (Boys Orphanage). As children grew older, the Sociedad de Beneficencia had fewer places for them. Efforts were made to place children older than three in custodial care. Many of these foster children were treated as unpaid servants, living with but not as part of the family. If they were lucky, affective bonds between them and the families formed despite the legal arrangements. To facilitate this tendency, the society was among the first state-sanctioned institutions to find a way to define women's role in foster parenting. Changing the wording of the placement contracts demonstrated how the society was recognizing that women's emotional bonding and strong roles were essential to the future of orphans.

The society often allowed females to sign contracts for foster children because it realized that children needed mothering, the one thing denied them in orphanages. It did not break the law by turning children over to women because adults who signed placement contracts had no legal guardianship over their wards unless they later petitioned for such rights. If married women wanted to become guardians, they needed their husbands to sign the documents. Placement contracts offered by the society changed over time.

In 1903 Joaquín Cullen, attorney for the Sociedad de Beneficencia, drew up a contract that he believed reflected its needs and those of the parents and children. The contract explicitly identified the foster parent as a female who would be "obliged to proceed like a caring mother [*madre cariñosa*], and [attend] to the child's moral and religious training, and satisfy all the costs of sustenance for the person she is receiving into her care." The specific references to mothers and a new dimension of affective responsibility had been integrated into the contract.[26]

In contrast to the society's image of women completely linked to motherhood, Argentine feminists defined the modern woman as a mother who also enjoyed economic and social liberation. One of the first female physicians, Elvira Rawson de Dellepiane, believed that medically defined hygiene was the only method to protect modern mothers so that they could carry out their biological and social missions. Her doctoral thesis, published in 1892, began by contrasting women's reproductive role and their lack of civil rights:

> Women are destined to fulfill the most important role in the reproduction of the species. [Nevertheless] they have a delicate constitution and have been reduced by their delicate mission and by customs to carry out a secondary public role. They are deprived of the freedoms enjoyed by the other sex, forced to suffocate their passions, provided a constantly insufficient education. . . . [They] are deprived of exercise and confronted by dangers that compromise their life and destiny. In hygiene they find the saving guide to emerge unscathed from the various stages of their evolution while maintaining the functional integrity of their organs generally and particularly those that dominate their existence, i.e. their reproductive organs.[27]

When Rawson de Dellepiane discussed marriage, she argued that women entered another state of evolution, one that transformed their emotional life. "With this act [of marriage] not only does one fulfill the sacred mandate to be fruitful and multiply, women develop new sentiments such as caring for their husbands and motherly love, ones that purify all sentiments [and] moralize customs."[28] If poor women did not love their husbands and abandoned their children, poverty, not the women, was to blame. Only a noble society could resolve the problem.[29]

The biblical reference in the section on marriage was Rawson de Dellepiane's strategy to both acknowledge and contest Catholic views of abstinence. Later in the chapter she argued that single, celibate, unmarried women were sicker and died earlier than married ones, and that poor unmarried women faced a life of libertinage and decadence. To prove her point, she examined mortality statistics for 1892 by sex and marital status and found that despite the rigors of childbirth, only 319 married women died during the year compared to 377 single women.[30]

The combination of a strong feminist belief in women's productive and reproductive missions was a hallmark of Rawson de Dellepiane's long career as a feminist and freethinker. She also played a pivotal role in the formulation of modern motherhood; her thesis was published before any local feminist tracts or popular medical texts about childbirth and mothering appeared. She later was a proponent of residences for needy women about to give birth or who had recently done so. She had no intentions of extolling women like Dalinda, who had died by the side of a road, and she probably would have protested executions such as that of Camila O'Gorman. In the future mothers would be in safe, secure homes. At the First Feminine International Congress, held in Buenos Aires in 1910, she was instrumental in obtaining a declaration, published by the congress criticizing foundling homes and arguing that mothers, single or married, were worthy of social assistance. Rawson de Dellepiane also proposed to the congress that laws be passed to permit investigations of paternity and to give all women the right to be guardians.[31]

Rawson de Dellepiane was not alone in her belief that the links between women and children needed to be defended by feminists. In 1914 Raquel Camaña, a well-known educator and feminist, published an article entitled "Femeneidad." There she directly linked motherhood to democracy, as well as to the need for mothers to care for their children:

> When a woman realizes she is about to become a mother, she will understand that it is her duty to nourish this future child not only with pure air, proper foods, and appropriate exercise, but also that she must mold this little soul with spiritual tranquility, good character, wholesome happiness, and with never ending optimism; that she should avoid the consequences of downtrodden spirits, anger, and nervous crisis. And under the influence of the laws of love, she will improve herself as well as her child. This is the solution of the human condition, one that will create a vibrant democracy [*democracia vital*] more important than political or industrial democracy.[32]

Unlike the feminists who waxed nostalgic about the love created by motherhood and the need to protect the poor mother, male physicians initially approached the issue of mothering more from the perspective of simply trying to lower the rate of infant mortality and abandonment. Most of their publications contained technical advice to ensure that children survived the first year. Male doctors wanted women to act as they were being advised to act, not as a special force in the family. The exception to this was Dr. Gregorio Aráoz Alfaro's 1899 *El libro de las madres*, which stated that women had social as well as biological responsibilities toward children.

Aráoz Alfaro tentatively broached women's special social role in the chapter "Educación moral e intelectual" (Moral and intellectual education), where he pointed out that "a child should regard his parents with tenderness [*cariño*] and respect." Nevertheless, it was the mother who should show affection. As he put it, "The really affectionate mother, one who cares for her children at play, knows when she should educate them and even later, when they go to school for several hours a day, it is in this house where these children will acquire notions of moral instruction." He defined this duty as "the most noble" one for a mother. This was one of the first challenges to the patriarchal order made by a male physician. Family law stated that it was the father's role to educate children, but this doctor clearly believed that maternal affections privileged women over men in the matter of educating young children.[33] For the most part, however, Aráoz Alfaro did not dwell on mother's affective nature because he was too busy placing birthing and infant care in a medical context.

José Penna and Horacio Madero, two other distinguished public health physicians, in 1910 also lauded women's affection as an instinctive weapon in the fight against infant mortality and abandonment:

> Protecting children is an instinctive act that begins by contemplating those tender beings and meditating on the harsh path with all the obstacles that these defenseless and weak things pursue in order to grow. They have only the tenderness and caring of their mothers who guard them against everything and save them with her immense love. Nevertheless, when there is a quirk of fate and a child is left to defend itself, the horrible destiny confronting that child is nudity, life as an orphan, abandonment to a slow death.[34]

According to Penna and Madero, only aberrant mothers consciously endangered their infants. These included upper-class women who were so vain and had so many social obligations that they refused to nurse and sent their children to wet nurses; poor working-class women whose need to earn money left them weak and unable to nurse; and wet nurses who sacrificed the health of their own children in order to sell their breast milk to others. From the perspective of these specialists, women's reproductive abilities were still directly linked to breast-feeding, and their qualities as mothers were linked to class issues.[35]

If mothers did not know how to take care of their children, the state would teach them. Mariano Etchegaray published a book premised on the notion that poor women lacked parenting skills. As he put it, "The family is incapable of transmitting this information to future generations because it lives in the most complete ignorance. After all, no one is born knowing how to raise children, just as no one is born with knowledge of agriculture or horticulture."[36] For this reason, Etchegaray advocated instruction in the subject in the public schools. Instead of worrying about politics, the new Dalindas would preoccupy themselves with scientific child raising.

Eliseo Cantón's work on the problems of pregnancy and child raising had much more positive views of working-class mothers. It made a strong case that Mothers Homes, subsidized by the state, would solve the economic problems that led women to abort or abandon children, or to undergo premature births. He portrayed future mothers as having the desire but not the opportunity to be good mothers, and also argued that the watchfulness of the state would ensure the opportunity.[37]

Until the introduction of child psychology as a central issue in child rearing, which occurred in Argentina after 1920, doctors were the principal sources of official medical information about women's reproductive capacities. Friends, midwives, and popular healers [curanderas] provided women with other opinions. Physicians' scientific knowledge, however, was more highly praised and valued at a time when Argentina was trying to improve its international reputation by lowering its infant mortality rate. State recognition of public health doctors made medicine an avenue of power for female as well as male doctors. Thus it is understandable that many of the early Argentine feminists were either physicians or writers on medical topics.

Public health physicians were often sought as consultants for government agencies, particularly in Buenos Aires. One such case was the 1890 investigation prompted by the mayor to lower infant mortality. Through the study and the Patronato Asistencia de la Infancia designed to implement it, the municipality had a clear opportunity to participate in the formation of new constructs of motherhood.

In the first report, in 1892, physicians Piñero and Podestá stated:

> Few mothers understand the importance of proper infant nutrition. Guided only by their affections and good intentions of giving their child the proper foods as they understand it, . . . they are surprised many times that after so much work and effort, everything seems to be for naught as symptoms set in that can come from nothing more than improper food.[38]

This, in general terms, is what we have already observed among the children who live in tenement dwellings, and this is what motivates the intervention of hygiene and municipal authorities. The society went far beyond hypothesizing. By 1898 it had 855 members, operated one day-care center, and was about to open another. Employees had attended to 25,801 day-care children and 3,481 children who remained overnight, of whom only seventeen had died. These numbers did not indicate the percentage of children returning each day because the statistics were designed to demonstrate the need for another center.[39]

In addition to *salas-cunas* (day care centers), a manual-trades school for urban children, and agricultural schools, in 1921 the organization also created a school to teach mothers how to take care of their children "according to the most modern concepts of scientific child-raising [*puericultura*]"; the objective was to ensure the health of young children. The fact that classes were given by upper-class women who belonged to the auxiliary Sociedad de Beneficencia, intimates that there were other agendas at work, specifically including the transmission of upper-class normative values about mothering to the working classes. Furthermore, the school was a blatant effort to obtain acceptable wet nurses for infants left in the care of the society. A mother who was enrolled received room and board, classes, and a small salary in return for breast-feeding another infant along with her own. The mother-student was allowed to leave the institution only once a month for three hours, unless hired by a family. In this scenario, mothers like the Difunta Correa would have been found nursing two children, not one.[40]

The school for mothers was not the only coercive mechanism implemented in Buenos Aires to teach mothers how to take care of their children. In 1908 the municipality created a new unit within its public assistance (public health) program. Known as the Infant Care Division (Sección Protección de la Primera Infancia), it soon began to create government institutions to deal with infant mortality and child care. In November 1911 the Municipal Council passed an ordinance setting aside 30,000 pesos to install five Institutos de Puericultura throughout the city where mothers could stay with their children, places that Dr. Emilio Coni believed to be superior to outpatient clinics because doctors could monitor the mothers.

> The advantages of this system are the following: it makes it impossible for children to be abandoned by their parents; it teaches mothers how to care for their children in the most careful fashion; it makes it possible for mothers to restimulate breast secretions whose decreased flow often prompted the mothers to come to the Instituto, and thereby make it possible for them to begin feeding their children again.[41]

The 1911 funds also paid for notices in French, Italian, English, Russian, and Turkish posted in such public places as maternity hospitals, the Civil Register Office, the Immigration Hotel, and offices dealing with mothers or children. The notice advised mothers that

> the best food for a child under the age of one is mother's milk. The child thus has the right to its mother's milk and the mother has the sacred responsibility

of providing that milk. Whoever has given that child its life cannot deny it her milk.[42]

The biological mission of mothers still being emphasized was the same one that made Dalinda so famous.

There are still many aspects of the campaign to construct a definition of mothering in Argentina that remain to be explored. Nevertheless, it is clear that in the case of its capital city, representatives of local and national governments had an extremely difficult time managing the care and education of orphaned and abandoned children. Even though the power of the Catholic Church had decreased, its impact on the civil code and the immigration of poor Europeans accustomed to an extensive system of church orphanages, encouraged high rates of child abandonment because images of mothers as martyrs had been complemented by those of women who voluntarily gave up their children. City officials discovered that they needed to find custodial families willing to provide not only the food and shelter legally required of parents but also the caring and affection they would have given their own biological children. To facilitate this process, the elite had to empower the affective and hygienic image of mothering. Gradually it developed a medical and psychological vocabulary to describe appropriate "mothering."

Urban and national reformers recognized that a successful campaign to promote good mothers and reduce the number of abandoned children involved a dual strategy. The first was to find ways to discourage poor mothers from abandoning their children. Mothers were taught, as Dalinda always believed, that it was their "natural" responsibility to care for all of their children, and it was the right of newborns to receive their mothers' breast milk. But the republican mother no longer had to sacrifice her own life because she now had to raise her child herself. She would care and nurture her offspring and would be aided in this process by the state. These views, added to medical and moral education, household advice, and reforms in the economic environment all supported working class families.

Advice emanating from the upper classes, government, feminists, and public health physicians about parenting ignored the father except for his financial support and focused upon the poor mother. This advice promoted a hygienized, caring, and activist vision of reproduction to replace earlier views of mothering as a passive martyrdom. In contrast, the cult of La Difunta Correa, perpetuated mostly by truck drivers who see her as their patron saint, extols women's dedication to their husbands. Dalinda asked for a miracle to save her infant son, but she did so only after blindly following her husband into the desert. Her story, as well as herbal and spiritual practices of folk-medicine practitioners, added to advice from female relatives, all served to create a lower-class counterhegemonic argument that always created tension when it conflicted with state discourse.

The second part of state strategy, not covered in this paper, guaranteed the empowerment of women in the family through legal reform. Attempts to limit the ideological influence of the church were seen in campaigns advocating divorce, legal recognition of illegitimate children, equal rights of *patria potestad* for fathers and mothers, and adoption. These efforts proved to be much more difficult than public health campaigns directed at the poor. Nevertheless, without confronting these issues, the construction of modern mothering norms and the plight of abandoned children could never be addressed in an adequate fashion.

By the 1930s the bodily and symbolic nature of mothering had been challenged, reshaped, and redefined. Mothers were important not only for their wombs and breasts but also for their knowledge, emotional commitment, and awareness of patriotic duty. Initially absent from the body politic through patriarchal clauses of the civil code, women were written "into" mothering as a legal process by 1926. Earlier religious versions of the passive biological mother were infused with greater responsibility and activity through efforts of feminists and public health officials anxious to lower infant mortality rates and encourage mothers to keep their children. The heart of the caring mother, along with the breast of the hygienized mother were embedded into the republican vision of motherhood. Children now needed mothers' laps, their emotional nurturing, and their knowledge of scientific mothering. And although the male-dominated popular religious cult continued to idealize La Difunta Correa, the state-approved modern mother wouldn't have been caught dead in La Difunta's situation.

• NOTES

The author wishes to thank Nancy R. Hunt, Doris Sommer, Daniel Balderston, Osvaldo Barreneche, Eva Johnson, and Gary Hearn for their comments on earlier drafts.

1. Quoted in Susana Chertudi and Sara Josefina Newbery, *La Difunta Correa* (Buenos Aires: Editorial Huemul, 1978), 122.

2. For an extensive set of legends and powers attributed to La Difunta Correa, see ibid.

3. Marifran Carlson, *¡Feminismo! The Woman's Movement in Argentina from its Beginnings to Eva Perón* (Chicago: Academy Chicago, 1988), 47–48; Lily Sosa

de Newton, *Diccionario biográfico de mujeres argentinas* (Buenos Aires: privately printed, 1972), 254–55.

4. Elisabeth Bronfen, *Over Her Dead Body: Death, Femininity and the Aesthetic* (Manchester: Manchester University Press, 1992), 219.

5. Ibid., 181.

6. Valerie Fildes, Lara Marks, and Hilary Marland, *Women and Children First: International Maternal and Infant Welfare, 1870–1945* (London and New York: Routledge, 1992).

7. Texts and paintings of angelitos in Mexico from the colonial period to the present can be found in "El arte ritual de la muerte niña," a special bilingual issue of *Artes de México* 1 (1992); Nancy Scheper Hughes discusses this issue in *Death without Weeping: The Violence of Everyday Life in Brazil* (Berkeley: University of California Press, 1992).

8. Peter W. Ward, *Birth Weight and Economic Growth: Women's Living Standards in the Industrializing West* (Chicago: University of Chicago Press, 1993). Although birth weights have not been studied in Argentina, statistics on infant mortality in Buenos Aires can be found in Victoria Mazzeo, *Mortalidad infantil en la ciudad de Buenos Aires (1856–1986)* (Buenos Aires: Centro Editor de América Latina, 1993).

9. Dr. Henry F. Helmholz, "Principles Governing Organization of Maternal and Child-Health Services," *Eighth Pan American Child Congress* (Washington, D.C., 2–9 May 1942) (Washington, D.C.: Government Printing Office, 1948), 262–64.

10. AGN, Sociedad de Beneficencia, Leg. 57, fojas 449–50. Case of María Sampó vs. the Sociedad de Beneficencia, 14 December 1912.

11. Jane Jenson, "Representations of Gender: Policies to 'Protect' Women Workers and Infants in France and the United States before 1914," in *Women, the State, and Welfare*, ed. Linda Gordon (Madison: University of Wisconsin Press, 1990), 152–53. On the concept of the "good-enough mother" see Donald Woods Winnicott, *Babies and Mothers* (Reading, Mass.: Addison-Wesley, 1987).

12. Clarissa W. Atkinson, *The Oldest Vocation: Christian Motherhood in the Middle Ages* (Ithaca: Cornell University Press, 1991). The rise of male physicians is discussed on 230–32.

13. Foundling wheels were found in many convents and charitable institutions in Europe and Latin America. They consisted of a revolving wheel with compartments to place a baby in. Similar to a revolving door, they were designed in such a way that the person depositing the child could not be seen by those inside the institution.

14. John Boswell, *The Kindness of Strangers: The Abandonment of Children in Western Europe from Late Antiquity to the Renaissance* (New York: Vintage, 1988, 1990). For later time periods, see Rachel Fuchs, *Abandoned Children: Foundlings and Child Welfare in Nineteenth-Century France* (Albany: SUNY Press, 1984); David Ransel, *Mothers of Misery: Child Abandonment in Russia* (Princeton: Princeton University Press, 1988); David I. Kertzer, "Gender Ideology and Infant Abandonment in Nineteenth-Century Italy," *Journal of Interdisciplinary History* 22.1 (1991): 1–25. See also David I. Kertzer, *Sacrificed for Honor: Italian Infant Abandonment and the Politics of Reproductive Control* (Boston: Beacon Press, 1993).

15. AGN, Sociedad de Beneficencia, Casa de Expósitos, Leg. 99, foja 334.

16. Municipality of Buenos Aires, *Patronato y asistencia de la infancia en la capital de la República; Trabajos de la Comisión Especial* (Buenos Aires: El Censor, 1892), 6–12; Alberto B. Martínez, *Censo general de la población, edificación, comercio e industrias de la ciudad de Buenos Aires*, 3 vols. (Buenos Aires: Compañía Sudamericana de Billetes de Banco, 1910), 2:64.

17. Municipality of Buenos Aires, *Patronato*, 7.

18. Ibid., 8; Martínez, *Censo general* (1909), 2: 63–64, 70.

19. Juan Carlos Rébora, *La familia (boceto sociológico y jurídico)*, 2 vols. (Buenos Aires: Juan Roldán, 1926), 1:224.

20. Argentine Republic, *Código Civil de la República Argentina* (Buenos Aires: Pablo E. Coni, 1874), Título III, Art. 1, 2, 4, 44, Título VI, VII.

21. Argentine Republic, *Código civil*, Título VII.

22. Fuchs, *Abandoned Children*, 7–8.

23. Ibid., 17–18.

24. Fuchs, passim.

25. Ann Taylor Allen, *Feminism and Motherhood in Germany, 1800–1914* (New Brunswick: Rutgers University Press, 1991), 145–46, 177–79.

26. AGN, Sociedad de Beneficencia, Leg. 57, fojas 180–81, New contract for child placement, 1903.

27. Elvira Rawson de Dellepiane, *Apuntes sobre higiene en la mujer: Tesis Inaugural* (Buenos Aires: Pablo E. Coni e Hijos, 1892), 9.

28. Ibid., 31–32.

29. Ibid., 33.

30. Ibid., 42.

31. *Primer congreso femenino internacional de la República Argentina* (Buenos Aires: A. Ceppi, 1911), 219, 304, 428–29.

32. Raquel Camaña, "Femeneidad," *Atlántida* 13 (1914): 108–10.

33. Dr. Gregorio Aráoz Alfaro, *El libro de las madres* (Buenos Aires: Cabaut, 1922), 251–53. The part cited did not include changes that appeared in the 1922 edition.

34. José Penna and Horacio Madero, *La administración sanitaria y Asistencia Pública de la ciudad de Buenos Aires*, 2 vols. (Buenos Aires: Guillermo Kraft, 1910), 1:417.

35. Ibid., 423–24.

36. Mariano Etchegaray, *Higiene y puericultura* (Buenos Aires: Imprenta G. Kraft, 1915), 150.

37. Eliseo Cantón, *Protección á la MADRE y al HIJO; Puericultura intra- y extrauterina; Profilaxia del aborto, abandono e infanticidio. MATERNIDAD-REFUGIO* (Buenos Aires, 1913), 1–17.

38. Intendencia Municipal, *Patronato Asistencia de la Infancia de la Capital de la República* (Buenos Aires: Intendencia Municipal, 1992), 313–14.

39. Patronato Asistencia de la Infancia, *Memoria* (1898), 18, 33.

40. Proyecto de reglamento, Patronato de la Infancia, *Libro de Actas*, t. 11, 2 March 1921, ff. 231–34. I would like to thank Dra. Noemí Girbal de Blacha for this reference.

41. Emilio R. Coni, *Higiene social. Asistencia y previsión social. Buenos Aires caritativa y previsor* (Buenos Aires: Imprenta de Emilio Spinelli, 1918), 82–83. The quotation is from 91.

42. Printed in Esther Kaminsky, *Puericultura (Protección a la primera infancia en la República Argentina), Tesis* (Buenos Aires: La Semana Médica, 1914), 49.

Garzonas y Feministas in Cuban Women's Writing of the 1920s

La vida manda
by Ofelia Rodríguez Acosta

In April 1928 feminist columnist Mariblanca Sabas Alomá[1] wrote a series of articles in the popular weekly magazine *Carteles* on the subject of female homosexuality[2] (or *garzonismo*,[3] as it was called in Cuba at the time). In these articles, Sabas Alomá, speaking in the name of progressive feminism, articulates a homophobic discourse that identifies lesbianism as a social disease plaguing Cuban society and argues against those who associate it with feminist values. The terms of her discussion and the very choice of her subject matter reflect the impact on Cuban society during this period of competing discourses on feminism, "free love" or sexual liberation for women, and homosexuality.

Many feminist intellectuals of the period, reacting to assumptions about their sexual orientation, were outspoken homophobes. Even feminists such as Sabas Alomá, who represented the progressive wing of the women's movement in Cuba at the time, exhibited homophobic attitudes with reactionary defensiveness.

Sabas Alomá characterized lesbianism as a crime against nature and a vice representing "la lujuria, el desenfreno y las desviaciones sexuales" (lust, licentiousness, and sexual deviance)[4] that, resulting from the oppression of women under capitalism, would disappear with the advent of socialism. She calls lesbianism an "asqueroso gusano que está corroyendo hasta las entrañas a toda una generación de mujeres" (a disgusting worm that is eating away at the very womb of a whole generation of women).[5]

The "scientific" discourse on female sexuality most well known in Cuba in this period was that developed by Spanish biologist Gregorio Marañón whose theories circulated widely in Latin America in the 1920s.[6] The popularity of this kind of medicalized, "scientific" discourse on female sexuality emerged at a time when the "free-love" movement had begun to impact certain sectors of Cuban society. Increasing access to economic independence and education, and the advent of birth control, made the concept of "free-love" viable for some women and opened up a certain space for lesbians. Female sexual "liberation" was emerging in the public eye as a force that had to be reckoned with. Clearly, female sexuality in general and lesbian sexuality in particular could no longer be controlled simply through ignorance and denial. In response to the need to police women's sexual freedom, a discourse was developing that assumed the superior stance of the (need we say, male) scientist/doctor.

Marañón presents a view of lesbianism deeply steeped in the concept that homosexuality of any kind is an aberration, an abnormality, a tragic defect. He also draws close links between sexually "liberated" women and lesbians. For Marañón, the bottom line is that if a woman either displays a high level of sexual desire or is unwilling to indulge her husband sexually, suffers depressions, doesn't enjoy domestic life, or is not happy in her marriage, she must be a lesbian. Lesbians are sexually passionate, assertive women with "viriloid traits" who are inclined toward participation in the public sphere. A "real" woman who conforms to the "prototype of femininity" is always sexually available to her husband but wants sex for herself only as a means to keep her man and get pregnant, seeing marriage and maternity as her highest mission in life. The possibility that sexual and marital mores have been established according to the principles of heterosexual male privilege is not even considered by Marañón.

As we have seen, Sabas Alomá has no qualms about the view of lesbians as deviant, aberrant, and masculinized women. However, she strongly disagrees with what she considers to be Marañón's attempt to equate lesbianism and feminism.[7] "No se masculiniza la mujer en el nuevo ejercicio de derechos, responsabilidades y deberes que hasta ahora habían sido privativos del hombre" (Women are not masculinized by their new exercise of the rights, responsibilities and duties that used to be limited to men).[8] Feminism, she argues, proposes moving to a higher phase in the evolution of humanity in which women participate actively as citizens in the public sphere, while *garzonismo* has been around since the days of "Safo y de Victoria Colonna," and is as old as any other "vice." In her view, feminism and lesbianism are diametrically opposed. "La garzona, lejos de constituir una etapa del feminismo, florece y supervive *a pesar del* feminismo" (The garzona, far from constituting a stage of feminism, emerges and survives *despite* feminism), she states.[9] She ridicules the tendency of the majority of the population to stereotype feminists as "masculine" women and insinuates that Marañón's ideas have contributed to this view:

> Feminista, entonces, es . . . un tipo negado de belleza y de gracia, con la voz baritonal, el genio endemoniado, la frase insultante para el sexo fuerte siempre a flor de labios, cuello, corbata, antiparras, ademanes hombrunos, y ¡horror de los horrores!, la sombra acusadora de un bigote incipiente, ¡coqueteando con las teorías del doctor Gregorio Marañón!

> (A feminist, then, is . . . a type who has forsaken beauty and grace, has a deep voice, a hellish temper, an insulting phrase for the strong sex always on her lips, coat and tie, spectacles, manly gestures, and—horror of horrors—the accusing shadow of a budding mustache, flirting with the theories of doctor Gregorio Marañón!)[10]

Sabas Alomá does not agree with Marañón's theory that homosexuality is exclusively the product of biological factors. She agrees that there probably is some kind of biological potential, but she insists that there are important social factors that make it a social reality. Her deep-seated homophobia leads her to conclusions that are profoundly misogynist. In her view, potential homosexuality is unleashed by the ineptness of "unfit" mothers, whom she sees as "uneducated," "unliberated" women. Implying—with her invocation of the womb ("la matriz")—that feminists are not the mothers of lesbians, she states that "*feminismo* no es, ni será nunca, matriz generadora de esa 'masculinización' de la mujer" (Feminism is not, and will never be, the womb that generates the masculinization of women).[11] Only 10 percent of women who marry have the "scientific" capacity to educate their children properly. "En el 90 por ciento de las restantes están las madres de las *garzonas*" (The mothers of the *garzonas* are among the remaining 90 percent).[12] In support of her view she prints a letter from the treasurer of the Alianza Nacional Feminista, Leticia de Arriba de Alonso, "La Marquesa de Tiedra,"[13] who congratulates her on her antilesbian campaign and declares that a woman who is "esencialmente apta para la maternidad" (essentially apt for maternity) could never be the mother of a *garzona*. On the contrary, women who have been oppressed and confined to the private sphere, and who have "no worldly experience or real education" are, in her view, more likely to commit errors in child rearing that might unleash the biological potential of homosexuality. Using tropes that could be read as inversions of those associated with birthing ("las entrañas" [innards or womb] and the parasitic "gusano" [worm]), Sabas Alomá in turn asserts that with the liberation of women offered by socialist feminism the disgusting worm of lesbianism will be purged.

Alternative voices were heard in defense of lesbianism, however. In response to her first article, Sabas Alomá received, and subsequently published, a letter from the lawyer and creative writer Dr. Flora Díaz Parrado stating that lesbians are "un tipo justo dentro de la incongruencia humana" (a logical type within human incongruence) and that their behavior is more acceptable than that of the servile woman.[14] She is actually quite audacious in her vindication of lesbianism, daring to take an openly positive position. Once again the female internal organs are invoked, but this time as a site for the revolutionary birth of lesbianism: "La *garzona* . . . tiene una revolución íntima, muy honda, en la entraña" (The *garzona* . . . represents an intimate revolution, very deep within the womb). She identifies World War I as the catalytic social phenomenon that led to what she sees as a worldwide trend toward lesbianism as a step in the evolution of "the woman of the future." Díaz Parrado also reminded Sabas Alomá that popular views are susceptible to change and that just as today they laugh ironically at their ancestors' perception of epileptics and mentally ill people as moral deviants, so too may her contemporaries' negative view of lesbians one day be seen as ridiculous.

This open-mindedness regarding lesbianism is reiterated in Ofelia Rodríguez Acosta's[15] novel of 1929, *La vida manda*, which contains—within a predominantly heterosexual narrative—a highly audacious subtext that presents lesbianism as a liberating identity for some women.[16]

Born in Cuba in 1902, Ofelia Rodríguez Acosta was an outspoken feminist and prolific creative writer. *La vida manda*, her second novel, was a commercial success, quickly going through two editions and provoking intense debates. Much of the uproar against the novel came from right-wing Catholic women within the feminist movement who were scandalized by Rodríguez Acosta's outspoken views on sexuality, in favor of free love and reproductive freedom. Mariblanca Sabas Alomá responds to the novel's critics in her review of the novel:

> Juzgar el libro de Ofelia con las antiparras arcaicas y antipáticas de la moral al uso, es ridículo, risible, tonto. Quede para los ineptos y para los mediocres. El lector inteligente lo tomará en sus manos libre de prejuicios.
>
> (To judge Ofelia's book through the antagonistic and archaic lens of common-

place ethics is ridiculous, laughable, and moronic. Leave that to the inept and the mediocre. Intelligent readers will pick it up without prejudice.)[17]

Early on in her review—and contradicting her call for a nonprejudiced reading—she reassures the reader in passing that the novel's protagonist and, by implication, its author as well, is a "real woman": "Novela de una mujer, de *toda una mujer*, por una mujer" (A novel about a woman, about a *real* woman, by a woman).[18] In this way Sabas Alomá reinforces a heterosexual reading of the text and deflects attention away from the novel's subversive subtext.

Characterizing *La vida manda* as "quizás . . . el único libro valiente escrito en Cuba de muchos años acá" (possibly . . . the only courageous book that has been written in Cuba in many years),[19] Sabas Alomá declares that "a Cuba le ha nacido su novelista" (Cuba's novelist has been born).[20] However, despite the generalized critical acclaim afforded Rodríguez Acosta in the years immediately following the novel's publication, in none of the literary histories written after 1940 does she receive more than passing mention. This is all the more alarming in light of the fact that her novelistic project constitutes a pioneering effort in the development of an explicitly feminist contemporary novel in Latin America.

Unlike most of the female characters in early-twentieth-century feminist novels written by Latin American women, *La vida manda* portrays a protagonist who is not well-to-do, married, and trapped in the domestic sphere, nor is she a virgin, a mother, a nun, or a prostitute. She is, rather, a clerical worker exploring the options available to a single woman who aspires to achieve economic independence through salaried employment and, in defiance of social conventions, rejects marriage and domesticity, asserting the freedom to pursue nontraditional relationships based on equality. The novelistic project is centered on an audacious disarticulation of the parameters of gender, sex, love, family, and motherhood, traditionally seen as inseparable.

In *La vida manda*, the protagonist, whose name is Gertrudis (in a likely reference to Gertrude Stein and to the nineteenth-century Cuban writer Gertrudis Gómez de Avellaneda), is seen as an active subject who is in the process of forging her own identity. From the outset of the novel, she is characterized as a strong and independent woman with clear ambitions to "be somebody," who overtly identifies with feminism and socialist ideals and is outspoken in her political views. Gertrudis is a "self-made woman" whose confidence stems from the fact that she is able to support herself through participation in the work force.

An outstanding feature of this novel is the experimentation that it presents in its portrayal of sexuality and relationships. Rodríguez Acosta engages the discourse on "free love" that circulated in Cuba in this period and tests its viability for women. Central to the subversive vision that Gertrudis represents is a belief in the possibility of free unions based on desire, respect, honesty, and equality. The protagonist never expresses a desire to follow the traditional route of marriage and domesticity, which are in no way presented as a goal for the realization of female potential.

In fact, Rodríguez Acosta consciously questions a whole range of conventions related to women's sexuality and socially assigned roles. Gertrudis's sexual desire and pleasure occupy a central place in her world. Even while still a virgin, Gertrudis is portrayed as a desiring subject and sexual aggressor. She is the antithesis of the blushing bride, and actively seeks out sexual satisfaction as she asserts her right to erotic fulfillment. Bored and physically unsatisfied in the traditional engagement/marriage track, Gertrudis leaves her fiancé for a male lover whom she hopes can satisfy her sexual curiosity and desire.

The sexual aspect of her relationship with her lover Damián is predominant. As a young woman involved in a sexual relationship outside wedlock, Gertrudis never flinches at the idea of defying social conventions and has a matter-of-fact belief that it is her prerogative to lead the life she chooses. However, it is precisely her relationship with Damián that provides the framework for the failure of Gertrudis's utopian vision.

Through the relationship between the protagonist and her lover, Rodríguez Acosta tests the viability of the "free-love" discourse and finds it to be lacking as a solution to women's subordination in the traditional marriage arrangement. Gertrudis becomes aware of how her values have been manipulated by her lover for his convenience. Discovering that Damián is "happily" married and has no intention of leaving his wife and children, Gertrudis realizes that he had encouraged her belief in "free-love" as a strategy to maneuver her into a relationship that, devoid of commitment and responsibility, he found very convenient.

> ¡Y qué bien encontrabas que yo fuera una mujer sin prejuicios, indómita, emancipada de preceptos y convencionalismos sociales! . . . Indudablemente resulta muy cómodo para ti.

> (You were pleased to find that I was a woman with no prejudices, untamed, free of preconceptions and social conventionalisms! . . . Undoubtedly you found that very comfortable.)[21]

There is no attempt on the part of the author, however, to suggest that traditional marriage is preferable or superior to the "free union." In fact, not one successful marriage appears in the novel and there are no families that are in any way complete. Nor are there any male characters in the novel who could be construed as appropriate partners for any woman.

The novel contains a subtext of lesbian identity and homoeroticism that provides a subversive alternative within a predominantly heterosexual text. The presence of this theme in the novel, though muted, is significant and can be read as a closeted affirmation of lesbianism as a viable path for women seeking self-realization.

As Gertrudis is making inroads into the intellectual scene in Havana, she is introduced to Delia Miranda, a well-known poet who is a lesbian. Delia's lesbianism is never named, a narrative gesture that parallels the social invisibility of lesbians in Cuban society at the time (and in most other Western societies for that matter). The scenes involving Delia are implicit and muted in such a way that many readers simply would not notice what is going on. Delia's lesbian identity as portrayed by Rodríguez Acosta is solely based upon her expression of lesbian desire, not upon any overt characterization by the narrator or by the other characters. There is no physical or psychological stereotyping of Delia in the novel. In fact, she is never described physically, and there is no mention of her mannerisms or style of dress. Although she is clearly independent and assertive, she is not once described as masculine. She is emotionally well balanced and shows no signs of social stigmatization. A successful poet, she represents a model of female creativity. All in all, Delia is clearly a positive character in the novel.

Delia is the only person in the novel truly able to recognize Gertrudis's value and potential. Throughout the novel, when the two women speak of each other, they use a profoundly humanizing language that contrasts with the objectifying language used by the male characters in their references to the protagonist.

> [Gertrudis] encarna nuestro tiempo. Ella vive ahora . . . [es] una mujer que trabaja, lucha, es pobre, y al mismo tiempo sabe pensar . . . practica la libertad de amar . . . ninguna religión.

> ([Gertrudis] embodies our times. She lives in the here and now . . . [she is] a woman who works, struggles, is poor, and who can also think . . . she practices free love . . . [is] not affiliated with any religion.)[22]

Rodríguez Acosta gives the reader the key to an appropriate reading of this novel from the perspective of lesbian aesthetics, acknowledging the use of silence in a way that was not theoretically articulated as a lesbian textual strategy until decades after this novel was written. Delia herself points out the communicative function of silence in closeted lesbian interactions:

—¿En qué me ha conocido usted, Delia? —En sus silencios. Sus silencios son de una elocuencia irrebatible, a veces, desconcertante. Ponerles atención, es verla a usted llorar, añorar, pensar descarnadamente: amar. . . .

("How have you come to know me so well, Delia?"
   "Through your silences. Your silences are irrefutably eloquent and, at times, disconcerting. To pay attention to them is to see you cry, to see you yearn, to see your thoughts exposed: to see you love.")[23]

One must read between the lines, watch for the authorial intention in the silences. The unspoken is that which signals the existence of a "love that dare not speak its name." The way in which the interaction between Gertrudis and Delia is narrated leaves little doubt their encounters are highly sexualized. When they were first introduced, "Delia la examinó de arriba a abajo" (Delia examined her from head to toe).[24] A comment made by Gertrudis provokes a glance from Delia that Gertrudis literally reads as a sign; a neon sign nonetheless. The gaze, with its subversive possibilities, communicates that which is silenced and socially repressed.[25] The sign's flickering on and off in this account could be seen as a reference to the fragmentation of Delia's socially recognized identity and to the need for code-like communication as a strategy for circumventing the silence imposed on lesbians and gays. Just like the flashing lights of a neon sign, these flashes would light up and then quickly go dark, mirroring the brief, fleeting peeks that Delia allows into her true identity, as if testing the waters. The first time the two women are alone together, Gertrudis controls the terms of their conversation. Employing phrases heavy with ambiguity—for example, "You know that I know who you are"— she establishes a certain level of complicity while at the same time imposing a clear distance between herself and the other woman. Nevertheless, insofar as their conversation makes it clear that Gertrudis acknowledges Delia's sexual orientation and accepts it without reproach, this can be read as an audacious moment in the novel:

[Delia:] —¿Quiere usted ser mi amiga?
[Gertrudis:] —No; yo no quiero tener amigas.
[Delia:] —¿Por qué ese aislamiento? ¿Quiere usted amortajarse en vida? ¡Es tan dulce la amistad!
[Gertrudis:] —Profésala usted, si quiere. Hoy por hoy, yo me basto sin ella. . . . Yo puedo tratarla a usted cuantas veces la vea. Me siento un poco comprendida por usted; pero si fuéramos amigas, quizá se echaría todo a perder. Usted sabe que yo sé quién es usted.
[Delia:] —¿Y me censura?
[Gertrudis:] —No.

[Delia:] —¿Me compadece?

[Gertrudis:] —Tampoco.

[Delia:] —Soy así de un modo inevitable.

[Gertrudis:] —Sea usted como usted quiera, y por lo que quiera. Lo único que a mí me interesa de usted es su corazón.

([D:] Would you like to be my friend?

[G:] No; I don't care to have any friends.

[D:] Why isolate yourself? Do you want to mummify yourself while still alive? Friendship is so sweet!

[G:] You can profess it if you like. For the present I can do without it. . . . I can relate to you whenever I run into you. I feel as if you understand me a little; but if we were friends, perhaps everything would turn out wrong. You know that I know who you are.

[D:] Do you censure me?

[G:] No.

[D:] Are you sorry for me?

[G:] No, I'm not.

[D:] I can't help being this way.

[G:] Be as you like and for whatever reason. To me, all that matters about you is your heart.)[26]

The next time the two women are alone, Delia dares to express her feelings for Gertrudis more explicitly. Delia's declaration of love for Gertrudis is not explained by the narrator at all. It simply appears in the flow of events and is left to speak for itself. This time Delia controls the terms of their conversation. Her direct and candid manner frightens Gertrudis. Taken off guard by Delia's declaration, she feels confused and vulnerable:

Delia le tomó una mano, que calentó entre las suyas, y con voz queda:

— . . . la quiero, Gertrudis, hasta el sacrificio. No lo olvide usted; recuérdelo siempre. . . .

—Delia, calle usted. ¡Calle usted, por favor! Me trastornan sus palabras porque no puedo razonar. Ha hecho usted mal en elegir este momento para decírmelas; estoy indefensa. Pero, de todos modos, creo [que] no ha debido hacerlo nunca. ¡Qué lástima! Pierdo su casi amistad. Porque, usted sabe, yo no soy mujer que soporta estas situaciones. Le ruego me deje usted en la próxima esquina.

(Delia took one of her hands and warming it between her own, she whispered: "I love you, Gertrudis, to the point of sacrifice. Don't forget it; always remember that. . . ." "Hush, Delia. Please, don't go on like this! Your words confuse me because I can't rationalize them. It's not fair of you to have chosen this moment to say this to me; I'm vulnerable. But, anyway, I don't think you should have ever said it at all. This is a shame! Now I lose your semi-friendship. Because, you know, I'm not the kind of woman who can put up with this kind of situation. I beg you to drop me off at the next corner.")[27]

Despite her deep affinity with Delia, Gertrudis is unable to consider the possibility that her ideal of a truly egalitarian relationship might be found with someone of the same sex. Gertrudis cannot see beyond the parameters of that which is socially acceptable,[28] but Rodríguez Acosta is intent upon stretching those parameters. Rodríguez Acosta's presentation of the relationship between Delia and Gertrudis opens a space for the possibility of erotic fulfillment devoid of the duplicity and sexist manipulation present under the guise of heterosexual romance.

One of the most transgressive moments of the text is a scene that takes place at a small gathering of intellectuals at which everyone is drunk. The intricate detail with which the two characters' movements are described reveals a profoundly erotic exchange and hints at a level of sexual contact between the two women that could not have been presented directly in a text such as this. The erotic dynamics are centered on their eye contact. As Beatriz Sarlo states: "Things can be done with the eyes, that it is not yet licit to do with the hands (and may never be)." The gaze, explains Sarlo, "follows an erotic script, that if written for the hands would be far too daring."[29]

[Gertrudis] se sentó, justamente frente a Delia. Los demás jugaban y gritaban en absoluta independencia. Gertrudis se sentía excitada, intranquila hasta el último repliegue de su carne y de su alma. . . . Sintió clavada en ella como ponzoñoso aguijón la mirada buída de Delia. Inmóvil, se puso a mirarla ella también. . . . La mirada de Gertrudis, hipnotizada, bajó hasta los labios de Delia, que se estremecía voluptuosamente. . . . Se agitó pecaminosamente en la larga, interminable, dulce mirada de la otra mujer. Delia sonreía triunfalmente. Esa sonrisa húmeda y palpitante, despertó a Gertrudis. La bebida se le subía a la cabeza.

([Gertrudis] sat down right in front of Delia. Everyone else was playing cards and talking loudly in absolute independence. Gertrudis felt excited, restless down to the last fold of her skin and to the bottom of her soul. . . . She felt Delia's sharp gaze piercing her like a venomous prod. Immobilized, she returned her gaze. As if hypnotized, Gertrudis's gaze descended to the lips of Delia, who was trembling voluptuously. She was stirred by the long, neverending, and sweet gaze of the other woman. Delia smiled triumphantly. Gertrudis was awakened by this damp and palpitating smile. The liquor was going to her head.)[30]

Gertrudis jumps up from her seat, rushes over to where the others are play-ing cards and, "sintiendo la atracción del vicio con íntimos temblores en el alma" (attracted to the debauchery with an intimate trembling of her soul),[31] begins betting recklessly. "What pleasure to lose everything in such heated excitement!" exclaims Gertrudis. She submits herself completely to the game and feels compelled to transgress, "con un ansia cada vez más grande de faltar, de ser mala, de llegar al fondo de todas las cosas" (with an ever stronger desire to err, to be bad, to reach the depths of everything).[32] The air becomes thick and, blacking out, she imagines that she is "pos-sessed" by all the guests at the party. "Toda quemada de deseos, ardió espontáneamente" (Burning with desire, she went ablaze with spontaneous combustion).[33] Scenes of her very first sexual experiences run through her mind and then, in a dreamlike state, she is led away by a nebulous figure and "Sus deseos fueron calmados físicamente, sin que ella supiera cómo ni por quién" (All of her desires were satisfied, without her knowing how or by whom).[34] Later she wonders who it could have been: "Was it Damián?" she asks herself, or "Félix? Antonio? Delia?"[35] The fact that Delia's name is included on the list of her possible lovers is a direct acknowledgment of the potential of lesbian sexuality that corroborates the encoded homoerotic ref-erences in the earlier passages. Interestingly enough, the three other people on the list were not even at the party.

The above scene is the last time Delia appears in the novel. Because the erotic implications were so obvious to the sensitive reader and their logical outcome so subversive, it was too transgressive to follow the thread of the relationship between the two women to its final consequences. It is left, therefore, as an unanswered interrogative and, as such, as an open possibil-ity. The scene occurs about four-fifths of the way through the novel and the only further mention of the relationship between the two women comes when some of Gertrudis's office mates slanderously spread the rumor that she and Delia are lovers.

Having lost faith in the possibility of finding personal realization through romantic partnership, Gertrudis adjusts the focus of her utopian vision toward the formation of a new generation with advanced sexual ethics and gender values. Gertrudis makes a deal with her former fiancé to have a child. There is no illusion of romance between the potential parents. Rodríguez Acosta presents this choice matter-of-factly as a perfectly rea-sonable one[36] and at the same time demonstrates clearly the different per-spectives taken by the two potential parents in this situation and how those perspectives correspond to the characters' gender positions. Gertrudis understands that for Antonio the arrangement is of interest only because it will allow him to have sex with her. "La aventura tenía para él un sabor picante, con rescoldo de viejos e insatisfechos apetitos" (For him the affair was spiced with the flavor of his past unsatisfied desires).[37] She also realizes that he most likely sees it as a way of getting back at her for breaking off their engagement. However, for Gertrudis, having a child is a desperate attempt at giving meaning to her life by having an influence on future generations. Quoting Oscar Wilde, she states, "Si la vida es un problema para mí, yo también soy un problema para la vida" (If life is a problem for me, I too am a problem for life).[38]

The choice of Antonio as the father of her child is a significant one. This is the man who beat her when she broke off relations with him, making her painfully aware of the gender-based physical limitations that prevented her from defending herself. It is as if, by resorting to motherhood as her final chance for self-realization, she were resigning herself to a role that had been biologically assigned to her as a woman, and were accepting a predestined gender role in a reversal of the transgressive gender strategies that she had so wholeheartedly embraced earlier in the novel. This strategy, however, also proves to be a false one. As a result of her pregnancy, Gertrudis loses her job. The child dies soon after birth, leaving Gertrudis alone, unemployed, and devastated.

At the beginning of *La vida manda*, Gertrudis is described as a young woman with a strong sense of self-confidence who sees herself as an emerging citizen and participant in the public sphere. By the end of the novel, however, she has completely lost this sense of security, of self as subject. As the narrator tells us, she has forgotten that she has a voice, that is, the ability to express herself, to articulate and interpret her own reality:

> Hacía cuatro días que no hablaba. Había olvidado su propia voz. . . . Su espíritu estaba en la misma posición, como su pensamiento. De espaldas a la vida.

> (She had not spoken for four days. She had forgotten her own voice. . . . Both her spirit and her thoughts had turned their backs on life.)[39]

When the novel ends, the protagonist's ideal of economic independence and sexual liberation has resulted a self-deluding utopia, her chances at artistic or intellectual realization have been squelched, her dearest relatives have died, her only male ally has taken a diplomatic post abroad, her aspiration to realization through motherhood has been frustrated through her baby's death, and she has even been fired from her clerical position with the government. As if all that were not enough, her gesture of ultimate rebellion, the taking of her own life, backfired. Blinded in the process of her aborted suicide attempt, she loses her vision (that is, her utopian impulse), and appears completely insane:

> Había abierto ya sus ojos y no veía aún. ¿Qué sucedía? Los cerró y tornó a abrirlos. ¡Nada! Toda su alma se quedó de pronto en silencio. Un pavoroso silencio de muerte. Una luz invisible, interior inmanente, empapó su pensamiento todo. Comprendió: ¡Ciega!

> (She had opened her eyes but she still couldn't see. What was happening? She closed them and then opened them again. A dreadful deadly silence. An inherent, internal and invisible light inundated her thoughts. She understood: She was blind!)[40]

The novel closes with this curiously ambiguous image of contrast between life and death, opening and closing, speech and silence, cognition and lack of action, illumination and blindness.

One could suggest that Gertrudis at first held the vision that as a wage-earning, sexually "liberated," white, heterosexual Cuban woman she would be allowed to participate fully in her society alongside her male compatriots. By the end of the novel, however, it has become clear that the character's vision of inclusion in civic life and freedom from patriarchal fetters is not viable within the heterosexual framework. Male privilege remains intact both in the labor force and in the heterosexual "free unions," and women continue to experience the oppression of truncated lives, submission, and silence.

It would be a mistake to assume that Rodríguez Acosta is writing against feminism by illustrating the pitfalls of the lifestyle of independent women. There is not an exaggeration of the evils of "free love" or of women's life outside the domestic sphere. The protagonist does not become a prostitute or a nun, nor does she yearn for a second chance to live out the traditional heterosexual marriage plot. In fact, Gertrudis's attempted suicide parallels the strategies employed by actual Latin American women of the 1920s and 1930s, such as the poet Alfonsina Storni, who under similar conditions of tragic frustration attempted to live outside the limitations and rigid social conventions scripted for their gender.

On the other hand, the role of the lesbian subtext in this novel—although muted—is utopian, not tragic. Delia is portrayed as a truly autonomous, successful woman and she represents an option for self-realization that Gertrudis is unable to accept. Gertrudis is blind to an alternative that Delia can see quite clearly. Adrienne Rich offers insight into the impact of such forms of denial on female self-fulfillment:

The lie keeps numberless women psychologically trapped, trying to fit mind, spirit, and sexuality into a prescribed script because they cannot look beyond the parameters of the acceptable. . . . The lesbian trapped in the "closet," the women imprisoned in prescriptive ideas of the "normal" share the pain of blocked options, broken connections, lost access to self-definition freely and powerfully assumed.[41]

Although Rodríguez Acosta does not explicitly condone homosexuality, there is clearly an absence in the novel of any ideal model of female sexuality or womanhood that would exclude a lesbian identity, which is quite significant given the rampant homophobia of the mainstream feminist movement in Cuba at the time and the generalized social invisibility of lesbians in Latin American society. Her portrayal of Delia, the lesbian poet, contradicts the terms of Marañón's discourse on lesbianism as an aberration rooted in biological factors, and also contradicts Sabas Alomá's view of lesbianism as a social disease and vice brought on by unfit mothers under capitalism. By presenting a positive lesbian character in her novel, Rodríguez Acosta intervenes in the debate on female homosexuality and suggests that feminists open their eyes to the possibility that lesbianism can be a liberating identity for women.

• NOTES

1. A founding member of the Grupo Minorista, Sabas Alomá participated actively in many other progressive cultural organizations of the period. She founded the short-lived magazine *Astral* in 1922 and wrote for several newspapers in the 1920s and 1930s such as *Carteles*, *Bohemia*, and *Avance*. In 1923 she attended the first Congreso Nacional de Mujeres de Cuba, and in subsequent years she attended many similar events both in Cuba and abroad. In 1930 she published her collection *Feminismo: cuestiones sociales—crítica literaria* (Havana: Editorial Hermes, 1930), which presented in book form her journalistic articles on women's issues. Her poetry was anthologized by Juan Ramón Jiménez and Camila Henríquez Ureña in their *La poesía cubana en 1936* (Havana: Institución Hispanocubana de Cultura, 1937). For more information on Sabas Alomá, see K. Lynn Stoner's study *From the House to the Streets: The Cuban Women's Movement for Legal Reform 1898–1940* (Durham: Duke University Press, 1991), 89–97.

2. See Mariblanca Sabas Alomá, "Pepillitos y garzonas," "Feminismo contra garzonismo," and "Génesis económica del garzonismo," April 1928. Included in *Feminismo*, 95–113.

3. This term was coined in Cuba consequent to the popularity of the novel *La Garçonne* by Victor Margueritte (Paris: E. Flammarion, 1922), which circulated in Spanish translation in Cuba in the 1920s and had a major impact on the debates around the free-love movement. The novel's protagonist is a young woman whose

sexual adventures include lesbian liaisons. *La Garçonne* was also published in English translation in at least five printings from 1923 onward (London, A. M. Philpot), and in Russian translation in 1926 (Riga, Knigo O. D. Strok).

4. Sabas Alomá, *Feminismo*, 98.

5. Ibid., 104.

6. Gregorio Marañón, *Estudios de fisiopatología sexual*, Colección Marañón, vol. 20 (Barcelona: Manuel Marín Editor, 1931).

7. Clearly, the personal implications are deeply threatening to Sabas Alomá as well.

8. Sabas Alomá, *Feminismo*, 109.

9. Ibid., 97.

10. Ibid., 47.

11. Ibid., 97.

12. Ibid., 99–100.

13. Ibid., 101–2.

14. Ibid., 106–8.

15. For more information on Ofelia Rodríguez Acosta, see Stoner, *From the House to the Streets*, 97–102.

16. Ofelia Rodríguez Acosta, *La vida manda* (Madrid: Biblioteca Rubén Darío, 1929). A second edition appeared in 1930.

17. Sabas Alomá, *Feminismo*, 235.

18. Ibid., 231.

19. Ibid., 235.

20. Ibid.

21. Rodríguez Acosta, *La vida manda*, 151.

22. Ibid., 143.

23. Ibid., 80–81.

24. Ibid., 35.

25. Paraphrased from Adrienne Rich's essay, "Compulsory Heterosexuality and Lesbian Existence," in *The Lesbian and Gay Studies Reader*, ed. Henry Abelove, Michèle Aina Barale, and David M. Halperin (New York: Routledge, 1993), 227–54.

26. Rodríguez Acosta, *La vida manda*, 103–4.

27. Ibid., 146.

28. Ibid., 7.

29. Beatriz Sarlo, *El imperio de los sentimientos* (Buenos Aires: Catálogos, 1985), 127. In her study of Argentine serial fiction for women in the 1920s, Sarlo, using Lacanian terms, speaks of the erotic function of the gaze in the literary conventions of popular literature:

> Si lo que el otro quiere decir está prohibido sólo la mirada puede . . . disolver, con sus mensajes ambiguos, las prohibiciones éticas o sociales. En este sentido, es más difícil de descodificar, pero más poderosa que la lengua, porque no [hay una] teoría de la mirada: los ojos dicen más que las palabras y . . . son . . . mensajeros que comunican lo que las convenciones sociales no esperan o reprimen en la lengua oral. (128)

(If what the other wants to say is forbidden, only the gaze, with its ambiguous messages, can dissolve the social and ethical taboos. In this sense, it is harder to decodify but more powerful than language, because [a] theory of the gaze [does] not [exist]: the eyes say more than words and . . . they are . . . messengers that communicate that which, according to social conventions, is not expected or is repressed in oral speech.)

30. Rodríguez Acosta, *La vida manda*, 92–94.
31. Ibid., 194.
32. Ibid.
33. Ibid., 195.
34. Ibid.
35. Ibid.
36. Rodríguez Acosta was an outspoken supporter of equal rights for children born out of wedlock. An example of the radical stance taken by those who led the campaign can be found in Sabas Alomá's articles on the subject:

La moral del futuro valorizará definitivamente el derecho de maternidad: toda mujer podrá o no tener un hijo o varios hijos, según le convenga, según lo desee, dentro del matrimonio o fuera del matrimonio, sin que en sus determinaciones a este respecto intervenga otro factor que no sea su propia determinación. ("Contra el torno, otra vez," in *Feminismo*, 123)

(The ethics of the future will give definitive value to maternity rights: each woman will be free to have a child or several children, according to her convenience, according to her wishes, within marriage or outside it, and no factor other than her own judgment will intervene in her decision-making process.)

37. Rodríguez Acosta, *La vida manda*, 235.
38. Ibid., 236.
39. Ibid., 250.
40. Ibid., 252.
41. Rich, "Compulsory Heterosexuality and Lesbian Experience," 244.

Daniel Balderston

Excluded Middle?

Bisexuality in
Doña Herlinda y su hijo

In late 1994 I gave a paper on the cinema of Jaime Humberto Hermosillo at the queer studies conference at the University of Iowa, and in it used the word *bisexual* to describe the character Rodolfo, the son in *Doña Herlinda y su hijo* (Doña Herlinda and her son).[1] In one of those comments from the audience for which one is forever grateful, someone (still unknown to me) asked where the bisexuality was in Rodolfo and in the film. I had thought the answer was transparent because by the end of the film he is married and the father of a son and also still involved in a passionate relationship with the musician Ramón. But several more viewings of the film—and a reading of the contentious but not overly persuasive book by Marjorie Garber, *Vice Versa: Bisexuality and the Eroticism of Everyday Life*—have returned me to the question from the audience, for Hermosillo's 1984 film, like the more recent *Wedding Banquet*, posits the gay male relationship as primary and the heterosexual marriage as a screen created as a response to parental pressure.

The late 1970s and early 1980s were a moment of effervescence for the nascent gay liberation movement in Mexico, with the emergence of small but vibrant groups, the Frente Homosexual de Acción Revolucionaria (FHAR) in Mexico City and Grupo Orgullo Homosexual de Liberación (GHOL) in Guadalajara, and the forging of international connections between the Mexican activists and their U.S. counterparts, particularly in San Francisco.[2] Luis Zapata had published *El vampiro de la Colonia Roma* in 1979 (later translated as *Adonis García*), José Joaquín Blanco published his important essay "Ojos que da pánico soñar" in 1981, and the FHAR was publishing *Política sexual: Cuadernos del Frente Homosexual de Acción Revolucionaria*, the first (undated) issue of which circulated in three thousand copies.

Before 1984 Hermosillo had made at least one implicitly homoerotic film, the 1974 *El cumpleaños del perro* (The dog's birthday). It concerns the murder of a young wife by her athlete husband and the protection granted him by a former employer, who eventually murders his own wife when she protests too loudly that her husband has become an accomplice to the first crime. There is nothing overtly sexual about the relation between the two men, and some quite explicitly sexual situations between the young athlete and his new wife. Yet the emotional core of the film is clearly the bond between the athlete and the singularly unattractive older man. As Francisco Sánchez notes in his essay on Hermosillo, at the time the film came out he and other critics were uncertain what to call that bond. He quotes from a review that he himself wrote at the time: "Hay una posibilidad de que los protagonistas de *El cumpleaños del perro* estén señalados por una inclinación homosexual, pero también hay otras muchas posibilidades: relación padre-hijo, sentimiento fraterno, camaradería viril o, simple y sencillamente, afinidad electiva de dos machos mexicanos" (It is possible that the protagonists of *The Dog's Birthday* are marked by a homosexual inclination, but other possibilities also exist: a father-son relationship, a fraternal feeling, virile camaraderie or, simply, the elective affinity of two Mexican machos),[3] a comment that Sánchez immediately qualifies as "Tonterías, yo sólo le estaba dando vueltas a la simulación, no queriendo aceptar lo que era por demás evidente, que Hermosillo nos había obsequiado la primera película gay de nuestro cine" (Pure foolishness: I was just going round and round in a pretense, not willing to accept what was more than obvious, that Hermosillo had given us the first gay film in our cinema).[4] But although gay subtexts were present in this and several others of Hermosillo's 1970s films, *Doña Herlinda* looks in retrospect like a response to the "coming-out" narratives of the post-Stonewall period, which impacted strongly in Mexico as elsewhere, a filmic example of which is the 1982 *Making Love*.[5] But these narratives are inflected by Hermosillo with a Mexican twist, here provided by the dominating (and perhaps domineering) presence of an archetypal Mexican mother, Doña Herlinda.

Rodolfo, though he may seem the "macho" of the gay couple, is a weak figure pulled in opposite directions by the two strong individuals in his life, his lover Ramón and his mother Doña Herlinda. Ramón says to him at one point, "Define yourself," but Doña Herlinda has already defined her son as "perfectly ambidextrous." Garber reminds us of the connection in the early Wilhelm Fliess and Sigmund Freud theories of bisexuality between handedness and sexual orientation, so Doña Herlinda is calling on strong cultural models when she asserts—surreptitiously, as always—her son's "native" bisexuality. Her precise statement is that he was born left-handed but that she made him into a perfect ambidexter; his bride's family has already confessed that Olga, the bride-to-be, is left-handed (which would imply lesbianism in the same old theories, an idea hinted at when Olga quickly shifts from skirts to pants).

The sexual politics in the gay couple are set out fairly overtly early in the film. Rodolfo is portrayed with deliberate touches of the filmic image of the famous film actor Jorge Negrete (whom he somewhat resembles),[6] though updated with a beeper in his belt: he wears cowboy boots and white pants, and his appearances in the film, beginning with the opening street scene in which he crosses from the plaza in front of the cathedral of Guadalajara toward the boardinghouse where Ramón lives, are frequently enlivened with the mariachi music about Guadalajara and Jalisco, the very songs sung in so many films by Negrete, considered the very archetype of the macho Mexican male.[7] In the early scene in the boardinghouse, Rodolfo explodes with jealousy at Ramón's friendship with another boarder, Eduardo, who is shown in one scene carving wood and in another knocks on Ramón's door to ask for the return of his hammer. Ramón will have none of Rodolfo's implication that he is attracted to Eduardo: "Es bien buga," he says. Now *buga* (*bugarrón* in the Caribbean) is an equivocal term in Mexican and Caribbean slang; the new *Oxford Spanish Dictionary* defines it as "straight," but a fuller translation would be "straight-acting, but willing to fuck gay men." In working-class Mexico and elsewhere in Latin America (and in working-class New York at least until 1930, as shown by the research of George Chauncey), sexual identity has more to do with roles played than with the sex of the partners; on this point see the eloquent article by Tomás Almaguer.[8] Ramón is saying that he is interested in being "used as a woman" not by a "straight" man but in a gay relationship; he is defining himself, that is, as an "international," someone whose maps of sexual identity have been redrawn according to modern U.S. and European models.[9] Interestingly, he is apparently of a lower class background than

Rodolfo,[10] who resolutely refuses the "international" categories, and whose behavior throughout the film is marked by gender and class privilege. What Almaguer, following Carrier, calls the "bisexual escape hatch"[11] shapes Rodolfo's resistance to the imposed "international" sexual categories, which seem to demand that he "come out" or "define himself" as gay.

And yet things are not so simple in the gay couple. Were the "Mexican" or "Latin American" sexual mapping as dominant as Almaguer and others have held, we would expect that Rodolfo would consistently take the "active inserter" role, while Ramón would be cast into the "anal receptive, *pasivo* sexual role."[12] Given the type-casting of Rodolfo as Jorge Negrete and Ramón as a long-haired, pretty, smooth ephebe, it is no surprise that in one early scene in the film Rodolfo is cast as the top, but a later scene unequivocally shows him as the bottom (although in both scenes the men are shown only from the waist up). This looks like "international" behavior, which would demand a remapping and renaming of Rodolfo as gay. But Rodolfo escapes anyway, through the emphatic public devices of marriage and fatherhood.

The straight couple in the film, Rodolfo and Olga, also proves more complicated than first meets the eye. Though there are a few embraces or gestures of Rodolfo's arm around Olga's shoulder, there is relatively little physical passion there. And Olga confirms in a conversation with Ramón that for her too this has been a marriage of convenience, to get away from dictatorial parents (or, as she puts it, to go from the *dictadura* [harsh dictatorship] of her parents to the *dictablanda* [soft dictatorship] of Doña Herlinda). Olga so quickly moves from a rather severe skirt and blazer ensemble to pants suits with ties and even jeans, and is so emphatically interested in pursuing a career, volunteer work with Amnesty International, and her studies (of German of all things, seemingly in response to her father's foreign accent) that she is decisively rejecting the role of the submissive, martyred Mexican wife and mother. She is a "new woman" in an explicitly international mode, while her husband clings to an earlier model of Mexican male identity.

Garber, in one of the few persuasive moments in her book, has argued that bisexual plots always involve triangles, and that the third side of the triangle is often the most interesting. In this case, the relationship that emerges between Olga and Ramón is fascinating. Connected only through Rodolfo, they forge a friendship or complicity that is reminiscent of the women's pictures of the forties, and indeed the gender ambiguities are considerable. Ramón is the more feminine of the two, while Olga in her ties and pants suits plays a very butch number to his (though at the end of the film, during the baptism, they are dressed the same, in white jackets, ties, and blue slacks, their haircuts similar). The scenes in which the two look radiantly into the cradle are in ironic counterpoint to Rodolfo, the biological father of the baby, who is out in the patio reciting a poem to his mother and her guests. Ramírez Berg, commenting on this relationship, declares: "There's one gentle scene like this after another in the film, and they accumulate to depict a new social order based on the politics of cordial communal interest and mutual respect";[13] his reading no doubt takes Hermosillo too straight, since the director undoes his utopian solutions with cognitive dissonances—here, the gender reversal that casts Olga as butch and Ramón as femme, in contradiction to so much that is explicit elsewhere in the film. Indeed, it is to Ramón that Olga confesses, "Siempre deseo cosas contradictorias" (I always desire contradictory things), a statement that bears as much on Rodolfo as on herself.

The poem Rodolfo is reciting, meanwhile, is Manuel Acuña's "Nocturno" (a poem he earlier memorized in the sauna with the help of Ramón, who seems to have a better memory for poetry than he does, despite his pretensions as a "declamador"). This poem by the Mexican romantic poet is famous for its association with the poet's suicide in 1873, and the dedication of it to Rosario de la Peña has spawned the persistent theory that Acuña committed suicide after being rejected by Rosario. In this context, though, what is most jarring about the poem is the poet's yearning for a world where he would share his life with his beloved Rosario and also with his beloved and saintly mother (to whom he dedicates a series of other poems). The middle stanzas of the poem, read by Rodolfo with great emotion at the end of the film, are

> A veces pienso en darte mi eterna despedida,
> borrarte en mis recuerdos y hundirte en mi pasión;
> mas si es en vano todo y el alma no te olvida,
> ¿qué quieres tú que yo haga, pedazo de mi vida,
> qué quieres tú que yo haga con este corazón? . . .
>
> ¡Qué hermoso hubiera sido vivir bajo aquel techo,
> los dos unidos siempre y amándonos los dos;
> tú siempre enamorada, yo siempre satisfecho,
> los dos una sola alma, los dos un solo pecho,
> y en medio de nosotros, mi madre como un dios!
>
> (Sometimes I think of saying goodbye to you forever
> erasing you from my memories and sinking you into my passion
> but if it is all in vain and the soul does not forget
> what do you want me to do, piece of my life,
> what do you want me to do with this heart?

How beautiful it would have been to live under that roof,
the two of us united forever and loving one another;
you always in love, I always satisfied,
the two of us a single soul, the two a single heart,
and between us, my mother like a god!)[14]

This melodramatic lyric is worthy of being transformed into a bolero or
canción ranchera of the kind sung by Lucha Villa earlier in the film, in the
scene in which Doña Herlinda lends her handkerchief to the weeping
Ramón, so eloquently discussed by José Quiroga in "(Queer) Boleros of a
Tropical Night."[15] If the Acuña poem is dedicated implicitly in the film to
Ramón (rather than to Rodolfo's wife, Olga), Hermosillo is playing here
with multiple ironics. What was impossible in the Mexico of 1873, the coex-
istence of passionate love with the bourgeois family, and is posed as a
utopian dream of a home with both the beloved Rosario and the beloved
mother is made real in the film. Rodolfo has it all: a household where he
shares life simultaneously with Ramón and with Olga. Ramón is his "com-
padre" by virtue of being the godfather of the son at the baptism, and is
more obviously paternal in his relation to his godson than is the biological
father himself. And all of this in a household presided over, administered,
by Doña Herlinda herself. When Rodolfo and Olga return from their honeymoon in Hawaii, a period during which Ramón toyed with finding his
own way into the gay community but is prevented from doing so by the
ever-meddling Doña Herlinda, it is she who proposes the ultimate wedding
present for the complicated ménage: architectural drawings showing various new rooms added to the house, including a tower room where Ramón
can practice his French horn. The already opulent house must be quite literally expanded into the walled garden to accommodate the new extended
family, and all of this at the initiative of the matriarch.

So overpowering, indeed, is Doña Herlinda that one begins to wonder
who is in charge of the complex relationships between Ramón, Rodolfo,
and Olga. When Ramón dances with a girl at the resort in Chapala so as to
annoy Rodolfo (who does indeed become visibly jealous), Doña Herlinda
intervenes by saying that *she* is too jealous of Ramón to allow him to dance
with other women. When Ramón is tempted to pick up a man during
Rodolfo and Olga's honeymoon in Hawaii, Doña Herlinda's presence again
interferes. Similarly, Rodolfo seems weak and indecisive when his mother is
in action. Ramón's heartfelt cry—"Definite"—uttered when Rodolfo's
engagement to Olga is being defined by others, is the closest we come to a
conventional gay liberation narrative in the film. Doña Herlinda, however,
proceeds by refusing to define her terms; her only reference to bisexuality,

as noted above, comes when she calls Rodolfo "perfectly ambidextrous." It is precisely because of her refusal to define the relationships taking place under her roof that their polymorphous perversity can flourish.[16] Stephen O. Murray calls the arrangements worked out in the film "more wish-fulfillment (a fairy tale?) than representative, even of the upper class,"[17] and indeed Joseph Carrier's says of his some seventy-five informants, mostly in Guadalajara (though of a lower class background than Rodolfo and his mother), that "*none* of my respondents has looked upon homosexual encounters as behavior generally acceptable to his family, nonhomosexual friends, or to society at large."[18]

Doña Herlinda y su hijo transgresses gay cultural expectations as much as it tries to educate straight audiences. The "families we choose"[19] in this film are annoyingly conventional, perhaps, but that seems to be Hermosillo's point: that for an utterly normal and unimaginative gay (or perhaps bisexual) man like Rodolfo, pleasing his mother is the safest way of pleasing himself. Ramón and Olga, the more sympathetic of the younger generation in the film, clearly turn the bizarre situation to their mutual advantage. The fag hag friend of Ramón's at the conservatory is scandalized by the conventional nature of her friend's dreams, but he seems happy with the panoramas that open for him in the new house. And Doña Herlinda can preside over the entire arrangement with poise and self-possession: she knows that she has made it all happen.

In an interview with Hermosillo in *Cineaction* by Florence Jacobowitz, Richard Lippe, and Robin Wood, which took place after the screening in Toronto of the third film in the *tareas* series, Lippe comments:

> You are interested in gay thematics but your films aren't restricted to gay themes. Do you ever find yourself thinking "I should do a gay film" just because you're gay? How do you feel about that or how do you judge your films and your work in relation to your identity as a person? Do you feel a commitment to do a certain amount of work that is gay orientated?[20]

Hermosillo responds:

> I never plan my films in that way. It's only most of the time the necessity of telling a story.[21]

The need to tell a story is inclusive, and does not necessitate the choice of gay material or the avoidance of it. Hermosillo is acutely conscious, though, of the fact that there are limits to what he can do. In the same interview he explains that in the third work in the *tareas* series he showed mother-son incest, but that the producers would not entertain the idea of a father-son incest plot. Perhaps the mother figure in *Doña Herlinda* is the inscription in Hermosillo's films of censorship and self-censorship. Hermosillo himself has commented on the negative aspects of Doña Herlinda in the interview quoted above,[22] but this only serves to open questions posed but not resolved in the film (and elsewhere in his cinema) on the extent to which he is parodying or critiquing Mexican family structures, and on just how radically he is challenging those structures as they impinge on the expression of sexual desire.

In a country where the Monument to the Mexican Mother sits a short block from the downtown intersection of Reforma and Insurgentes in the capital, it is not too far-fetched to hear an echo of the name of the famous Frida Kahlo painting *Madre México y yo* (Mother Mexico and I) in the title of this film. In any case, in the course of the film Doña Herlinda is identified so thoroughly with Mexico—with its cuisine, its art, its sexual mores, its dreams of order and progress—that Olga's comment on the "dictablanda" (soft dictatorship) of Doña Herlinda serves to identify her with the national party, the PRI. Like the party, she holds everything together in her anaconda-like deadly grasp. The pop political science terms used by Olga, "dictadura" for her parents' regime and "dictablanda" for Doña Herlinda's, reinforce the identification of Doña Herlinda with the PRI, with its democratic trappings and consensual framework but ultimately dictatorial powers.

Ramírez Berg has called *Doña Herlinda y su hijo* a "Utopia of tolerance."[23] Perhaps, if we remember that most utopias, starting with Thomas More's, have a strong authoritarian streak. Hermosillo himself, in the interview already cited, expresses considerable reservations about the "dictablanda" of Doña Herlinda:

> Well, I don't think that Doña Herlinda is a very positive character. She's very sinister, too, because otherwise she wouldn't have asked her son to marry that woman. She helps her son to be happy as a gay man. She's very sinister. She's controlling things the way she wants but she's not giving them freedom.[24]

A bit later in the interview he adds: "She's a nice character but some things she does are not fine, but it's beautiful to have those kinds of contradictions in the character."[25] Contradictions: the very word used by Olga to define her objects of desire, and apparently a touchstone of Hermosillo's esthetics.

In his essay on Hermosillo in the catalog published by the Cineteca Nacional, Francisco Sánchez notes that even in his first films in the 1960s and 1970s Hermosillo was interested in dissonant sexualities and in "freaks," and that the homoerotic elements only gradually became central to his filmography. Indeed, after *Doña Herlinda* Hermosillo has not continued making what one might call "gay" films, though *Clandestino destino* has one gay male character (out of four) and plays with the possible bisexual nature of the other three characters. In any case, both before and after *Doña Herlinda* Hermosillo has homosexuality present as only one element of a sexual spectrum, and, having said that, the anomalous nature of *Doña Herlinda* itself in the international context of gay filmmaking become more clear, in that in his "gayest" film Hermosillo insistently inscribes homosexuality in the context of the Mexican family structure and seemingly takes for granted the natural bisexuality of one of its main characters.[26] *Doña Herlinda* is not a "coming out" film but a "bringing back in" film, in which the homosexual side of one of the central characters is accommodated within the family structure.

• NOTES

I am grateful to Oscar Chong and Jorge Ruffinelli for help in gathering material on Hermosillo, including videotapes of many of his films, and to José Quiroga and Donna Guy for their readings of several versions of this paper.

1. The 1984 film is available from Macondo Video.

2. For a good account of the emergence of gay liberation movements in Mexico, see Ian Lumsden, *Homosexualidad, sociedad y estado en México*, trans. Luis Zapata (Mexico City: Solediciones; Toronto: Canadian Gay Archives, 1991), 63–78, which includes a brief discussion of the work of Luis Zapata and of Hermosillo as emblematic of the period. On the activities of GHOL in Gualajara (where Hermosillo has been based since the late 1970s), see Joseph Carrier, *De los otros: Intimacy and Homosexuality among Mexican Men* (New York: Columbia University Press, 1995), 180–84.

3. Francisco Sánchez, *Hermosillo: Pasión por la libertad* (Mexico City: Cineteca Nacional, 1989), 14.

4. Ibid., 14.

5. On the bisexual plot in *Making Love*, see Marjorie Garber, *Vice Versa: Bisexuality and the Eroticism of Everyday Life* (New York: Scribner's, 1995), 393–94.

6. In a story in the same volume as the narrative version of "Doña Herlinda y su hijo," Jorge López Páez writes that his character Emmanuel "resulta una combinación perfecta de Pedro Armendáriz, Jorge Negrete y Pedro Infante y ciertos detalles de Carlos López Moctezuma" (was a perfect combination of Pedro Armendáriz, Jorge Negrete, and Pedro Infante, with certain details of Carlos López Moctezuma): *Doña Herlinda y su hijo y otros hijos* (Mexico City: Fondo de Cultura Económica, 1993), 8.

7. John King refers to the "ebullient machismo of Jorge Negrete"—see *Magical Reels: A History of Cinema in Latin America* (London: Verso, 1990), 50—and Charles Ramírez Berg notes "Jorge Negrete's ready smile and unselfconscious demeanor singing songs celebrating *machismo*" in his *Cinema of Solitude: A Critical Study of Mexican Film, 1967–1983* (Austin: University of Texas Press, 1993), 5.

8. Tomás Almaguer, "Chicano Men: A Cartography of Homosexual Identity and Behavior," in *The Lesbian and Gay Studies Reader*, ed. Henry Abelove, Michèle

Aina Barale, and David M. Halperin (New York: Routledge, 1993), 255–73.

9. See Carrier, *De los otros*, 193–95.

10. It is hard to say anything very definite about Ramón's class, because when his parents come to visit from the North, it is apparent that they are cultured and bourgeois, though not in the same ostentatious (and urban) way as Doña Herlinda and Rodolfo.

11. See Almaguer, "Chicano Men," 259.

12. Ibid., 261.

13. Ramírez Berg, *Cinema of Solitude*, 132.

14. Manuel Acuña, *Obras: Poesías, teatro, artículos y cartas*, ed. and intro. José Luis Martínez (Mexico City: Editorial Porrúa, 1949), 191–92.

15. José Quiroga, "(Queer) Boleros of a Tropical Night," *Travesia: Journal of Latin American Cultural Studies* 3.1–2 (1994): 199–213.

16. In the López Páez story "Doña Herlinda y su hijo," Ramón is the narrator, commenting frequently on the perfect communication that existed between Doña Herlinda and Rodolfo, who seem almost telepathic in their messages in unison.

17. Stephen O. Murray, "Family, Social Insecurity, and the Underdevelopment of Gay Institutions in Latin America," in *Latin American Male Homosexualities*, ed. Stephen O. Murray (Albuquerque: University of New Mexico Press, 1995), 41.

18. Carrier, *De los otros*, 14. He reiterates the point on 61.

19. I am thinking of course of the fine book by Kath Weston, *Families We Choose: Lesbians, Gays, Kinship* (New York: Columbia University Press, 1991).

20. Florence Jacobowitz, Richard Lippe, and Robin Wood, "An Interview with Jaime Humberto Hermosillo: The Necessity of Telling a Story," *Cineaction* 31 (1993): 43. In the same issue, see Robin Wood, "*Homework* Times Three," *Cineaction* 31 (1993): 28–32.

21. Jacobowitz, Lippe, and Wood, "An Interview with Jaime Humberto Hermosillo," 43.

22. Ibid., 42.

23. For a virulent attack on *Doña Herlinda* and on Hermosillo's work in general, see Jorge Ayala Blanco, *La condición del cine mexicano* (Mexico City: Editorial Posada, 1986), 356–75. Ayala Blanco observes: "Cruel paradoja: Hermosillo era cada día más festejado y cada día filmaba peor" (A cruel paradox: every day Hermosillo became more famous and yet every day made worse films) (366). His observations on the amateur acting, poor sound, and cinematography are quite telling, in my opinion.

24. Jacobowitz, Lippe, and Wood, "An Interview with Jaime Humberto Hermosillo," 42.

25. Ibid.

26. However unlikely the living arrangement in the film, the notion of a more fluid bisexuality in Mexico than in the United States is borne out in the literature, as for instance in Joseph Carrier's "Mexican Male Bisexuality," in *Bisexualities: Theory and Research*, ed. Fred Klein and Timothy J. Wolf (New York: Haworth Press, 1985), 75–85, esp. 83–84.

13 *Eduardo P. Archetti*

Multiple Masculinities

The Worlds of Tango and Football in Argentina

This chapter focuses on the meanings of masculinity displayed in classical tango texts and in football arenas.[1] Since the end of the 1920s Argentine exports to Europe and the world have included tango music, choreography, singers, and musicians. Football (soccer) players have been another export. Over the years, tango and football have become representative of performing Argentines and a pervasive global image of "genuine" Argentine cultural products. Very few Argentines will deny that tango and football certainly played and still play the double role of public mirrors and models of masculinities.

Cornwall and Lindisfarne observe that different images and behaviors contained in the notion of masculinity are not always coherent and that "they may be competing, contradictory and mutually undermining."[2] Competing masculinities are produced and negotiated in different social arenas with different actors. The world of tango is explicitly made of the complex relations between men and women. In contrast, the world of football is exclusively male, an encounter in the stadium (and in the history of clubs and competitions) between competing groups of male players and supporters. Consequently, analysis of tango lyrics and football chants must reflect the complexities of models and idioms of masculinity.

Men deploy their manhood in social contexts where class origin, historical experiences, rituals, and accepted or subversive discourses are constitutive elements. Thus, gendered social and cultural differences exclude an explicit consideration of a "hegemonic" masculinity in Argentine society.[3]

The analysis of tango lyrics is rooted in the classical period of the *tango-canción* (tango-song) from 1917 to 1935. Most significant tango narratives were produced in that period and the texts chosen are key elements in the existing charter of Argentine tango "mythology."[4] Tango poetics relates not only to "universal" emotions like sadness, happiness, fear, and anxiety but also to those of love, pride, guilt, shame, and honor. All are fundamental in the articulation of individual identity and sociocultural processes.

The tango, dispossessed of its history and particularities, has been transformed in the Argentine society of today into the "mythical" language of gendered emotions. It is, in spite of different attempts to transform its authoritative framework, a kind of "frozen" universe of meanings. Jorge Luis Borges suggested that, as in the case of the *Iliad*, all tango texts may melt into a single poem, or that an ambitious poet will be able to write such a poem.[5] This observation still makes sense.

Tango lyrics reflect different types of love: love as duty, passion, deep friendship, and, finally, romantic love.[6] The first modern *tango-canción* that we know of was "Mi noche triste" (My sad night), written by Pascual Contursi in 1917. This lyric inaugurated a new narrative of failed romance told by a man in an intimate and confessional form.[7] The "theme" of love as something almost impossible is common. The men of these stories love with such intensity that the risk of rejection is correspondingly overwhelming. At the same time, lyrics revalorize (hetero)sexuality, sexual relations, and sensual love.

A constant topic is women who abandon men. These texts portray a sad man remembering his lost happiness. In all cases the listeners (readers) are confronted with a couple living together without being married. They have no children and the woman is always leaving the house. In literal terms, she is "stepping out" into the open world. In contrast, the image of a man passing through an identity crisis, unable to control the situation, is melancholically reiterated. The way he speaks about sadness, nostalgia, the loss of happiness, and the fear of loneliness is sincere and passionate.

In other classic texts, the locus of sentiments (and inevitable abandonment) is in the cabaret.[8] Women leave the house to enter the fascinating space of the cabaret.[9] In this setting, they are represented as *milonguitas* (young unmarried women from middle-lower-class families and born in a barrio or suburb). They are sensual and egoistic, and have self-confidence that emanates from their beauty and elegance. The *milonguita* escapes from the barrio, from poverty perhaps, and from a future as a housewife, to the center of Buenos Aires, to the excitement, luxury, and pleasure that the best cabarets offer to young, ambitious, and beautiful women. From the man's perspective, this life is superficial; lyrics emphasize that the loss of female chastity and indulgence in pure sensuality lead to suffering and loneliness when youth vanishes, and, in the end, the women in these songs are abandoned by rich but unreliable men. However, underpinning the texts is a recognition that the cabaret can provide a space of "freedom" and material advancement if sensuality is coupled with "authentic love." Women's (and men's) pure sensuality and their selfish interest in material security are portrayed in many tangos as being as destructive as passion. The drama of these tangos derives from the speaker's comparison of himself, a virtuous and truly loving man, to the *milonguita* who is seduced by material gains and immediate pleasures, and to the *bacán* (rich man) who promises the world and uses his money to seduce women.

Who is the narrator? It seems that the "man of the tango" is middle-aged, single, middle-class;[10] that he has grown up in a barrio and now is living in the center of Buenos Aires, enjoying leisure time with his friends (*la barra*) in daily visits to coffeehouses (in many tangos called "the home"); and that he has had "great" love affairs or, at least, "one" that has marked him profoundly. Eventually, this man developed a romantic and nostalgic view of the past. He has loved and desires to love again, but he is not looking for marriage and conventional family life.[11] The image of the ideal woman he presents is no longer associated with virginity and chastity, as was the case of the traditional romantic novels of the same period.[12] He does not expect subordination and traditional respect from the woman. Caught in the notion of romantic love, he expects his feelings will be understood and that she will love him with the same intensity. Loyalty and fidelity are the product of love and not of convention and authority.

The modernity of tango lyrics lies precisely in their presentation of uncertainties related to the exercise of romantic choice. In this type of lyric the basic elements in the cultural construction of romantic love are intimacy, companionship or friendship, the existence of mutual empathy, and the search for sexual pleasure. The distortion of one of these, such as too much emphasis on sexual pleasure, creates an emotional imbalance leading to unhappiness, loneliness, and nostalgia. The universalization of romantic love in these texts is highly dependent on a definition of a "self" that can choose in accordance with deep emotions and thus achieve a full realization of him/herself, and the lyrics point to the dangers arising from the existence of a world dominated by *milonguitas* and *bacanes*.

It appears that given the difficulty of realizing romantic love, male narrators envisage only one solution for the women and, it should be stressed, for themselves: namely, a return to the forms of love and chastity associated with traditional family roles. In this discursive context the image, both of the *milonguita* and of the ungrateful son, are contrasted to that of the idealized mother.[13] Maternal love is exalted and closely associated with ideas of purity, suffering, sincerity, generosity, and fidelity. A mother's love is the only permanent feeling and is embedded in a web of relations characterized by loyalty and where unselfishness dominates. The tango thus presents romantic love as less "pure" than a love based exclusively on moral duty. For a loving mother, there is no place for calculation, second thoughts, or hidden intentions. The idealized mother is the source of boundless love and absolute self-sacrifice. This kind of love seems complete, while the love of the *milonguita* and even of the male narrator (as compared with his mother) may just be a malevolent deceit. The *milonguita* cannot be transformed into a "mother," and, conversely, the "mother's" world excludes the nightlife of the public sphere. In other words, a *milonguita* will never be a wife, or a mother of many children. Hence, for the chaste mother, romantic love is impossible, just as motherhood is impossible for the *milonguita*.[14] Moreover, the mother is precisely the figure one cannot choose; and thus, also in this sense, she represents an absolute contrast.

In the complex relationships between the *milonguita*, the "mother," and the "son" (the narrator is always a son, never a father) the idea of guilt related to sinful behavior is one of the central moral elements connecting personal responsibility and conformity to social norms. Many classic tango texts express the dilemmas and the conflicts related to the pursuit of desire in a social context regulated by fixed rules of behavior. A son's love and consideration for his mother makes it possible for protagonists to recognize that emotions are closely connected to social norms. Romantic love challenges the accepted perception that feelings, pleasures, and excitements are culturally constructed. Instead they are perceived as "subversive" to family life and ordered biological reproduction.

The tango's discourse apparently suggests that motherly love, as the ideal representation of the reproducer, is an everlasting emotional state, and that the *milonguita* and the son need to understand this emotion as a precondition for experiencing new ones. The tango does not assert that abandoning romantic love is something positive. The conflicts and the psychological and moral dilemmas are presented, and at the same time the "mother" is depicted as a model of fidelity and continuity. The introduction of guilt understandably attempts to call attention to moral issues and to mitigate the image of men/people pursuing only their desires and narrow interests. At the same time, the tango narrative clearly shows that the elaboration of guilt is based on the experience and understanding of other emotions like joy, disappointment, jealousy, fear, happiness, and anxiety.

Tango poetics attempts to place the audience in a mood of melancholy and nostalgia for something important that has been lost. It is not by accident, then, that the great tango poet Enrique Santos Discépolo defined tango as "a sad thought that can be danced." This process of remembering previous suffering presupposes the capacity to pardon: the abandoned man transforms his disillusionment into a promise of deep friendship or the "sinful son" comes back home asking for forgiveness. Therefore, the act of forgiveness is made possible by a personal sense of guilt. However, the discourse of honor and shame coexists with the discourse of guilt. The tango presents another solution: that of vengeance. Let us explore this answer.[15]

The romantic lover and the powerful and cynical rich man (*bacán*) are not the only male archetypes in the tango narrative. One of the key figures is the *compadrito*. He is an elegant seducer whom no woman is able to resist, and is admired because of his courage, physical strength, and capacity to cheat where necessary. The *compadrito* has a defiant and hostile attitude toward other men. In the code of honor defended by the *compadrito*, violence and fighting establish and reproduce social hierarchies. Borges always preferred these texts, where the mission of tango was "to give Argentines the inner certainty of having been brave, of having performed in accordance with the requirements of daring and honor."[16] The social destiny of this rebellious man was thus based on a kind of ethic of "the man who is alone and expects nothing from others."[17] The figure of the *compadrito* is quite different from the man in search of happiness through romantic love (see "El porteñito" [1903] and "El taita" [1907]).[18] He is very concerned with women's loyalty but in a context where men expect obedience and submission from their women. He is a character from the outskirts, not the center, of the city. He is not a man of the cabaret, and most of the time he roams a local territory inhabited by other men like him. In this context male honor is very dependent on female sexual behavior. In some cases the betrayal by the women is punished by death, but in most, the woman is described as weak, unable to resist temptation.[19] The "other man" takes advantage of her moral fragility, and, consequently, is punished.

As I have pointed out above, in the romantic texts the abandoned man tries to understand and to forgive, he becomes a "full moral person" because his actions are guided by authentic feelings and genuine passion. However, the women are not perceived as weak but rather as autonomous and in a way, very determined. Such female independence serves as a contrast to many texts dealing with the moral discourse of honor and shame where the woman is portrayed as fragile and in need of protection. In the discourse of romantic love women can decide for themselves whom to love. In such cases the chosen man is responsible only for himself and not for her decisions and feelings. Thus this view of romantic love represents a break with traditional perceptions of women, reflecting also a new way of constructing male identity.

Many tangos between 1917 and 1930 present the figure of the *compadrito* in a deep identity crisis. In "La he visto con otro" (I have seen her with another man) the betrayed man will not kill her: while crying, he will try to forget her. In "Bailarín compadrito," the *compadrito* abandons his suburb and becomes a well-known cabaret dancer. In this process, he transforms himself into the opposite of a *compadrito*, becoming a kind of bourgeois "dandy" hiding his social origin and past life. In "Malevaje," the *compadrito* surprisingly falls in love. As a consequence of his feelings, he lost his "hope, courage, and wishes to be brave" and abandoned his "malevolent and ferocious past life." Thus, love comes to be seen as having a real transformative capacity: the *compadrito* will now avoid fighting and feels afraid of dueling because he can be killed or, if he kills, will suffer negative consequences.[20] The *compadrito*, in the last verse of the tango, begs the woman, "please, by God, tell me what you gave me / I am so transformed / I don't know who I am."[21]

Who is a "real" man: the romantic lover, the *bacán*, the *compadrito*, or the *compadrito* in crisis? Who is a "real" woman: the independent lover, the *milonguita*, the "mother," or the dependent and treacherous women of the *compadrito* universe? The tango depicts different kinds of men and women, a world of archetypes, a mixture of fiction and reality, creating a complex universe of moral and individual choices and dilemmas. The contrasting models of masculinity and the emotional relations between men and women are conveyed through different discourses of agency, personhood, and identity. The poets of the tango presented alternatives, puzzles, and some solutions. I argue that tango is today socially meaningful, not entirely but largely, because it provides a framework by which people recognize personal events, social contexts, and accepted cultural emotions, and the boundaries that separate them. The poetics of tango (as well as the music and the choreography) provides some means (and not all) by which gender identities are modeled in the public sphere.[22]

In a previous analysis of football fans' chants I have tried to depict the general cultural logic of this performance. In this essay I will concentrate on an analysis of the "discourses" of the supporters and their vanguard, the militant fans. The fans, in their constant activity, creating anthems, inventing nicknames, waving banners, and producing an endless series of chants, dedicate themselves to classifying and evaluating objects and actions. This way of classifying not only refers to a moral order, to what ought to be done and what ought not to be done, but also expresses a type of knowledge as to why things are as they are. In the ritual of football the moral order, whether subverted or not, whether lasting or transitory, lends itself to a sort of male evaluation of the value of autonomy, dependency, control, freedom, dignity, self-esteem, and loyalty to commitments. It is, accordingly, a world full of explicit and implicit meanings. It is a world in which symbolic frontiers appear clearly, starting from thoughts about a set of important social relations: father/son, adult/child, and "real man"/homosexual. Being a child or a boy or a homosexual entails the danger of losing autonomy. This is related also to "enduring," an explicit ideology on the importance of resisting pain and disappointment.[23]

One of the secrets of football is that it can still, despite its critics, be defined as a game. Games are generally associated with the exercise of imagination and the gratuitous search for difficulty. That is why the ultimate reward of football is always a reward for difficulties and rarity. The maximum event is seen as an aesthetic work, as a creation, as if the final product were the result of improvisation, intuition, and risk. At the same time, football creates conditions of equality among the players, in theory eleven on one side against eleven on the other, all with the same capacities and powers.

This condition of equality in the football stadium undoubtedly permits a rupture of the hierarchies of daily life and social structure. Furthermore, it is valid not only for the "central" players but also for the "peripheral" actors, the fans. Every Sunday football match creates a special world in clear contrast with the world of factory, office, or family. Because it allows the suspension of a certain social order, participants are granted a certain license. Football as a game has the power to decenter authoritarian rules and to recenter basic egalitarian feelings. The stadium thus offers men and those about to be men, the adolescents and children who accompany their fathers, a site where they can construct an order and a world that are strictly masculine. There an explicit moral discourse takes place, one that establishes boundaries between what is allowed and what is not allowed, between good and evil, and finally between the positive and negative aspects of what is ideally defined as masculine.

In the symbolic world of Argentine fans there are traditional verses called *hijos nuestros* (our sons) chanted for expressing the superiority of one team over the other. This chant is not a modern invention and has certainly existed since the first stages of the game in Argentina. What is the significance of this chant? Undoubtedly, "our sons" refers to a relation of paternity: son refers to father, whether known or unknown. When one group of fans refers to another in this way, alluding to the nature of the relationship between the two clubs, the effect of contempt and disdain is secured through the symbolic transformation of the other into child or son.

These chants presuppose the loss of the opponents' autonomy and the fact that they cannot act like real men. One does not expect rebellion or victory from a son: the son has to accept the authority, power, and orders of the father. At the same time, converting a person into a father means awarding a status of authority, respect, and power. The relationship between father and son does not refer to a symmetrical relationship where understanding and mutual respect prevail; instead, the central point comes to be subordination. This chant from the River Plate fans summarizes this type of relationship: "Calamar, calamar, calamar / ya sabemos que te vas para la B / te lo dice tu papá / que se llama River Plate" (Shellfish, shellfish, shellfish / We know you go to the B [the second division] / Your father tells you so / And he's called River Plate).[24]

The automatic response to an alleged relation of paternity is usually the traditional "sons of bitches" (*hijos de puta*), chanted loudly until "our sons" is drowned out. It is interesting to note that in these cases the insulted fans will never reply with an "hijos nuestros" unless this is substantiated by the statistics of the matches played. Accordingly, "hijos nuestros" expresses a relation of paternity and subordination that can be proved statistically.

The condition of being a child does not appear in many chants at present, and I do not think it did much in the past either. In the past Boca Juniors fans used to chant to River Plate fans: "River tenía un carrito / Boca se lo quitó / River salió llorando / Boca salió campeón" (River had a little cart / Boca took it away / River got up crying / Boca became champion), and "Vea, vea, vea / qué cosa tan fulera / ahora los de River / toman leche y mamadera" (Look, look, look / What a clumsy lot / Now the River boys / Suck a baby's bottle). Obviously, it does not allude to a filial relationship but, rather, to the condition of childhood, or to the lack of maturity, autonomy, and independence. The disqualification comes about by converting the other into a child; his condition as an adult, as an independent, autonomous man, is thereby denied. At present one of the favorite chants of the rival groups of fans against San Lorenzo de Almagro fans runs as follows: "Aquí está la famosa barra de San Lorenzo / la que no tiene cancha / la que se fue al descenso / ahora le pusieron un supermercado / y la mandan los domingos / a hacer los mandados" (Here's the famous San Lorenzo gang / Who haven't got a field / Who were pushed aside / So they set up a supermarket / And they send them on Sundays / To do the shopping). Presumably, no one but children would go shopping on Sundays, a day when "real men" are at the football stadium.

The short presentation of an event will serve to bring out one of the main concerns of contemporary militant fans. In 1984 in a match for the Libertadores Cup between Olimpia de Paraguay and Independiente of Argentina, played at level pegging, cleanly and with no violence, almost at the end of the second half it was a draw, 2–2. In those short, dramatic final minutes Independiente took the third goal and the victory. After the shout for the goal, and while the ball was going back to center field for what was to be a pointless further kickoff, the stands and the terracing of the red side of Independiente joined in a stentorian, unanimous shout: "Y ahora, y ahora / me chupan bien las bolas" (Now, now / They're really sucking me off properly). This was said with the typical jumps and fists raised towards the area of the stands occupied by five thousand or so Paraguayans who, it should be mentioned, had arrived at the stadium with posters praising Argentine democracy and condemning the Stroessner dictatorship.

The immediate question is why in the moment of victory did the fans choose to offend the losers, to humiliate them? The affirmation of masculinity depends upon depriving the other of his masculinity. The conquered, the weak, in other words the one who is not a "real man," has to do, or be supposed to do, things that go against his nature. The fans have created a vast repertoire where the construction of sexuality and a world divided between men and fake men, that is homosexuals, comes to be the central aspect.[25] One example among many: "Cordobés, cordobés / limpiáte bien el culo / que te vamos a coger" (Cordoban, Cordoban / Wipe your bottom well / Cordoban we're coming to screw you).[26] This relation looks more personal in the following chant: "Sol y luna, sol y luna / sol y luna, sol y luna / la poronga de Labruna / en el culo de Labruna" (Sun and moon, sun and moon / Sun and moon, sun and moon / Armando's dong / In Labruna's ass).[27]

The famous "Bambino Veira case" or "incident" has in recent years become the privileged context for creating chants.[28] Viera was accused of molesting a boy, making his nickname "Bambino" sound somewhat ironic. The rival fans of San Lorenzo shouted: "Compañero, Bambino, zapatero / la concha de tu madre / le pagaste al portero / le pagaste a la cana / te cogiste al pibe / hijo de la puta madre" (Mate, Bambino, cobbler / Your mother's cunt / You paid off the doorkeeper / You paid off the cop / You were screwing a boy / You son of a bitch).[29]

In all these chants what seems clear is that the fans of one team or particular central actors (a trainer, a player, or a manager) are the real machos, the real men, able to force the other fans or social actors to play the homosexual. It is interesting to note that the homosexuals are those who let themselves be humiliated, those who do not defend their masculine identity with sufficient force. A popular chant, sung by many fans in three recent seasons, is a clear threat against the players if they do not win, warning them of what might happen to them: "Vamos, vamos a ganar / que si no, los vamos a vejar" (Come on, come on we're going to win / Otherwise we're going to take them). Those who do the taking are the strong, the real men, and in no case see themselves as homosexuals. This distinction between the passive and the active role is illustrated clearly in the rhymes alluding to the "Veira case": for the rivals of San Lorenzo, Bambino is downgraded into a "son of a bitch" and the San Lorenzo fans reclaim his role as macho. In no case is there an explicit moral sanction on behavior judged as abnormal. The rival fans do not say that Bambino is a homosexual.

The field of sexuality is in turn a world of rules and prohibitions that refer to morality, to what is permitted and accepted in a particular society, to a range of expectations in which it is possible to play and experiment with unsatisfied fantasies and desires. Similarly, the sexuality displayed in a particular relationship is bound up with sensual and sentimental aspects that articulate both individual and gender identity. The fans, by choosing the field of discourse of sexuality, call upon all these levels, and therefore transform the traditional content of the discourses. The explicit introduction of sexuality into the public arena of football is a recent change that is worth stressing. In doing this, the fans are in a way breaking a taboo, a set of rules: sexuality is being converted into a public, open discourse (many would say an expression of the coarseness and "bad taste" of the popular classes). My hypothesis is that the "conversation" set up between rival groups of fans takes place at the level not of the comic but of the tragic.

The "tragic" effect is secured by breaking a rule, namely the norm of heterosexuality. This breach, it is worth stressing, is done by a person (individual, player or trainer, or a social being, a particular group of fans) with whom people sympathize and can identify. From the viewpoint of the San Lorenzo fans, Bambino is not repulsive, but at the same time not so good that one cannot identify with him. If Bambino were entirely evil as a character, this positive identification would not exist. The same could be said of the other personalities mentioned in the chant. However, the presence of transgression does not eliminate the rule that defines "normality," namely, that normal sexuality is that between persons of different sexes. Tragic themes are usually related with the type of existential dilemmas that may be particularly prominent in the field of sexuality.

This observation does not imply that the normality of heterosexuality is not considered. However, the chants referring to it are very much in the minority, and those I have compiled have to do with the traditional grudge against the English. When they lost against England in the 1966 World Cup, the fans of River later chanted: "Y si la Reina / se baja su tapado / el viejo Onega / le clava su poronga" (And if the Queen / Gets down on all fours / Old Onega / Will nail her yam). When there was a win over England in the 1986 World Cup, one of the most popular chants during the celebrations was "Thatcher, Thatcher, Thatcher / ¿dónde estás? / Maradona te anda buscando / para metértela por detrás" (Thatcher, Thatcher, Thatcher / Where are you? / Maradona's looking for you / To screw you from behind).[30] How is the meaning of this type of obsession by militant fans to be interpreted? I think the interpretation invites an obvious psychoanalytic interpretation: the chants display protective inversion mechanisms, because they combine the sadistic fantasies of the macho with his deep doubts as to his own masculinity. These doubts evidently stimulate the making of this type of affirmation.[31] This interpretation assumes, without much discussion, that all the psychological symbols have a special meaning at the motivational level. I do not deny that this may be true for many fans, but it is hard to know it without interviewing every one of them. I think that the examples I have given can be treated not as personal symbols but as symbols that constitute a public field of discourse where there is no need to operate with the hypothesis of profound motivation.[32] This enables us to distinguish the origin of the chants, which may be in the unconscious or even form part of the dream repertoire, from their operational meaning, that is, the creation of a public tragic effect. The conversion into an element of public discourse is a feature of a general attitude and not of the free expression of individual emotions, as I have sometimes emphasized in this text.

Clearly, homosexual relationships, in the case we are concerned with, refer to a public arena where symbols operate at a collective level. The fans dramatize these relationships, and their ritual use refers on the one hand to a sensual aspect, in this case sexual relations, the anus and the penis, and on the other to an ideological aspect where what is affirmed is strength, omnipotence, violence, and the breaking of the other's identity. In this process what appears as the central concern is the construction of a certain type of masculinity, a sort of prototype of the militant fan. What is important about this tragic effect is that it makes it possible for intrapsychic conflicts to be expressed in a cultural idiom and through the license of a ritual such as football.

The fans, accordingly, construct a metaphorical field. They are not passive beings; they see themselves and act as true protagonists. This metaphorical field is constructed on the basis of what we may call analogical extension: the enemies, the defeated, who are the chief subject of the chants, are described in terms of homosexuality, which is the subsidiary subject. This is present in the chants presented above. However, another example will be useful to bring this type of argument out clearly. It is traditional in a game against Brazil or Brazilian teams for Argentine fans to chant: "Y ya lo ven, y ya lo ven / Brasil está de luto / son todos negros / son todos putos" (we all know / Brazil's in mourning / they're all niggers / they're all queer). The main subject, Brazil, is associated with the category of niggers and queers.

The chants function as metaphors by selecting, emphasizing, suppressing, and organizing aspects that make it possible for gender identity to be dramatized; placing heterosexuality in suspension does not imply that it does not exist in the field of the normal. The transgression is referred to specifically in order to reinforce the rules. It is the other who, by allowing himself to be penetrated and humiliated, recalls the importance of masculinity as the language of domination. Physical violence is an extension to the field of practice of this type of conceptual construction.

I can summarize this section by saying that the "worst" image of a real man seems to be that of being a child, boy, and homosexual. These are the positions of maximum heteronomy and marginality in the range of relations of social forces in Argentine society. The Argentine fans are reflecting in their chants on the problematic content of the relations between fathers and sons, between adults and children, and, finally, between real men and homosexuals. The construction of a positive masculine identity means that one must overcome the negative, and somewhat arbitrary, aspect of these power relationships. Football serves to rethink and recall the limits and dangers of any transgression. Likewise, and quite clearly, it refers to those conceptual aspects where the classification of distinct types of social relationship is the privileged thematics of ritual.

• BY WAY OF CONCLUSION

Football allows perception of a world as socially constructed by its various actors, especially by the peripheral players, the fans and their militant vanguard. In this cultural world, the idioms of masculinity tell us something about the way in which packages of social and individual identity are constructed through the dramatization that can be found in linguistic codes. At the same time the actors appear as "moral actors" in the sense that they assign value to particular objects and particular actions. It is, accordingly, a world full of explicit and implicit meanings. It is a world in which symbolic frontiers appear clearly, starting with thoughts about a set of important social relations: father/son, adult/child, and "real man"/homosexual.[33] On these, obviously, the actors ponder in other less public contexts, with less show, and without the smell of police tear gas. Thus, relations between men can partially be understood in terms of dominance, control, and power.[34]

The social and symbolic world of tango tell us about the importance of love for women in creating a positive masculine image. The emphasis is placed on emotional control and, thereby, on the search for "authentic" and "romantic" love. I have tried to demonstrate that the epos of honor and shame, where the narrator tells stories of vengeance and death, will be replaced by the importance of expressing authentic feelings as a way of constructing personal dignity. Romantic love in the tango is perceived as a kind of rebellion against a conception of domestic love based on the "sacralization" of the familial space. In the universe of tango the father, omnipresent in the discourses of football, is absent. Consequently, the tango lyrics will never emphasize marriage, a kind of *pax matrimonialis*, as the only possible way to happiness. "Man the reproducer" is replaced by "man the lover," a "suffering man" unable to control women.

The comparative masculinities depicted in the universes of tango and football appear as fluid, ambiguous, on occasion contradictory, perhaps subversive of a dominant and hegemonic heterosexual Argentine masculinity based on the institutionalization of men's dominance over women. The active men in the ritual arenas of football and tango are dispossessed of social power and wealth and, therefore, less concerned with the reproduction of the image of a dominating middle-class "pure" heterosexual male.[35]

• NOTES

1. The tango texts analyzed constitute the core of "classic" songs. They are very much played, and past and present singers and popular orchestras will always include them in their repertoires. The poetics of tango was a historical product of the city of Buenos Aires but now is undoubtedly part of the ballads of a turbulent nation. The gathering of football texts (chants and songs) has been based on my attending in Buenos Aires thirty-four first-division football matches during four months in 1984, five months in 1988, and two months in 1994. During this period I did not follow a given club or group of fans.

2. Andrea Cornwall and Nancy Lindisfarne, "Dislocating Masculinities: Gender, Power and Anthropology," in *Dislocating Masculinities*, ed. Cornwall and Lindisfarne (London: Routledge, 1994).

3. Different military governments and many nationalist writers in the 1920s considered "subversive" the ideal image of the Argentine male seen in many tango texts in my paper. This, I hope, will be clear later in the text.

4. There is general agreement among tango historians on the centrality of this period: see Darío Cantón, *¿Gardel, a quién le cantás?* (Buenos Aires: Ediciones de la Flor, 1972); Simon Collier, *The Life, Music and Times of Carlos Gardel* (Pittsburgh: University of Pittsburgh Press, 1986); Horacio Ferrer, *El tango. Su historia y evolución* (Buenos Aires: A. Peña Lillo, 1960); Blas Matamoro, *La ciudad del tango* (Buenos Aires: Editorial Galerna, 1982); Horacio Salas, *El tango* (Buenos Aires: Planeta, 1986); and Noemí Ulla, *Tango, rebelión y nostalgia* (Buenos Aires: Centro Editor de América Latina, 1982). Marta E. Savigliano, in *Tango and the Political Economy of Passion* (Boulder: Westview Press, 1994), has shown how the "exotic" tango became a world cultural commodity during these years. On the role of "dangerous" sexual women, especially prostitutes, in the creation of gender anxiety in Buenos Aires see Donna J. Guy, *Sex and Danger in Buenos Aires* (Lincoln: University of Nebraska Press, 1991).

5. Jorge Luis Borges, *Evaristo Carriego*, in *Prosa completa*, vol. 1 (Barcelona: Bruguera, 1980), 93.

6. Niklas Luhmann, *El amor como pasión* (Barcelona: Ediciones Peninsula, 1985).

7. See "Mi noche triste" (1917), "La cumparsita" (1924), "Amurado" (1927), and "Farolito de Papel," in Eduardo Romano, *Las letras del tango: Antología cronológica: 1900–1980* (Rosario: Editorial Fundación Ross, 1991). Romano has produced the best chronological anthology of tango lyrics. Each text is reproduced with a short (and fascinating) history of who sang and recorded it. This makes it possible to "measure" the historical persistence of the different songs.

8. The cabaret in Buenos Aires and the rest of the world posed a concrete challenge to the cult of domestic life and family parties or celebrations. The cabaret was not a typical family entertainment like, for instance, the circus, vaudeville, restaurants, theater, or movies. Rather, it serviced the sexual or erotic fantasies and desires of adult men and women. The cabaret was a modern arena for taking time out and for many women to "step out" of control (see Lewis A. Erenberg, *Steppin' out: New York Nightlife and the Transformation of American Culture* (Chicago: University of Chicago Press, 1981); Peter Jelavich, "Modernity, Civic Identity, and Metropolitan Entertainment: Vaudeville, Cabaret, and Revue in Berlin, 1900–1933," in *Berlin, Culture and Metropolis*, ed. Charles W. Haxthausen and Heidrun Suhr (Minneapolis: University of Minnesota Press, 1990); Harold B. Segel, *Turn-of-the Century Cabaret* (New York: Columbia University Press, 1987); and Jerrold Siegel, *Bohemian Paris: Culture, Politics, and the Boundaries of Bourgeois Life, 1830–1930* (New York: Viking, 1986); as well as Matamoro, *La ciudad del tango*.

9. See "Flor de fango" (1917), "Margot" (1919), "Mano a mano" (1920), "Zorro gris" (1920), "El motivo" (1920), "Ivette" (1920), "Milonguita" (1920), "Pompas de jabón" (1925), "Che Papusa oí" (1927), "Muñeca brava" (1928), "Milonguera"

(1929), "Mano cruel" (1929), "¿Sos vos?" (1930), all in Romano, *Las letras del tango*.

10. It could be questioned how truly middle-class they are, because many of the tango lyricists were working-class and often anarchist.

11. How does this fit into the middle-class image and the fact that many of them are unemployed?

12. Beatriz Sarlo, *El imperio de los sentimientos* (Buenos Aires: Catálogos, 1985).

13. See "Flor de fango" (1917), "Margot" (1919), "Madre" (1922), "Nunca es tarde" (1925), "Milonguera" (1929), and "La casita de mis viejos" (1931), all in Romano, *Las letras del tango*.

14. On contrasting images of women and motherhood in Argentina, see Guy, this volume.

15. See "Mano a mano" (1920) and "La casita de mis viejos" (1931) in Romano, *Las letras del tango*. I have developed these ideas at length in other papers: see Archetti, "Argentinian Tango. Male Sexual Ideology and Morality," in *The Ecology of Choice and Symbol. Essays in Honour of Fredrik Barth*, ed. Reidar Grønhaug (Bergen: Alma Mater, 1991), and "Models of Masculinity in the Poetics of the Argentinian Tango," in *Exploring the Written. Anthropology and the Multiplicity of Writing*, ed. Eduardo P. Archetti (Oslo: Scandinavian University Press, 1994).

16. Borges, *Evaristo Carriego*, 91.

17. Borges, preface to *El compadrito*, ed. Jorge Luis Borges and Silvina Bullrich (Buenos Aires: Emecé Editores, 1956), 8.

18. Both included in Romano, *Las letras del tango*.

19. See "Desdén" (1927) and "La gayola" (1929), in Cantón, *¿Gardel, a quién le cantas?*, 84, 132.

20. See "La he visto con otro" (1926), "Malevaje" (1928) and "Bailarín compadrito" (1929) in Romano, *Las letras del tango*.

21. Ibid, 151–52.

22. Fito Paéz, an Argentine rock idol and a talented composer, has recently argued that the themes of classical tango lyrics are as pertinent as the rock songs written by him and others in expressing feelings, emotions, and cultural values (*El País*, 6 July 1995, 34). For rock and popular Argentine singers to perform tango songs is no longer a sign of "decadence," of a "trip to the past."

23. Archetti, "Place et fonctions du comique (ou) du tragique dans le 'discours' des 'supporters' du football argentin," in *Anthropologie du sport. Perspectives critiques*, ed. Jacques Ardoino and Jean-Marie Brohm (Paris: Quel Corps?, 1991), and "Argentinian Football: A Ritual of Violence?" *International Journal of the History of Sport* 9.2 (1992): 209–35.

24. Or when, appealing to tradition, they chant: "Vamos, vamos los villeros / vamos a ganar / que nacieron hijos nuestros / hijos nuestros morirán" (Come on, come on slum lads / We are going to win / They were born our children / Our children they will die). Many of the "cantitos" do not rhyme, but some do. They are usually sung to the tune of a current hit song. The use of very current hits is taken as a sign of ingenuity on the part of the fans because what is a popular song one day may be forgotten the next.

25. My analysis is mainly focused on "key" teams of the Argentine first divi-

sion—Boca Juniors, River Plate, San Lorenzo de Almagro, Independiente, and Racing, called the "five great teams"—and on important but less "legendary" teams such as Huracán, Estudiantes de La Plata, Gimnasia y Esgrima, and Newell's Old Boys. The "five great" are from different suburbs of Buenos Aires. These clubs, well known internationally because they have exported outstanding players to European football since the 1920s, can also be seen as the only "national teams" with supporters all over Argentina.

26. More examples: "Huracán, Huracán / por el culo te la dan" (Huracán, Huracán / They'll give you it up the ass); "Hinchada, hinchada hay una sola / hinchada es la de Boca / que le rompe el culo a todas" (Fandom, fandom, there is only one / That's Boca's fans / That will break the asses of the lot of them); "Vea, vea, vea / que equipo más boludo / ahora, a la salida / le rompemos bien el culo" (Look, look, look / What a fucked up team / On the way out / We'll really break their ass); "Despacito, despacito / le rompemos el culito" (Slowly, slowly / We'll break their little ass); "Mandarina, mandarina / que se metan en el culo / el apodo de gallinas" (Tangerine, tangerine / Let them stuff it up their ass / Their nickname Hen); "River no te me borrés / River no te me borrés / no jugués a la escondida / porque a la salida / te vamos a coger" (River you won't escape me / River you won't escape me / Don't play at hide-and-seek / For on the way out / We're going to screw you); "Oh, oh, oh, por el horto / oh, oh, oh por el horto; Veo, veo / que ves / una cosa / que la historia / se repite otra vez / los volvemos a coger" (Oh, oh, oh, up your asshole / Oh, oh, oh, up your ass; Look, look / What can you see / What a thing / It's history / It's repeating itself again / We're going to screw them again).

27. More examples: "Pan y vino / Pan y vino / pan y vino / la poronga de Menotti / en el culo del Bambino" (Bread and wine / Bread and wine / Bread and wine / Menotti's dong / In Bambino's ass); "Señor Armando / señor Armando / a su cuadrito lo cojemos caminando" (Mr. Armando, Mr. Armando / We'll screw your little team on the way); "Ruso, ruso / el tano te la puso" (Ruso, Ruso / The Wops stuffed it up you); "Donde puso el huevo Tarabini / yo no sé, yo no sé" (Where Tarabini laid the egg / I don't know, I don't know); "Soy de Boca, soy de Boca / qué puto yo soy" (I'm Boca, I'm Boca / What a fag I am) (sung by the San Lorenzo fans); "Con cariño, con cariño / la pija de Menotti / en el culo de Coutinho" (Tenderly, tenderly / Tenderly, tenderly / Menotti's prick / In Coutinho's ass); "Qué feo, qué feo / qué feo debe ser / venirse desde el Parque / para verse coger" (How, horrible, how horrible / How horrible it must be / To come all the way from the Parque / Only to get yourself screwed); "Vale diez palos verdes / se llama Maradona / y todos los de River / le chupan bien las bolas / y cuando va a la cancha / la doce le agradece / todo lo que Dieguito se merece" (He's worth ten greenbacks / He's called Maradona / And everyone from River / Sucks him off properly / And when he comes onto the ground / The twelfth man thanks him / For all that Dieguito deserves).

28. Veira was a famous San Lorenzo de Almagro player in the 1960s. A brilliant technical striker, he was also well known for his flamboyant "playboy" life. He later become a coach. In 1980 he was accused of raping a young boy who approached him asking for an autograph, and was put in prison for a short period. While the trial continued, he became a successful coach in Argentina, Colombia, and Spain. Finally,

in May 1992 he was sentenced to four years in prison. He appealed and in 1994 was declared innocent.

29. More examples of the Bambino Viera chants: "Bambino prestáme a la Pepa / y yo te presto a mi sobrino" (Bambino lend me Pepa / And I'll lend you my nephew), Pepa being the nickname of Veira's wife. The San Lorenzo fans reply: "Cuidado, cuidado / el Bambino está afuera" (Watch out, watch out / Bambino's about); or, "Yo te la meto / te la dejo / el Bambino se coge a todos los putos" (I'll stuff it up / I'll leave it in / Bambino will fuck all the fags).

30. One of the few groups of fans that continually asserts the value of "normal" heterosexual intercourse are those of Gimnasia de la Plata, who often chant: "Para ser un hincha del Lobo / hay que tener / una botella de vino / y una mina al lado" (To be a Lobo fan / You have to have / A bottle of wine / And a woman in your bed).

31. Marcelo Suárez Orozco, "A Study of Argentine Soccer: The Dynamics of the Fans and Their Folklore," *Journal of Psychoanalytic Anthropology* 5.1 (1982): 7–27.

32. About this distinction, see Gananath Obeyesekere, *Medusa's Hair* (Chicago: University of Chicago Press, 1984), 14–18.

33. Lancaster has convincingly shown that the stigma of the homosexual in Nicaragua derives not just from anal passivity and penile activity in particular but from "passivity" and "activity" in general: "Subject Honor and Object Shame: The Construction of Male Homosexuality and Stigma in Nicaragua," *Ethnology* 27.2 (1988): 111–25, and *Life Is Hard: Machismo, Danger, and the Intimacy of Power in Nicaragua* (Berkeley: University of California Press, 1992), 242–43. This sexual ideology seems very common in Latin American popular culture. The Argentine middle class tends to perceive this behavior as perverse and consequently not as a real expression of masculinity. Peter Loizos has observed that Greeks accept male heterosexual penetration as real and as dominating male behavior: "A Broken Mirror: Masculine Sexuality in Greek Ethnography," in *Dislocating Masculinities*, ed. Andrea Cornwall and Nancy Lindisfarne (London: Routledge, 1994), 71.

34. On the historical relation between the social and symbolic universes of tango and football, see Archetti, "Estilos y virtudes masculinas en *El Gráfico*: la creación del imaginario del fútbol argentino," *Desarrollo Económico* 139 (1995).

35. On the contrasting and coexisting models of masculinity in Spain and Greece, see Angie Hart, "Missing Masculinity? Prostitutes' Clients in Alicante, Spain," in *Dislocating Masculinities*, ed. Cornwall and Lindisfarne, and Loizos, "A Broken Mirror."

Part Four

Redefinitions

14 *Francine Masiello*

Gender, Dress, and Market

The Commerce of Citizenship in Latin America

La sudaca irá a la venta. —Diamela Eltit, *El cuarto mundo*

In August 1994 visual artist Juan Dávila caused a minor scandal when reproductions of his painting of Simon Bolívar in drag circulated throughout Chile. The "Liberator" of Spanish America was portrayed with rouge and lipstick; beneath a flowered cape and a military uniform, he exposed the breasts of a woman. This camp representation of one of South America's most revered founding fathers drew immediate protests from Venezuelan and Colombian diplomats and irritated Chilean officials. As a result, FONDART, the sponsoring organization of fellowships for Chilean artists, rejected Dávila's petition for funding and refused to entertain future proposals from individual applicants. The episode is certainly reminiscent of the NEA's uproar over the work of Robert Mapplethorpe and Andrés Serrano, but Dávila's project also brings to mind a number of contradictions about the reception and interpretation of modern Latin American culture.

Can we reduce the artist's rendition to a simple example of postmodern camp? A playful confusion of images that borders on the absurd? Possibly so, but Dávila's portrait also offers other readings, reminding us how the gendered body shapes both the political forum and the theater of commerce and trade. Dávila's work calls specific attention to the role that gender and sexuality play in defining Latin American subjects; it interrogates fixed notions of identity passed on from founding fathers. Indeed, as Chilean critic Raquel Olea has shown,[1] Dávila's painting reminds us that the national project depends on a masculine, heterosexual body to organize memory and history. It also suggests that others have the right to construct an image of the national hero and to reverse the common aesthetic and symbolic legacies that have excluded considerations of gender. In the same vein, Dávila shows us that patriotism is also a commercial construct, based on the wholesale packaging and trade of poses, gestures, styles, and dress. In fact, this portrait forms part of a large installation piece entitled *Utopia* (1988), in which Dávila tests concepts of gender and nation on a canvas of images, all assembled from religious relics, tourist postcards, and mass-culture objects, and underscoring the ready-made tokens of exchange from which national symbols are born. The work thus evokes the excesses of commodity trade in general while mocking the state-endorsed traffic in nostalgia and invented tradition.

I begin with this example in order to make the case that gender in Latin America is often represented as a visual spectacle on the national political stage. Moreover, the accoutrements of gender—cosmetics, dress, and pose—are treated as commodities to be bought and sold in the image-making service of the nation. In effect, from the time of the nineteenth-century independence wars through the recent transition to democracy, patterns of dress and sexuality have formed part and parcel of the Latin American political imagination. At times, gendered representations bestowed validity upon national projects—for example, images of the warrior hero or the "republican mother" were used to dignify the newly independent countries following their freedom from Spain. Toward the century's close, the marketing of gender images and dress served the liberal state as a vehicle to modernize culture. Dress, when monitored under the aegis of fashion, created the illusion of choice and freedom within clearly marked boundaries of decorum. Moreover, with this discourse in hand, Latin America was able to compete with European style and keep pace with trends from abroad. Fashion thus strengthened the projects of the modern state; it also endorsed a mode of citizenship related to sales and commerce. How to act as a modern person in the nation was set out through prescribed behaviors and through standards of dress and speech. They all conferred a limited range of identities upon individuals as a part of a fledgling democracy. This was reinforced through projects of secular education and the ideological controls of the press, which directed consumer tastes and controlled private desires. In this way, they regulated the *style* of being a citizen.

The current *fin de siglo* is not lacking for comparisons with the time one hundred years ago. Once again, the state faces the task of reconsolidation, this time under a neoliberal agenda for a free-market economy. With the globalization of capital, the control of labor and markets and the advancement of a mass media project that seriously constrains local culture, citizenship is redefined as performance, while fashion, sales, and the camera lens create a peculiar politics of identity. This predominantly visual mode belonging to the media orients our understanding of the public and private dimensions of life; it shapes electoral campaigns and consumer preferences and conditions us for immediate gratifications. Dress and style count more than any program of collective well-being and needs.

Nevertheless, while the state posits a need for fixed subjectivities and stable positions of meaning, the free play of artifice and shifting identities proliferates without relief. In this respect, when alternative gendered identities emerge, erupting below the tightly woven fabric of patriotic discourse, they often supply an emancipatory potential, a proposal for democratic action. The play of appearances thus overrides state and media control and, like Dávila's portrait, invites a powerful critique of the commodification of form. A closer look at the nineteenth century in comparison with our current times reveals interesting links between gender, dress, and the commerce of the modern state.

A first, curious case emerges around the theme of "la monja alférez," or the "ensign nun." One of the classic legends of Latin America, especially in Mexico and the Andean nations, the story of Catalina de Erauso is about a seventeenth-century Basque nun who flees the convent and, dressed as a man, joins the army of Conquistadors traveling from Mexico to Chile.[2] Her masculine disguise enables her to participate in the conquest of the Araucanian Indians; it also allows her a number of adventures with women of the creole elite. A swashbuckler and pursued assassin, Catalina de Erauso repeatedly escapes the law and seeks refuge in the convent. In some versions, she returns to Spain as a nun or finds religious solace in Mexico; in other stories, she is shot at sea or dies of natural causes in the New World. Interestingly enough, the lesbianism of the Basque nun was not directly brought into question; instead, what attracted the attention of historians was the permissiveness of the Catholic Church and the corruption of the Spanish crown. This tale was carried forth with many variants but acquired renewed interest in the nineteenth century as a way to express concern about the relationship between Latin America and Spain and then to ventilate anxiety about the growth of commerce in the postindependence years. A contrast of two versions of this tale reveals the evolution of these concerns. The first is an 1848 story by José Victorino Lastarria, one of

Chile's most important political figures;[3] the second is an account of "la monja" supplied by positivist historian Diego Barros Arana and published in the *Revista de Santiago* in 1872.[4]

In Lastarria's tale, entitled "El Alférez Alonso Díaz de Guzmán," the nun as ensign is in love with another officer but pretends to be upset about that soldier's engagement to a woman named Angelina. Anchored in a discussion about truth and deception, the novella takes cross-dressing as a metaphor for verbal duplicity and bilingual speech. It is not unplanned, for example, that the ensign in moments of undress (a naked, essential self?) speaks to her brother in the Basque language; by contrast, Castilian (as the language of colonial law) becomes the medium of cloaked intentions and mistruths. The nun, when dressed as a man, becomes a symbol of the colonial failure to regulate its subjects under a single civic code.[5] Lastarria resolves this crisis by removing the ensign's disguise at the end of his novella; she confesses her love for a military man and later plunges into the sea. Order is thus brought to the colony and the suspicion of deviance is arrested.

This tale from 1848 is a reflection on the errors of the colonial regime and its failure to standardize rules of speech and dress in the service of civic virtue. Yet the slippage of Lastarria's story line reveals that the element of cross-dressing, however morally questionable for the author, is in fact the driving force behind fiction; it allows for the story to accelerate and expand, and creates a machine for the production of a New World discourse.

By contrast, Diego Barros Arana's account—published nearly twenty-five years later—proliferates in radically different ways so that the nun's travels come to signal the excessive liberties of women in commercial society. Citing a text of 1653, Barros Arana tells of the nun's adventures in Mexico, where she travels as a merchant in the company of a sixteen-year-old girl. As she takes to the business of commerce and sales, the nun protects the identity of her companion, threatening to kill anyone who dares to unveil her. Catalina de Erauso thus proceeds until her death in 1650, somewhere on the trade routes between Mexico and Vera Cruz. In Barros Arana's presentation, the woman is pure ambiguity; she first befriends a gentleman and later challenges him to a duel; she forbids her companion to converse with men yet allows for her betrothal. In this respect, she is both the accomplice and enemy of men. Moreover, she denies her companion any voice in the tale so that the girl remains a shadow of others with no expressions of feelings or reason.

The scene corresponds to the irrationality of a new form of itinerant commerce in Latin America, and parallels a late-nineteenth-century anxiety for progress and change. In the context of an "on-the-road" story governed by business and eros, the status of women demands revision; now, they stand accused of delinquency in matters of citizenship and honor but still remain essential for the process of modernization. Again, the ensign nun fulfills a double function: she signals deviant behavior as well as an aesthetic potential. Barros Arana celebrates the discovery of a seventeenth-century tale yet calls into question the volatility of the nun and her roamings in the world of commerce. Women, in this case, suggest an anxiety about lucrative ventures; hence, the concern for institutional order, so important to writers like Lastarria, is now redirected to include matters of money and trade.

Lest this anecdote be removed from its context, it should be noted that Barros Arana's account very much coincides with the logic of other texts published in the *Revista de Santiago*. Directed by Augusto Orrego Luco and engaging the participation of the most important political and cultural figures in Chile at the time, the journal gave marked attention to the demands of citizenship in a new society along with a fiercely anticlerical claim for secular rule. The *Revista de Santiago* attempted to modernize the legal codes of Chile; contributors thus argued for the separation of church and state, and for a reformed civil code with permission for secular marriage. They also extended a broad appeal for female education as if to control, by a standardization of training, the proliferation of dispersed female identities observable in Chile. The *Revista de Santiago* often tried to catalogue the Chilean population: body counts of the deceased, the number of immigrants who reached the shores of Valparaíso, school enrollments, membership lists in civic societies, and inventories of names and addresses formed part of a discourse about modernity, regulating populations and naming all local subjects. In this obsessive context, elements of disguise, or excess in dress or decorum, were perceived as ways to sabotage the state and confuse the identities of citizens.

The great fear in this instance is simulation and deception, named by intellectuals such as the Argentine José Ingenieros (1902) as the great pathology of modern times.[6] Taking his cue from Darwin, he sought to explain the struggle for life as an activity producing constant behavioral mutations and leading to mimetic compulsions. The man of character, who was committed to action and strongly anchored in his beliefs, was now replaced, in the *fin de siglo*, by the "hombre amorfo," chameleon-like in appearance and credo.

Latin American newspapers and magazines of the time are replete with articles about the dangerous extravagance of dress and disguise and, as a remedy, offer guidelines for the conduct of readers. Most often, they fear cross-dressing as the principal metaphor for these sinister deceits and discreetly recommend conventional good taste to control deviant behaviors.

The Argentine newspaper *La Tribuna*, in a column of social commentary, recommends appropriate dress:

> La mujer con corbata, chaleco, gabán y pantalones y un hombre con sortijas, pulseras, bermellón y rizos, tienen mucho que entender. Esto es, tienen que entender que no entienden las leyes de buen gusto.

> (A woman with tie, vest, jacket, and pants, and a man with earrings, bracelets, hair dye and curls, have a lot to learn. They must understand that they do *not* understand the rules of good taste).[7]

Here, style and fashion are obvious points of distinction for a new consumer society; "good taste" is a social regulator, a way to control abuse and excess. Nevertheless, those who would dictate the rules of dress also understand that fashion creates a fiction of its own, catering to impostors and fakes, who test the laws of inheritance through various forms of disguise. In this respect, the fiction of dress is the only truth in the climate of modernization; it becomes the equivalent of pleasure. This new economy of style dominates the *fin de siglo* and also creates a number of apprehensions about the proper identity of citizens. With its immigrants, anarchists, rural migrants, and countless *arrivistes*, the city bespeaks chaos. Again, this confusion is expressed through an active concern for nonstandard dress and confused gender identity.

Demanding to regulate the consumer habits of citizens and clarify who's who in society, Nicolás Bolet Peraza appends a photograph of contemporary life to his article "La mujer nueva" (The new woman).[8] The print shows seven persons: one in a riding habit, several in suits with bowler hats, a bearded figure near a bicycle, another guiding a wheel; several with neckties, a few with boots. The caption reads, "Confusión de sexos, ¿Quién es quién?" (Confusion of sexes: Who's who?). Bolet Peraza then supplies a long essay on recommended dress for women in society. Although the masquerade may very well mark the *fin de siglo*, he issues a call for order and for the disentanglement of social relations created by gender confusion:

> La mujer en calzas es una provocación que se presenta a tres autoridades: a la Sociedad, a la Higiene, y a la Estética. La estética es, por ahora, la más ofendida de las tres. Dice que la mujer ha ido a copiar la moda salvaje; que ha ido a copiar el traje de las mujeres Esquimales; dice que las formas femeninas, cuyo mérito escultórico consisten en ciertos pleonasmos de contorno que no caben en el prosaico vestido del varón, pierden todo su encanto natural. Y la Sociedad alega que los pantalones y el *sport* en la mujer la desenfemenizan y hombrean; y por último, la Higiene abre su gran libro estadístico, para probar

con resultados de observación, que el traje masculino, cuando no viste formas masculinas, tiene sus inconvenientes; y como quiera que la mención de esos inconvenientes se lo guarda la Higiene para exponerlos en la Clínica, resulta que los profanos nos quedamos en ayunas de inconvenientes. . . . Queda la cuestión de gustos.

(A woman in pants provokes three public authorities: Society, Hygiene, and Aesthetics. Aesthetics, for the moment, is the most offended of the three. "Aesthetics" opines that woman has copied the style of savages; that she has copied the outfits of Eskimo women. It claims that feminine form, whose sculpted beauty consists of various redundancies not apt for the prosaic suits of men, loses all its natural charm. And "Society" alleges that pants and jackets defeminize woman and make her masculine. Finally, the field of "Hygiene" opens its great book of statistics to prove empirically that masculine dress when not used by masculine forms, carries its inconveniences. . . . And then there's the question of taste).[9]

As might be expected, Bolet Peraza opposes masculine dress for women; nevertheless, he endorses *regulated* market forms of female enhancement. In typically turn-of-the-century mode, he urges the sale of cosmetics and medicinal beauty cures. In particular, the "Píldoras tocológicas," invented by Dr. Bolet himself and advertised repeatedly in the pages of his magazine, promise to restore natural color to women, to bring vitality to the eyes, and to provide a lasting change in appearance. His cure, of course, is attached to a vision of the fragmented female body that promises an interest in profit and sales.[10]

As a new market strategy for introducing readers to consumer society, journalists urged the purchase of cosmetics while they standardized dress for women. This narrative move linked female identity to an economy of sales as it also revealed anxieties about the increasing autonomy of new populations in Latin American cities.

Caras y Caretas (1898–1939), Argentina's long-running cultural magazine, synthesized a national concern about racial and sexual difference that is productive for our discussion here. If, in the Chilean example, the question of cross-dressing was related to the effects of the colonial experience and the rise of modern commerce, in Argentina, cross-dressing as a topic in journalism was linked very directly to official xenophobia. In this respect, José Ingenieros's text, previously cited, coincides with attitudes registered on the pages of *Caras y caretas*. In both instances, simulation and disguise are evoked to explain the crisis of a nation. Patriotic rhetoric is built from the naming and localization of difference and from denouncing those impostors who menace the modern state.

For all its commentary about upper-class social life in Argentina—the elite coteries and the banquets of the rich and famous—*Caras y caretas* devotes even more attention to immigration, carnival, and perversion, juxtaposing these different topics as forms of provocation. Thus, alongside the photographs of recent arrivals from Europe, labeled "la galería de inmigrantes," *Caras y caretas* published photos of famous cross-dressers, and masked participants in carnival festivities.[11] In these terms, the new century in Argentina hosted a sideshow of misfits whose presence was evoked in cultural debate to show the failures of democracy. Even the modern government was metaphorically linked to the spectacle of circus.[12]

Equally important in the pages of the journal were the women immigrants from Europe who chose to dress as men. *Caras y caretas* supplied a regular gallery of photographs of cross-dressed foreign women who had reached Argentine shores. In search of work, they dressed as men and mixed with local elites. Such was the case of Dafne Vaccari, an Italian political activist, who assumed the identity of Arturo de Aragón;[13] or the case of Carlos Lambra, an Englishwoman dressed as a man who taught music to Argentine women of privilege.[14] Abundant references of this kind were usually politically motivated, designed to expose wayward subjects who stray from national coherence, but also to indicate the improper gendering of particular social actions. The corrective, then, was found in *regulated* work for women, controlled by emerging industry that organized not only their labor but their bodies, their dress, and appearance. Finally, it is not surprising that as *Caras y caretas* poked fun at the excesses of carnival, it also carried a considerable number of advertisements on cosmetics, depilatories, corsets, and hair dyes.[15]

Is there universal accord about the marketing demands placed on women? Are there any refutations to this discourse on female dress? Interestingly enough, women writers launched a direct attack on proposals of this kind through the vehicle of the feminist press. In an early, vitriolic critique of the restrictions placed on women within the discourse on fashion, Argentine feminist Juana Manso de Noronha wrote in her periodical, *Album de señoritas*:

> La muger es esclava de su espejo, de su corsé, de sus zapatos, de su familia, de su marido, de los errores, de las preocupaciones; sus movimientos se cuentan, sus pasos se miden, un ápice fuera de la linea prescripta, ya no es muger, ¿es el qué? . . . un ser mixto sin nombre, un monstruo, ¡¡un fenómeno!!
>
> (Woman is a slave of her mirror, her corset, her shoes, her family, her husband, her errors, her concerns; her movements are measured, her steps are

counted. An inch off the prescribed mark, and she is no longer a woman. What is she? . . . a mixed being without a name, a monster, a phenomenon!!)[16]

The implications here are obvious: should women stray from prescribed roles and dress, they will be dismissed as monsters.

In a more tempered voice, later women journalists of the nineteenth century regularly challenged the impositions of fashion. *La Alborada del Plata*, a publication of Juana Manuela Gorriti, protested the stays of the corset and the hoop skirt; contributors also opposed the kind of clothing that would separate women of different classes.[17] Literature of the past *fin de siglo* expressed considerable concern about fashion and style and the ways in which human subjectivity was controlled by the consumer market.[18] It also became a challenge of early feminists to find new ways of cutting the so-called social fabric, as editors from Uruguay wrote in their magazine called *La Tijera* (1876). Reversing the codes of sartorial obligation, the writers slyly alerted their readership when they wrote: "Todos sabemos lo que significa 'La Tijera' en manos de una mujer." (We all know the meaning of "Scissors" [*La Tijera*] when placed in a woman's hands.) The possibility of subversion is cut from the cloth of society.

In this respect, a counterinstitutional force is defined by free association among women; they sewed a community together through education and political training, through the formation of alternative subjectivities not necessarily regulated by the state. In defense of female collaboration, one anonymous woman cited Garnier: "Dividir el trabajo es *asociarlo*; porque la división del trabajo, convierte el trabajo individual en un trabajo colectivo entre todos los cooperantes del producto, y es una de las manifestaciones de la sociabilidad humana" (To divide the work force is to *regroup* it . . . into collective labor shared by all participants in the process; and this is one of the manifestations of human sociability).[19] Seeking new forms of female association, a number of autonomous intellectual groups arose in the late nineteenth century, determined to emphasize autonomy and a different "look" for women.

In Argentina, for example, anarchist women congregated under the banner of La Voz de la Mujer (1895–1896) in order to forge a collective identity eluding control by the state. The eponymous periodical of this group negotiated new representations of women not to be shaped by the dictates of the fashion magazines but by the female sexual desires. The newspaper thus counseled its female readers to recognize the demands of their bodies and to find satisfaction and pleasure in the promise found in anarchist thought.[20] One of the questions posed through the run of the paper is why women of working-class background have fewer rights of self-expression as seen in style or sexual pleasure than the women of high society who freely indulge their passions. But the materiality of these female bodies, divided by class and privilege, ultimately leads to a question of citizen rights in the nation. For the readers of *La Voz de la Mujer*, a participatory voice is assured when they join the ranks of the anarchist movement.

These late-nineteenth-century debates are, in reality, discussions about a different kind of female visibility in the bedroom, home, and public sphere. In the final analysis, they extend the discussion of dress and style to the visual imagery of citizenship itself. One could argue that these examples are not only about the construction of utopian communities of women but more importantly about issues of embodiment and representation. By emphasizing corporeality as the basis of citizen rights, they reverse discussion about our sense of the classical public sphere as a space for disembodied minds and transparent spirits. More fundamentally, they centrally evoke questions of unregulated desire and challenge the state monopoly over the marketplace of representation.

In this process, it might be asserted that individual private subjects, elevated from the time of the Renaissance as actors in the theater of modernity, need to be redefined when gender enters as a category of analysis; the presence of gendered subjects shifts the debate to include an idea of the body, public, and market. For this reason, the matter of dress acquires special importance as it situates sexual bodies as vehicles for commodified goods; their heightened visibility is then politically charged. Nevertheless, the regulation of dress and identity, controlled by market and state, produces—in spite of itself—alternative dramas of representation.

Contemporary writers and artists also address these shifting representations and the ways in which the body is forcibly propelled into the market arena. Indeed, the presence of the marketplace dominates much of recent literature and film. In *Duerme* (1994), Mexican novelist Carmen Boullosa writes about a woman from colonial times who chose to dress as a man, thus reminding us of the story of Catalina de Erauso discussed earlier in this essay.[21] But unlike the nineteenth-century treatments of the swashbuckler nun, Boullosa suggests that one can *buy* variants of identity and freedom; everything can be purchased or traded according to the rules of the market. Cross-dressed wealthy creoles are thus exchanged with servants or foreign subjects. Like the magic enacted by indigenous communities to protect deviant subjects from harm, Boullosa also describes the magic of money to enact such transformations; with coins of exchange, individuals purchase their freedom and alter their public identity. In this way, male and female, Indian and white, Mexican and foreign are portrayed as sliding categories that, once commodified in the market, can also be purchased and sold.

From a different perspective, Chilean writers Carmen Berenguer and Pedro Lemebel sustain a less optimistic inquiry in a series of short, experimental videos bearing the title "Postal del Sur." The first of the series, produced in 1990 at the moment of the Chilean transition to democracy, is related to the second, produced in 1992, and sets up questions about the relation of the human body to market-driven forms of identity. The first tape presents a dull image of television snow blocked off by the letters MU, the written equivalent of the sound of cows. This initial, silent segment is followed by a simple sign, "Sonido de la carne en el tráfico al mercado" (Sound of flesh en route to the market). Here, a paradoxical silence set against an onomatopoeic word for sound (MU) necessarily raises the topic of censorship; it also reinforces the idea of the neoliberal market as a place for the dismemberment of bodies, a slaughterhouse where citizens are reduced to the status of animals and led to their eventual death. The new Chile, pushed on the road to democracy through the efforts of market and media, produces animal sounds without voices, images without action.

Although contemporary theory emphasizes the need to create individuals who might participate in the public sphere, in fact, it presupposes the existence of interlocutors who speak without visible trace, as minds without bodies or language without tongues. By contrast, the marginal figures who do not enter the public arena are configured differently: these individuals enter the camera lens to become photographs without voices, still poses without movement, standing as public spectacle without a right to expression. They thus exist in silent corporeality, coming into view only as commodities for trade. The perspective of the state strips these marginal figures of the power to initiate action; like a game of simulacra and doubling, it allows the appearance of jesters who mimic the actions of others but never take charge of the show.

Nevertheless, the market-driven environment always expresses fissures; a complex web of unpredictable meanings emerges in the public space, altering the static vision of bodies and producing new concepts of agency and change. In the second video by Berenguer and Lemebel, we see a still black-and-white photo of the back of a headless woman; about her neck lies a set of seven razors, laced together like pendants on a necklace. Unexplained for the viewer is the use of the razors; as instruments of transformation, their operation is hidden from sight. Nor is it clear who will utilize these tools in the altering female appearance. The subsequent scene, now with human movement and filmed in color, captures a frontal shot of a woman's torso, with seven threaded clusters taped to her chest as if they were hair or electrodes. Again, the question of female activity is still left unanswered. Nevertheless, despite the forceful dehumanization perpetrated by the camera's gaze, a resistance begins to emerge, heard in the powerful rhythms of the woman's breathing, suggestive perhaps of simple survival or the inaugural sound of a voice. From what began as an oppressive still frame, the female subject assumes agency in the scene.

This somewhat optimistic view of human potential to override market force frequently surfaces in contemporary avant-garde texts. A final example supplied by the writings of Diamela Eltit is instructive in this regard. Eltit's novel *Lumpérica* (1983) addresses questions of representation when she describes the female body under the tyranny of the masculine gaze.[22] Here, she locates the basis of authoritarian power in sight and representation; in other words, vision is the basic epistemological privilege with which to control the other.[23] In *Lumpérica*, the light of a publicity billboard shines down upon a public plaza in a poor section of Santiago and, by accident, illuminates the body of a woman. This person acquires social meaning by the force of the electric sign; as a result, she exists as a fragmented image, not as a constituted whole. Even her name in the novel, "L. Iluminada," is a function of the mechanical lamp. The spotlight thus affects a symbolic economy of identity, value, and language; it is the source of all discursive power and, despite its irrationality, it regulates all relations of exchange and the market value of those observed.

This gaze exercises a particular violence on human beings and feelings, reducing persons to object status. The figures who cross the plaza are highlighted like commercial products: "están aquí lamiendo la plaza como mercancías de valor incierto" (they are here licking the plaza like commodities of undetermined value).[24] Moreover, the anonymous power of the spotlight especially focuses on the gender-specific features of L. Iluminada as a woman; around the materiality of this gendered spectacle, political authority is affirmed. Diamela plays with the technological and ideological dominance of the gaze insofar as it determines identity and manipulates appearance and meaning. Reading in an allegorical mode, I want to assume that it represents the vigilant eye of the state, which validates the kinds of objects to be placed in market circulation.

In this context, Eltit inserts a paradoxical question: "¿Cuál es la utilidad de la plaza pública?" (What is the usefulness of the public plaza?)[25] Cleared of its original function as a site of festivity and unrepressed chaos, the plaza is now at the mercy of an apparatus of representation. Nevertheless, and here is the liberating response of Eltit's subject, a new form of chaos is introduced by the chance interventions of the electrical sign whose multiple permutations of light produce unanticipated forms of alterity. Thus, at the end of the novel, the character exceeds the power of the spotlight; the narrative focalization shifts from the billboard to the woman observed. As if to take charge of her body, she alters her physical appearance: with scissors and mirror in hand, she proposes an independent mode of self-perception beyond the gaze of the billboard lamp. Then the natural light of dawn illuminates pedestrian traffic in the city: "La gente era ahora heterogénea, mujeres, hombres, estudiantes" (The crowd was now heterogeneous with women, men, students).[26] Interestingly enough, nature creates and regulates ordered subjects, but it is a slippage of market and state—allegorized by the billboard as its lights scan the female body—that inaugurates a train of unpredictable subjectivities, unplanned actions. Paradoxically, the state produces a free game of signifiers in spite of itself; it generates alternative forms of meaning that lead to gendered agency and political change.

These contemporary writers and artists—like their nineteenth-century forebears—insist on linking corporeality to the experience of modernization. Indeed, they show that (neo)liberal rule was never a disembodied process; moreover, the visual display of difference serves an argument for liberalism itself. I hope to have shown that Latin American modernity is bound to a program of regulated tastes and desires. It identifies particular expressions of gender with commodity form and also endorses social relations in which gender is offered for trade or sale. Nevertheless, the spectacle of representation often prompts alternative forms of identity and alliance; it requires us to rethink the ways in which the body has been used to create "national subjects." As a correlative to artistic responses, it is not surprising in this respect that a large number of Latin American social movements insist on the body as a point of departure to defend human rights and economic advancement; that powerful activists congregate today around issues of sexual choice; that informal sectors reveal a high female component, with housewives unions in barrios placing successful claims on democratic rule through negotiation with the market; and last year, as a border war was building between Ecuador and Peru, that the *New York Times*[27] reported the strong intervention of eighteen women's groups, whose participants put their bodies on the battle line to denounce the claims of nationalism. Lacking in monumentality, these actions test the gaze of power and propose new dimensions of agency to offset traditional expressions of consensus. It behooves us, then, as critics to reinsert the gendered body in our discussions of aseptic neoliberal exchange, to show the gendered body as an originating point of discourse, community, and action.

• **NOTES**

1. Raquel Olea, "Libertad de arte y otros imaginarios," *La Epoca*, 19 August 1994.

2. Considerable attention has been given to this story, including a film starring María Félix (1944). For recent scholarship, see Stephanie Merrim, "Catalina de Erauso: From Anomaly to Icon," in *Coded Encounters: Writing, Gender and Ethnicity in Colonial Latin America*, ed. Francisco Javier Cevallos-Candau, J. A. Cole, N. M. Scott, and N. Suárez-Araúz (Amherst: University of Massachusetts Press, 1994), 177–205, and Lucas G. Castillo Lara, *La monja alférez* (Caracas: Editorial Planeta Venezolana, 1992).

3. José Victorino Lastarria, "El Alférez Alonso Díaz de Guzmán," *Obras completas de Don J. V. Lastarria* (Santiago: Imprenta Barcelona, 1913), 12:53–78.

4. Diego Barros Arana, "La monja alférez," *Revista de Santiago* 1.1 (1872): 225–34.

5. For a different treatment of this story, see Bernardo Subercaseaux, *Cultura y sociedad liberal en el siglo XIX* (Santiago: Aconcagua, 1981), 97–99.

6. José Ingenieros, *La lucha por la simulación en la vida*, intro. Aníbal Ponce (Buenos Aires: Ramón J. Roggero, 1949).

7. Luis Varela [Orión, pseud.], untitled, *La Tribuna*, 15 August 1870, 2.

8. Nicolás Bolet Peraza, "La mujer nueva," *Las Tres Américas* 26 (August 1896): 900–902.

9. Ibid.

10. The marketing of cosmetics was always perceived as a possibility for men to profit from the distribution of goods among a female audience. On this, see the unsigned essay "Dos palabritas a las damas," *Las Tres Américas* 1 (November 1894): 598.

11. *Caras y caretas* gave evidence of a lively tradition of crossed identities: folk customs of women dressed in pants and men garbed in skirts (no. 307, 1904); an Indian man who dressed as a woman in order to protect the children of his tribe, in "El hombre-mujer descubierto en Viedma" (no. 189, 1902). The magazine even carried an unsigned article entitled "Animales que se disfrazan" (1922).

12. Political activity was often explained as a charade. Thus the debates between Mitre and Alsina or the crisis of 1890 were represented as great parties of political masqueraders. Even the title of the magazine, *Caras y caretas*, suggests that dissimulation is the basis of modern reality. On this topic, see my "'Gentlemen,' damas y travestis: Ciudadanía e identidad cultural en la Argentina del fin de siglo," in *La imaginación histórica en el siglo XIX*, ed. Lelia Area and Mabel Moraña (Rosario: UNR Editora, 1994), 297–309.

13. *Caras y Caretas* 407 (1906).

14. Ibid., 346 (1905).

15. Even masculinity can be purchased for a price: "Hágase un hombre," reads an advertisement of *Caras y caretas*: "¿De qué modo? Yo le diré: llene el siguiente cupón y a vuelta de correo le enviaré mis folletos: VIGOR y SALUD. Están llenos de informaciones para los hombres" (1902: 3). The point here is that a gendered identity is material to be bought and sold.

16. Juana Manso de Noronha, "Educación de la muger," *Album de señoritas* 8 (17 February 1854): 58–59.

17. E. del T., "El lujo," *La Alborada del Plata* 2.3 (23 January 1880).

18. Regarding fashion and style as a topic of conflict in narrative, it is worth consulting the prose fiction of Argentine writers Juana Manuela Gorriti (*El Oasis en la vida*, 1888) and Emma de la Barra (*Stella*, 1905), or the Peruvian Mercedes Cabello de Carbonera (*Blanca Sol*, 1889).

19. Unsigned, "División de la enseñanza y el trabajo," *La Alborada del Plata* 8 (6 January 1878): 2.

20. For selections of texts drawn from *La voz de la mujer* along with commentary, see my *La mujer en el espacio público: El periodismo femenino en la Argentina del siglo XIX* (Buenos Aires: Feminaria, 1994).

21. Carmen Boullosa, *Duerme* (Mexico City: Alfaguara, 1994).

22. Diamela Eltit, *Lumpérica* (Santiago: Planeta, 1991).

23. Ernesto Laclau and Chantal Mouffe, *Hegemony and Socialist Strategy: Towards a Radical Democratic Politics* (New York: Verso, 1985), 59, have referred to this process of representation as the basic political mechanism of the state. I am indebted to them in these pages.

24. Eltit, *Lumpérica*, 11.

25. Ibid., 45.

26. Ibid., 208.

27. *New York Times*, 30 January 1995.

15 · Arnaldo Cruz-Malavé

"What a Tangled Web!"

Masculinity, Abjection, and the Foundations of Puerto Rican Literature in the United States

Resistance to power does not have to come from elsewhere to be real, nor is it inexorably frustrated through being the compatriot of power. It exists all the more by being in the same place as power.

—Foucault

It's on the ruins of what surrounds me that I build my manhood.

—Fanon

For Alberto, *toda la sangre*

Hovering like some rare bird over land and sea, the protagonist of the Puerto Rican Luis Rafael Sánchez's tale of foundations, "¡Jum!" (Hm!), straddles the village's border.[1] But with his ass "pressed tight enough to choke his buttocks,"[2] the "sissy . . . the queer . . . the queen" who is the protagonist in the villagers' taunts is not just a sign for a monstrous other. He is rather *the* opening that, in an allegory reminiscent of Octavio Paz's myth of national origins,[3] allows for permeability, for penetration. Neither masculine nor feminine affiliation, institutional ritual nor gossip sustains his identity. Instead, his shifting signification is propped up by a heterotopian series in which the most disparate signifiers are invoked in order to summon the other—the external, the noncommunal—by means of lubricity, lubrication: the white linen suit, the talc "May's Dream," the eau de toilette "Com tu mí" (Cum to me), the comb, the ring, and the jar of petroleum jelly.[4] With a narrative tone halfway between the ironic distance of a *chiste colorao*, or

An earlier version of this essay appeared in *differences: A Journal of Feminist and Cultural Studies*.

dirty joke, and the identification of sentimental pathos, cruelty and kindness, Sánchez describes how that unnamed and unnameable character who
is the homosexual searches, with assiduous despair, as in a horror film, all
communal spaces for a safe haven—a room of his own:

> En cada recodo, en cada alero, en las alacenas, en los portales, en los anafres,
> en los garitos. . . . Los hombres, ya seguros del relajo, le esperaban por el cocal
> para aporrearle a voces. . . .
> —¡Mariquita! ¡Loqueta!
> —¡Maricastro!
> Las mujeres aflojaban la risita por entre la piorrea y repetían quedito. . . .
> —¡Mujercita!
> Hasta el eco casquivano desnudó su voz por el río con un inmenso jjj uuu
> mmm.
>
> (In every corner, under the eaves of every home, in the cupboards, in the
> doorways, in the ovens, in the gambling halls. . . . The men, confident now in
> their jiving, would wait for him by the coconut grove to slug him with their
> words. . . . "Sissy!" "Fairy!" "Big Faggot!" The women would unleash their
> hushed laughter through the pus of their rotten gums and softly repeat. . . .
> "Girly!" Even the empty-headed echo stripped off his voice once by the river
> with a huge hhh mmm.)[5]

But the homosexual here, like the abject in Kristeva,[6] is neither subject
nor object. Before him one can invoke only an approximating word—an
insistently repeated insult that falls on his amorphous body in an attempt to
mold it, to give it shape. An attempt whose very repetition is but an indication of the homosexual's nonexistence, of his ghostly state. Dead man,
specter, the homosexual, let's say, is a hole, and through that hole slips in all
that otherness that the community seeks to repel—treason:

> —¡Que el hijo de Trinidad es negro reblanquiao!
> —¡Que el hijo de Trinidad es negro acasinao!
> —¡Que el hijo de Trinidad es negro almidonao!
>
> ("'Cause Trinidad's son is a whitified nigger!" "'Cause Trinidad's son is a
> social-club nigger!" "'Cause Trinidad's son is a starched-up uppity nigger!")[7]

An entangled sort of precariousness, one could say, joins the village and
the protagonist, Trinidad's son. For the community that repudiates him
is also living haltingly, stalked by whiteness and power, permanently
besieged. And its insults, desperately brandished on the homosexual's body,
bounce back to its own communal body like blows in order to reveal in the

end, rather than the fixity of a secured identity, the precariousness of a norm that must be constituted compulsively in the expulsion not of the radically different but of the proximate other, of Trinidad's son.[8] Like the homosexual's body, the black body in "¡Jum!" is spectral, undefinable, and unformed, and its borders must be delimited and shored up by what Judith Butler has called the compulsive performance of the prohibition, of the Law:[9]

> —¡Que se pone carbón en las cejas!
> —¡Que es mariquita fiestera!
> —¡Que los negros son machos!
> —¡Y no están con ñeñeñés!

> ("'Cause he draws on eyebrows with charcoal!" "'Cause he's a flaming sissy!" "'Cause black men are real men!" "And don't go for all that prissiness!")[10]

So it is that "¡Jum!"—which seems at first to reproduce that terrorizing logic that demands that every representation of the homosexual be relegated to the arena of expiation and martyrdom, that piously prescribes that we identify with him solely on his deathbed, returning him thus to the communal fold—invokes a disturbing and incongruous mix, akin to the Puerto Rican tradition of the grotesque, in which, as in Francisco Oller's nineteenth-century painting *El Velorio* (The wake), the Puerto Rican nation is finally, and joyfully, gathered around an image of death.[11] For "¡Jum!" is as much a wake as it is a feast—as much a celebration as a crucifixion. And in it every blow delivered against the homosexual's body accumulates until it forms, as has been lucidly shown by Agnes Lugo-Ortiz, another body: the community's choral corps(e). Assembled on the very edge of the village, the river bank, this chorus sings, in a sort of counterpoint typical of literary *negrismo* and reminiscent of the exorcising logic of the Cuban Nicolás Guillén's "Sensemayá: Chant to Kill a Snake,"[12] its ritual foundational song: "El agua hizo glu glu. Entonces que no vuel—va no—vuel—va, / el hijo de Trinidad / glu . . . / que / glu . . . / no / glu . . . / vuelva / glu . . . / se / glu . . ./ hundió!" (The water went gloo gloo. And then don't come—back don't —come—back, / Trinidad's son / gloo . . . / don't / gloo . . . come back / gloo . . . / he / gloo . . . / sank!)[13]

The constitution of the community, Sánchez, then, seems to say, with a sangfroid whose very contrast underscores the terror that founds it, is not merely an act of expulsion but of cannibalism—literally an absorption. For the community here has been wise enough not to waste any of the abject's body's parts, not even his dying breath, in order to found, in close counterpoint, its identity. But has the abject, I wonder, a word of his own, a nondialectical rhythm, a breath that may not be profitably used for that counterpoint? Is there, that is, a space of his own—a space not complicitous with the binary structure of sacrifice—from which to articulate his identity or toward which to orient it? Or are there other channels—channels of his own—through which to resist abjection? And if he were to come out of the river and travel along the foreseeable paths, retrace the route of his crucifixion, would he be able then to subvert the structure that repudiates him and absorbs him? Or would he end up falling once again into abjection's tangled web?

Much of Puerto Rican literature in the United States, both the production of the first generation of U.S.-born Puerto Rican, or Nuyorican,[14] writers as well as that of the homosexual exile writers of the Puerto Rican generation of 1970s,[15] has been written from this *des-tierro*, this landlessness/this banishment, this river of abjection. Elsewhere I have shown how, emerging from the context of the Third World political movements of the 1960s, one of the most representative currents of Nuyorican literature sought to found, through the demystification of social relations, an authentic space for the Puerto Rican nation and for the self.[16] And I have further argued how, in consonance with the model of internal colonialism, prevalent then, this current set out to "unmask" the complicity of the colonized with the social relations that maintained his or her oppression—to transcend, that is, those hierarchical relations between master and slave that contain the identity of one in that of the other and that Fanon, no doubt their most sagacious analyst, called "dual narcissism."[17] And I have moreover identified an evolution in this demystifying current of Nuyorican literature that consists of the disappearance of that utopian element, of that transcendent foundational space for the community and the self that it was the poet's task to unveil. There is in the later work of an author as representative as Pedro Pietri, for instance, a demystifying intention that, as a result of the absence of an anchoring foundational space, ends up multiplying and disseminating ad infinitum. As in his play *The Masses Are Asses*, Pietri's characters unmask themselves in rapid succession without being able however to leave that binary space of expulsion and banishment that is here, as in so much of Nuyorican literature, the bathroom, *el toilet*.[18]

Allow me now to return to this evolution of the demystifying foundational gesture of Nuyorican literature in order to suggest that in the works that we may call its founding texts, that impossibility of transcending the binary structure of abjection was already present. And that to a great extent the strength and pathos of Nuyorican texts such as Piri Thomas's *Down These Mean Streets* (1967), Miguel Piñero's *Short Eyes* (1975), and the anthology *Nuyorican Poetry* (1975), edited by Piñero and Miguel

Algarín,[19] derive from the fact that in them the attempt to transform that structure into the hypostasis of an authentic ethnic, or national, space is fully assumed and imploded—taken to its limits. It has been said that with the appearance of Nuyorican literature in the late 1960s, a new American marginal identity is born. But I would rather say that Nuyorican literature emerges in the gap that opens up when the transcendental subject that sustains Fanon's epistemology implodes and that its origins are in that lack of foundations, in its coming to terms with the condition of reversibility and implication that constitutes "Puerto Ricanness" in the United States. "Ricans are funny people," declares a "white" character in *Short Eyes*; in a world ruled by ferociously defended racial and sexual limits, they represent, like the homosexual in "¡Jum!," the porous, the permeable—treason: "If a spic pulls a razor blade on you . . . and they ain't no white people around . . . get a spic to watch your back, you may have a chance."[20] The founding texts of Nuyorican writing, I propose, then, persistently comment on that porous, treacherous condition that constitutes "Puerto Ricanness," but not so much in order to transcend it as in order to use it to authorize themselves—to find within it, that is, modes of resistance and validation.

Homi Bhabha has suggested that the effectiveness of Fanon's thought lies still not so much in its yearning for "the total transformation of Man and Society" as in its being always in a state of emergence, of unresolved contradiction, "never dawning without casting an uncertain dark."[21] And in this sense recent analyses of *Black Skin, White Masks* may show that despite the vigilance with which Fanon turns to his own body in order to unveil the masks of his complicity with the structures that oppress him ("O my body, make of me always a man who questions!" is the prayer with which he ends his book),[22] his efforts to transcend the binary relations of expiation are also built on the expulsion of the other—of the homosexual.[23]

Contrasting the relationship between family and state in Europe and the Caribbean, Fanon argues that whereas in Europe a "normal" family produces a "normal" citizen in conformity with the state, in the Caribbean "a black child, having grown up within a normal family, will become abnormal at the slightest contact with the white world."[24] Unlike in Europe, in the Caribbean, "abnormality" is caused not by the family but by the state. And he concludes: "Like it or not, the Oedipus complex is far from coming into being among blacks. . . . An inability on which we highly congratulate ourselves."[25]

And it's just that this *inversion* of the relationship between family and state in the Caribbean is symptomatic of the general psychological structure that organizes the two pathologies that rule social relations between whites and blacks: negrophobia and paranoia. These two pathologies are economies of inversion and, like the former inversion of family and state, they also describe chiasmatic figures. In the end, the white man who is afraid of the erect phallus that is the black man in Western culture, argues Fanon, also desires him; just as the white man who imagines himself persecuted by the black man, also pursues him, summons him up. "Fault, guilt, denial of guilt, paranoia—one is once again," states Fanon, "in homosexual territory."[26]

And certainly the territory in which Fanon feels himself immersed and from which he tries to extricate himself is the same one surveyed by Freud in his exemplary cases of Schreber and the "Wolf-Man."[27] Cases in which the patient's phobia and paranoia lie in fact in the neurotic repudiation of what he desires—the passive copulation with the father, what Freud called elsewhere the "negative Oedipus complex."[28] It might become understandable, then, why Fanon might have wanted to exorcise the Oedipus complex, so susceptible of reversibility, from within the Caribbean family and how, in order to do so, he had to relegate—to banish, so to speak—all discussion of Martinican homosexuality to the footnotes of his text. Footnotes in which he further assures us—after reviewing the traditional case of Martinican men who dress up like women and are called *comères* (godmothers) and the no less typical case of fellow countrymen who have been forced by economic circumstances to serve in the metropolis as "passive pederasts"— that he has not as yet had "the chance to establish the overt presence of pederasty in Martinique" and that it must certainly be what he calls a direct "result of the absence of the Oedipus complex in the Caribbean."[29]

It seems, then, that before the dangerous advancement of the homosexual territory that threatens to overwhelm all relations between the colonizer and the colonized, containing them in its chiasmatic grasp, Fanon has tried to preserve a space for romance, safeguarded from inversion, where eros might not be implicated in the binary relations of expulsion, where desire may neither be defined in opposition to repudiation nor be susceptible to turning into its apparent opposite. A space that would be both an origin for and an anticipation of the mature object relations that will some day exist when whites and blacks alike take off the masks of their "dual narcissism."

But in works like *Short Eyes* and *Down These Mean Streets*, there is no space for romance outside the binary relations of expiation, and even if throughout such works their characters successively and ferociously attempt to delimit desire from repudiation, they all end up falling once again into abjection's implicated web. *Bildungsromane* of sorts, these texts are rites of passage that figure the Nuyorican subject's attempt to gain authority, to emerge, as it were, as a passage into maturity and maleness. But upon concluding the ritual, upon leaving the initiatory precinct of the jail to return to his family, Julio "Cupcakes" Mercado, the protagonist of *Short Eyes*, knows that he has gained that heterosexual space at a cost—at the cost of his contamination—and that he carries with him "the jail,"[30] its relations of expiation. And similarly, Piri, the protagonist of *Down These Mean Streets*, upon finishing his voyage of education, ascends for the last time onto the *rufo*, the rooftop of his dreams, in order to realize that all of his ambition to gain a name, a territory, a "turf," through the performance of machismo, through racial affiliation, or a conjugal union,[31] is a mirage, equivalent to drug addiction, and begins to descend, without assurances but hopeful, onto abjection's "mean streets"—streets ruled by the "other," "the Man"—while, in the background, a "sad-assed bolero" is heard announcing the defeat of all illusion, of all romance.[32]

Carlito, the eponymous character of *Carlito's Way*, philosophizes. Speaking of sexual relations with "faggots" in jail, he says: "Bad news. Once a guy starts on that you got to put him down—pretty soon you don't know who's the poger and who's the pogee."[33] And certainly in *Short Eyes*, *Down These Mean Streets*, and *Nuyorican Poetry*, homosexual practices occupy that zone of reversibility where the Nuyorican author's struggle to emerge from the spectral state of abjection to which he is subjected by "internal colonialism," by "the System," by "the Man," always inevitably falls back on contested territory. In them, one could say, the "queen" and the "faggot" are not so much the antithesis of their "macho" characters and poetic personae as that "proximate other" in whose likeness the latter see reflected the catastrophic condition of their own manhood, what in one of his poems anthologized in *Nuyorican Poetry*, Algarín describes as the "cockless," *mongo* (flaccid) state of the Nuyorican condition.[34] No wonder, then, the insistence on homosexuality in these texts. And if it is true that their characters and poetic personae desperately try to overcome that reversible and ghostly condition that simultaneously emblematizes homosexual practices and the Nuyorican condition, it is also true that they must assume it, incorporate it. More than a repudiation of homosexuality, it seems, then, that much like the short story "¡Jum!," Nuyorican texts exhibit its problematic absorption. So that a blurb from the original edition of *Down These Mean Streets* introduces it in an unwittingly perceptive way: "Piri Thomas describes the passionate, painful search to validate his manhood, for which, with dead-pan cool, he had to fight, steal, *submit to buggery* . . . take any dare, any risk" (emphasis added). To validate masculinity with its ruin, to submit to sodomy, to "buggery," in order to construct a male national identity, there's the paradoxical foundational project that Nuyorican texts set for themselves.

But, as Carlito rightly warns, once the bodies of two men are joined, once they are tangled up in "sodomy," in homosexual practices, who's to say who's the giver and who's the taker, who attacks and who surrenders, if he who gives it surrenders, or if he who takes it devours? Once, that is, the bodies of two men embark on an erotic act, however conventional and predictable it may be, who's to say for sure what final figure will contain that movement? Who'll remain standing? Who'll end up on his knees?

But it is precisely to this paradoxical and precarious movement that *Short Eyes* and *Down These Mean Streets* submit themselves, all the while attempting to channel it and to contain it through a rhetoric of displacement and of transfiguration, respectively.

As in a dramatization of Althusser's notion of ideology,[35] the characters of *Short Eyes* appear before us, emerge into the light and onstage by being interpellated by the prison guard, by the Law, who in addition warns them that they must answer because "your ass is mine."[36] And so it is that in *Short Eyes* sodomy is what subdues the subject, what subjects *and* subjectifies him, fixing him in place within the network of distinctions of the prison system, assigning him a name and a space. And all of its characters, the guards as well as the inmates, are defined in real or symbolic relation to sodomy: they either penetrate or are penetrated, they are either "daddies" or "stuff" in a hierarchical, unilinear chain of abjection.

Just as in Foucault power cohabits with resistance,[37] here abjection and eros share the same path: sodomy. And even if the play's characters attempt, through an asymmetrical erotic choreography, to keep desire at bay by transforming it into repudiation, by compulsively reproducing the abjection to which the prison system subjects them, that very repetition begins also to undermine the distinctions that the system had sought to fix in place. Thus in what is perhaps the pivotal scene in Piñero's play, the desire of one of its characters, Paco, for the "Puerto Rican pretty boy," Julio "Cupcakes" Mercado, threatens to disrupt that hierarchical chain of subjections on which the prison system is based by inverting its directionality and offering instead the possibility of "going both ways."[38] Turning to the linguistic repertoire of Puerto Rican seduction, from the falsely humble confessional plea—

Oyeme, negrito . . . tú me tiene[s].

(Listen, *negrito*, . . . you're driving me.)[39]

—to the defiantly luring dare—

Cupcakes: [E]cha, que está[s] caliente, Paco.
Paco: Pue[s] ponme frío

(Cupcakes: Get away, you're hot, Paco.
Paco: Then cool me off),[40]

—by way of hyperbolic adulation—

Cupcakes, [nene lindo], que dio[s] bendiga la tierra que tú pise[s]

(Cupcakes, pretty babe, may god bless the ground you step on)[41]

—Paco transforms the place of expulsion, the bathroom, into a romantic space.

But faced with the threat of disruption, the system engenders its own "pure" object of sacrificial restoration, the presumed molester of girls, Clark Davis, in the lingo of the jail, "Short Eyes"—a character whose sole qualification for occupying the abject place of the "stuff" rests on his being the other, the marked one, "the freak." And all of Paco's desire for Cupcakes, now transformed into violence, is discharged upon him.

And not only Paco but all of the characters who participate in the rape and murder of "Short Eyes" are also implicated in this inversion of abjection into desire—an inversion that forces them to resort to displacement as a strategy of containment. For deep down all of the inmates desire Cupcakes, and Cupcakes, walking among them like a tantalizing delicacy, losing at the card games so as to have to bend down and do push-ups, summoning them all with the eloquent promise of the culinary moniker that identifies him, also desires to be desired. So that, in the end, the displacement of all of the characters' desire onto the murder of "Short Eyes" is simply revealed as just that: a strategy of containment. And the strength of their desire is accurately and paradoxically confirmed by the brutality with which the latter must be contained, by the ferociousness with which it must be denied.

If *Short Eyes* seeks to assume and transform that state of abjection represented in Nuyorican foundational texts by homosexual practices through displacement, *Down These Mean Streets* tries to assume it and to contain it through a rhetoric of transfiguration. Invoking the paradoxical Hegelian dialectic that affirms that all self-consciousness in-itself and for-itself exists only by virtue of its recognition by another self-consciousness,[42] Fanon argues that to the degree that the Caribbean black man has not been able to make himself acknowledged by the white man through struggle, he has not yet attained that condition of self-consciousness that would confirm his humanity; he does not exist.[43] Unlike the American black man who "battles and is battled,[44] the Caribbean black man, Fanon affirms, does not occupy even the predictable space of contestation.[45] Consumed by that paternalist animal that is European culture, "unable ever to be sure whether the white man considers him self-consciousness in-itself and for-itself," the Caribbean black man must devote himself incessantly, Fanon explains, "to uncovering resistance, opposition, challenge"[46] in order to prove through them his own existence.

Piri Thomas and Puerto Rican writing in the United States are, I believe, in an analogous position to that of the Caribbean black man in European culture. Situated between the lost maternal paradise of Puerto Rican roots and the paternal world of assimilation, straddling two contradictory systems of racial classification—that of American society and of the Puerto Rican family—that configure blackness respectively as an ontology and as a condition, oscillating between adolescence and adulthood, Piri Thomas desperately seeks an identity from which to make himself visible, from which to emerge. But standing in that not-yet-recognized invisible middle ground, Thomas will make his first gesture of affirmation not so much to express a repressed identity as to engage in a practice: to go against the Law, to trespass the limit, to penetrate alien turf, to transgress. And in penetrating enemy territory to discover in the blows, the bruises, the cuts that the structures of "the System" heap on his skin, his own body. To realize that he exists: to feel his flesh, to taste his blood, and to hope that out of that gushing wound is born, as out of a martyr's stigma a flower, the valor, the stone-faced coolness, the rigidity before one's opponent, and the heart that prove, in the midst of the forlornness of the wound, the presence of that redeeming quality, intangible and elusive, that is masculinity:

> Then . . . everybody starts dealing . . . [and you] feel somebody put his damn fist square in your damn mouth and split your damn lip and you taste your own sweet blood—and all of a sudden you're really glad you came . . . you're glad somebody punched you in the mouth; you're glad for another chance to prove how much heart you got.[47]

So it is that in *Down These Mean Streets* the chapter on the protagonist's initiation into manhood culminates with a visit to the apartment of some Puerto Rican "faggots,"[48] for the "faggot" incarnates for the "macho" that state of abjection through which his own masculinity is constituted. And even if he may thus represent the final trial to which the "macho" must subject himself in expectation of the transfiguration of his body by the signs of masculinity, he can also conjure up the terrifying image of his possible fixation in that state, of his inability to transfigure abjection.

The entire homosexual adventure of Piri and his friends in this chapter is traversed by the fear of cannibalism, by the fear, that is, of being absorbed or sucked in by the other—the homosexual hypostatized as a hole, a vacuum, an anus, or a devouring mouth. And in fact the trial to which Piri and his friends subject themselves is that of the practice of fellatio. Impassive, like heroes withstanding their enemy's assault, the characters of *Down These Mean Streets* bear on their body the "outrage" of the "blows."[49] But, with each suction, with each "blow," they feel their body distending and dispersing, disappearing in the homosexual's avid mouth, conforming to its rhythm, to its breath. And while the homosexual's mouth sucks their member, their "joint," they in turn inhale a huge cigarette of marihuana, a "king-sized joint," gobbling it up.[50] It seems, then, that the symmetry between the "faggot" and the "macho" has managed to expand dangerously. Exhausted, spectral, the "macho" and the "faggot" are confused and fused. They are now one single entwined body, a body that shares orifices in which it would be impossible to disentangle receptivity and aggression.

But at the very moment in which the bodies of the "macho" and the "faggot" are entangled, leveling their differences, there appears, as in *Short Eyes*, the violence that restores the system, transforming desire into repudiation; and Piri, emerging from his spectral state over the screeching sound of the beating of a "faggot," begins to ascend onto the *rufo*, the rooftop, of his dreams, from which he now projects himself as owner of "his" barrio and of himself, as "king," as "boss," as "man," transfiguring himself thus on the ruins of his own virility.

It is a partial, precarious solution, which the novel itself takes care to dissolve. In the end, Piri begins to descend, as we have said above, from the *rufo* of his identity onto abjection's "mean streets," confirming thus his inability to acquire a territory of his own through the performance of machismo, through racial affiliation or a national romance. Looking at himself in the mirror, he now feels all of the masks with which his false attempts at plenitude had covered his face fall off, and in their place he sees not the much anticipated transcendental subject of Fanonian epistemology but a hole: "I felt as though I had found a hole in my face and out of it were pouring all the different masks that my *cara-palo* face had fought so hard to keep hidden."[51]

It is in that hole, in that opening onto the other—intervened mouth or anus, site of transaction and decantation—where I would like to place the work of that other Puerto Rican author who at the first seems to shun all affiliation with the demystifying poetics of foundational Nuyorican texts: the self-defined homosexual 1970s émigré Manuel Ramos Otero. No other Puerto Rican writer has so insisted on founding his writing solely on what could destroy it, on abjection. And no other has so surrendered to the communicating and excluding paradoxes that rule the relationship between the master and the slave.[52] And no one else has so dared to assume the language of the torturer in order to make visible at last—bruised and battered—his own body. At the beginning of this essay I asked myself whether the abject could emerge from his *des-tierro*, from his landlessness/his banishment, whether he could constitute a voice of his own, or whether he would be destined irrevocably to fall back once again into abjection's tangled web. And emerging from the decaying Hudson River piers in the painting by Angel Rodríguez-Díaz on the cover of one of his books, *Página en blanco y stacatto* (Blank page and staccato), Ramos Otero seems to answer this question for us. Wrapped up in a *modernista* kimono and brandishing the umbrella of one of his poems against the storm,[53] Ramos Otero, unperturbed, walks on. Is he, then, on his way to vindicate or to assimilate, to surrender or to attack? Is he, like the repressed, returning from an origin buried there in the city's very edge? Or is he, like a specter, traveling to the center to reclaim his image, his rightful place? Oscillating between these two poles, using the very paths of abjection, Ramos Otero, with his kimono and his umbrella, summons us to that traveling theater[54] that is his walk—a pure will to exist, dispossessed of all grounding, contingent but also alone, fierce and forlorn.

• NOTES

I would like to thank Alberto Sandoval Sánchez, Doris Sommer, Efraín Barradas, and Rubén Ríos Avila for their comments on an earlier draft of this essay.

1. The protagonist's liminal condition is established from the very first paragraph of "¡Jum!," in Sánchez's *En cuerpo de camisa* (San Juan: Ediciones Lugar, 1966): "Que era ave rarísima asentando vacación en mar y tierra" (They said he was a very rare bird vacationing both on land and sea) (57).

2. "Que el hijo de Trinidad se prensaba los fondillos hasta asfixiar el nalgatorio" (That Trinidad's son pressed his ass tight enough to choke his buttocks), ibid.

3. I am referring here to the categories of "the open" and "the closed" as they relate to national identity and gender in Paz's classic book on Mexicanness, *El laberinto de la soledad* (The labyrinth of solitude) (Mexico City: Fondo de Cultura Económica, 1959). For an excellent analysis of Piri Thomas's *Down These Mean Streets* from the perspective of Paz's categories, see Marta E. Sánchez, "Revisiting Binaries of Race and Gender: Piri Thomas's *Down These Mean Streets* and the Construction of a Puerto Rican Ethnic Nationalist Subject" (unpublished; University of California, San Diego).

4. Sánchez, "Revisiting Binaries of Race and Gender," 60.

5. Ibid., 57–58.

6. Julia Kristeva, *Powers of Horror: An Essay on Abjection* (New York: Columbia University Press, 1982), 1–2.

7. Sánchez, "Revisiting Binaries of Race and Gender," 59.

8. In *Sexual Dissidence* (Oxford: Oxford University Press, 1991), Jonathan Dollimore argues in favor of what he calls the "perverse dynamic" that subverts through the "unstable proximate" the norm, the Law.

9. Judith Butler, *Gender Trouble: Feminism and the Subversion of Identity* (London: Routledge, 1990).

10. Sánchez, "Revisiting Binaries of Race and Gender," 58.

11. Positioning the dead child around whom the nation gathers below a traditionally roasted pig, Oller turns his national allegory into a grotesque tale of incorporation, of cannibalism. As in "¡Jum!," the nation here is constituted in and through the death of an other. But if we consider that since the nineteenth century Puerto Rico's colonial status has been figured as an infantile condition or as death, that other against whom the nation is constituted is also itself. One could argue, then, that Oller's painting belongs to a tradition in which the Puerto Rican nation is paradoxically constituted, emerges as it were in and through an act of self-annihilation, in which the representation of its failure to constitute itself as a nation also provides the opportunity for a joyous act of self-affirmation, of national foundations. For an analysis of infantilization as a trope in Puerto Rican writing, see Juan G. Gelpí *Literatura y paternalismo en Puerto Rico* (San Juan: Universidad de Puerto Rico, 1993). For a meditation on impotence and lack as a means of authorization in Puerto Rican literature, see my "Toward an Art of Transvestism: Colonialism and Homosexuality in Puerto Rican Literature," in *¿Entiendes? Queer Readings, Hispanic Writings*, ed. Emilie Bergmann and Paul Julian Smith (Durham: Duke University Press, 1995), 137–67.

12. Like "¡Jum!," Guillén's poem "Sensemayá" (1934), in *Antología mayor* (Mexico City: Editorial Diógenes, 1972), may be read as an act of communal constitution through the exorcism of an "evil" other—an act whose dual structure is formally reproduced by the African-American musical structure, typical of *negrista* poetry, of "call and response." Similarly, in "Community at Its Limits: Orality, Law, Silence and the Homosexual Body in Luis Rafael Sánchez's '¡Jum!'" in *¿Entiendes? Queer Readings, Hispanic Writings*, ed. Emilie Bergmann and Paul Julian Smith (Durham: Duke University Press, 1995), 115–136, Agnes I. Lugo-Ortiz has shown how, in "¡Jum!," the community is constituted through an equivalent African-Caribbean dialogic musical structure whose aim is the homogenization of all voices in what the Cuban anthropologist Fernando Ortiz has described as a moment of "rapture" or *arrebato* (quoted in Lugo-Ortiz, 124–26).

13. Sánchez, "Revisiting Binaries of Race and Gender," 62.

14. The term *Nuyorican* was originally used by Puerto Ricans on the island as a pejorative term for emigrants, most of whom settled in New York. In the late 1960s Puerto Rican writers began to reclaim the term and thus reaffirmed the immigrant community's specific experiences, history, and social practices. See Miguel Algarín's "Nuyorican Language" in *Nuyorican Poetry: An Anthology of Puerto Rican Words and Feelings*, ed. Miguel Algarín and Miguel Piñero (New York: Morrow, 1975). For an overview of Nuyorican literature, see the special issue of the *ADE Bulletin* 91 (1988): 39–62.

15. I am referring here to Puerto Rican gay writers of the so-called generation of the 1970s who, toward the late 1960s, exiled themselves in the United States, where

they have written most of their work—writers such as Víctor Fragoso (*El reino de la espiga* [New York: Nueva Sangre, 1973] and *Ser islas/Being Islands* [New York: El Libro Viaje, 1976]); Manuel Ramos Otero; Carlos Rodríguez Matos (*Matacán* [Madrid: Playor, 1982] and *Llama de amor vivita: Jarchas* [South Orange, N.J.: Ichali, 1988]); Alfredo Villanueva Collado (*Grimorio* [Barcelona: Murmurios, 1986], *En el imperio de la papa frita* [Santo Domingo: Colmena, 1989], *La voz de la mujer que llevo dentro* [New York: Arcas, 1990], and *Pato salvaje* [New York: Arcas, 1991]); and Alberto Sandoval Sánchez (*Nueva York Tras Bastidores/ New York Backstage* [Santiago, Chile: Editorial Cuarto Propio, 1993]). See also Rafael Ramírez, *Dime capitán: Reflexiones sobre la masculinidad* (Río Piedras, Huracán, 1993), and Carlos Rodríguez Matos, "Actos de Amor: Introducción al estudio de la poesía puertorriqueña homosexual y lesbiana," *Desde Este Lado/From This Side* 1.2 (1990): 23–24.

16. Arnaldo Cruz-Malavé, "Teaching Puerto Rican Authors: Identity and Modernization in *Nuyorican* Texts," *ADE Bulletin* 91 (1988): 45–51.

17. Frantz Fanon, *Peau Noir, Masques Blancs* (Paris: Editions du Seuil, 1952), 9–10.

18. In Pedro Pietri's *The Masses Are Asses* (Maplewood, N.J.: Waterfront, 1984), Piri Thomas's *Down These Mean Streets* (New York: New American Library, 1968), and Miguel Piñero's "Paper Toilet" (in *Outrageous* [Houston: Arte Público, 1986]) and *Short Eyes* (New York: Hill & Wang, 1975), as we shall see, the bathroom, the toilet, and the "tearoom," both as a place of abjection and desire, are the privileged sites of Nuyorican literature.

19. Miguel Algarín and Miguel Piñero, eds., *Nuyorican Poetry: An Anthology of Puerto Rican Words and Feelings* (New York: Morrow, 1975).

20. Piñero, *Short Eyes*, 28.

21. Homi K. Bhabha, "Interrogating Identity: Frantz Fanon and the Postcolonial Prerogative," *The Location of Culture* (New York: Routledge, 1994), 41.

22. Fanon, *Peau Noir, Masques Blancs*, 190.

23. For a parallel reading of the interaction of homosexuality and race in Fanon, see Dollimore, *Sexual Dissidence*, 344–47.

24. Fanon, *Peau Noir, Masques Blancs*, 119.

25. Ibid., 125–26.

26. Ibid., 150.

27. Freud, "The Case of Schreber," *The Standard Edition of the Complete Psychological Works of Sigmund Freud* (London: Hogarth Press and Institute of Psycho-analysis, 1958), 12:9–82, and "The Case of the Wolf-Man," in *The Wolf-Man by the Wolf-Man*, ed. Muriel Gardiner (New York: Hill & Wang, 1991), 153–62.

28. See, for example, "A Child Is Being Beaten," *The Standard Edition of the Complete Psychological Works of Sigmund Freud* (London: Hogarth Press and Institute of Psycho-analysis, 1955), 17:179–204.

29. Fanon, *Peau Noir, Masques Blancs*, 148.

30. Piñero, *Short Eyes*, 119.

31. The most important romantic relationship in *Down These Mean Streets* is the protagonist's with Trina, whom he calls his "Marine Tiger," referring to the ship in which so many Puerto Ricans migrated to New York and, metonymically, to the

mass migration of Puerto Ricans to the United States after World War II. *Down These Mean Streets* could be read thus as the attempt to unite the descendants of earlier Puerto Rican migrations, such as the protagonist, with their Puerto Rican roots through their union with the then most recent migration. It could be read, that is, as a sort of "national romance," which ends up failing. On the "national romance" in Latin America, see Doris Sommer's brilliant *Foundational Fictions: The National Romances of Latin America* (Berkeley: University of California Press, 1991).

32. Thomas, *Down These Mean Streets*, 314.

33. Edwin Torres, *Carlito's Way* (New York: Avon, 1993), 42.

34. Algarín and Piñero, *Nuyorican Poetry*, 52.

35. Louis Althusser, "Ideology and Ideological State Apparatuses (Notes Towards an Investigation)," *Lenin and Philosophy and Other Essays* (New York: Monthly Review Press, 1971).

36. Piñero, *Short Eyes*, 5.

37. Michel Foucault, "Power and Strategies," *Power/Knowledge: Selected Interviews and Other Writings, 1972–1977*, ed. Colin Gordon (Brighton: Harvester, 1980), 134–45.

38. Piñero, *Short Eyes*, 69.

39. Ibid., 66.

40. Ibid., 67.

41. Ibid.

42. G. W. F. Hegel, *Phenomenology of Spirit*, trans. A. V. Miller (Oxford: Oxford University Press, 1977).

43. Fanon, *Peau Noir, Masques Blancs*, 177ff.

44. Ibid., 181.

45. Diana Fuss has argued that in *Peau Noir, Masques Blancs* Fanon's theory of the black man as an other, as a "phobic projection of a distinctly Western imaginary," uncovers a "deeper, more insidious level of orientalism" in which the black man is even excluded from participating in alterity, as otherness is claimed by the white man. Diana Fuss, "Interior Colonies: Frantz Fanon and the Politics of Identification," *Diacritics* 24.2–3 (1994): 20–42. Fanon's distinction between the ontological condition of the American and Antillean black man would accord with these two levels of exclusion identified by Fuss.

46. Fanon, *Peau Noir, Masques Blancs*, 182.

47. Thomas, *Down These Mean Streets*, 67.

48. Ibid., 63–70.

49. Ibid., 68.

50. This symmetry is pointed out by Robert Reid-Farr in his excellent analysis of *Down These Mean Streets* in his doctoral dissertation "Conjugal Union: Gender, Sexuality, and the Development of an African-American National Literature" (Yale University, 1994).

51. Thomas, *Down These Mean Streets*, 306.

52. For an examination of abjection in Ramos Otero's work, see in particular his "Vida ejemplar del esclavo y el señor" y "Loca la de la locura," both published in *Cuentos de buena tinta* (San Juan: Instituto de Cultura Puertorriqueña, 1992). On the importance of the Hegelian dialectic of the master and the slave in his work, see

his interview by Columbia University's Center for American Cultural Studies in *Dispatch* 5.1 (1986): 14–16. For an analysis of abjection in Ramos Otero's writing, see my "Toward an Art of Transvestism," 137–67.

53. The poem on which this painting is based is "Esta es la segunda parte del *Ulysses*," from *El libro de la muerte* (New York: Waterfront; Río Piedras: Cultural, 1985), 10.

54. "Teatro rodante" is the expression used by Ramos Otero in his description of this painting in "Descuento," *Página en blanco y stacatto* (Madrid: Playor, 1987), 105, available in English translation by Rod Lauren as "The Untelling," *The Portable Lower East Side* 5.1–2 (1988): 85–111.

Sylvia Molloy

From Sappho to Baffo

Diverting the Sexual in Alejandra Pizarnik

Escribir un solo libro en prosa en lugar de poemas o fragmentos. Un libro o una morada en la cual refugiarme.

[To write only one book of prose instead of poems or fragments. A book or a home where I could find shelter.]

—Alejandra Pizarnik, diary entry, 28 September 1962

In a mock table of contents for her *La bucanera de Pernambuco, o Hilda la polígrafa* (The pirate of Pernambuco, or Hilda the polygraph), Alejandra Pizarnik cites a section of that text as dedicated "A Safo y a Baffo" (To Sappho and Baffo).[1] Like Muriel Rukeyser's hortatory "Not Sappho, Sacco," in "Poem Out of Childhood,"[2] Pizarnik's mock dedication swerves from Sappho through phonetic repetition and distortion, even as it names her. Rukeyser's swerve points to the political; in effect, her full declaration reads: "Not Sappho, Sacco. / Rebellion pioneering among our lives." No less rebellious, Pizarnik chooses, however, the farcical gesture: in bringing together Baffo and Sappho, she is performing an act of literary vandalism, both honoring and defacing the sapphic monument (and the complex narratives it stands for), calling attention to the lady as she literally draws a mustache ("Baffo" is "whiskers" in Italian) on her face.

Susan Gubar interprets swerves such as Rukeyser's (observable in other poets, from Amy Lowell to Robin Morgan) as gestures of distrust; distrust, in general terms, of Sappho as a (poetic/lesbian) precursor and (poetic/lesbian) collaborator, but also distrust of "a single standard for writers defining themselves by their sexual difference."[3] In such a spirit, I first thought I would approach lesbian sexuality in Pizarnik's work through sapphic distrust, as manifested through parody and the grotesque, and then connect it to the ambiguous status of the sexual, as a decisive element of self-figuration, in Pizarnik's work. Yet naggingly, as I tried to pursue this slippery construct, now as Sappho-Baffo the mustachioed lady, now as Sappho *and* Baffo, a Beckettian collaborative pair, in the most obvious place, that is, in the verbal vertigo of *Los poseídos entre lilas* and *La bucanera de Pernambuco*, I was reminded of another sapphic pair or, rather, of other sapphic crisscrossings, where Sappho and Baffo might find a more fruitful incarnation. I refer, of course, to Pizarnik's *La condesa sangrienta* (The bloody countess), the text at once dazzling and elusive on which I have chosen to focus my commentary.[4]

The mention of parody might seem unexpected in connection with a text that, in chronicling one long obsessive act of cruelty, seems unlikely to sustain the destabilizing reading that parody demands. I want to argue that, although not overtly parodic, *La condesa sangrienta*, as a borderline text constantly staging its own *liminality*, opens itself to such a reading. By *liminality* I do not mean the "experience of limits," conventionally or morally speaking that *La condesa sangrienta* relates on an anecdotal level but the instances of textual, perceptual, and ideological *friction*, the constant blurring and resetting of boundaries, put into practice by the text. One such instance of friction is to be found in the preface itself, where, as in all prefaces, the enunciation of the text is negotiated. The understated, rigorously economical tone of this preface, so reminiscent of the Borges of mock book reviews and of *Historia universal de la infamia*, does not appear to be coincidental. Mimicking Borges, Pizarnik presents her text as a review of Valentine Penrose's biography of the bloody countess.[5] In so doing, she seems to reclaim the narrator's stance in *Historia universal de la infamia*, that of a "tímido que no se atrevió a escribir cuentos y que se distrajo en falsear y tergiversar . . . ajenas historias" (a shy young person who dared not write stories and so amused [her]self by falsifying and distorting . . . the tales of others).[6] The fact that Pizarnik's strategies for "falsifying and distorting" are themselves very similar to those of *Historia universal de la infamia* (enumerations, breaks in narrative continuity, focus on a few scenes), although of no direct use to me here, lends additional credence to my statement. Pizarnik too, in telling the tale of another, is telling herself. But what part of that self is she telling?

I must stray now from Borges and consider the precise nature of Pizarnik's ventriloquism beyond that prologue, the dynamics of female-female borrowing, more precisely of female-female collaboration. Indeed, this is a text of female, and exclusively female textual transactions, of a female, and exclusively female gaze. (I could have said just as well: This is a text of female, and exclusively female, sexual transactions, of a female, and exclusively female, erotic gaze.) Pizarnik, a woman, reads the reading performed by another woman, Valentine Penrose, on yet a third woman, Erzébet Báthory. The recipient of the double gaze, the woman on which the double reading is performed is, in turn, a *gazer*: her erotic pleasure is principally derived from the *spectacle* of the torture of women, the systematic *piercing* of women, practiced by herself, by her servants, or by clever machines like the Iron Maiden. As in Wilde's *Salome*, the gazer here is a vehicle for voyeuristic desire, desired when and while desiring.

What does the gaze alight upon and what does it retain? A cursory comparison between Valentine Penrose's text and that of Pizarnik's will show that the former has been picked over, *ravaged* one might say, by a lacerating reading that—excising contextual links, privileging emblematic scenes of desire and cruelty—has successfully denarrativized Penrose's text. It has turned the story of Erzébet Báthory's life into a series of tableaux vivants, held together only by the countess's (and her reader's) scopophilia, a re-*vision* more than a re-*counting* of female cruelty.[7] Much more than Penrose, Pizarnik lingers on the countess's gaze, tells us that she suffered from terrible pain in her eyes,[8] punctuates the text with references to the countess's erotic gaze: "La condesa, sentada en su trono, contempla" (The countess, on her throne, looks on); "La condesa contempla desde el interior de la carroza" (From inside her carriage the countess looks on).[9] The use of the Spanish *contemplar* (both to look on and to contemplate), reinforces the framing power of that gaze, stressing its aesthetic quality, as does the enthralled description of the torture itself, consistently involving piercing: "De pronto, los senos maquillados de la dama de hierro se abren y aparecen cinco puñales que atraviesan a su viviente compañera" (Suddenly, the painted breasts of the Iron Maiden open and five daggers emerge, piercing her live companion).[10] "Esta sombría ceremonia tiene una sola espectadora silenciosa" (This somber ceremony has only one silent spectator), writes Pizarnik deceptively,[11] for, although obviously voyeuristic, this layered same-sex gaze is, above all, associative: Pizarnik, Penrose, the countess, her acolytes, and, clearly, their readers are caught up in one continuous, collaborative act of female visual lust. Of each and every one of them it might be said, as Pizarnik writes of the countess, "En lo esencial, vivió sumida en un ámbito exclusivamente femenino. No hubo sino mujeres en sus noches de crímenes" (Essentially, she lived immersed in an exclusively female realm; there were only women in her crime-filled nights).[12]

The story of Erzébet Báthory, as filtered by Penrose, affords Pizarnik two particularly fruitful ways of inscribing lesbian desire. As it relates to the gothic, *La condesa sangrienta* allows for the narrative figuration of the unspeakable (already obsessively present in Pizarnik's poetry), a trope, as Eve Sedgwick has shown, for a deviant sexuality that must remain unnamed.[13] If the countess's exploits are not exactly silenced, the deliberate economy of Pizarnik's text, the way it has of cutting itself short, constantly point to *more*: to a more horrible, a more lascivious, a more ecstatic, to a more than can ever be named. And, as it relates to vampire narratives (an automatic connection, even if the countess is not "technically" a vampire, and one that Cortázar, in his rereading of the Báthory legend,[14] does not hesitate to spell out), *La condesa sangrienta* points to the female monstrous, to the never quite seen, to, as Sue-Ellen Case has so eloquently argued, the "disappeared" lesbian: vampires, as is notorious, have no reflection in the mirror.[15]

Yet this faux-vampire does project an image of sorts, a reflection endowed (as specular images usually are in Pizarnik)[16] with considerable drive: "nadie tiene más sed de tierra, de sangre y de sexualidad feroz que estas criaturas que habitan los fríos espejos" (no one thirsts more for earth, for blood, for ferocious sexuality than the creatures inhabiting cold mirrors).[17] I wish to look closely at that reflection as it is considered in one section of *La condesa sangrienta*, "El espejo de la melancolía" (The mirror of melancholia), emblematic of the liminality I mentioned earlier. Although it cannot be considered a lesbian disappearing act—it has too much "presence"—it is, I propose, a spectacle of diversion: as much a *mise en abyme* of sexual desire, as constructed by the lesbian gaze, as a *speculation* on the impossibility of liberating that desire. In it, Pizarnik brings together three aspects of the countess that, in Penrose's text, appear to bear no relation to one another, and has them signify together. "Vivía"—the section begins, quoting directly from Penrose—"delante de su gran espejo sombrío, el famoso espejo cuyo modelo había diseñado ella misma" (She lived before her great dark mirror, the famous mirror that she herself had designed).[18] And Pizarnik adds: "Podemos conjeturar que habiendo creído diseñar un espejo, Erzébet trazó los planos de su morada" (We may conjecture that, while believing that she was designing a mirror, she was laying down the plans for her dwelling).[19] The familiarization of the mirror, the notion of an uncanny rendered unexpectedly secure—this is a *comfortable* mirror, with armrests (shaped like a pretzel, says Penrose, a homey touch Pizarnik wisely avoids)—is unsettling only for those not participating in the specular ceremony. Pizarnik's mirror-dwelling, like Benjamin's etui-like interior,[20] is the private realm of the subject, the stage for his/her phantasmagorias. In it, the countess makes a spectacle out of herself—for herself. It is, in reality, a dwelling within a dwelling: unlike Penrose, whose countess moves from one residence to another, from her townhouse in Vienna's Blutgasse to her castle in Csejthe, Pizarnik takes pains to confine the countess to her castle and to stress her physical isolation. Shunning the exterior for the interior, the blood street for the blood castle, Pizarnik's recluse countess withdraws, additionally, into the privacy of her mirror.

Significantly, "El espejo de la melancolía" is the only section of *La condesa sangrienta* in which lesbianism is mentioned, specifically in connection to, or rather, within the frame of, the sheltering mirror:

> Y a propósito de espejos: nunca pudieron aclararse los rumores acerca de la homosexualidad de la condesa, ignorándose si se trataban de una tendencia inconsciente o si, por lo contrario, la aceptó con naturalidad, como un derecho más que le correspondía. En lo esencial, vivió sumida en un ámbito exclusivamente femenino. No hubo sino mujeres en sus noches de crímenes. Luego algunos detalles son obviamente reveladores: por ejemplo, en la sala de torturas, en los momentos de máxima tensión, solía introducir ella misma un cirio ardiente en el sexo de la víctima. También hay testimonios que dicen de una lujuria menos solitaria. Una sirvienta aseguró en el proceso que una aristocrática y misteriosa dama vestida de mancebo visitaba a la condesa. En una ocasión las descubrió juntas, torturando a una muchacha. Pero se ignora si compartían otros placeres que los sádicos.

> (On the subject of mirrors: rumors about the countess's homosexuality were never verified. It was unclear whether it was an unconscious tendency or if, on the contrary, she accepted it naturally, as one more right to which she was entitled. Essentially, she lived immersed in a purely female world. There were only women in her crime-filled nights. And then there are the obviously telling details: for example, in the torture chamber, in the moments of great-est tension, she herself would introduce a burning taper into the vagina of the victim. There is also evidence of a less solitary lust. During the trial a servant asserted that a mysterious, aristocratic lady, dressed as a young man, visited the countess. On one occasion she discovered them together, torturing a young woman. But it is not known whether they shared less sadistic pleasures.)[21]

The mirror prompting this reflection of/on lesbianism is also, held up by Pizarnik, a mirror that blurs. No sooner does it register that it equivocates: the Countess's lesbianism is a rumor, it is never verified, it is unclear, it may have been unconscious, or else have been an entitlement (that is, a right, not a pleasure). In sum, there is no *public* knowledge that it existed: it is private, a *secret*. But then, adds Pizarnik, there are the *obviously telling* details, those spied on by the servant, by Pizarnik, by us readers. We know.

On the surface, Penrose's text is more straightforward and voluble on the subject, diagnosing the countess's lesbianism as an astrological fatality of sorts:

> In the matter of women's horoscopes, any negative aspect received by Mercury from the Moon when the Moon itself is in Mars, causes a homosexual tendency. That is why the lesbian is often also sadistic: the influence of Mars, a male and a warrior, guides her, and her spirit, influenced by those cruel weapons, does not hesitate to wound, especially in love, what is beautiful, young, loving and feminine.[22]

Penrose's homophobic construction of the evil lesbian, typical of certain decadent French texts (for example, Rachilde's *Monsieur Vénus*) is complemented by chatty references to seventeenth-century lesbianism, stemming more, one suspects, from the desire to titillate than from a need for historical accuracy. Some of it is rather gaudy, like her description of the flagellating Hungarian tribads, a narrative Pizarnik might have used perhaps to her advantage in one of her later, garish *Textos de sombra*, but for which she has little use here. Neither a conventional "evil lesbian," nor a member of a flamboyant community, Pizarnik's countess stands out alone in the mirror, a figure of defiance. Her very excess is a sign of resistance. It is as a figure of disruption that she makes lesbian sense.[23]

If I have spoken of diversion regarding this mirror scene it is because it does not focus solely on the countess's equivocal lesbianism but shifts to another paradigmatic image, another subject construction, that of the melancholic. The countess, Pizarnik tells us, "padecía el mal del siglo XVI: la melancolía" (suffered from melancholia, the disease of the sixteenth century).[24] Enter the figure of "el melancólico," the melancholic (the gendered Spanish prose imparts the decisive coup de grace), effectively degendering and abstracting the female figure in the mirror. And it is around this figure of *replacement*—the masculine melancholic displacing the blurred lesbian—that Pizarnik writes one of the most *personal* pages of her work, one that might be seen both as an autobiographical statement and as an aesthetic program.

It may be useful at this point to make clear that I am not arguing for a historically lesbian countess, nor reading modern sexualities into a seventeenth-century character, nor reading sexualities *tout court* into twentieth-century renderings of that character, nor reclaiming Pizarnik-as-lesbian through her rendering of the countess. What I am trying to do is to trace

Pizarnik's dealings with the lesbian, once she summons that lesbian into the sheltered mirror-dwelling of her text; to follow Pizarnik's act as she brings the lesbian out fleetingly only to cross-dress her, with a sleight of hand facilitated, once more, by the mirror—now you seen her, now you don't— into *el melancólico*, a male (or rather degendered) figure of acedia. Less grotesque than a Sappho with Baffo, than the lady with whiskers, the lesbian here has, nonetheless, been de-faced.

I propose that this specular defacing process, staged in the countess's mirror, this naming while denying, is a constant in Pizarnik's work, so rich in splintered subjectivities, in pronominal gaps, in absent gender markers, in hiatus, so secretive and deliberately *unreferrable*. Here, in this mirror scene, is Pizarnik's own philosophy of the boudoir. A boudoir turned closet, it is the site of the most extreme, most transgressive representation of desire and, at the same time, allows for the muting of that desire, its displacement, its indifference:

> Creo que la melancolía es, en suma, un problema musical: una disonancia, un ritmo trastornado. Mientras *afuera* todo sucede con un ritmo vertiginoso de cascada, *adentro* hay una lentitud exhausta de gota de agua cayendo de tanto en tanto. De allí que ese *afuera* contemplado desde el *adentro* melancólico resulte absurdo e irreal y constituya "la farsa que todos tenemos que representar". Pero por un instante—sea por una música salvaje, o alguna droga, o el acto sexual en su máxima violencia—, el ritmo lentísimo del melancólico no sólo llega a acordarse con el del mundo externo, sino que lo sobrepasa con una desmesura indeciblemente dichosa; y el yo vibra animado por energías delirantes.

> (I believe that melancholia is, in sum, a musical problem: a dissonance, a disturbed rhythm. While *outside* everything occurs with the vertiginous rhythm of a cataract, *inside* there is the exhausted slowness of the water-drop falling from time to time. That is why that *outside* contemplated from the melancholic's *inside* seems absurd and unreal, "the farce in which we must all perform." But for an instant—thanks to a wild music, to some drug, or to sex in its most violent form—the slow rhythm of the melancholic not only matches that of the outside world but surpasses it with an excess that is unbelievably joyous; and the "I" vibrates, moved by delirious energies.)[25]

Of the Countess's encounters with her mysterious cross-dressed companion, Pizarnik had written: "It is not known whether they shared less sadistic pleasures." The question this last paragraph prompts is: "Do less sadistic pleasures exist?" That sexuality must be imagined "in its most violent form" in order to operate the break, the *coming out*, bespeaks the matching violence with which it has been repressed. That the lesbian break, in *La condesa sangrienta*, can be conceived only as transgressive, as an erotic death rattle, and then only through the layers of a twice-read gothic vampire tale, shows the magnitude of that repression, the resilience of Pizarnik's closet.

In one of the brief flashes that compose her fragmentary self-reflection in "Caminos del espejo," from *Extracción de la piedra de locura*, Pizarnik writes: "Pero el silencio es cierto. Por eso escribo. Estoy sola y escribo. No, no estoy sola. Hay alguien aquí que tiembla" (But silence is certain. That is why I write. I am alone and I write. No, I am not alone. There is someone here who trembles).[26] This essay has attempted to restore, or to begin to restore, that trembling silent other, closeted in Pizarnik's mirror.

· **NOTES**

1. Cited in Cristina Piña, *Alejandra Pizarnik* (Buenos Aires: Planeta, 1991), 171.

2. Muriel Rukeyser, "Poem Out of Childhood," *The Collected Poems of Muriel Rukeyser* (New York: McGraw-Hill, 1982), 3.

3. Susan Gubar, "Sapphistries," in *The Lesbian Issue* (essays from *Signs*), ed. Estelle B. Freedman, Barbara C. Gelpi, Susan L. Johnson, and Kathleen M. Weston (Chicago: University of Chicago Press, 1985), 107.

4. Alejandra Pizarnik, *La condesa sangrienta* (Buenos Aires: Aquarius, 1971). All English translations are my own unless noted otherwise. A complete English version of *La condesa sangrienta*, "The Bloody Countess," may be found in *Other Fires: Short Fiction by Latin American Women*, ed. Alberto Manguel (New York: Clarkson N. Potter, 1986), 70–87.

5. Valentine Penrose, *Erzébet Báthory, la comtesse sanglante* (Paris: Mercure de France, 1962).

6. Jorge Luis Borges, *Historia universal de la infamia*, in *Obras completas* (Buenos Aires: Emecé, 1974), 291; *A Universal History of Infamy* (New York: Dutton, 1972), 12.

7. Changes with respect to Penrose's text are of interest here: Penrose goes back and forth between Erzébet Báthory and Gilles de Retz, establishing a parallel between female and male erotic violence; Pizarnik all but erases the masculine from her book, doing away with the notorious *maréchal* the better to highlight the countess.

8. Pizarnik, *La condesa sangrienta*, 33.

9. Ibid., 13, 18.

10. Ibid., 14.

11. Ibid., 10.

12. Ibid., 44. For women as spectators, and the spectacle of female monstrosity, see Linda Williams, "When the Woman Looks," in *Re-Vision: Essays in Feminist Film Criticism*, ed. Mary Ann Doane, Patricia Mellencamp, and Linda Williams (Frederick, Md., University Publications of America and American Film Institute,

1984). For additional very useful reflections, see Mary Ann Doane, "Film and the Masquerade: Theorizing the Female Spectator," *Femmes Fatales: Feminism, Film Theory, Psychoanalysis* (New York: Routledge, 1991), and Patricia White, "Female Spectator, Lesbian Specter: *The Haunting*," in *Inside/Out: Lesbian Theories, Gay Theories*, ed. Diana Fuss (New York: Routledge, 1991).

13. Eve Kosofsky Sedgwick, *Between Men: English Literature and Male Homosocial Desire* (New York: Columbia University Press, 1985), 94. Interestingly, the same conjunction of aristocracy and homosexuality that Sedgwick notes in the trope of the "unspeakable" is at play in the case of the countess, whose high social station not only gives her total freedom but puts her above the law. She is, in more senses than one, *untouchable*.

14. Julio Cortázar, *62: Modelo para armar* (Buenos Aires: Sudamericana, 1968); in English, *62: A Model Kit*, trans. Gregory Rabassa (New York: Pantheon, 1972).

15. For a good discussion on the identification of vampire and lesbian, see Sue-Ellen Case, "Tracking the Vampire," *Differences* 3 (1991): 1–20.

16. See for example, in *Arbol de Diana*, poem 14: "El poema que no digo, / el que no merezco. / Miedo de ser dos / camino del espejo; / alguien en mí dormido / me come y me bebe." (The poem I do not say, / the one I do not deserve. / Fear of being two / on the way to the mirror: / someone asleep within me / is eating me, drinking me.) Alejandra Pizarnik, *Obras completas* (Buenos Aires: Corregidor, 1993), 75. Also, Pizarnik's remarks on mirrors to her interviewer Marta Moia. To the question "Whom do you see in the mirror?" Pizarnik answers: "A la otra que soy" (The other that I am). Alejandra Pizarnik, *El deseo de la palabra*, ed. Antonio Beneyto and Marta I. Moia (Barcelona: Ocnos, 1975), 250.

17. Pizarnik, *La condesa sangrienta*, 44.

18. Ibid., 43.

19. Ibid.

20. Walter Benjamin, "Paris, Capital of the Nineteenth Century," in *Reflections* (New York: Harcourt Brace Jovanovich, 1978), 155.

21. Pizarnik, *La condesa sangrienta*, 44.

22. Penrose, *Erzébet Báthory*, 25.

23. I strongly disagree here with David William Foster's reading of Pizarnik's *La condesa sangrienta* as a mere reproduction of the "evil lesbian" model. *Gay and Lesbian Themes in Latin American Writing* (Austin: University of Texas Press, 1991), 101. Foster's contention that the countess, in that capacity, "horrifies because her sexuality resists virtually any strategy of accommodation within a scheme of 'legitimate' [*sic*] sexuality, heterosexual or homosexual" (101), reveals, quotation marks notwithstanding, a disturbingly normative view of sexual practices. It is precisely the resistance of this lesbianism, its *irreducibility* to the "legitimate" (for who is to lay down the rules for the "legitimate" or the "illegitimate"?) that render Pizarnik's text so provocative. It is not so much "horrifying" as it is challenging: *It will not go gently into the norm.*

24. Pizarnik, *La condesa sangrienta*, 45.

25. Ibid., 46.

26. Alejandra Pizarnik, *El infierno musical* (Buenos Aires: Sudamericana, 1968), 43.

Bibliography of Gender and Sexuality Studies on Latin America

Abreu Esteves, Martha de. *Meninas perdidas: Os populares e o cotidiano do amor no Rio de Janeiro da Belle Époque*. Rio de Janeiro: Editora Paz e Terra, 1989.

Acevedo, Zelmar. *Homosexualidad: Hacia la destrucción de los mitos*. Buenos Aires: Ediciones del Ser, 1985.

Acosta-Belén, Edna, and Christine E. Bose. *Researching Women in Latin America and the Caribbean*. Boulder: Westview Press, 1993.

Adam, Barry D. "Homosexuality without a Gay World: Pasivos y Activos en Nicaragua." *Out/Look* 1.4 (1989): 74–82.

———. "In Nicaragua: Homosexuality without a Gay World." *Journal of Homosexuality* 24 (1993): 171–81.

Aguiar, Flávio. "Homossexualidade e repressão." *Sexo e Poder*. Ed. G. Mantega. São Paulo: Editora Brasiliense, 1979.

Alarcón, Norma. "Chicana's Feminist Literature: A Re-Vision through Malintzín/or Malintzín: Putting Flesh Back on the Object." In Moraga and Anzaldúa, 182–90.

Almaguer, Tomás. "Chicano Men: A Cartography of Homosexual Identity and Behavior." *The Lesbian and Gay Studies Reader*. Ed. Henry Abelove, Michèle Aina Barale, and David M. Halperin. New York: Routledge, 1993. 255–73. Also in *Differences* 3.2 (1991): 75–100.

Alonso, Ana María, and María Teresa Koreck. "Silences: 'Hispanics,' AIDS, and Sexual Practices." *The Lesbian and Gay Studies Reader*. Ed. Henry Abelove, Michèle Aina Barale, and David M. Halperin. New York: Routledge, 1993. 110–26. Also in *Differences* 1 (1989): 101–24.

Alonso, José Antonio. *Sexo, trabajo y marginalidad urbana*. Mexico City: Editorial Edicol, 1981.

Alvarez, Sonia. *Engendering Democracy in Brazil: Women's Movements in Transition Politics*. Princeton: Princeton University Press, 1990.

Anzaldúa, Gloria. *Borderlands/La Frontera: The New Mestiza*. San Francisco: Spinsters/Aunt Lute Press, 1987.

———. "To(o) Queer the Writer—Loca, escritora y chicana." *InVersions: Writings by Dykes, Queers and Lesbians*. Vancouver: Press Gang, 1991. 249–63.

———, ed. *Making Face, Making Soul/Haciendo Caras: Creative and Critical Perspectives by Women of Color*. San Francisco: Aunt Lute Press, 1990.

Arango R., María Clara. "La educación sexual: La educación que siempre ocurre." *Educación Hoy* 8.47–48 (1978): 3–182.

Arboleda G., Manuel. "Peru: Gay Activism Takes Hold within a Complex Multi-Ethnic Society." *Advocate* 445 (29 April 1986): 29–33.

———. "Social Attitudes and Sexual Variance in Lima." In Murray 1995, 100–10.

Arce, Andrés, and Modesto Elizeche Almeida. *La violación sexual en el Paraguay: Aspectos psicológico, social y jurídico*. Asunción: Centro Interdisciplinario de Derecho Social y Economía Política, Universidad Católica, 1993.

Archetti, Eduardo. "Argentinian Tango: Male Sexual Ideology and Morality." *The Ecology of Choice and Symbol: Essays in Honour of Fredric Barth*. Ed. Reidar Grønhaug. Bergen: Alma Mater, 1991. 280–96.

———. "Estilos y virtudes masculinas en *El Gráfico*: La creación del imaginario del fútbol argentino." *Desarrollo Económico* 139 (1995): 419–42.

———. "Models of Masculinity in the Poetics of the Argentinian Tango." *Exploring the Written: Anthropology and the Multiplicity of Writing*. Ed. Eduardo Archetti. Oslo: Scandinavian University Press, 1994. 97–122.

Ardila, Rubén. "La homosexualidad en Colombia." *Acta psiquiátrica y psicológica de América Latina* 31 (1985): 191–210.

Argüelles, Lourdes, and B. Ruby Rich. "Homosexuality, Homophobia, and Revolution: Notes toward an Understanding of the Cuban Lesbian and Gay Male Experience." 2 parts. *Signs* 9 (1984): 683–99 and 11 (1985): 120–36.

Arias Londoño, Melba. *Mujer, sexualidad y ley*. Bogotá: Unidad de Psicoterapia y Sexualidad Humana, 1988.

Arriazola Alfaro, Mario. *El lenocinio en el derecho nacional y la represión de la trata de personas y de la explotación de la prostitución ajena*. Mexico City: privately printed, 1965.

Balderston, Daniel. "The 'Fecal Dialectic': Homosexual Panic and the Origin of Writing in Borges." In Bergmann and Smith, 29–45.

Bao, Daniel. "Invertidos sexuales, tortilleras and maricas machos: The Construction of Homosexuality in Buenos Aires, Argentina, 1900–1950." *Journal of Homosexuality* 24.3–4 (1993): 183–219.

Barradas, Efraín. "Epitafios: el canon y la canonización de Manuel Ramos Otero." *La Torre* 7.27–28 (1994): 319–38.

———. "El machismo existencial de René Marqués." *Sin Nombre* 8.3 (1977): 69–81.

Barrán, José Pedro. *Historia de la sensibilidad en el Uruguay.* 2 vols. Montevideo: Ediciones de la Banda Oriental/Facultad de Humanidades y Ciencias, 1989.

Barrancos, Dora. *Anarquismo, educación y costumbres en la Argentina de principios de siglo.* Buenos Aires: Editorial Contrapunto, 1990.

———. "Anarquismo y sexualidad." *Mundo urbano y cultura popular.* Ed. Diego Armus. Buenos Aires: Editorial Sudamericana, 1990.

Barruel de Lagenest, H. D. *Lenocínio e prostituição no Brasil.* Rio de Janeiro: Agir, 1960.

Bastos, José C. "Homossexualidade masculina." *Jornal Brasileiro de Psiquiatria* 28 (1979): 7–11.

Behar, Ruth. *Translated Woman: Crossing the Border with Esperanza's Story.* Boston: Beacon Press, 1993.

Behares, Luis E. "La subcultura homosexual en Montevideo." *Relaciones* 64 (1989): 13–24.

Bejel, Emilio. "*Fresa y chocolate* o la salida de la guarida." *Casa de las Américas* 35.96 (1994): 10–22.

Bellinghausen, Hermann, ed. *El nuevo arte de amar: Usos y costumbres sexuales en México.* Mexico City: Cal y Arena, 1990.

Bellucci, Mabel. "Anarquismo, sexualidad y emancipación femenina: Argentina alrededor del 900." *Nueva Sociedad* 109 (1990): 148–57.

Benedetti, G. "Transsexualismo e transvestismo." *Revista Geográfica Universal* 62 (1980): 87–94.

Bergmann, Emilie L., and Paul Julian Smith, eds. *¿Entiendes? Queer Readings, Hispanic Writings.* Durham: Duke University Press, 1995.

Besse, Susan K. "Crimes of Passion: The Campaign Against Wife Killing in Brazil, 1910–1940." *Journal of Social History* 22.4 (1989): 653–66.

———. *Restructuring Patriarchy. The Modernization of Gender Inequality in Brazil, 1914–1920.* Chapel Hill: University of North Carolina Press, 1996.

Blair, Doniphan. "Gay Men in Nicaragua." *Advocate* 422 (1985): 48–51.

Blanco, José Joaquín. "Ojos que da pánico soñar." *Función de medianoche.* Mexico City: Era, 1981. 183–90.

Blanco, José Joaquín, and Luis Zapata. "¿Cuál literatura gay?" *Sábado*, cultural supplement to *Unomásuno* 310 (8 October 1983): 11.

Bleys, Rudi C. *The Geography of Perversion: Male-to-Male Sexual Behavior Outside the West and the Ethnographic Imagination, 1750–1918.* New York: New York University Press, 1995.

Bolton, Ralph. "Machismo in Motion: The Ethos of Peruvian Truckers." *Ethos* 17.4 (1979): 312–42.

Bossio, Enrique. "Interview with a Gay Activist." *The Peru Reader: History, Culture, Politics.* Ed. Orin Starn, Carlos Iván Degregori, and Robin Kirk. Durham: Duke University Press, 1995. 477–81.

Boulous, R., et al. "Perceptions and Practices Relating to Condom Use among

Urban Men in Haiti." *Studies in Family Planning* 22.5 (1991): 318–25.

Braiterman, Jared. "Fighting AIDS in Brazil." *Coming Out.* Ed. S. Likosky. New York: Pantheon, 1990. 295–307.

Brant, Herbert J. "Camilo's Closet: Sexual Camoflague in Denevi's *Rosaura a las diez.*" *Bodies and Biases: Sexualities in Hispanic Cultures and Literature.* Ed. David William Foster and Roberto Reis. Hispanic Issues 13. Minneapolis: University of Minnesota Press, 1996. 203–16.

———. "'La mariconería de la barra': Homoeroticism and Homophobia in Denevi's 'Michel.'" *Romance Languages Annual 1995.* Ed. Jeanette Beer, Patricia Hart, and Ben Lawton. West Lafayette: Purdue Research Foundation, 1996. 379–84.

———. "The Mark of the Phallus: Homoerotic Desire in Borges' 'La forma de la espada.'" *Chasqui* 25.1 (1996): 25–38.

Bravo Martínez, Mariana. *Incesto y violación: Características, implicaciones y líneas.* Santiago de Chile: Ediciones Academia, Universidad Academia de Humanismo Cristiano, 1994.

Bruce-Novoa, Juan. "Homosexuality and the Chicano Novel." *Confluencia* 2.1 (1986): 69–77.

Bruschini, Maria Cristina A., and Fúlvia Rosemberg, eds. *Vivência: História, sexualidade e imagens femininas.* São Paulo: Editora Brasiliense, 1980.

Carballo-Diéguez, Alex. "Hispanic Culture, Gay Male Culture, and AIDS: Counseling Implications." *Journal of Counseling and Development* 68 (1989): 26–30.

Cardín, A. *Guerreros, chamanes y travestis: Indicios de homosexualidad entre los exóticos.* Barcelona, 1984.

Carrier, Joseph M. "Cultural Factors Affecting Urban Mexican Male Homosexual Behavior." *Archives of Social Behavior* 5.2 (1976): 103–24.

———. *De los otros: Intimacy and Homosexuality among Mexican Men.* New York: Columbia University Press, 1995.

———. "Family Attitudes and Mexican Male Homosexuality." *Urban Life* 5.3 (1976): 359–76.

———. "Gay Liberation and Coming Out in Mexico." *Gay and Lesbian Youth.* Ed. Gilbert Herdt. New York: Haworth Press, 1989. 225–53.

———. "Mexican Male Bisexuality." *Bisexualities: Theory and Research.* Ed. Fritz Klein and Thomas J. Wolf. New York: Haworth Press, 1985. 75–85. Also in *Journal of Homosexuality* 11 (1985): 75–85.

———. "Miguel: Sexual Life History of a Gay Mexican American." *Gay Culture in America.* Ed. Gilbert Herdt. Boston: Beacon Press, 1992. 202–24.

———. "Participants in Urban Mexican Male Homosexual Encounters." *Archives of Social Behavior* 1 (1971): 279–91.

———. "Sexual Behavior and the Spread of AIDS in Mexico." *Medical Anthropology* 10 (1989): 129–42. Also in *The AIDS Pandemic*, ed. R. Bolton (New York: Gordon & Breach, 1989), 37–50.

Carrier, Joseph M., and J. Raúl Magaña. "Use of Ethnosexual Data on Men of Mexican Origins for HIV/AIDS Prevention Programs." *The Time of AIDS.* Ed. Gilbert Herdt and Shirley Lindenbaum. London: Sage, 1992. 243–58.

Carrillo, Ana María. "Los adolescentes y la sexualidad." *Fem* 13.79 (1989): 9–17.

Carvalho, Tamara Teixeira de. "Hippie de ayer, yuppie de hoy: Disciplinamiento sexual y canon corporal." *Nueva Sociedad* 109 (1990): 141–47.

Case, Sue-Ellen. "Seduced and Abandoned: Chicanas and Lesbians in Representation." In Taylor and Villegas, 88–101.

Castillo, Ana. "La Macha: Toward a Beautiful Whole Self." In Trujillo, 24–48.

Castro, María. *El lesbianismo como una cuestión política*. Mexico City: Ponencia, 1987.

Castro-Klaren, Sara, Sylvia Molloy, and Beatriz Sarlo, eds. *Women's Writing in Latin America*. Boulder: Westview Press, 1991.

Caulfield, Sueann. "Getting into Trouble: Dishonest Women, Modern Girls, and Women-Men in the Conceptual Language of Vida Policial, 1925–1927." *Signs* 19.1 (1993): 146–76.

Caulfield, Sueann, and Martha de Abreu Esteves. "Fifty years of Virginity in Rio de Janeiro: Sexual Politics and Gender Roles in Juridical and Popular Discourse, 1890–1940." *Luso-Brazilian Review* 30.1 (1993): 47–74.

Centro Latinoamericano de Demografía, Fondo de Población de las Naciones Unidas, Ministerio de Salud Pública, and Organización Panamericana de la Salud. *Mujer y fecundidad en Uruguay: Factores determinantes directos de la fecundidad y sus implicaciones en salud*. Montevideo: Ediciones Trilce, 1994.

Chávez-Silverman, Suzanne. "The Look That Kills: The 'Unacceptable Beauty' of Alejandra Pizarnik's *La condesa sangrienta*." In Bergmann and Smith, 281–305.

Chiñas, Beverly Newbold. "Isthmus Zapotec Attitudes toward Sex and Gender Anomalies." In Murray 1995, 293–302.

Colinson, Helen, ed. *Women and Revolution in Nicaragua*. London: Zed Books, 1990; distributed in the U.S. by Humanities Press, Atlantic Highlands, N.J.

Congreso Colombiano de Sexología. *Terapia y educación sexual*. Bogotá: ICFES, Instituo Colombiano para el Fomento de la Educación Superior, 1984.

Cordero Morera, Sigifredo, and José Durán Umana. *Delitos sexuales: Jurisprudencia penal*. San José, Costa Rica: Investigaciones jurídicas, 1993.

Córdova Plaza, Rosio. "De cornudos, dejadas y otras especies: Un estudio de caso sobre sexualidad en el campo veracruzano." *América Indígena* 52.3 (1992): 137–46.

Cornwall, Andrea, and Nancy Lindisfarne. *Dislocating Masculinity: Comparative Ethnographies*. London and New York: Routledge, 1994.

Corrêa, Mariza. *Os crimes da paixão*. São Paulo: Brasiliense, 1981.

Cruz-Malavé, Arnaldo. "Para virar al macho: La autobiografía como subversión en la cuentística de Manuel Ramos Otero." *Revista Iberoamericana* 59.162–163 (1993): 239–63.

———. "Toward an Art of Transvestism: Colonialism and Homosexuality in Puerto Rican Literature." In Bergmann and Smith, 137–67.

Daniel, H., and R. Parker, eds. *Sexuality, Politics and AIDS in Brazil*. London: Falmer Press, 1993.

de Alba, Alicia Gaspar. "Tortillerismo: Work by Chicana Lesbians." *Signs* 18 (1993): 956–63.

Del Río, E. *El amor en los tiempos del SIDA*. Mexico City: Editorial Grijalbo, 1988.

Deutsch, Sandra McGee. "Gender and Sociopolitical Change in Twentieth-Century Latin America." *Hispanic American Historical Review* 71.2 (1991): 259–306.

Di Liscia, María H., María S. Di Liscia, María J. Billorou, and Ana M. Rodríguez. *Acerca de las mujeres: Género y Sociedad en La Pampa*. Santa Rosa: Universidad Nacional de la Pampa, 1994.

Dourado, Luiz Angelo. *Homossexualismo masculino e feminino e delinquência*. Rio de Janeiro: Zahar, 1967.

Doyle, Iracy. *Contribuição ao estudo da homossexualidade femenina*. Rio de Janeiro: Lux, 1956.

Dundes, Alan, and Marcelo Suárez Orozco. "The *Piropo* and the Dual Image of Women in the Spanish-Speaking World." *Parsing through Customs*. Ed. Alan Dundes. Madison: University of Wisconsin Press, 1987.

Dynes, Wayne R. "Portugayese." In Murray 1995, 256–63.

Educación sexual: América Latina y Área del Caribe/ Sex Education: Latin America and the Caribbean. Guayaquil: Departamento de Información y Educación de APROFE, 1974.

Engel, Magali. *Meretrizes e doutores: O saber médico e a prostituição na cidade do Rio de Janeiro, 1845–1890*. São Paulo: Brasiliense, 1990.

Espin, Oliva M. "Cultural and Historical Influences on Sexuality in Hispanic/Latin Women: Implications for Psychotherapy." *Pleasure and Danger: Exploring Female Sexuality*. Ed. Carol Vance. London: Routledge, 1984. 149–63.

———. "Issues of Identity in the Psychology of Latina Lesbians." *Lesbian Psychologies*. Ed. Boston Lesbian Psychologies Collective. Urbana: University of Illinois Press, 1987. 35–55.

Espinosa Molina, Claudio. *Crímenes sexuales*. Santiago: Editorial Neupert, 1969.

Farmer, P. *AIDS and Accusation: Haiti and the Geography of Blame*. Berkeley: University of California Press, 1992.

Fecundidad en la adolescencia: Causas, riesgos y opciones. Washington, D.C.: Organización Panamericana de la Salud, 1988.

Ferguson, Ann. "Lesbianism, Feminism and Empowerment in Nicaragua." *Social Review* 21.3–4 (1991): 75–97.

Fernández-Olmos, Marguerite. "Luis Rafael Sánchez and Rosario Ferré: Sexual Politics and Contemporary Puerto Rican Narrative." *Hispania* 70.1 (1987): 40–46.

Figueroa, Alvin Joaquín. "Feminismo, homosexualidad e identidad política: el lenguaje del otro en *Felices días, tío Sergio*." *La Torre* 5.20 (1991): 499–505.

Figueroa Perea, Juan Guillermo. "Algunas reflexiones sobre la representación social de la sexualidad femenina." *Nueva Antropología* 12.41 (1992): 101–21.

Fiol-Matta, Licia. "The 'Schoolteacher of America': Gender, Sexuality, and Nation in Gabriela Mistral." In Bergmann and Smith, 201–29.

Fonseca, Guido. *História da Prostituição em São Paulo*. São Paulo: Editora Resenha Universitária, 1982.

Forrest, K. A., D. M. Austin, M. I. Valdés, E. G. Fuentes, and S. R. Wilson. "Exploring Norms and Beliefs related to AIDS Prevention among California Hispanic Men." *Family Planning Perspectives* 25 (1993): 111–17.

Foster, David William. *Cultural Diversity in Latin American Literature*. Albuquerque: University of New Mexico Press, 1994.

————. *Gay and Lesbian Themes in Latin American Writing*. Austin: University of Texas Press, 1991.

————. "Latin American Literature." *Encyclopedia of International Lesbian and Gay Culture*. Ed. Claude J. Summers. New York: Holt, Rinehart & Winston, 1995, 425–31.

————, ed. *Latin American Writers on Gay and Lesbian Themes: A Bio-Critical Sourcebook*. Intro. Lillian Manzor-Coats. Westport, Conn.: Greenwood Press, 1994.

Foster, David William, and Roberto Reis, eds. *Bodies and Biases: Sexualities in Hispanic Cultures and Literatures*. Minneapolis: University of Minnesota Press, 1996.

Franco, Jean. *Plotting Women: Gender and Representation in Mexico*. New York: Columbia University Press, 1989.

French, William. "Prostitutes and Guardian Angels: Women, Work, and the Family in Porfirian Mexico." *Hispanic American Historical Review* 72.4 (1992): 529–53.

Fry, Peter. "Léonie, Pombinha, Amaro e Aleixo: Prostituição, homossexualidade e raça em dois romances naturalistas." *Caminhos cruzados: Linguagem, antropologia, ciências naturais*. Ed. Alexandre Eulálio. São Paulo: Editora Brasiliense, 1983.

————. "Male Homosexuality and Afro-Brazilian Possession Cults." In Murray 1995, 193–220.

————. *Para inglês ver: Identidade e política na cultura brasileira*. Rio de Janeiro: Zahar, 1982.

Fry, Peter, and Edward MacRae. *O que é homossexualidade*. São Paulo: Brasiliense, 1983.

Fusková, Ilse, and Claudina Marek. *Amor de mujeres: El lesbianismo en la Argentina, hoy*. Buenos Aires: Planeta, 1994.

Fusková-Komreich, Ilse. "Lesbian Activism in Argentina: A Recent But Very Powerful Phenomenon." *The Third Pink Book*. Ed. A. Hendriks, R. Tielman, and E. van der Veen. Buffalo: Prometheus Books, 1993. 82–85.

Gandolfo, Elvio E. "Montevideo sexual, una reflexión a pie." *Nueva Sociedad* 109 (1990): 80–89.

Gaspar, Maria Dulce. *Garotos de programa: Prostituição em Copacabana e identidade social*. Rio de Janeiro: Zahar, 1985.

Gelpí, Juan. *Literatura y paternalismo en Puerto Rico: Estudio del canon*. Río Piedras: Editorial de la Universidad de Puerto Rico, 1993.

Gicci, Francisco. *Educación sexual: Consejos a los padres*. Buenos Aires: Mercateli, 1914.

Giel, R. "Tropical Tribades: A Report on Homosexuality and Lesbian Relationships in Surinam." *Bijdragen tot de Taal-Land en Volkenkunde* 115 (1990): 311–15.

Goldberg, Jonathan. "Sodomy in the New World: Anthropologies Old and New." *Social Text* 29 (1991): 45–56.

Goldwert, Marvin. "Mexican Machismo: The Flight from Femininity." *Psychoanalytic Review* 72.1 (1985): 161–69.

Gomezjara, F., E. Barrera, and N. Pérez. *Sociología de la prostitución*. Mexico City: Ediciones Nueva Sociología, 1978.

González, Deena J. "Masquerades: Viewing the New Chicana Lesbian Anthologies." *Out/Look* 15 (1991): 80–83.

González Blanco, Alberto. *Delitos sexuales en la doctrina y en el derecho positivo mexicano.* 3d ed. Mexico City: Editorial Porrua, 1974.

González Rojo, Enrique. "El papel de feminismo en la revolución sexual." *Fem 27* (1978): 48–53.

Graham, Sandra Lauderdale. "Slavery's Impasse: Slave Prostitutes, Small-Time Mistresses, and the Brazilian Law of 1871." *Comparative Studies in Society and History* 33.4 (1991): 669–94.

Green, James N. "The Emergence of the Brazilian Gay Liberation Movement, 1977–1981." *Latin American Perspectives* 21 (1994): 38–55.

Grupo Ceres. *Espelho de Venus: Identidade social et sexual da mulher.* São Paulo: Editora Brasilense, 1981.

Grupo Mujer y Sociedad. *Mujer, amor y violencia: Nuevas interpretaciones de antiguas realidades.* Bogotá: Universidad Nacional de Colombia, Tercer Mundo Editores, 1991.

Gruzinski, Serge. "Las cenizas del deseo: Homosexuales novohispanos a mediados del siglo XVII." *De la santidad a la perversión: O de por qué no se cumplía la ley de Dios en la sociedad novohispana.* Ed. Sergio Ortega. Mexico City: Editorial Grijalbo, 1986. 169–215.

Guerra-Cunningham, Lucía, ed. *Mujer y sociedad en América Latina.* Mexico City: Editorial del Pacífico, 1980.

Guerrero, Manuel de Jesús. *El machismo latinoamericano.* New York: Plus Ultra, 1977.

Guridi Sánchez, Jorge. *Ensayo sobre dogmática del delito de incesto en el derecho penal.* Mexico City: UNAM, Facultad de Derecho y Ciencias Sociales, 1961.

Gutiérrez, Ramón A. *When Jesus Came, the Corn Mothers Went Away: Marriage, Sexuality and Power in New Mexico, 1500–1846.* Stanford: Stanford University Press, 1991.

Guy, Donna J. "Future Directions in Latin American Gender History." *Americas* 51.1 (1994): 1–9.

———. "Medical Imperialism Gone Awry: The Campaign against Legalized Prostitution in Latin America." *Science, Medicine and Cultural Imperialism.* Ed. Teresa Meade and Mark Walker. New York: St. Martin's Press, 1991. 75–94.

———. *Sex and Danger: Prostitution, Family and Nation in Argentina.* Lincoln: University of Nebraska Press, 1991.

———. "White Slavery, Public Health, and the Socialist Position on Legalized Prostitution in Argentina, 1913–1936." *Latin American Research Review* 23.3 (1988): 60–80.

Guzmán, Mario. "Los homosexuales en México." *Continedo,* 1971, 44–54.

Hahner, June. *Emancipating the Female Sex. The Struggle for Women's Rights in Brazil, 1850–1940.* Durham: Duke University Press, 1990.

Hernández, Juan Jacobo, and Rafael Manrique. "El movimiento gay/lésbico en México." *Del Otro Lado* 15 (1994): 12–15.

Herrera-Sobek, María. "*La Delgadina*: Incest and Patriarchal Structure in a Spanish-Chicano *Romance-Corrido*." *Studies in Latin American Popular Culture* 5 (1986): 90–107.

Hidalgo, Hilda, and Elia Hidalgo-Christensen. "The Puerto Rican Cultural Response to Female Homosexuality." *The Puerto Rican Women*. Ed. Edna Acosta-Belén. New York: Praeger, 1979. 110–23.

———. "The Puerto Rican Lesbian and the Puerto Rican Community." *Journal of Homosexuality* 2 (1976–1977): 109–21.

"Homosexuality in Cuba: A Threat to Public Morality?" *Connexions: An International Women's Quarterly* 2 (1981): 18–19.

Howes, Robert. "The Literatures of Outsiders: The Literature of the Gay Community in Latin America." *Latin American Masses and Minorities: Their Images and Realities* (SALALM) 30 (1987): 288–304.

Jáuregui, Carlos Luis. *La homosexualidad en la Argentina*. Buenos Aires: Ediciones Tarso, 1987.

Jiménez Cadena, Álvaro. "¿Educación sexual sin castidad?" *Revista Javeriana* 62.604 (1994): 297–317.

Jones, Brooke. "Cuban Lesbians." *off our backs* 10 (1980): 6, 16.

Jornada de denuncia a la violencia contra la mujer. Santo Domingo: CIPAF, Ediciones Populares Feministas, 1981.

Kaminsky, Amy. *Reading the Body Politic: Feminist Criticism and Latin American Women Writers*. Minneapolis: University of Minnesota Press, 1993.

Kimball, Geoffrey. "Aztec Homosexuality: The Textual Evidence." *Journal of Homosexuality* 26.1 (1993): 7–24.

Knaster, Meri. *Women in Spanish America: An Annotated Bibliography from Pre-Conquest to Contemporary Times*. Boston: G. K. Hall, 1977.

Knecher, Lidia, and Marta Panaia, comps. *La mitad del país. La mujer en la sociedad argentina*. Buenos Aires: Bibliotecas Universitarias, Centro Editor de América Latina, 1994.

Kutsche, Paul. "Situational Homosexuality in Costa Rica." *Anthropology Research Group on Homosexuality Newsletter* 4.4 (1983): 6–13.

———. "Two Truths about Costa Rica." In Murray 1995, 111–37.

Kutsche, Paul, and J. Bryan Page. "Male Sexual Identity in Costa Rica." *Latin American Anthropology Review* 3 (1991): 7–14.

Kuznesof, Elizabeth Anne. "Sexual Politics, Race and Bastard-Bearing in Nineteenth-Century Brazil: A Question of Culture or Power?" *Journal of Family History* 3.16 (1991): 241–60.

Lancaster, Roger N. *Life Is Hard: Machismo, Danger, and the Intimacy of Power in Nicaragua*. Berkeley: University of California Press, 1992.

———. "Subject Honor and Object Shame: The Construction of Male Homosexuality and Stigma in Nicaragua." *Ethnology* 28.2 (1988): 111–26.

———. "'That We Should All Turn Queer?' Homosexual Stigma in the Making of Manhood and the Breaking of a Revolution in Nicaragua." *Conceiving Sexuality: Approaches to Sex Research in a Postmodern World*. Ed. Richard Parker and John Gagnon. New York: Routledge, 1995. 135–56.

Landes, Ruth. "A Cult Matriarchate and Male Homosexuality." *Journal of Abnormal and Social Psychology* 35 (1940): 386–97.

Lane, Erskine. *Game-Texts: A Guatemalan Journal*. San Francisco: Gay Sunshine Press, 1978.

Lavrin, Asunción, ed. *Sexuality and Marriage in Colonial Latin America*. Lincoln: University of Nebraska Press, 1989.

———. *Women, Feminism, and Social Change in Argentina, Chile, and Uruguay, 1890–1940*. Lincoln: University of Nebraska Press, 1995.

Leiner, Marvin. *Sexual Politics in Cuba: Machismo, Homosexuality and AIDS*. Boulder: Westview Press, 1994.

Lerer, María Luisa. *Sexualidad femenina: Mitos, realidades y el sentido de ser mujer*. Buenos Aires: ESA/Plan, 1986.

Leyland, Winston, ed. *My Deep Dark Pain Is Love: A Collection of Latin American Fiction*. San Francisco: Gay Sunshine Press, 1983.

———, ed. *Now the Volcano: An Anthology of Latin American Gay Literature*. San Francisco: Gay Sunshine Press, 1979.

Lidid Céspedes, Sandra. "Sida, empuje conservador e indiferencia." *Nueva Sociedad* 109 (1990): 116–23.

Lima, Délcio Monteiro de. *Comportamento Sexual do Brasileiro*. Rio de Janeiro: Livraria Francisco Alves, 1978.

———. *Os Homoeróticos*. Rio de Janeiro: Editora Francisco Alves, 1983.

Londoño E., María Ladi. "Sexualidad femenina como práctica de libertad." *Nueva Sociedad* 109 (1990): 90–98.

———. "Sexualidad y placer de la mujer. Un estudio de caso." *La realidad colombiana*. Ed. Magdalena León de Leal. Bogotá: Asociación Colombiana para el Estudio de Población (ACEP), 1982. 152–63.

Loyola, Maria Andrea. *Aids e sexualidade: O ponto de vista das ciências humanas*. Rio de Janeiro: Universidade de Estado do Rio de Janeiro, 1994.

Lugo-Ortiz, Agnes. "Community at Its Limits: Orality, Law, Silence, and the Homosexual Body in Luis Rafael Sánchez's 'Jum.'" In Bergmann and Smith, 115–36.

Lumsden, Ian. *Homosexualidad, sociedad y estado en México*. Trans. Luis Zapata. Mexico City: Solediciones, Colectivo Sol; Toronto: Canadian Gay Archives, 1991. Also in English: *Homosexuality, Society and the State*. Toronto: Canadian Gay Archives, 1991.

———. *Machos, Maricones and Gays: Cuba and Homosexuality*. Philadelphia: Temple University Press, 1996.

MacRae, Edward. "A construção da igualdade: Identidade sexual e política no Brasil da 'Abertura.'" Campinas: EDUNICAMP, 1990.

———. "Os respetáveis militantes e as bichas loucas." *Caminhos cruzados: linguagem, antropologia, ciências naturais*. Ed. Alexandre Eulálio. São Paulo: Editora Brasiliense, 1983. 99–111.

Maduro, Otto. "Extracción de plusvalía, represión de la sexualidad y catolicismo en Latinoamerica." *Fem* 5.20 (1981–1982): 21–28.

Mafud, Julio. *La conducta sexual de la mujer argentina*. Buenos Aires: Editorial Distal, 1991.

———. *La conducta sexual de los argentinos*. Buenos Aires: Editorial Distal, 1988.

Magaña, J. Raul, and Joseph Carrier. "Mexican and Mexican-American Male Sexual

Behavior and the Spread of AIDS in California." *Journal of Sex Research* 28 (1991): 425–41.

Maldonado Vázquez, Salvador. *Ensayo sobre orientación sexual para México y Latinoamérica*. Mexico City: Editorial Diana, 1976.

Mantega, Guido. *Sexo e poder*. São Paulo: Editora Brasiliense, 1979.

Manzor-Coats, Liliana. Introduction to *Latin American Writers on Gay and Lesbian Themes: A Bio-Critical Sourcebook*. Ed. David William Foster. Westport, Conn.: Greenwood Press, 1994. xv–xxxvi.

———. "Who Are You, Anyway? Gender, Racial and Linguistic Politics in U.S. Cuban Theater." *Gestos* 11 (1991): 163–74.

Maranhão, Odon Ramos. *Manual de sexologia médico-legal*. São Paulo: Editora Revista dos Tribunais, 1972.

Marroquín, Rolando. "Investigación sobre actitudes hacia la planificación familiar y la educación sexual, en una muestra de 200 madres de Tecoluca." *América Indígena* 35.4 (1975): 797–831.

Martin, Bernice. "La sacralización del caos: El simbolismo en la música 'rock.'" *Estudios Públicos* 48 (1992): 227–85.

Martínez, Elena M. *Lesbian Voices from Latin America: Breaking Ground*. New York: Garland, 1995.

Martínez-Alier, Verena. *Marriage, Class and Colour in Nineteenth–Century Cuba: A Study of Racial Attitudes and Sexual Values in a Slave Society*. London: Cambridge University Press, 1974; Ann Arbor: University of Michigan Press, 1989.

Martínez-Maza, Otoniel, Diana M. Shin, and Helen E. Banks. *Latinos and AIDS: A National Strategy Symposium*. Los Angeles: Center for Interdisciplinary Research in Immunology and Disease, 1989.

Martínez Roaro, Marcela. *Delitos sexuales: Sexualidad y derecho*. 4th ed. Mexico City: Editorial Porrúa, 1991.

Masiello, Francine. *Between Civilization and Barbarism: Women, Nation, and Literary Culture in Modern Argentina*. Lincoln: University of Nebraska Press, 1991.

———. "'Gentlemen,' damas, travestis: Ciudadanía e identidad cultural en la Argentina del fin de siglo." *La imaginación histórica en el siglo XIX*. Ed. Lelia Area and Mabel Moraña. Rosario: Universidad Nacional de Rosario Editora, 1994. 297–309.

———. *La mujer y el espacio público: El periodismo femenino en la Argentina del siglo XIX*. Buenos Aires: Feminaria, 1994.

Matory, J. Lorand. "Homens montados: Homossexualidade e simbolismo da possessão nas religiões afro-brasileiras." *Escravidão e invenção da liberdade: Estudos sobre o negro no Brasil*. Ed. J. Reis. São Paulo: Brasiliense, 1988.

McCreery, David. "Una vida de miseria y vergüenza: Prostitución femenina en la Ciudad de Guatemala." *Mesoamérica* 7.11 (1986): 35–59.

Mendès-Leite, Rommel. "The Game of Appearances: The 'Ambigusexuality' in Brazilian Culture of Sexuality." *Journal of Homosexuality* 25.3 (1993): 271–82.

Mendoza, Vicente T. "El machismo en México." *Cuadernos del Instituto Nacional de Investigaciones Folklóricas* 3 (1962): 75–86.

Mexico. Consejo Nacional de Población. *Encuesta nacional sobre sexualidad y familia en jóvenes de educación media superior, 1988.* Mexico City: Consejo Nacional de Población, 1988.

———. Secretaría de Salud, Dirección General de Planificación Familiar. *Informe de la encuesta sobre conocimiento, actitud y práctica en el uso de métodos anti-contraceptivos de la población masculina obrera del área metropolitana de la ciudad de México.* Mexico City: Secretaría de Salud, 1990.

Miller, Francesca. *Latin American Women and the Search for Social Justice.* Hanover, N.H.: University Press of New England, 1991.

Misse, Michael. *O Estigma do Passivo Sexual.* Rio de Janeiro: Achiamé, 1979.

Molloy, Sylvia. "Disappearing Acts: Reading Lesbian in Teresa de la Parra." In Bergmann and Smith, 230–56.

———. "La política de la pose." *Las culturas de fin de siglo en América Latina.* Ed. Josefina Ludmer. Rosario: Beatriz Viterbo Editora, 1994. 128–38.

———. "Too Wilde for Comfort: Desire and Ideology in Fin-de-Siècle Spanish America." *Social Text* 31–32 (1992): 187–201.

Molyneaux, Maxine. "Mobilization without Emancipation: Women's Interests, State, and Revolution." *Transition and Development: Problems of Third World Socialism.* Ed. Richard P. Fagen, Carmen Diana Deere, and José Luis Coraggio. New York: Monthly Review Press, 1986.

Monreal, Tegualda. "Determining Factors Affecting Illegal Abortion Trends in Chile." *New Developments in Fertility Regulations: A Conference for Latin American Physicians.* Airle, Va.: Pathfinder Fund, 1976.

Monsiváis, Carlos. "Control y condón: La revolución sexual mexicana." *Nueva Sociedad* 109 (1990): 99–105.

———. "La mujer en la cultura mexicana." *Mujer y sociedad en América Latina.* Ed. Lucía Guerra-Cunningham. Mexico City: Editorial del Pacífico, 1980. 101–17.

———. "Paisaje de batallas entre condones: Saldos de la revolución sexual." *Nuevo arte de amar: usos y costumbres sexuales en México.* Mexico City: Cal y Arena, 1992.

———. "¿Pero hubo alguna vez once mil machos?" *Fem* 18 (1981): 9–20.

———. "Sexismo en la literatura mexicana." *Imagen y realidad de la mujer.* Ed. Elena Urrutia. Mexico City: SEPDiana, 1979. 102–25.

Montaner, Carlos Alberto. "Sexo malo." *Informe secreto sobre la revolución cubana.* Madrid: Ediciones Sedmay, 1976. 173–77.

Montero, Oscar. "Before the Parade Passes By: Latino Queers and National Identity." *Radical America* 24.4 (1993): 15–26.

———. *Erotismo y representación en Julián del Casal.* Amsterdam: Rodopi, 1993.

———. "Julián del Casal and the Queers of Havana." In Bergmann and Smith, 92–112.

Moraga, Cherríe, and Gloria Anzaldúa, eds. *This Bridge Called My Back: Writings by Radical Women of Color.* 2d ed. New York: Kitchen Table Press, 1983.

Morales, Edward S. "HIV Infection and Hispanic Gay and Bisexual Men." *Hispanic Journal of Behavior Sciences* 12 (1990): 212–22.

Moreau de Justo, Alicia. "Educación sexual y educación moral." *Hacia la extinción de un flagelo social.* Buenos Aires: Fabril Financiera, 1937.

Moreira, Rita. "Lésbicas: O alto preço de uma opção de vida." *Revista Espacial* 5 (1980): 36–39.

Mosonyi, Esteban Emilio. "La sexualidad indígena vista a través de dos culturas: waraos y guajibos." *Boletín Americanista* 26.34 (1984): 179–91.

Mott, Luiz. "A Aids e os Médicos no Brasil." *Ciência e Cultura* 39.1 (1987): 4–13.

———. "Antropologia, população e sexualidade." *Gente* 1 (1984): 89–103.

———. *Escravidão, homossexualidade e demonologia.* São Paulo: Icone, 1988.

———. "The Gay Movement and Human Rights in Brazil." In Murray 1995, 221–30.

———. "Homossexuais negros no Brasil e na África." *Os Afro-Brasileiros.* Ed. Roberto da Mota. Recife: Editora Mecejana, 1985.

———. "A homossexualidade no Brasil: Bibliografia." *Latin American Masses and Minorities* (SALALM) 30 (1987): 592–609.

———. *O lesbianismo no Brasil.* Porto Alegre: Mercado Aberto, 1987.

———. "Quinientos años de homosexualidad en las Américas." *Conducta impropia* (Lima) 4–5 (1993): 21–24.

———. *O sexo proibido: Virgens, gays e escravos nas garras da inquisição.* Campinas: Editora Papirus, 1989.

———. "A violação dos direitos humanos dos homossexuais no Brasil." *Boletim da Associação Brasileira de Antropologia* 19 (1993): 6.

Mujer y sociedad en América Latina. Buenos Aires: Consejo Latinoamericano de Ciencias Sociales, 1991.

Mujeres e iglesia: Sexualidad y aborto en América Latina. Washington, D.C.: Catholics for a Free Choice-USA/Distribuciones Fontamara, 1989.

Munín, Alicia, and Regina G. Schlüter. *Turismo y sexo: Aproximación a un estudio sobre prostitución y turismo en Argentina.* Buenos Aires: Centro de Investigaciones en Turismo, 1985.

Murraro, Rose Marie. *Sexualidade da mulher brasileira.* Petrópolis: Vozes, 1983.

———, ed. *Sexualidade, liberação e fé: Por uma erótica cristão. Primeiras indagações.* Petrópolis: Vozes, 1985.

Murray, Stephen O. "Heteronormative Cuban Sexual Policies and Resistance to Them." *GLQ* 2.4 (1995): 473–77.

———. "'Homosexual Occupations' in Guatemala?" *Journal of Homosexuality* 21 (1991): 57–64. Also in Murray 1995, 71–79.

———, ed. *Latin American Male Homosexualities.* Albuquerque: University of New Mexico Press, 1995.

———. "Lexical and Institutional Elaboration: The 'Species Homosexual' in Guatemala." *Anthropological Linguistics* 22 (1980): 177–85.

———. *Male Homosexuality in Central and South America.* Gai Saber Monograph 5. San Francisco: Instituto Obregón, 1987.

———. "Male Homosexuality in Guatemala: Possible Insights and Certain Confusions from Obtaining Data by Sleeping with the Natives." *Out in the Field: Reflections of Lesbian and Gay Anthropologists.* Ed. Ellen Lewin and William Leap. Urbana: University of Illinois Press, 1995. 236–60.

———. "Stigma Transformation and Relexification in the International Diffusion of 'Gay.'" *Beyond the Lavender Lexicon: Gay and Lesbian Language.* Ed. William Leap. New York: Gordon & Breach, 1996. 215–40.

————. "The 'Underdevelopment' of 'Gay' Homosexuality in Mesoamerica, Peru, and Thailand." *Modern Homosexualities*. Ed. Ken Plummer. London: Routledge, 1992. 29–38.

Murray, Stephen O., and Manuel Arboleda G. "Stigma Transformation and Relexification: *Gay* in Latin America." In Murray 1995, 138–44.

Murray, Stephen O., and Wayne Dynes. "Hispanic Homosexuals: A Spanish Lexicon." In Murray 1995, 180–92.

Nazal Manzur, María Eugenia. *El delito de corrupción de menores*. Santiago: Universidad Católica de Chile, 1968.

Negrón-Muntaner, Frances. "Echoing Stonewall and Other Dilemmas: The Organizational Beginnings of a Gay and Lesbian Agenda in Puerto Rico, 1972–1977." 2 parts. *Centro* 4.1 and 4.2 (1992): 77–95 and 98–115.

Nicholson, Roberto. "Educación sexual del adolescente." *Criterio* 48.1725 (9 October 1975): 554–57.

Nieto S., Elba María. *El delito de la violación sexual en Honduras: causística*. Cuadernos "Visitación Padilla" 2. Tegucigalpa: Comité Hondureño de Mujeres por la Paz, 1989.

Novo, Salvador. *Las locas, el sexo, los burdeles*. Mexico City: Novaro, 1972.

"Nuestra época sexual: Lo público de lo privado." Special dossier. *Nueva Sociedad* 109 (1990): 77–185.

Nuñez Noriega, Guillermo. *Sexo entre varones: Poder y resistencia en el campo sexual*. Hermosillo: El Colegio de Sonora, Universidad de Sonora, 1994.

Okita, Hiro. *Homossexualidade: Da opressão à libertação*. São Paulo: Proposta Editorial, 1981.

Ortiz, Ricardo L. "Sexuality Degree Zero: Pleasure and Power in the Novels of John Rechy, Arturo Islas, and Michael Nava." *Journal of Homosexuality* 26.2–3 (1993): 111–26.

Parker, Richard G. "AIDS in Urban Brazil." *Medical Anthropology Quarterly* 1 (1987): 155–75.

————. *Bodies, Pleasures and Passions: Sexual Culture in Contemporary Brazil*. Boston: Beacon Press, 1991.

————. "Changing Brazilian Constructions of Homosexuality." In Murray 1995, 241–55.

————. "Masculinity, Femininity and Homosexuality: On the Anthropological Interpretation of Sexual Meaning in Brazil." *Journal of the History of Sexuality* 2 (1986): 679–82. Also in the *Journal of Homosexuality* 11.3–4 (1985): 155–63.

————. "Youth Identity and Homosexuality: The Changing Shape of Sexual Life in Contemporary Brazil." *Gay and Lesbian Youth*. Ed. Gilbert Herdt. New York: Haworth Press, 1989. 269–89. Also in Portuguese: *Sexo e Prostituição*. Rio de Janeiro: Gráfica Record Editora, 1967.

Pérez, Emma. "Sexuality and Discourse: Notes from a Chicana Survivor." In Trujillo, 159–84.

Perlongher, Néstor. "Avatares de los muchachos de la noche." *Nueva Sociedad* 109 (1990): 124–34.

————. *O negócio do michê: Prostituição viril em São Paulo*. Rio de Janeiro:

Laemmert, 1986. Also in Spanish: *La prostitución masculina*. Buenos Aires: Ediciones de la Urraca, 1993.

———. *O que é Aids*. São Paulo: Brasiliense, 1987.

Piedra, José. "His/Her Panics." *Dispositio* 16.41 (1991): 71–93.

———. "Nationalizing Sissies." In Bergmann and Smith, 370–409.

Pollak-Eltz, Angelina. "Antropología y sexualidad: la familia negra en Venezuela." *Megafón* 9.17–18 (1986): 66–77.

Puleo, Alicia. "Perspectivas antropológicas de un problema de crítica literaria." *Escritura y sexualidad en la literatura hispanoamericana*. Madrid: Fundamentos, 1990. 9–20.

Quiroga, José. "Fleshing Out Virgilio Piñera from the Cuban Closet." In Bergmann and Smith, 168–80.

———. "(Queer) Boleros of a Tropical Night." *Travesia* 3.1–2 (1994): 199–213.

Rago, Margareth. *Do cabaré ao lar: a utopia da cidade disciplinar, Brasil 1890–1930*. Rio de Janeiro: Paz e Terra, 1985.

———. *Os prazeres da noite: Prostituição e códigos da sexualidade feminina em São Paulo (1890–1930)*. Rio de Janeiro: Paz e Terra, 1991.

Ramírez, J., E. Suarez, G. de la Rosa, M. A. Castro, and M. A. Zimmerman. "AIDS Knowledge and Sexual Behavior among Mexican Gay and Bisexual Men." *AIDS Education and Prevention* 6 (1994): 163–74.

Ramírez, Rafael L. *Dime capitán: reflexiones sobre la masculinidad*. Río Piedras: Ediciones Huracán, 1993.

Ramos, Juanita, ed. *Compañeras: Latina Lesbians*. New York: Latina Lesbian History Project, 1987.

Ramos–Frías, José A. *Estudio criminológico y médico-legal de la homosexualidad*. Mexico City: Virginia, 1966.

Randall, Margaret. "To Change Our Own Reality and the World: A Conversation with Lesbians in Nicaragua." *Signs* 18 (1993): 907–24.

Reinhardt, Karl J. "The Image of Gays in Chicano Prose Fiction." In Murray 1995, 150–57.

Ribeiro, Leonídio. *Homossexualismo e endocrinologia*. Rio de Janeiro: Francisco Alves, 1938.

Rivero, Eneida B. "Educación sexual en Puerto Rico." *Revista de Ciencias Sociales* 19.2 (1975): 167–91.

Rodrigues, José Carlos. *Tabu do corpo*. Rio de Janeiro: Achiamé, 1975.

Rodríguez Castelo, Hernán. *Léxico sexual ecuatoriano y latinoamericano*. Quito: Ediciones Libro Mundi, 1979.

Rodríguez Matos, Carlos. "Actos de Amor: Introducción al estudio de la poesía puertorriqueña homosexual y lesbiana." *Desde Este Lado/From This Side* 1.2 (1990): 23–24.

———. *POESIdA: An Anthology of AIDS Poetry*. New York: Ollantay Press, 1996.

Román, David. "Performing All Our Lives: AIDS, Performance, Community." *Critical Theory and Performance*. Ed. Janelle Reinelt and Joseph Roach. Ann Arbor: University of Michigan Press, 1992.

———. "¡Teatro Viva!: Latino Performance and the Politics of AIDS in Los Angeles." In Bergmann and Smith, 346–69.

Rosero Bixby, Luis. *La actividad sexual en Costa Rica*. San José: Asociación Demográfica Costarricense, 1984.

Saítta, Sylvia. "Anarquismo, teosofía y sexualidad: Salvador Medina Onrubia." *Mora* 1 (1995): 54–59.

Salas, Luis. *Social Control and Deviance in Cuba*. New York: Praeger, 1979.

Salessi, Jorge. "The Argentine Dissemination of Homosexuality, 1890–1914." In Bergmann and Smith, 49–91.

———. *Médicos, maleantes y maricas: Higiene, criminología y homosexualidad en la construcción de la Nación Argentina (Buenos Aires 1871–1914)*. Rosario: Beatriz Viterbo, 1995.

———. "Tango, nacionalismo y sexualidad. Buenos Aires: 1880–1914." *Hispamérica* 60 (1991): 33–54.

Salessi, Jorge, and Patrick O'Connor. "For Carnival, Clinic, and Camera: Argentina's Turn-of-the-Century Drag Culture Performs 'Woman.'" In Taylor and Villegas, 256–74.

Sandoval, Alberto. "Staging AIDS: What's Latinos Got To Do with It?" In Taylor and Villegas, 49–66.

Santa Indez, Antônio Leal de. *Hábitos e atitudes sexuais dos brasileiros*. São Paulo: Editora Cultrix, 1983.

Santiago, Luis. "Twenty Years of Puerto Rican Gay Activism." *Radical America* 25.1 (1993): 40–48.

Sarduy, Severo. "Escritura/Travestismo." *Mundo Nuevo* 20 (1968): 72–74.

Sarlo, Beatriz. *El imperio de los sentimientos*. Buenos Aires: Catálogos, 1985.

Schaefer-Rodríguez, Claudia. "The Power of Subversive Imagination: Homosexual Utopian Discourse in Contemporary Mexican Literature." *Latin American Literary Review* 17.33 (1989): 29–41.

Scheper-Hughes, Nancy. *Death without Weeping: The Violence of Everyday Life in Brazil*. Berkeley: University of California Press, 1992.

Schneider, Luis Mario. "El tema homosexual en la nueva narrativa mexicana." *Casa del Tiempo* 5 (1985): 82–86.

Schrifter Sikora, Jacobo. *La formación de una contracultura: homosexualismo y sida en Costa Rica*. San José: Guayacán, 1990.

Schrifter Sikora, Jacobo, and Johnny Madrigal Pana. *Hombres que aman hombres*. San José: Ediciones Ilep-SIDA, 1992.

Schulz, Bernhardt Roland. "La Manuela: Personaje homosexual y sometimiento." *Discurso Literario* 7.1 (1990): 225–40.

Schwartz, Kessel. "Homosexuality as a Theme in Representative Contemporary Spanish American Novels." *Kentucky Romance Quarterly* 22 (1975): 247–57.

Seminar on Feminism and Culture in Latin America. *Women, Culture, and Politics in Latin America*. Berkeley: University of California Press, 1990.

"El Sexo en México." Special dossier. *Nexos* 12.139 (1989): 29–80.

"Sexuality and Christianity: An Attempt at Reconciliation." In *Women in Dialogue: (Mujeres para el Diálogo), Puebla Mexico, January 27 to February 13, 1979: Translations of Seminar Sessions Held "Outside the Walls" During CELAM III*. Notre Dame: Catholic Committee on Urban Ministry, 1979. 24–29.

Shaw, Deborah. "Erotic or Political: Literary Representations of Mexican Lesbians." *Journal of Latin American Cultural Studies* 5.1 (1996): 51–63.

Shaw, Donald. "Notes on the Presentation of Sexuality in the Modern Spanish American Novel." *Bulletin of Hispanic Studies* 59.3 (1982): 275–82.

Silva, Aguinaldo. *Primeira carta aos andróginos*. Rio de Janeiro: Pallas, 1985.

Silvera, Makeda. "Man Royal and Sodomites: Some Thoughts on Afro-Caribbean Lesbians." *Sight Specific: Lesbians and Representation*. Ed. Lynne Fernie. Toronto: A Space, 1988. 36–43.

Simo, Ana María, and Reinaldo García Ramos. "Hablemos claro." *Mariel: Revista de Literatura y Arte* 2.5 (1984): 9–10.

Slade, Doren L. "Marital Status and Sexual Identity: The Position of Women in a Mexican Peasant Society." *Women Cross-Culturally: Change and Challenge*. Ed. Ruby Rohrlich-Leavitt. The Hague: Mouton, 1978. 129–48.

Smith, Lois M., and Alfred Padula. *Sex and Revolution: Women in Socialist Cuba*. New York: Oxford University Press, 1996.

Smith, Paul Julian. *The Body Hispanic: Gender and Sexuality in Spanish and Spanish American Literature*. Oxford: Oxford University Press, 1989.

Soares, Luiz Carlos. *Rameiras, ilhoas, polacas: A prostituição no Rio de Janeiro do Século XIX*. São Paulo: Atica, 1992.

Sobre mulher e violência: Perspectivas antropológicas da mulher. Vol. 4. Rio de Janeiro: Zahar, 1985.

Sommer, Doris. *Foundational Fictions: The National Romances of Latin America*. Berkeley: University of California Press, 1991.

Steele, Cynthia. *Politics, Gender and the Mexican Novel, 1968–1988: Beyond the Pyramid*. Austin: University of Texas Press, 1992.

Stepan, Nancy. *The Hour of Eugenics: Race, Gender and Nation in Latin America*. Ithaca: Cornell University Press, 1991.

Stephen, Lynn. *Zapotec Women*. Austin: University of Texas Press, 1992.

Stern, Steve J. *The Secret History of Gender: Women, Men and Power in Late Colonial Mexico*. Chapel Hill: University of North Carolina Press, 1995.

Stoner, K. Lynn. "Directions in Latin American Women's History, 1977–1984." *Latin American Research Review* 22.2 (1987): 101–34.

———. *Latinas of the Americas: A Source Book*. New York: Garland, 1989.

Suárez-Orozco, Marcelo. "A Study of Argentine Soccer: The Dynamics of Its Fans and Their Folklore." *Journal of Psychoanalytic Anthropology* 5.1 (1982): 7–28.

Taggart, James M. "Gender Segregation and Cultural Constructions of Sexuality in Two Hispanic Societies." *American Ethnologist* 19.1 (1992): 75–96.

Taylor, Clark L. "How Mexicans Define Male Homosexuality: Labeling and the *Buga* View." *Kroeber Anthropological Society Papers* 53–54 (1978): 106–28.

———. "Legends, Syncretism, and Continuing Echoes of Homosexuality from Pre-Columbian and Colonial Mexico." In Murray 1995, 80–99.

———. "Mexican Male Homosexual Interaction in Public Contexts." *The Many Faces of Homosexuality: Anthropological Approaches to Homosexual Behavior*. Ed. Evelyn Blackwood. New York: Harrington Park, 1989. 117–36. Also in *Journal of Homosexuality* 11.3 (1986): 117–36.

Taylor, Diana, and Juan Villegas Morales, eds. *Negotiating Performance: Gender, Sexuality, and Theatricality in Latin/o America*. Durham: Duke University Press, 1994.

Teixeira, N. *Juventude Transviada*. Leimeira: Editora Letras de Província, 1966.

Trevisan, João Sivério. *Devassos no Paraíso: A homosexualidade no Brasil, da colónia à atualidade*. São Paulo: Editora Max Limonad, 1986. Also in English: *Perverts in Paradise*. London: Gay Men's Press, 1986.

Trujillo, Carla, ed. *Chicana Lesbians: The Girls Our Mothers Warned Us About*. Berkeley: Third Woman Press, 1991.

Umpierre, Luz María. "Lesbian Tantalizing in Carmen Lugo Filippi's 'Milagros, Calle Mercurio.'" In Bergmann and Smith, 306–14.

Uribe, Olga T. "Modelos narrativos de homosexualidad y heterosexualidad en el reino de los sentidos de *Canon de alcoba*: 'Ver,' 'Oír' y 'El recogimiento,' tres textos de Tununa Mercado." *Latin American Literary Review* 22.43 (1994): 19–30.

Vain, Leonor, ed. *Mujer golpeada: Primer encuentro nacional de centros de prevención de la violencia doméstica y asistencia a la mujer golpeada*. Buenos Aires: Editorial Besana, 1989.

Vargas, Ava, ed. *La casa de citas en el Barrio Galante*. Mexico City: Grijalbo, 1991.

Vega Centeno B., Imelda. "Ser joven en el Perú: socialización, integración, corporalidad y cultura." *Allpanchis* 25.41 (1993): 177–210.

Viel, Benjamín. "Patterns of Induced Abortion in Chile and Selected Other Latin American Countries." *Epidemiology of Abortion and Practices of Fertility Regulation in Latin America: Selected Reports*. Washington, D.C.: Pan American Health Organization, 1975.

Villanueva Collado, Alfredo. "Machismo vs. Gayness: Latin American Fiction." *Gay Sunshine* 29–30 (1976): 22.

———. "Meta(homo)sexualidad e ideología en dos novelas antiburguesas peruanas." *Confluencia* 7.2 (1992): 55–63.

Whitam, Frederick L. "*Os Entendidos*: Gay Life in São Paulo in the late 1970s." In Murray 1995, 231–40.

Whitam, Frederick L., and Robin M. Mathy. *Male Homosexuality in Four Societies: Brazil, Guatemala, the Philippines, and the United States*. New York: Praeger, 1986.

Worth, Dooley, and Ruth Rodriguez. "Latina Women and AIDS." *Radical America* 20.6 (1986–87): 63–67.

Yarbro-Bejarano, Yvonne. "De-constructing the Lesbian Body: Cherríe Moraga's *Loving in the War Years*." *The Lesbian and Gay Studies Reader*. Ed. Henry Abelove, Michèle Aina Barale, and David M. Halperin. New York: Routledge, 1993. 595–603. Also in Trujillo, 143–55.

———. "Expanding the Categories of Race in Lesbian and Gay Studies." *Professions of Desire: Lesbian and Gay Studies in Literature*. Ed. George E. Haggerty and Bonnie Zimmerman. New York: MLA Publications, 1995. 124–35.

———. "The Lesbian Body in Latina Cultural Production." In Bergmann and Smith, 181–97.

Young, Allan. *Gays Under the Cuban Revolution*. San Francisco: Grey Fox Press, 1981.

Zalduondo, Barbara de, and Jean Maxius Bernard. "Meanings and Consequences of Sexual-Economic Exchange: Gender, Poverty and Sexual Risk Behavior in Urban Haiti." *Conceiving Sexuality: Approaches to Sex Research in a Postmodern World*. Ed. Richard Parker and John Gagnon. New York: Routledge, 1995. 157–80.

Zavala de Cosio, María Eugenia. *Cambios de fecundidad en México y políticas de población*. Trans. Jorge Ferreiro. Mexico City: El Colegio de México/Fondo de Cultura Económica, 1992.

Contributors

Eduardo P. Archetti is Professor of Social Anthropology at the University of Oslo in Norway. His current research is on constructions of masculinity in Argentina.

Daniel Balderston is Professor of Spanish and Portuguese at Tulane University and chair of the Task Force on Gay and Lesbian Issues of the Latin American Studies Association (LASA). He specializes in Argentine literature and cultural studies.

Peter Beattie is Assistant Professor of History at Michigan State University. He specializes in the history of the Brazilian military.

Rob Buffington is Assistant Professor of History at St. John's University. He specializes in intellectual history and criminology in Mexico.

Sueann Caulfield is Assistant Professor of History at the University of Michigan. She specializes in Brazilian women's history.

Arnaldo Cruz-Malavé is Associate Professor of Spanish at Fordham University. He specializes in Puerto Rican and U.S. Latino studies.

Donna J. Guy is Professor of History at the University of Arizona and president of the Conference on Latin American History (CLAH). She specializes in women's history and economic history.

Roger N. Lancaster is Associate Professor of Anthropology at George Mason University. He is currently working on a book on the queer body.

Francine Masiello is Professor of Spanish and Comparative Literature at the University of California, Berkeley. She specializes in Argentine literature and culture, especially of the nineteenth century and the avant-garde.

Nina Menéndez is Assistant Professor of Spanish at the University of Florida, specializing in early-twentieth-century Cuban women's writing.

Sylvia Molloy is Albert Schweitzer Professor of Spanish and Comparative Literature at New York University. Her current research is on gender and sexuality studies of decadence in late-nineteenth-century Spanish American literature.

Oscar Montero is Associate Professor of Spanish at the City University of New York. He specializes in Spanish-American *modernismo* and contemporary Cuban literature and cultural studies.

José Quiroga is Associate Professor of Spanish at George Washington University. He is currently working on a book on homosexuality and the Cuban Revolution, and another on Latin American poetry.

Ben Sifuentes Jáuregui teaches Spanish at Wesleyan University. He is finishing a book entitled "Facing Masculinity: Gender, Performativity, Transvestism in Contemporary Latin American Literature."

Yvonne Yarbro-Bejarano is Associate Professor of Spanish at Stanford University, specializing in sexuality studies on both Mexican and U.S. Latino literature and culture.

Index